WESTERN RESPONSES TO TERRORISM

WESTERN RESPONSES TO TERRORISM

Edited by

ALEX P. SCHMID

and

RONALD D. CRELINSTEN

FRANK CASS
LONDON • PORTLAND, OR

First published in 1993 in Great Britain by
FRANK CASS PUBLISHERS
Newbury House, 900 Eastern Avenue,
London, IG2 7HH, England

and in the United States of America by
FRANK CASS PUBLISHERS
c/o ISBS
5804 N.E. Hassalo Street
Portland, Oregon 97213-3644

Website: http://www.frankcass.com

Copyright © 1993 Frank Cass & Co Ltd
Reprinted 1998

British Library Cataloguing in Publication Data

Schmid, Alex P.
    Western Responses to Terrorism
    I. Title   II. Crelinsten, Ronald D.
    303.625
    ISBN 0-7146-4521-4 (cloth)
    ISBN 0-7146-4090-5 (paper)

Library of Congress Cataloging in Publication Data

Western responses to terrorism / edited by Alex P. Schmid and
Ronald D. Crelinsten.
        p.   cm.
    "This group of studies first appeared in a Special Issue of Terrorism
and Political Violence, Vol. 4, No. 4 (Winter 1992) published by
Frank Cass & Co. Ltd."—T.p. verso.
    This volume derives from a conference organized by the European
Student Association AEGEE.
    Includes bibliographical references and index.
    ISBN 0-7146-4521-4—ISBN 0-7146-4090-5 (pbk.)
    1. Terrorism—Europe—Congresses. 2. Terrorism—Terrorism—Europe
Prevention—Congresses. I. Schmid, Alex Peter. II. Crelinsten,
Ronald D.
    HV6433.E85W47 1993
303.6'25'094—dc20   93-9572
                                                                        CIP

This group of studies first appeared in a Special Issue of
Terrorism and Political Violence, Vol.4, No.4 (Winter 1992)
published by Frank Cass & Co. Ltd.

Printed in Great Britain by
Antony Rowe Ltd., Chippenham, Wilts.

Contents

Acknowledgements

Given that this volume derives from a conference, we are first and foremost indebted to the wide range of academicians and practitioners, most of whom contribute to this volume, who came to Leiden in 1989 where, without any financial incentive, they provided a wealth of observations and recommendations which is quite beyond the reach of a single writer. We would also like to express our sincere thanks to the enthusiastic students of the European Student Association AEGEE (Association des Etats Généraux des Etudiants de l'Europe),[1] who organized the conference and brought it to fruition. Without their organizational abilities, this two-day conference would simply not have been possible.

In particular, Alex Schmid would like to express his gratitude to Ingrid van Loo, Wijnand Nuts, Caspar Wenckebach, Barend Post, Wendela van Oosterom, Christine André de la Porte, Christien Reigersman, Willem Sodderland, Francine Lulofs, Christine Boreel, Renee Boreel, Victorine Bos, Martine Visser 't Hooft, Bemmie Schorer, Margje Vosselman, Karen Jeneson, Ginet Bunker, Anouk van Schaardenburg, Denise Kentie, Annette van Kalmthout, Elsbeth Tiedemann, Fleur van Dunné, Jannekje Meinesz, Edith Reinen, Joan Koene, Denise Krul, Alexander van Dedem, Remco van de Horst, Maarten Korthuis, Nic van Neerynen, Jeroen Bruins Slot, Heleen Brameyer, Luc Matter, Barbara Kuipers, Ninette Kokke, Dominique Laimböck, Marjon Vrouwenvelder and the Jaarclub 'Rockfort'.

At the Center for the Study of Social Conflict (Leiden University), which also helped to organize the conference, Alex Schmid would like to thank Jan Brand for bringing the bibliography into good shape and to Angela van der Poel for harmonizing the various manuscripts for the conference proceedings.

The editing and preparation of the final manuscript for publication would not have been possible without the help of Iffet Ozkut, whose skill in editing, proof-reading, and bibliographic research, as well as her patience, encouragement and enthusiasm during the difficult task of paring the manuscript down to size, made it possible to meet the submission deadline. Ronald Crelinsten would also like to thank Vishwanath C. Hassan and his impeccable work on the many tables in this volume and to Charles Stuart, who put most of the final changes into the computer.

Finally, both editors would like to express their gratitude to David C. Rapoport for his support, encouragement and advice while bringing this volume to publication. We would also like to thank Randal Gray, Journals Editor at Frank Cass & Co. Ltd., for his invaluable collaboration during the production process. To Cyrille Fijnaut, Ariel Merari, Stephen Sloan and G. Davidson Smith, all of whom provided excellent chapters to the original volume that must, alas, be published elsewhere, we express our deep gratitude.

NOTES

1. AEGEE is a European Students' Association which aims to promote European co-operation and integration. Since it considers the emergence of a European public opinion to be a pre-condition for European unity, AEGEE is striving to motivate public opinion in this direction. AEGEE was founded in 1985 by students of Les Grandes Ecoles in Paris. Since then AEGEE-branches (so-called antennae) have been founded in more than 60 European university towns. AEGEE antennae regularly organize events covering all aspects of European culture, economics and politics.

PART I
THE PROBLEM

Editor's Introduction: Western Responses to Terrorism

ALEX P. SCHMID AND
RONALD D. CRELINSTEN

"To me the most urgent problem of our time is the problem of
discovering a way of overcoming evil without becoming
another form of evil in the process"

Laurens van der Post

This volume is the outgrowth of a congress organized by the *Association des Etats Généraux des Etudiants de l'Europe* (AEGEE) and the Center for the Study of Social Conflicts (COMT) of Leiden University on 16–17 March 1989. Its title was 'Towards a European Response to Terrorism: National Experiences and Lessons for the Europe of 1992'. With the prospect of a Europe without frontiers, the problem of a common anti-terrorist policy gained new urgency. While nations like the United States and Israel had developed certain response models for coping with terrorism, which model of anti-terrorist policies should be adopted by the countries of the European Community? Should it be a German model with features like *Berufsverbot* and high-security prisons like Stammheim? Should it be a British model, based on counter-insurgency experience gained in Palestine, Malaya, Cyprus and Northern Ireland? Or is it possible to learn from other European nations in order to develop a new model combining effectiveness with democratic acceptability?

The congress was meant to stimulate public discussion on a matter which security experts generally prefer to discuss among themselves. The invited speakers and panelists came from ten countries and included academic scholars, retired military and intelligence experts, lawyers, politicians and journalists. For the present volume, the Greek conference paper could not be included as it was never completed in written form. One case, France, was never expanded into a full article but the original is included for the sake of completeness. In addition, we invited two more authors (Stahel and Vetschera) to highlight their nation's response. Altogether, the present volume covers the national experiences of eight European countries. Unfortunately, we could find no scholar willing to describe critically how the Turkish government copes with terrorism. Since Turkey is Europe's most affected country, the lessons to be learned from Turkey are especially important. To write about terrorism seems to be as dangerous as being considered a terrorist in Turkey, where the 'cure' for terrorism has been almost as bad as the 'disease' of insurgent terrorism prior to 1980:

> Since the last military coup of September 1980, the following developments took place: 650,000 persons were arrested and imprisoned. 212,000 of them were brought to trial; 4,500,000 are on a black list; 914,000 have been removed from their jobs; 14,000 lost Turkish citizenship; 48 persons were executed; 170 died from torture.[1]

As this sombre list illustrates, terrorism can have as great an impact on domestic political life as on international affairs. A nation like Lebanon has been nearly destroyed by it. Superpowers have been affected by it (President Carter's embassy hostage crisis and President Reagan's Irangate). Europe's future, too, might be affected by the doings of small groups of terrorists. This volume, then, is meant to contribute to a neglected but necessary debate.

In the first two contributions, Alex Schmid outlines the conceptual and practical problems surrounding the control of terrorism in democratic societies. In the third article, A.J. Jongman then surveys the incidence of terrorism, both domestic and international, in Western Europe in the 20-year period since 1968, when counter-terrorism first became a major policy issue in the West. At the same time, he highlights problems surrounding the recording of incidents and the conflicting assumptions that underlie the best known data bases.

The next eight chapters are eight national studies from Europe. First, Alex Schmid looks at international and domestic terrorism in the Netherlands and the ways in which the Dutch government dealt with them. Next, Fernando Jiménez surveys the Spanish government's response to the terrorist threat in Spain, with particular emphasis on the Basque question. Gilbert Guillaume then briefly surveys the kinds of terrorism encountered by France and recent legal, diplomatic and police responses. In the next chapter, Kurt Groenewold focuses on the Federal Republic of Germany's struggle against the Red Army Faction, particularly the legal and administrative dimensions of the government's response. Having himself undergone the Federal Republic's special procedures for prosecution of the Red Army Faction, as defense attorney for some Faction members, Groenewold highlights the intricate ways in which the legal and administrative procedure was altered in the name of counter-terrorism.

Donatella della Porta describes in detail the Italian state's fight against terrorism, including analysing how the Red Brigades were defeated by special amnesty laws. David Bonner examines the British government's different measures to combat terrorism both in Britain itself and in Northern Ireland. He also assesses their effectiveness and their sensitivity to civil liberties. Albert Stahel provides a glimpse of a country usually ignored in the literature on terrorism: Switzerland. Stahel shows how Switzerland serves as a logistical base for both European and international terrorism. Finally, Heinz Vetschera examines another oft-neglected nation, Austria, reminding the reader of both its historical links with terrorism and its contemporary experience.

The next six contributions take a broader look at more regional approaches to counter-terrorism and the problems of international co-operation. The first two focus on the newly emerging European Community: F. Korthals Altes' Dutch perspective on the difficulties of co-ordinating national policies and Meliton Cardona's chronicle of European regional and international efforts to co-operate. Paul Bremer next presents an American perspective on international co-operation, highlighting more recent successes in legal prosecution of international terrorists. Then Richard Clutterbuck surveys the chequered history of negotiations policy in hijacking and hostage-taking, both in the public and the private sector, and examines the key issues involved. M.P.M. Zagari returns to the European Community with the European Parliament's activities in counter-terrorism and the idea of establishing a European juridical area, with a European Court to try international terrorist cases. Finally, Richard Clutterbuck discusses the implications of a unified Europe with no internal border controls for identifying terrorist and criminal suspects.

In our conclusion, we survey the range of approaches that have been taken toward countering terrorism over the past 25 years and assess their relative effectiveness as well as their acceptability to democratic values. In discussing Western trends in counter-terrorism, we focus in particular on the military option, which has received considerable attention in recent years, and on the psychological approach, which has received very little attention at all. Finally, we discuss how to maintain a balance between effectiveness and democratic acceptability in Western responses to terrorism and attempt to identify the most common ways in which this balance has been threatened.

The original conference upon which this volume is based was held in March 1989. Since then, the world has changed dramatically. The emergence of Europe as a major political and economic entity has been accompanied by the reunification of Germany and the emergence of Eastern European democracies, the collapse of the Soviet Union and its empire and the end of the Cold War, the 1991 Gulf War and related realignments in the Middle East and significant electoral change in many Western nations. The vision of a 'New World Order', with its 'peace dividend', that was heralded when the Cold War ended has been clouded by economic hardship, both in the new states emerging from the ashes of the Soviet Empire and in the West, and by the emergence of ethnic and nationalist warring and anti-immigrant and anti-refugee violence in Europe. Add to this the increasingly influential role of religious fundamentalist thought in the political life of nations both East and West, for example Afghanistan, Algeria, Israel, Turkey, even the United States, and the electoral gains of right-wing extremists in France, Germany and Italy. With these profound and dramatic changes has come a transformation of terrorism and political violence in general. The increasing importance of religiously-inspired, right-wing, nationalist or anti-foreign violence and the increasing recognition, as highlighted in many contributions to this volume, that domestic and international forms of terrorism are often closely connected, necessitate a rethinking of traditional approaches both to the study of terrorism and to its control by democratic states.

By looking back over the past two and a half decades of terrorism when a new era in international affairs is just beginning, we hope that this volume will serve to highlight the need to rethink traditional concepts of both terrorism and counter-terrorism and to develop new approaches for the democratic control of terrorism in a rapidly changing world.

NOTES

1. *Milliyet*, Nov. 1989, as quoted in *Volkskrant* (Amsterdam), 29 Nov. 1989, p.10.

The Response Problem as a Definition Problem

ALEX P. SCHMID

To escape the defeatist position that 'one man's terrorist is another man's freedom fighter', this essay distinguishes four arenas of discourse on terrorism: an academic one (where a consensus definition is offered); a state discourse (where definitions are generally wide and vague); a public one (as reflected in the media's usage of the term 'terrorism'); and, finally, that of the 'terrorists' and their sympathisers (where the focus is on political ends, while avoiding a discussion of means). To escape the choice between a crime model of terrorism, which focuses on the illegal means only, and a war model, which portrays terrorism as a continuation of politics, a legal definition of terrorism is proposed as the peacetime equivalent of war crimes, thereby moving into an arena of discourse where there is much international agreement. Such definition of terrorist acts would narrow what can be rightfully considered terrorism, but broaden the consensus as to the unacceptability of terrorist methods.

The definition of what constitutes 'terrorism' varies from society to society, from government to government and, to a lesser degree, even from academic author to academic author. Such diversity of definition is problematic when one strives to develop a common policy against 'terrorism'. If one country has a broad definition and the other a narrow one, a clear and consistent consensual policy will be an elusive goal. How can we escape from this definitional quagmire?

Four Arenas of Discourse on 'Terrorism'

We can begin by distinguishing four different arenas of discourse on non-state terrorism:

1. The academic discourse. The universities offer an intellectual forum where scholars can discuss terrorism without being suspected of sympathising with terrorists.

2. The state's statements. The official discourse on terrorism by those who speak in the name of the state.

3. The public debate on terrorism. The way our open societies are structured, this arena is largely co-extensive with the views and suggestions met in the media.

4. The discussion of those who oppose many of our societies' values and

support or perform acts of violence and terrorism against what they consider repressive states.[1]

Taking each arena in turn:

1. When academic scholars look at terrorism, their perspective – as researchers, not necessarily in their role as citizens – differs from that of those charged with law enforcement against insurgent terrorists. To use a distinction of T. R. Gurr: the latter are 'firefighters', while the former should be mere 'students of combustion'. Their distance should allow them more perspective.

Over the past few years, this author has attempted to discover what the academic perspective on terrorism is by communicating with other members of the research community. The instruments used were lengthy questionnaires mailed to many authors in the field. On this basis, an academic consensus definition of 'terrorism' is attempted. I was glad to find considerable academic acceptance of its basic elements. No less than 81 per cent of the respondents from the academic community found my first attempt at definition partially or fully acceptable.[2] The comments and criticism of over 50 scholars helped me to refine and reconceptualize this first definition. The result is the following definition:

> Terrorism is an anxiety-inspiring method of repeated violent action, employed by (semi-)clandestine individual, group or state actors, for idiosyncratic, criminal or political reasons, whereby – in contrast to assassination – the direct targets of violence are not the main targets. The immediate human victims of violence are generally chosen randomly (targets of opportunity) or selectively (representative or symbolic targets) from a target population, and serve as message generators. Threat- and violence-based communication processes between terrorist (organisation), (imperiled) victims, and main targets are used to manipulate the main target (audience(s)), turning it into a target of terror, a target of demands, or a target of attention, depending on whether intimidation, coercion, or propaganda is primarily sought.[3]

2. Such a precise but lengthy definition is not likely to be used by governments. Compare this 'academic' definition with two government definitions, the German and the British:

German Federal Republic, Office for the Protection of the Constitution (1985): 'Terrorism is the enduringly conducted struggle for political goals, which are intended to be achieved by means of assaults on the life and property of other persons, especially by means of severe crimes as detailed in art. 129a, section 1 of the penal code (above all: murder, homicide, extortionist kidnapping, arson, setting off a blast by explosives) or by means of other acts of violence, which serve as preparation of such criminal acts';[4]

United Kingdom (1974): 'For the purposes of the legislation, terrorism is the use of violence for political ends, and includes any use of violence for the purpose of putting the public or any section of the public in fear'.[5]

The British definition, in particular, is very broad and could be interpreted to include conventional war as well as nuclear deterrence. Unfortunately, the 'European' TREVI (Terrorism, Radicalism, Extremism and political Violence) group definition has been modelled on the British one, except that it excludes the contingency of war: 'Terrorism is defined as the use, or the threatened use, by a cohesive group of persons of violence (short of warfare) to effect political aims'.[6] The European Convention to Combat Terrorism (1977) did not use any definition in order not to get stuck in a political debate. It simply listed crimes and 'depoliticized' these in order to circumvent restrictions on extradition. However, this avoidance of the problem was no solution as various controversies around extradition in the following years made clear.

3. What is the image of terrorism in the media? In another questionnaire, editors of news agencies, television, radio and the press were asked what kind of (political) violence their medium labelled 'terrorism'. Table 1 summarises which particular acts of violence these editors defined as acts of terrorism and reveals a declining consensus about labelling certain acts of violence as 'terrorism'.

TABLE 1

ANSWERS TO THE QUESTION: 'WHAT KIND OF (POLITICAL) VIOLENCE DOES YOUR MEDIUM COMMONLY LABEL "TERRORISM"?'

Type of violence using	Percentage of editors label 'terrorism'
Hostage taking	80%
Assassination	75%
Indiscriminate bombing	75%
Kidnapping	70%
Hijacking for coercive bargaining	70%
Urban guerrilla warfare	65%
Sabotage	60%
Torture	45%
Hijacking for escape	35%

Other categories mentioned by individual respondents were: murder by an organisation; land mines; attacks on security forces in rural areas and robbery.

While the European Convention for the Suppression of Terrorism assumes all hijackings to be acts of terrorism for the purposes of extradition,[7] editors do make a distinction between a hijacking for escape and one for coercive bargaining. In this particular case, I think that the majority of editors are closer to the mark than the drafters of the European convention. If you are sitting in an aircraft and the hijacker only asks the pilot to fly to Rome instead of Tirana, you will feel much less terrorised than when he or she demands the liberation of 700 prisoners from the Iranian government. In the first case, the pilot can, through a change of behaviour, escape from the threat of being killed. In the second case, his and the passengers' attitude or behaviour does not matter, since the addressee is not identical with the threatened group of people.

In the same way, a kidnapping can be terroristic or not. When only money is asked from an abducted millionaire, the situation is less frightening than when political concessions are asked from a government in return for the victim, as when the German industrialist Hanns-Martin Schleyer was abducted by the German Red Army Faction in 1977. Apparently some hijackings and kidnappings are more terroristic than others. The same goes for 'assassination'. Some political assassinations are performed to kill a political opponent whose policies are contrary to those of the murderer. The murder of John F. Kennedy was not terroristic in this sense. A terroristic assassination, on the other hand, involves more parties than the killer and his victim. There are three parties instead of two (see Figure 1).

FIGURE 1

THE TRIANGLE OF INSURGENT TERRORISM

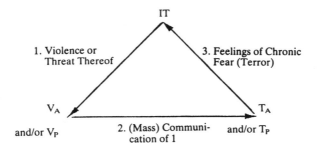

(IT = Insurgent Terrorist; V_A = Victim Belonging to the Camp of the State Authorities; V_P = Victim Being Part of the Public; T_A = The Authorities as Target; T_P = The Public as Target)

Source: Alec P. Schmid and Janny de Graaf, *Violence as Communication: Insurgent Terrorism and the Western News Media* (Beverly Hills: Sage, 1982), p.176.

As Figure 1 makes clear, there is a difference between the target of violence and the target of terror, between the victim and the opponent. The specific victim does not matter as much as with a traditional assassination. In a terroristic murder, one victim can easily be substituted for another since the effect on the ultimate target is what really counts. Hence one has to distinguish between a common assassination and one in the context of terrorism by labelling the first 'individuated political murder' and the second 'de-individuated political murder'.[8] In the first case, the victim usually knew his opponents and the threat posed to him before he was killed. In the second case, the victim is often not aware that he is a party to a conflict and the attack on his life comes unexpectedly.

Here we also arrive at the reason why terrorism terrorises. It does so because we are caught by surprise and are victimised arbitrarily and without provocation from our side. Suddenly, we are 'struck with terror'. Terror, then, is a state of mind. Terrorism is the calculated causing of extreme anxiety of becoming a victim of arbitrary violence and the exploitation of this emotional reaction for manipulative purposes.

4. I am aware that this is not the way the terrorists themselves and their sympathizers would describe their activities. During the AEGEE/COMT conference in Leiden some graffiti-painters calling themselves the 'Revolutionary Commando Marinus van der Lubbe' sent a letter to the local newspaper wherein they expressed their solidarity with the oppressed people in, among other places, Palestine, Ireland, Central America and Kurdistan. Literally, they said: 'It is clear that so-called terrorism is the logical and just resistance of the people against state terrorism, capitalism, racism, sexism and imperialism'.[9] Some contemporary terrorists call themselves 'freedom fighters', members of the anti-imperialist resistance, or 'Defense League'.

There is nothing new in this: in the Second World War the German occupation force called members of the Dutch resistance 'terrorists' while the latter's self-image was that they were patriots and resistance fighters. The point I wish to make here is that these terms are not exclusive. They are 'definitions' with different focal points: one in terms of means, the other in terms of goals.

Terrorism as the 'Peacetime Equivalent of War Crimes'

Which definition is the right one? A good definition is one to which many can agree. A broad definition – like 'terrorism is violence for political purposes' – is likely to be objected to by more people than a narrow one since it turns more practitioners of violence into terrorists. An academic definition which is too detailed, may be impractical. What is needed is a legal definition to which many can agree. I submit that such a legal definition already exists in the category of 'war crimes'.[10]

Fotion and Elfstrom (1986) have concluded that 'In contrast to the lack of clarity about what constitutes war, there is broad international agreement about what actions count as war crimes.'[11] It would be wise to profit from this consensus. Included among the acts prohibited by the laws of war are attacks on persons taking no active part in hostilities. This also includes members of the armed forces who have laid down their arms. The protection of the non-combatant and the innocent stand at the core of international humanitarian law as codified in the Hague Regulations and Geneva Conventions. The rules of war prohibit not only violence against captives but also hostage-taking as well as most other atrocities committed by terrorists.[12]

Terrorists have elevated practices which are excesses of war to the level of routine tactics. They do not engage in combat, as soldiers do. They strike preferably the unarmed.[13] The attack on the undefended is not an unsought side-effect but a deliberate strategy. Categorising acts of terrorism as war crimes is also appropriate in the sense that terrorists consider themselves as being at war with Western democracies.[14] What makes them different from soldiers, however, is that they do not carry their arms openly and that they do not discriminate between armed adversaries and noncombatants. Since they are not fighting by the rules of war they turn themselves into war criminals. Terrorism distinguishes itself from conventional and to some extent also from guerrilla warfare through the disregard for principles of chivalry and humanity contained in the Hague Regulations and Geneva Conventions.

I believe that Western policy-makers would do well to choose a restricted legal definition of terrorism as 'peacetime equivalents of war crimes'. Such a definition might exclude some forms of violence and coercion (such as attacks on the military, hijackings for escape and destruction of property) currently labelled 'terrorism' by some governments. However, a narrow and precise definition of terrorism is likely to find broader support than one that includes various forms of violent dissent and protest short of terrorist atrocities.

Other, lesser forms of political violence (e.g., against property) will still be illegal by national laws. However, terrorist offences could be considered federal crimes against humanity, requiring special treatment. If we have clarity on this front, nobody will be able to confuse terrorists and freedom fighters. 'Freedom fighters' who adhere to the rules of war should be given privileged treatment. 'Freedom-fighters' targeting civilians, on the other hand, should be dealt with as war criminals. Extradition problems, which now arise out of different interpretations about who is a terrorist, could then disappear. The good motive (like the fight for self-determination, freedom and democracy) can then no longer exculpate the bad deed of violence against the unarmed, the disarmed and the neutral bystanders.

The European Convention for the Suppression of Terrorism has been plagued by the lack of distinction between a 'criminal offence' and a 'political offence'.[15] By placing narrowly defined acts of terrorism in the context of 'war crimes', the dilemma of attributing a given act of violence to the criminal or political sphere disappears. Acts of terrorism, like war crimes, could be dealt with by a special European tribunal with special jurisdiction on terroristic offences.

NOTES

1. This classification has been inspired by Philip Schlesinger, Graham Murdock and Philip Elliott, *Televising 'Terrorism': Political Violence in Popular Culture* (London: Comedia, 1983). Schlesinger *et al.* differentiate between the official perspective, the alternative perspective, the populist perspective and the opposition perspective.
2. Alex P. Schmid, Albert J. Jongman *et al.*, *Political Terrorism: A New Guide to Actors, Authors, Concepts, Data Bases, Theories, and Literature* (Amsterdam: North-Holland Publishing, 1988), p.2.
3. Schmid *et al.*, *Political Terrorism*, p.28.
4. Ministry of the Interior. *Verfassungsschutzbericht 1984* (Bonn: Bundesministerium des Innern, 1985), p.17n.
5. Prevention of Terrorism (Temporary Provisions) Act of 1974; cited in E.F. Mickolus, *The Literature of Terrorism* (Westport, CT: Greenwood Press, 1980), p.295.
6. *Handelingen* (Dutch Parliamentary Proceedings) II, 1986/87, Bijlagen 19700, Hoofdstuk VI nr.30, p.5, as cited in Peter Klerks, *Terreur Bestrijding in Nederland 1970–1988* (Amsterdam: Ravijn, 1989), p.22.
7. Article 1, *Europees Verdrag tot bestrijding van terrorisme*, 1977.
8. Schmid *et al.*, *Political Terrorism* (note 2).
9. *Leidsch Dagblad*, 17 March 1989.
10. To my knowledge, Alfred P. Rubin was the first to relate terrorism to the laws of war. See: A.P. Rubin, 'Terrorism and the Law of War', *Denver Journal of International Law and Politics* 17/2–3 (1983), p.219.
11. N. Fotion and G. Elfstrom, *Military Ethics: Guidelines for Peace and War* (Boston: RKP, 1986), p.260.
12. L.P. Bremer III, 'Terrorism and the Rule of War', US Dept. of State, Bureau of Public Affairs, Current Policy No.947 (Text of address 23 April 1987), p.3.
13. Of the 782 international terrorist incidents listed by the US State Dept. for 1985, the smallest group of victims (7 per cent) consisted of military men; the largest group (27.5 per cent) consisted of 'other', that is, other than military and other than diplomats (9.5 per cent), politically affiliated and non-official public targets (7.25 per cent), private party (15.4 per cent) and business (23.75 per cent); US Dept. of State, 1986, p.3 (see also Jongman, this volume).
14. I have discussed this theme in more detail in A.P. Schmid, 'Force or Conciliation? An Overview of Some Problems Associated With Current Anti-Terrorist Response Strategies', *Violence, Aggression and Terrorism* 2/2 (1988), pp.152–5.
15. See M. Zagari (Rapporteur), *Verslag namens de Commissie juridische zaken en rechten van de burger over de bestrijding van het terrorisme*, Europees Parlement. Zittingsdocumenten, Document A2-155/89, 2 May 1989, p.14. (See also Zagari, this volume, p.291, for an English version of this text.)

Terrorism and Democracy

ALEX P. SCHMID

When there is a confrontation between the absolute politics of terrorism and the compromising politics of democracies, the former seems to be in a position of advantage. This essay discusses the strengths of democracies (non-violent change through elections, open criticism in and by the media, courts that protect the weak against the strong) as well as their weaknesses (freedom of movement and association, abundance of accessible targets and a legal system that requires solid proof). The weaknesses of democratic societies are increased by some features of the market system (it not only increases wealth but also inequality, sells weapons to supporters of terrorism, manages their banking and offers them access to the media through the commercial basis of the concept of news value). Ultimately, the struggle between terrorism and democracy is one for legitimacy and maintaining the latter is strategically more important for democratic governments than winning short-term victories through tactical 'quick fixes' which might seem effective but turn democracies into something that begins to mirror the terrorist opponent.

Democracy is rule by the majority while respecting the right of the minority. Terrorism is an instrument of rule of a tyrannic minority whether in or out of power. Democracy involves respect for rules when engaged in disputes and conflicts. Terrorism's strategy is based on transgressing rules of civilized conduct. Democracy involves tolerance of those who think differently. Terrorists are, in Marx's words, 'dangerous dreamers of the absolute'.[1] These are some of the dichotomies which create problems for democratic societies. By tolerating the intolerant, democracies allow terrorists to plan and prepare their strikes. By combating them with measured, rule-based force, democracies are at a tactical disadvantage in the conflict with an anonymous opponent showing no restraint.

How can democracies prevent terrorists from freely scheming and moving within our societies? The cross-border traffic between European states is already large today and will further increase in 1993 when the free movement of goods, capital and people becomes a reality. In 1987, for instance, the Dutch borders alone were crossed by 30,000 trains, 229,000 aircraft and 232,000 ships. Custom points were crossed by 114,000,000 people while 27,404 persons were refused entry. At the checkpoints, almost 4,000 pieces of weaponry and ammunition were confiscated.[2] If we relate this traffic generated by 15 million Dutch people to the traffic generated by all 326 million citizens of the European Economic Community – and those central Europeans who since 1989 enjoyed greater freedom of movement – the problem of discovering tiny groups of terrorists looks staggering. The opening of the borders is likely to create new opportunities for those who do not wish well to a united democratic Europe. They might profit more from the benefits of a single market than law-abiding citizens.

The main dilemma posed when democracies are confronted by terrorism is the one between ACCEPTABILITY and EFFECTIVENESS.[3] Anti-terrorist measures have to be acceptable to a democratic society. On the other hand they have to be effective against a particularly unsavoury type of attack. It looks as if we have to make a cruel choice: do we want to sacrifice some democratic substance in order to be effective against terrorism or do we have to tolerate a certain level of terrorism for the sake of maintaining the civil liberties and political rights which we cherish?

How, then, should democracies defend themselves? There are those who prefer inaction to strong counter-measures because they are afraid of the consequences of over-reaction. Their policy is not too different from those who are inclined to fatalism, arguing that nothing can stop determined terrorists. There are those who want to appease the terrorists by giving them what they want, hoping that they will not come back with new demands. On the other side of the middle road are those who plead for stern anti-terrorist legislation, emergency powers and draconian forms of punishment in the expectation that these will deter other would-be terrorists. Finally, there are those who would not refrain from the pro-active use of security forces, with some even advocating counter-terror by commando units.[4] The response will depend on two aspects: first, the nature and seriousness of the terrorist challenge, and second, the sources of strength and weakness in democratic society. The first aspect is the topic of A. J. Jongman's chapter in this volume. The second aspect is the one we shall turn to here.

Strengths of Democracy

Modern democracy which involves, among other elements, popular sovereignty in the form of majority rule, respect for minorities, equality before the law, and guarantee of basic civil and political rights[5] is less normal than we are accustomed to assume. There have been only 23 states in the world which have continuously permitted competitive elections since 1948. Fifteen of these are West European.[6] The least democratic region of the world, on the other hand, is the Middle East and Northern Africa. It is probably no accident that a good part of the terrorist threat to Western democracies comes from this region. Democracies are threatened both from outside and from within. The outside threat comes often from those countries where regimes rule without popular legitimation and where state terrorism is practised at home and sometimes also abroad. According to a 1987 count (see Table 1), there were 39 absolutist states in the world (none in Western Europe). In addition, 48 states were classified 'limited authoritarian' (none in Western Europe). Eleven were labelled 'partial democracies' (including Turkey). Another 25 were termed 'insecure democracies' (including Malta and Greece in Southern Europe, as well as Cyprus). Finally, this survey of 159 nations listed 28 'stable democracies' (17 in Western Europe). Among these are all the nations whose case studies are in this volume.

TABLE 1

DISTRIBUTION OF SYSTEMS OF GOVERNMENT (MID-1980s)

I STABLE DEMOCRACIES: Government based on free and fair elections, people enjoying freedom of expression and civil rights. *Current number*: 28.

II INSECURE DEMOCRACIES: powers of state are, in theory, logically based on popular choice, but democratic institutions function less well or are subject to infringements – as in less than honest elections. Typically, the military stand behind the government. It can oust the civilian government if necessary or desirable and has done so in the past. *Current number*: 25.

III PARTIAL DEMOCRACIES: those countries in which there are genuine democratic elements mixed with authoritarian powers. The authoritarian sector may be the monarchy, the military or a one-party civilian regime. Undemocratic rulers make real concessions to pressures and aspirations for democracy. *Current number*: 11.

IV LIMITED AUTHORITARIAN: private life is not controlled by the regime. The press is free to publish but may not criticize the regime, an elected assembly with little power and other aspects of constitutional government are present. *Current number*: 48.

V ABSOLUTIST OR TOTALITARIAN STATES: there are no rights against officialdom, there is no constitution that the rulers cannot change. Elections have no effects on power. Private life is also likely to be regulated by those in power. *Current number*: 39.

Source: Robert Wesson (ed.), *Democracy: A Worldwide Survey* (NY: Praeger, 1987), pp.xi–xiii. It should be noted that 'current' predates the recent changes in the former Soviet Union and Eastern Europe by several years.

The impression exists that insurgent terrorism is most rampant in Western democracies, in those societies which least deserve it. This impression is probably biased: because we have a free press, political violence against the state is more visible here. Yet there is some truth in this statement. Some features of democracy make it vulnerable to terrorism. Other features make democracies strong and resilient. Let me first point out the internal sources of strength of Western democracy:

1. Rulers can be removed without the use of violence in the process of forming new majorities through *free and fair elections*. The need for political violence to bring about social change is therefore greatly reduced;
2. Rulers can be criticised openly. Protest can take the form of demonstrations and accusations in the *media which are free*. The need to make oneself heard violently is greatly reduced;
3. In cases of conflicts between individuals, groups and the state, *courts act impartially* and more or less independent from the authorities. Minorities can get their rights through courts if majorities will not listen. This again reduces the need for violence.[7]

The existence of these three *conflict-reducing mechanisms* is a great source of strength for democracies, *if* these mechanisms are working properly. There have been cases where ruling parties created election obstacles by devising election districts in such ways as to create secure majorities. The gerrymandering that took place in Northern Ireland or in Sri Lanka are examples. This has arguably contributed to terrorism. In other cases, the courts and the police have not been impartial. Policemen who killed demonstrators without provocation and threat to their own lives without being brought before a court – such as in the case of Benno Ohnesorg, the West Berlin demonstrator who was killed during a demonstration against the Shah of Iran – offer dissenters a good argument for recourse to violence. The German June 2nd [1967] movement took its justification from this particular unpunished police killing. And where the media cannot ventilate the feelings and grievances of the populace, such as in the Basque country under the Franco regime, another element contributing to terrorism becomes active.

The point I wish to make is that democratic processes must be working properly in order to prevent domestic terrorism. Strong emphasis has to be placed not only on majority rule but also on minority rights. Grievances must be taken away as soon as they arise, before they coagulate into embittered action groups that go underground. Prevention is the first line of defence. Defence is more difficult once a terrorist group has been formed, since internal dynamics determine the group's behaviour as much if not more than external facilitating or inhibiting factors. In sum, then, the strengths of well-working democracies can minimise the probability that domestic terrorist groups emerge. However, they are no guarantee against threats from abroad.

Weaknesses of Democracies

Which elements of Western democracies facilitate political violence and terrorism? Democratic societies are open societies. This brings several dangers with it:

1. There is freedom of movement on a scale undreamt of before private cars, mass tourism and international migration. Immigrants and political refugees in Western Europe can offer infrastructures to international terrorism. They can be mobilised from abroad, as in the protests against Salman Rushdie's *The Satanic Verses* in early 1989. The volume of cross-border traffic in Western Europe is already so enormous that it is beyond systematic control.

Professional European terrorists like those of the Provisional IRA are usually not impeded by present borders (although two IRA terrorists were caught at the Dutch-German border in 1987). They have crossed borders in Europe for a long time and for them the changes introduced at the end of 1992 will not make much difference. State-supported terrorists from outside Europe might bring in their weapons through clandestine channels also used by drug-traffickers or they can count on the inviolability of diplomatic luggage and enter on false passports. The idea of replacing borders with computerised registration of the movement of suspected and wanted persons, which underlies the Schengen Information System (SISI), has not yet been put to a test.[8] It might not substitute for border checkpoints, however deficient.

2. There is freedom of association in Western democracies. The private lives of citizens are not the business of the state. Citizens want their privacy protected. This also provides the potential terrorist with a freedom of association and a freedom of movement unthinkable in more authoritarian states. The freedom provided by democracies can be abused for conspiracies against democracy itself. With regard to conspiracy, some European countries like Germany have strong laws (Article 129 StGB regarding participation in a criminal association), while others like the Netherlands have not (although this might change). So democracies are faced with a paradox: in order to give citizens greater freedom of private movement it might be necessary to increase control over the same citizens by a general obligation to carry, at all times, personal identification papers.[9] In some countries, the citizens are accustomed to it. In the Netherlands, for instance, people are not. In fact, several opinion polls have indicated that about half of the Dutch population is opposed to this. To carry identification papers is also very unpopular in the United Kingdom.[10]

This will create problems, since the first line of defense against terrorism is intelligence collection on a scale which also touches the law-abiding citizen and causes irritation with and opposition to creating a surveillance society/ The only solution to popular resistance against such control is, in my view, a strong parliamentary control over the collection and distribution of personal data. Perhaps the European Parliament can form a controlling body to control the controllers, such as the Security Intelligence Review Committee in Canada to make sure that powerful owners of data collection do not lead a life of their own, using it for party-political purposes as happened in the United States under the Nixon administration.

3. The third weakness of democracies is that terrorists find an abundance of targets in our open societies. We might protect some buildings and infrastructural facilities but since the terrorist strategy is not primarily a counter-force but a counter-value strategy this only means a shift in target selection. In societies where value is placed on all human life, almost any group of citizens can be victimized by terrorists to put pressure on the state. Target-hardening of all possible terrorist targets becomes an impossible task unless we want to turn our societies into police states. To take an example: it is said that Western airlines should be protected better, the way El Al is protected. Yet Israel is a garrison state that spends more than 30 per cent of El Al's total budget on security. None of our private airlines could afford such heavy expenditures.

4. The constraints posed by the legal system constitute the fourth weakness of democracies. The legal system of Western democracies requires solid proof of a person's guilt before he or she can be tried. The sophistication of terrorist organizations in their operation, however, makes it more difficult to convict seasoned terrorists than more primitive common criminals who more often than not confess and thereby provide evidence against themselves. The evidence that there is against terrorists sometimes does not stand up in court. Furthermore, national courts have repeatedly been blackmailed by terrorists, for instance through witness intimidation. The creation of a European tribunal for terrorists might be able to remove part of the direct threat of intimidation of jurors when these are not local people from the community wherein terrorists operate.

In addition to these democratic vulnerabilities, there are some stemming from our free market system.

Weaknesses of Free Market Societies to Terrorism

Western societies are characterized not only by a democratic system but also by a free market system. This free market system on the one hand supports the democratic system. On the other hand, however, it can also damage the democratic system. While we are all theoretically equal as citizens, we have different power in the market place. The dynamics of capitalist development creates wealth and inequality which the state cannot fully redress through taxation. Inequality creates grievances which can find their expression in various forms of political violence, not necessarily by those least well off but by those who feel morally outraged and obliged to defend an exploited or neglected underclass. The first modern terrorist movement was called the People's Will and consisted of upper-class Russian students who championed the cause of the people. The reference group with which students identify does not have to be a domestic one; it can be on the other side of the globe. In the Netherlands, for instance, there was a strong anti-apartheid movement which identified with the African National Congress. Some extremists linked to this movement have repeatedly attacked multinationals with investments in South Africa.

The dilemma of Western multinational corporations operating in non-democratic states is that they are obliged to collaborate with authoritarian and repressive regimes to protect their investments. They also tend thereby to strengthen such regimes, although, in the long run, they might be agents for destabilizing such regimes. Past association with non-democratic regimes by multinational corporations found support from powerful Western governments embracing almost any regime which was anti-communist no matter what its human rights record. With the Soviet Union's demise, this attitude is likely to change. Multinational corporations might in future receive less government backing in their dealings with authoritarian regimes. If so, they would do well to be more concerned about legitimizing their business in non-democratic societies than hitherto.

This brings me to another weakness of free market societies. Western business corporations have massively exported arms to countries supporting international terrorists. More recently whole factories for the waging of chemical and bacteriological warfare have been sold to unreliable and unpredictable Arab dictatorships:

- a whole poison gas factory has been constructed in Libya by German business firms. For example, from 1983 onwards, the firm Degussa sold hexamethylene-tetramine for the production of poison gas to the chemical factory near Rabta in Libya;[11]
- Iraq has constructed a factory for biological weapons south east of Baghdad and a Bavarian firm has provided highly toxic biological materials to the Iraqis. These biological weapons are, according to experts, especially suitable for sabotage and terror attacks.[12] There is a

large black – and sometimes not so black – market for explosives and small weapons. While some terrorist weapons used to come from the Eastern bloc, there has been ample capitalist involvement as well. Two examples:

- weapons used to kill Libyan dissidents in West Germany came from the United States through Rotterdam to the Libyan embassy in Bonn, imported by a business-minded ex-CIA agent;
- according to information from the German *Bundeskriminalamt*, the pistol used to kill Aldo Moro was imported into Italy from Austria, being among 150 Czechoslovak machine-guns which Mr Prokosch, an influential Austrian businessman, provided to the Red Brigades.

There can be no doubt that a Europe without borders needs much stricter controls on weapon and explosives sales and transports than in the past. All explosives ought to be tagged and, together with weapons and ammunition, should be declared 'strategic goods' which cannot be transported across European national borders without licences. The present end-user declarations system for international weapons sales has to be changed since some officials in some countries, like Yugoslavia before it broke up, offer them for sale. With regard to weapon exports, particular attention should be given to Belgium which, according to a recent parliamentary investigation, forms a major link in the international illegal arms trade. In Italy, the Mafia plays an important role in arms smuggling. It has provided weapons to right-wing organizations in return for assistance in drug traffic. Many British soldiers in Northern Ireland have died from weapons bought in the United States. Theft from army magazines in Western Europe is also a major source of supply.[13] Clearly, the future Europe will have to place more emphasis on the fight against arms smuggling, arms theft and illegal possession of firearms. By 1984 the European Convention for the Control of the Acquisition and Possession of Firearms by Individuals of 28 June 1978 had been ratified only by Luxembourg and the Netherlands and has been signed only by the Federal Republic of Germany, Greece, Ireland and the United Kingdom.[14]

Western European business should also think twice before marketing new types of weapons which are ideal for terrorists. To give an example: the Austrian weapon factory, Gaston-Glock, has designed a new pistol, the Glock-17, which consists largely of plastic. Only the barrel, the slide and the spring are from metal. Detection by X-ray machines will certainly be made more difficult. It has been reported in 1986 that Colonel Gaddafi was interested in purchasing between 100 and 300 Glock-17 plastic pistols.[15] Apparently, there is still truth in Lenin's saying that capitalists are willing to sell the rope with which they can be hanged.

Another support mechanism for terrorists in Western Europe is the financial one. In order to provide sleepers and active terrorists with the necessary financial means, terrorist organizations rely at least in part on the Western banking system. By protecting the identity and privacy of their clients, Western banks have also protected the business of terrorists. Here, too, more change is necessary than we have seen so far. Yet another way in which business has contributed to the financial strength of terrorists is by the paying of ransom to terrorist organizations in exchange for the lives of kidnapped employees and captains of industry. The insurance industry, which has insured companies against the risks of kidnapping, has payed large sums of money to terrorists – money which allows them to go on with their business of extortion and destabilization.[16]

A major element of the market society which facilitates terrorism is the fact that violence – both as information and as entertainment – is a commercial product for the Western media. Violence, no matter what the cause, always draws the attention of people. The production of violence, whether in fictional action series or in terrorist campaigns, creates audiences which can then be exposed to sales – but also to fear-messages. There is a structural parallel between the use of fictional violence by advertisers in the mass media and the use of real violence by terrorists. The main difference is that advertisers pay the media for their message while terrorists, by attacking newsworthy persons, create information which is freely distributed by the mass media system to mass audiences. In my study on Insurgent Terrorism and the Western News Media,[17] I found no fewer than 32 different ways in which the media can serve terrorists, one of them being the 'learning of new coercive techniques from media reports on terrorism'. Media coverage is also a form of gratification for most terrorists. They are major consumers of their own propaganda. Coverage of their deeds gives them a sense of identity and power.

For the media, terrorist news is good news in that it offers live drama and compelling pictures. Terrorist news items tend to be over-represented in our news programs. With the advertisers using fictional violence to sell us their products and the terrorists using real violence to manipulate our perception of the world and imprint their presence and power in our minds, television puts violence on the public agenda in a way that is disproportional to the amount of violence in our everyday experience in Western Europe. I also believe that fictional violence has a negative impact on the level of violence in society. The Swiss government passed a law in 1989 prohibiting gratuitous violence in video movies.

The larger problem of violence in commercially-sponsored television action series is, however, not dealt with. When French television was commercialized some years ago, analysts noted a rise in violent materials being shown. The opening of the borders for television in Europe is likely to have the same effect. Violence for entertainment and for selling commercials is not so innocent. All television is, to some extent, educational television. While terrorists might not need any more education in violence, would-be imitators of televised violence are a fact. Rambo has found an admirer not only in Ronald Reagan who promised to deal with terrorism 'in the spirit of Rambo'; he has also found imitators among common viewers such as Michael Ryan, the 1987 mass-killer in Hungerford, Great Britain.

It is time for a new maturity that recognizes that the media do much more than just report what happens in the world. The media, and especially television, are the central market square in today's global society. Yet television is not reality. Television is, as Joshua Meyrowitz has pointed out, 'a construction and reconstruction of reality'.[18] There have to be some rules, some guidelines, a code of ethics for those professionally engaged in putting reality together for us when violence becomes a method of getting into the news and of making the media work for terrorists. It is interesting to note that the problem of 'propaganda by the deed' was already the subject of governmental concern back in 1898 during an international conference wherein governments took measures to contain anarchist *attentats*. Following the suggestion of Germany and Austria, the governmental conference accepted a proposal to limit press coverage of anarchist assassinations.[19]

In February 1989 a 'political accord' was reached in Brussels about the future of European television within a Europe without borders. One issue on which European ministers agreed was that at least half of the programmes broadcast should be European products.[20] I think that European television should not only be helped against American and Japanese competition but also against terrorist producers of violence for media-based audience manipulation.

Conclusion

I have focused on what I perceive to be the main elements of strength and weakness in Western democracies facing terrorism. In order to cope better with intra-European as well as imported terrorism, we have to reduce our weaknesses and improve our strengths. I will not offer detailed recommendations here on how this could be done. There is, however, one point I want to stress.

The strength of a democratic state is an outflow of the legitimacy of its government. Where authorities respond to majority political demands and respect minorities' rights, terrorists cannot successfully exploit political issues to gain a degree of legitimacy themselves. In such circumstances, the terrorists' own tactics discredit them, depriving them of legitimacy. However, when democratic governments resort to illegal countermeasures against acts of insurgent terrorism, this is invariably exploited by the terrorists and their supporters, with a consequent decline in government legitimacy. The recourse to unlawful methods of repression by government actors is a temptation sometimes triggered and subsequently condoned by popular and opposition party demands to do something – 'anything' – to 'stop terrorism'. Those tactics which cannot stand the light of day will invariably backfire when they are exposed. The resulting loss of credibility will create political damage far greater than the gains achieved with quick fix methods. Irangate is a testimony to this.

Strategy has been defined as 'a process of inducing another party to choose action beneficial to oneself'.[21] An insurgent terrorist strategy is successful if it manages to bring a democratic government to a lawless over-reaction or to intimidate it into a spineless under-reaction. A democratic society, if it is self-confident and true to itself, can take many more blows and has more resilience than its numerically insignificant opponent. Ultimately, it is a question of not being demoralized while providing no signs of encouragement and hope to the terrorist side. In this psychological warfare, the media play a crucial role even if they do not want to acknowledge this. However, the management of perceptions by and through the media alone will not do and might even backfire when these are not based on solid achievements which show consistency and inspire credibility. A coherent Western democratic response to terrorism will, in addition, also require clarity and consensus as to what we wish to regard as terrorism and how we wish to combat it.[22]

NOTES

1. I was unable to find the source for this quotation.
2. Figures from *Volkskrant*, 12 July 1988, p.1. It should be kept in mind that the checks at the border with Belgium are almost non-existent for private cars, due to older Benelux agreements. The figures therefore refer mainly to sea- and air-traffic and land traffic at the German border.
3. This dichotomy has been stressed by the director of a private US school offering special courses designed to train anti-terrorist techniques. See Thomas Plate and Andrea Darvi, *Secret Police: The Inside Story of a Network of Terror* (NY: Garden City, 1981), p.57.
4. This scale is based on Frederick Y. Homer, 'Terror in the United States: Three Perspectives', in M. Stohl (ed.), *The Politics of Terrorism* (NY: Marcel Dekker, 1983), pp.162–5.
5. Axel Görlitz (ed.), *Handlexikon zur Politikwissenschaft* (Hamburg: Reinbeck, Rowohlt, 1973), Vol.1, pp.58–9.

6. Dennis A. Kavanagh, 'Western Europe', in Robert Wesson (ed.), *Democracy: A Worldwide Survey* (NY: Praeger, 1987), p.12.
7. Based on Wesson's, 'Introduction', in Wesson, *Democracy*, p.3.
8. Cf. Peter Klerks, *Het Schengen Informatiesysteem: Grenswachter aan de Europese Buitengrenzen, Privacy en registratie* 14/3 (Sept. 1989), pp.16–21.
9. Juan Linz has pointed out what few like to hear: 'Paradoxically, a democratic regime might need a larger number of internal security forces than a stabilized dictatorship, since it cannot count on the pervasive effect of fear'. J.J. Linz and Alfred Stephan, *The Breakdown of Democratic Regimes* (Baltimore: Johns Hopkins Press, 1978), p.61.
10. J. Naeye, 'Legitimatieplicht voor gekleurde Nederlanders' *Nederlands Juristenblad* 63/33 (Oct. 1988), pp.1193–98; P. van Reenen, 'Policing Europe After 1992: Co-operation and Competition', *European Affairs* 3/2 (Summer 1989), p.48.
11. Degussa owned 42.5 per cent of the shares of Degesch [*Deutsche Gesellschaft für Schädelingsbekämpfung*]. Degesch had also distributed 100,000kg of Cyklon-B to be used in Nazi gas chambers (see Jehudith Noach, 'Stress en Traumatisering', Master's Thesis in Clinical Psychology, Leiden Univ., 1990, p.225).
12. *Der Spiegel*, Nr.4, 1989, p.16ff. 'Mit dem Elend anderer Geschäfte machen?'; *Der Spiegel*, Nr.5, 1989, p.16ff. 'Hundertmal tödlicher als C-Waffen'
13. *Der Spiegel*, 27 July 1981 (Nr.31), quoting from a report by the Center for Contemporary Studies (ed.), *The International Arms Trade and the Terrorist* (London: Contemporary Affairs Briefing No.7, 1981).
14. See M. Zagari, this volume.
15. J.L. Scherer, *Terrorism* 1/2 (May 1986).
16. James Adams, *The Financing of Terror* (NY: Simon & Schuster, 1987), p.249.
17. A.P. Schmid and J. de Graaf, *Violence as Communication. Insurgent Terrorism and the Western News Media* (London: Sage, 1982).
18. J. Meyrowitz, 'Television's Covert Challenge', *Dialogue*, No.82 (April 1988), p.62.
19. Peter Klerks, *Terreur Bestrijding in Nederland 1970–1988* (Amsterdam: Ravijn, 1989), p.161.
20. *Volkskrant*, 28 Feb. 1989, p.4.
21. Tanter and Kaufman, in Y. Evron (ed.), *International Violence* (Jerusalem: Hebrew Univ., 1979), p.204.
22. Geoffrey M. Levitt, *Democracies against Terror. The Western Response to State-Supported Terrorism* (NY: Praeger, 1989), p.97.

Trends in International and Domestic Terrorism in Western Europe, 1968–1988

A. J. JONGMAN

An assessment of the problems related to trend analysis on international and domestic terrorism during two decades, beginning in 1968, including definitions, data collection, and sources, shows that propositions on terrorism in general are almost impossible to make and are not very useful for policy-making. Nevertheless conclusions are drawn about the number of incidents, number of casualties, types of incidents and target selection. Particular emphasis is placed on the margins of error and the differences based on the various data collection efforts.

While the first part concentrates on terrorism on a global scale, the second part deals with Western Europe in particular. Overall and national trends are provided for number of incidents, casualties, incident type, active groups and their tactics and target selection. Special attention is given to the spill-over effect from the Middle East and the selection of American targets. It is almost impossible to indicate an overall trend for Western Europe. Various European countries experienced and continue to experience severe domestic terrorist problems which in some cases appeared to be far more destructive and lethal than international terrorism.

A major conclusion is that researchers should be very careful with trend analysis on empirical data of terrorism, particularly on domestic terrorism. The trends vary from country to country depending on their specific political problems.

Terrorism is one of many problems in our societies that needs our attention, yet its importance should not be exaggerated. In most West European countries, the number of terrorist incidents is less than one per cent of the total number of criminal offences. The material damage caused by terrorist incidents is far less than the material damage caused by other forms of crime. Risks International estimated the material damage caused by international terrorist incidents at 33 million dollars for the year 1986.[1]

In comparison with other causes of death such as traffic accidents, drug-related murders, homicides and violence in the family, terrorism is a minor problem.

In the context of more than 100 million war deaths in this century, the number of victims of non-state terrorism makes no statistically significant difference. Yet as a tool for political violence – that can be wielded by just a single individual – contemporary terrorism has no rival in the textbooks of conventional military strategy. The rewards are high, and the risks relatively small. Perhaps that is the main reason why techniques of political terrorism have spread around the globe.

The media influence our images of terrorism. They generally emphasize rising trends in the amount and lethality of terrorism.[2] Is this trend real or not? Here, empirical data on political terrorism in Western Europe will be evaluated. The various existing data bases will be compared in order to determine their value for trend analysis. After briefly discussing the general trends for the whole world, in terms of incidents, casualties, regional distribution, target categories and types of incidents, we will take a closer look at the situation in Western Europe. Unfortunately, the majority of the available data bases concentrate on international or transnational terrorism while several European countries have more to fear from domestic terrorism.

Any assertion on trends in terrorism has to rely on data provided on a regular basis according to the same definition. Very few agencies in the world that collect data on terrorism fulfil these two conditions. The information on terrorism is scattered, incomplete and definitions have been adapted to new circumstances. The most suitable data for trend analysis have been provided by state agencies which carefully exclude from their public reports data that could undermine government policies. Unfortunately, these are the only reports that are used for trend analysis.

The annual reports on the patterns of terrorism issued by the US Department of State are by far the most widely quoted reports. Another well-known source is the reports of the insurance company, Risks International.[3] It issues weekly, monthly and quarterly reports, but unfortunately these are not publicly available. In more recent years, research institutes have started data collection efforts, including the University of Aberdeen and the Foundation for the Study of Terrorism in London (both UK), the Polemological Institute in Paris (FR), the Polemological Institute of Groningen University and the Center for the Study of Social Conflicts, Leiden University (both NE) and the Jaffee Center for Strategic Studies in Tel Aviv. There are private companies in the United States which collect data. NATO has established a working group on terrorism that has so far published two reports.[4]

Ted Robert Gurr critically evaluated the existing data bases on political violence. He found that the older data bases concentrating on the analysis of trends and characteristics of incidents were not well-suited to the analysis of other questions, such as the analysis of political context and causation. He highlighted the principal omissions in the publicly available data as follows:

(1) There are no comprehensive, current data sets on incidents of domestic terrorism. As a consequence, there can be no analyses of their trends, diffusion, or of the relations between transnational and domestic conflicts;

(2) There are no data sets which provide systematic information about the identities and characteristics of groups which use terrorist strategies. As a result, we cannot specify with any precision what kinds of groups are most likely to use terror, or the circumstances in which opposition groups shift toward or away from the use of terror, or trace and compare the life-cycles of violent political groups;

(3) There are no broadly-based data sets with coded information on the outcome of terrorist campaigns or on government responses to episodes of domestic terrorism. Therefore, it is not possible to anticipate the effects of success or failure on terrorist groups, nor to test the effects of different kinds of government policies toward domestic terrorism;

(4) There is no systematic compilation of information from case studies about ideologies, recruitment practices, organization, decision-making, or command and control in violent political groups. Therefore, the ways in which they operate and respond to changing circumstances and counterterrorism policies is largely a matter of speculation;

(5) There is no system or common framework for accumulating information on the psychological characteristics, recruitment, and careers of members of terrorist movements. Therefore, we have mostly impressionistic evidence about the kinds of people likely to join and lead terrorist organizations, and the kinds of incentives and threats which might induce them to alter their behaviour. Gurr concluded that many, perhaps most, of the important questions being raised cannot be answered adequately with the information presently available to scholars.[5]

Definitions

The number of recorded terrorist incidents in a data base is dependent on the definition used as well as the quality of the sources used for the data collection. In addition, recording procedures of data collectors influence the count. The CIA report for 1979, for instance, deliberately excluded, 'the assassinations and cross-border operations associated with the Arab-Israeli conflict, unless those incidents either victimized non-combatant nationals of states outside the principal area of conflict or became the object of international controversy'. This means that international incidents in the Middle East are considerably underreported.

In 1980 the CIA entirely revised its figures for the previous years. The reasons given were that the range of data sources they had previously used was too narrow and that they had now decided to include statistics on 'threats' and 'hoaxes'. This dramatically revised the figures upward. The CIA's 1980 report claimed 6,714 international terrorist incidents from 1968 to 1980, whereas their 1979 report totalled only 3,336. The US Department of State's statistics provide, by general agreement, the most comprehensive and accurate figures on incidents involving American citizens and property. Yet, what is an 'incident'? To give an example: the RAND Corporation chronology treated a wave of 40 bombings in the same city in the same night as a single incident, whereas the CIA's data base dealt with it as 40 separate incidents.

There are other major problems, such as erroneous information, conflicting reports from different or even from the same sources, and deliberate suppression or underreporting by the authorities.

Researchers of the Center for the Study of Social Conflicts at Leiden University and the French Polemological Institute in Paris collect data on all incidents of political violence, while other data collection efforts specifically concentrate on international terrorism. However, in some data bases, guerrilla activities are recorded as terrorist incidents when they are directed against civilians. While most researchers concentrate on acts by non-state agents, others, including the Jaffee Center and the French Polemological Institute, include acts by state agents when they are directed against the public-at-large or individuals not associated with a dissident organization involved in terrorism.

As Table 1 reveals, some data bases rely on just one or a few newspapers while others are based on various sources. The choice for a selection of sources is to a large extent determined by financial resources and manpower. Definitions, on the other hand, are based on conceptual and ideological considerations. In the following, the main conceptualizations are listed:

United States Department of State:

> Terrorism is premeditated motivated violence perpetrated against noncombatant targets by subnational groups or clandestine state agents, usually intended to influence an audience. International terrorism is terrorism involving the citizens or territory of more than country.[6]

Edward Mickolus:

> International/transnational terrorism is the use or threat of use, of anxiety inducing extranormal violence for political purposes by any individual or group, whether acting for or in opposition to established government authority, when such action is intended to

TABLE 1

SOURCES USED FOR DATA COLLECTION

Mickolus (1989)	Newsagencies (AP, UPI, Reuters), *Washington Post, New York Times*, Foreign Broadcasting Information Service, Big networks (ABC, NBC, CBS), Chronologies of the Nuclear Regulatory Commission and the FBI
Mickolus (1980)	US Department of State, FAA, USIA, US Senate and House of Representatives staff reports for congressional committees, Facts On File, Associated Press dispatches, *New York Times, Washington Post, Chicago Tribune, Detroit Free Press, The Economist*
COMT, Leiden University	*International Herald Tribune*
French Polemological Institute	*International Herald Tribune, Le Monde, Neue Zürcher Zeitung*
Jaffee Center	Mass media (primarily dailies, weeklies, periodicals), professional publications, government releases
State Department	Newspapers, diplomatic channels
Gurr	*New York Times*, regional news sources, scholarly literature
Risks International	Not specified
London Institute	Not specified
RAND	Newspapers and other sources
CIA	Not specified

influence the attitudes and behavior of a target group wider than the immediate victims and when, through the nationality or foreign ties of its perpetrators, through its location the mechanics of its resolution, its ramifications transcend national boundaries . . . Kidnappings solely motivated for money are not considered to be terrorist events unless ransoms are intended to finance the achievement of political goals . . . The chronology does not classify incidents as terrorism that relate to declared wars or major military interventions by governments, or guerrilla attacks on military targets conducted as internationally recognized acts of belligerency. If, however, the guerrillas were striking at civilians or the dependents of military personnel in an attempt to create an atmosphere of fear to foster political objectives, then the attacks are considered to be terrorism. Official, government-sanctioned military acts in response to terrorist attacks, such as the Israeli bombing, of the PLO headquarters in Tunis or the United States seizure of an Egyptian plane carrying the terrorists from the *Achille Lauro* incident, are not themselves coded.[7]

Jaffee Center:

> For purposes of data collection, a terrorist group is defined as an organization other than a state (although it may enjoy state support and/or act in the service of a state) that resorts to the systematic use of violence in order to achieve political ends. A terrorist incident is any violent activity conducted by a non-state organization in order to attain political objectives. (. . .) In addition to these categories, the JCSS data base monitors international terrorist activity conducted by direct emissaries of states on foreign territory. International terrorist incidents are defined as those events in which more than one country is involved. Nevertheless . . . we excluded incidents that formed part of an underground struggle conducted by rebels against a foreign army in their own country. Inclusion of violent events associated with struggles of this sort would considerably distort the picture of international terrorism . . . The statistics also refer to incidents carried out by states' agents when the attacks targeted either the public-at-large or individuals not associated with a dissident organization involved in terrorism. State-sponsored attacks against members of terrorist groups are considered part of a counter terrorism effort conducted by the state, and are excluded from this report.[8]

Ted Robert Gurr:

> [This chapter] surveys the use of 'terrorist' tactics by private groups for political purposes. The interpretative problems are sidestepped by using an empirical definition of this kind of 'political terrorism' that makes no *a priori* assumptions about what effects the users hope to accomplish by their actions or about how their would-be victims react. The definition has three objective elements. The first is that destructive violence is used, by stealth rather than in open combat. Explosives and incendiary devices are the archetypical weapons of political terrorism, but there are others, including sniping, kidnapping, hijacking, biological agents, and atomic devices, the latter thus far feared rather than used. The second element in the definition is that some, at least, of the principal targets are political ones. Political targets include public buildings, political figures and groups, and the military and the police. Terrorist tactics often are aimed at private targets as well, sometimes for dramatic effects, sometimes because of their political associations, sometimes simply because rebels have many axes to grind. The third definitional element is that these actions be carried

out by groups operating clandestinely and sporadically. This restriction is needed to distinguish the practitioners of terrorism from armed bands of rebels and revolutionaries who operate more or less continuously from areas that they control at least in part . . . All three elements must be present for an act or set of actions to be considered 'political terrorism' in the context of [this study]. The groups responsible for such actions are called 'terrorists' [here], but without assuming that they would describe their actions or aims in the language of terrorism.[9]

French Polemological Institute:

The recording of terrorist incidents by the French Polemological Institute is part of a broader data collection effort of all incidents of political violence. Its codings allow for eight types of incident that can occur in ten possible contexts, terrorism being one of them. It does not have a specific definition of terrorism but it uses the following codes for 'type of incident':

0 Spontaneous violence (riots, demonstrations, massacres . . .)
1 Attacks against property (or directed at property, understood as material interests or group symbols)
2 Attacks against persons (executions and political assassinations, assaults . . .)
3 Deprivation of liberty (hostage-taking, kidnapping, disappearances, imprisonment, internment, skyjacking)
4 Limited confrontations (rescues, ambushes, skirmishes, raids, fusillades . . .)
5 Significant battles (land, sea or air)
6 Shelling and bombardment
7 Other

These types of incidents can occur in the ten following contexts:

0 State conflict/armed interstate tension
1 Significant intrastate conflict (guerrilla, civil war)
2 Economic and social struggles (strikes, agrarian reform, etc.)
3 Terrorism
4 Religious confrontation
5 Ethnic or nationalist claims
6 Intracommunity confrontation (minorities, racism)
7 Legal violence (repression, etc.)
8 Violence involving a change in political regime (*coup d'état*, revolution etc.)
9 Other.[10]

Incidents: Numbers and Trends. Table 2 provides a comparison of the data provided by the above mentioned institutions across the two decades under study. In a few cases, data for 1988 are not given. The comparison clearly shows that the trends in the various reports vary according to the definition and the sources used to collect the data.

TABLE 2

COMPARISON OF RECORDED TERRORIST INCIDENTS
BY VARIOUS DATA SOURCES FOR THE PERIOD 1968–1988

Year	Risks Int. **	US State Dept. *	RAND *	CIA *	Mickolus *
1968	—	142	35	111	123
1969	—	214	51	166	179
1970	293	391	101	282	344
1971	278	324	52	216	301
1972	206	648	84	269	480
1973	311	564	163	275	340
1974	388	528	153	382	425
1975	572	475	89	297	342
1976	727	599	151	413	455
1977	1,257	562	143	279	340
Sub Total (1970–77)	*4,032*	*4,091*	*936*	*2,413*	*3,027*
1978	1,511	850			
1979	2,585	657			
Sub Total (1970–79)	*8,128*	*5,598*			

Year			Mickolus *	LIST *	INTER *	Imprimis I *	Imprimis II **
1980	2,773	760	501				
1981	2,701	496	471				
1982	2,492	477	423				
1983	2,838	485	428	495			
1984	3,525	598	471	597			
1985	3,010	785	526	812	408	812	6,375
1986	2,860	774	533	848	437	848	8,550
1987	3,089	832	503		377	875	12,750
Sub Total (1985–87)	*8,959*	*2,391*	*1,562*		*1,222*	*2,535*	*27,675*
1988	3,734	864			433		
TOTAL	*35,150 (1970–88)*	*12,025 (1968–88)*			*1,655 (1985–88)*		

* International/transnational terrorist incidents only
** Domestic and international terrorist incidents combined
Sources: Adapted from data published by US Department of State, CIA, RAND, Risks International, Imprimis, E.F. Mickolus, Jaffee Center for Strategic Studies, London Institute for the Study of Terrorism.

For example, both Risks International and the US Department of State have collected data since the end of the 1960s. Risks International recorded a total of 35,150 incidents between 1970 and 1988, while the US Department of State recorded a total of 13,572 incidents between 1968 and *1991*. The large difference can be explained by the fact that the US Department of State concentrated on international terrorism, while Risks International also included domestic incidents.

In the United States several agencies have collected data on terrorism. Table 3 compares the number of incidents recorded by five different US sources during 1970–77. Differences of more than 400 per cent exist, ranging from 4,091 incidents recorded by the US State Department to only 936 incidents recorded by the RAND Corporation.

TABLE 3

TERRORIST INCIDENTS RECORDED BY FIVE US DATA BASES
DURING 1970–1977

Risks International	4,032 incidents
US Department of State	4,091 incidents
Mickolus	3,027 incidents
CIA	2,413 incidents
RAND	936 incidents

Table 4 compares data from six different data bases for the more recent 1985–87 period. Again, large differences exist (200–300 per cent),

TABLE 4

TERRORIST INCIDENTS RECORDED BY SIX DATA BASES
DURING 1985–1987

Risks International	8,959 domestic and international incidents
IMPRIMIS II	27,675 domestic and international incidents
IMPRIMIS I	2,535 international incidents
US State Department	2,391 international incidents
Mickolus	1,562 international incidents
Jaffee Center	1,222 international incidents

ranging from a high of 2,535 international incidents recorded by Imprimis to a low of 1,222 international incidents recorded by the Jaffee Center. The maximum number of domestic and international incidents combined has been recorded by Imprimis, totalling more than three times the number Risks International recorded for the same period (30,120 vs. 8,959).

The trends over time differ across data bases as well. For example, both Risks International and the US State Department, while recording vastly different totals, show similar stable trends during the 1985–87 period, with a slight drop in 1986. The Jaffee Center for Strategic Studies, on the other hand, which limits its analysis to international terrorism, just as the US State Department does, not only recorded only half the number of incidents listed by the US State Department, but showed the opposite trend. The total number of incidents decreased from 1985 to 1987, with a peak in 1986.

The Foundation for the Study of Terrorism in London (Imprimis), which does make a distinction between international and domestic incidents, recorded slightly more incidents of international terrorism than the US State Department, but with a steady increase from 1985 to 1987. The data did not show a drop in the number of incidents in 1986 as the American data did. A steady increase over the three years was also found when domestic incidents were included as well (Imprimis II). The data of Edward Mickolus show a rising trend in the 1980s since 1982 that reached a peak in 1986 and decreased in 1987. For 1985–87, he therefore replicates the trend found by the Jaffee Centre and not the other American data bases.

The only two data bases that record incidents throughout the 1970s *and* the 1980s are Risks International and the US State Department (see Table 2). Because the former records domestic incidents as well as international ones, the absolute numbers are consistently higher throughout most of the two decades, as might be expected. During the 1970s Risks International records an annual average of 813 incidents/year while the US State Department records 560 incidents/year. Comparing these averages with those recorded for the 1980s shows that the combined data set of Risks International (domestic and international incidents) jumps to an annual average during 1980–88 of 3,002 incidents/year compared with a much more modest rise to 675 (international) incidents/year for the US State Department's data base.

This much higher increase in the average annual number of incidents recorded by Risks International suggests that the number of domestic terrorist incidents has gone up much more in the 1980s than the number of international incidents. This highlights once again the importance of determining what kinds of incidents are counted in a particular data base before comparisons are made. It also underscores how much information is lost by an exclusive focus on international terrorism.

Casualties: If we compare statistics on deaths and injuries compiled by the US State Department and Risks International, very different results emerge. The former recorded a total number of 7,664 deaths and 17,618 injured caused by international terrorist incidents in 1968–88. On the other hand, Risks International, which also included domestic incidents, recorded a total number of 28,110 deaths and 18,925 injured during 1970–83. Despite the shorter period, the latter data base records many more deaths than the former and the deaths outnumber the injuries, a result that is not typical of most statistics, where the number of injured usually surpasses several times the number of those killed. Edward Mickolus recorded a total number of 3,668 deaths and 7,474 injured for 1968–80.

Using the US State Department's figures, which cover both the 1970s and the 1980s, the annual average of casualties (dead and injured) shows an upward trend. The annual average number of deaths rose from 293 in the 1970s to 515 in the 1980s, while the annual average of injured rose from 599 to 1,251 from one decade to the next. When domestic incidents are included, using the data of Risks International, annual averages of deaths (2,003) and of injured (1,352) during 1970–83 are, of course, much higher. Mickolus' data, which only includes transnational incidents, show lower casualty rates comparable to those of the US State Department for the 1970s. For 1968–80, his data show annual averages of 282 deaths and 575 injured.

TABLE 5

RELATIVE FREQUENCY DISTRIBUTION OF TERRORIST INCIDENTS, IN PERCENTAGES, 1968–1987

	Risks 70–86 %	USSD 68–78 %	USSD 85–87 %	Mickolus 68–80 %	Mickolus 80–87 %
North America	3.0	9.3	0.2	10.0	6.0
Latin America	53.0	26.5	15.0	21.0	17.0
Western Europe	24.0	37.0	27.0	33.0	37.0
Sub-Sahara Africa	3.0	3.7	3.7	3.0	5.0
Asia	6.0	5.6	11.0	7.0	9.0
Middle East	12.0	16.1	42.7	21.0	26.0
Eastern Europe		0.4	0.1	1.0	0.7
Transregional			0.1		0.1
Oceania		0.03		1.0	

Geographic Distribution: Turning now to the geographic distribution of terrorist incidents, this too varies according to data source. Table 5 compares the relative frequency of terrorist incidents for different regions of the world across a variety of data bases. According to Risks International, more than half of the recorded incidents (53 per cent) in 1970–86 were recorded in Latin America and about a quarter (24 per cent) in Western Europe. By contrast, data bases limited to international terrorist incidents, such as those of the US State Department or of

Edward Mickolus, show higher percentages for Western Europe (27–37 per cent) and lower percentages for Latin America (15–26.5 per cent), indicating that international terrorism has affected Western Europe more than any other region of the world, while domestic terrorism has affected Latin America more. While Risks International records only 12 per cent for the Middle East from 1970–86, the other sources record higher percentages, particularly in the 1980s. This again most probably reflects definitional differences in what is recorded.

Trends in the 1980s: The various sources show different trends for the 1980s. According to the data of the US State Department, the average percentage of (international) incidents in Latin America decreased from 26.5 per cent in the 1970s to 19 per cent in the 1980s. For Latin America, the data of the US State Department show peaks in 1981, 1983 and 1986. Mickolus' data show peaks in 1980, 1981 and 1986 (see Table 6).

TABLE 6

PERCENTAGE SHARE OF TERRORIST INCIDENTS IN LATIN AMERICA, 1980–1987

	80 %	81 %	82 %	83 %	84 %	85 %	86 %	87 %	Total %
US State Department		23	20	25	14	15	21	13	19
Mickolus	22	22	17	17	12	16	21	13	17

According to the US State Department, the relative share of (international) terrorist incidents in Western Europe reached a peak in 1982 with 52 per cent, but it has steadily decreased since then to 18 per cent in 1987. On the other hand, Mickolus' data show a cyclical pattern with peaks in 1982 and 1985 (see Table 7).

TABLE 7

PERCENTAGE SHARE OF TERRORIST INCIDENTS IN WESTERN EUROPE, 1980–1987

	80 %	81 %	82 %	83 %	84 %	85 %	86 %	87 %	Total %
US State Department		43	52	39	39	28	20	18	34
Mickolus	37	42	45	29	37	44	32	28	37

In more recent years, there has been a considerable shift to the Middle East (see Table 8). According to the US State Department, the relative share rose from 16.1 per cent in the 1970s to 32 per cent in the 1980s.

TABLE 8

PERCENTAGE SHARE OF TERRORIST INCIDENTS IN THE MIDDLE EAST,
1980–1987

	80 %	81 %	82 %	83 %	84 %	85 %	86 %	87 %	Total %
US State Department		20	11	22	34	46	47	45	32
Mickolus	21	20	13	33	30	24	27	28	26

The data of the US State Department show a steeply rising trend during the 1980s from a low of 11 per cent in 1982 to a peak of 47 per cent in 1986. The data of Mickolus show a peak of 33 per cent in 1983; since then the percentage dropped over two years and rose again in 1986, but showed no steep rise.

Asia's share of recorded terrorist incidents rose steadily in the 1980s, from a low of 3 per cent in 1981 to 20 per cent in 1987, according to the US State Department. Mickolus' data show a similar trend, from a low of two percent in 1981 to a peak of 21 per cent in 1987. In Africa, both sources show more or less similar trends. The percentage shares fluctuated between two and nine per cent and both sources show a peak for the year 1984. Mickolus' data show a rising trend until 1984 and, thereafter, a clear downward trend.

The shares of Eastern Europe were less than one per cent in both sources. The data of the US State Department show a clear downward trend. For North America, the two sources show different trends and present different percentage shares (Table 9).

TABLE 9

PERCENTAGE SHARE OF TERRORIST INCIDENTS IN NORTH AMERICA,
1980–1987

	80 %	81 %	82 %	83 %	84 %	85 %	86 %	87 %	Total %
US State Department		6.0	7.0	2.0	0.8	0.5	0.3	0.0	2.3
Mickolus	11.0	9.0	13.0	5.0	2.0	2.0	4.0	5.0	6.0

After a peak of seven per cent in 1982 the relative share shows a downward trend approaching zero in 1987, according to the US State Department. However, the data of Mickolus show an opposite trend. After a peak of 13 per cent in 1982 and lows of two per cent in 1984 and 1985 the data show an upward trend reaching five per cent in 1987. Mickolus' percentages are also consistently higher than those of the US State Department.

Target Categories

While terrorist acts are often considered to be blind in their targeting, there are certain categories of preferred targets. However, because the existing data bases utilize different target categories, a unified picture is difficult to establish. For example, Tables 10–12 present data from three different sources for the year 1987 (and, for one, 1988 as well). The American State Department (Table 10) makes a distinction between facility attacks and attacks on persons. The category 'other' shows the highest percentages for both types of attacks, 51.3 per cent and 68.4 per cent respectively. This would seem to indicate that civilians are the main target of (international) terrorism. The majority of the facility attacks that are clearly identified are directed against business (24.8 per cent), while the majority of the attacks on a specific category of person are directed against the military (11.9 per cent).

TABLE 10

RELATIVE FREQUENCY DISTRIBUTION OF TARGET CATEGORIES, IN 1987, IN PERCENTAGES, ACCORDING TO US STATE DEPARTMENT

	Type of facility %	Type of victim %
Business	24.8	6.1
Government	8.7	7.3
Military	7.8	11.9
Diplomat	7.5	6.3
Other	51.3	68.4

The Israeli Jaffee Center (Table 11) does not make a distinction between the two types of attacks and it excludes the category 'military'. The data suggest a rather equal distribution of targeting against economic (30.8 per cent), political and adversary (26.5 per cent) and random public (26.0 per cent) targets in 1987, with diplomats being the targets in only 14.3 per cent of the incidents that year. For 1988 the Jaffee Center data show higher percentages for the categories 'political and adversary' and 'diplomatic', with increases of 3.6 and 4 per cent respectively, with a commensurate decrease of 5.7 per cent for the category 'random public'.

The French Polemological Institute, with a still different classification, records the greatest percentages for public officials (35.6 per cent) and anonymous civilians (30 per cent). The remaining two categories, members of clandestine organisations (16 per cent) and anonymous civilians in a visible category (18 per cent), are targeted only about half as much as the other two. The Institute's third category is the only one

TABLE 11

RELATIVE FREQUENCY DISTRIBUTION OF TARGET CATEGORIES,
IN PERCENTAGES, ACCORDING TO JAFFEE CENTER

	1987 %	1988 %
Political and adversary	26.5	30.1
Random public	26.0	20.3
Economic	30.8	31.1
Diplomatic	14.3	17.1
Unclear and other	2.4	1.1

that is clearly consistent with either state terrorism or the enforcement
terrorism of insurgent groups, although the Jaffee Centre's 'political and
adversary' category could also include such forms of terrorism.

TABLE 12

RELATIVE FREQUENCY DISTRIBUTION OF TARGET CATEGORIES IN 1987,
IN PERCENTAGES, ACCORDING TO ETUDES POLEMOLOGIQUES

(1)	Public officials	35.6%
(2)	Members of clandestine organizations	16.0%
(3)	Anonymous civilians	30.0%
(4)	Anonymous civilians but with a categorial visibility	18.0%

While it makes sense to distinguish between material targets and
human targets, American data bases often make a further distinction
between American targets and non-American targets. According to
Risks International, only four per cent of the domestic and international
attacks in 1986 were directed against American targets. The majority of
these anti-American attacks were bombings (85 per cent) largely directed
against American business (39 per cent). Other favourite targets for
bombings were American diplomats (20 per cent) and American police
and military (11.7 per cent). Assassinations were mainly directed against
US diplomats and American businessmen. Only one hijacking was
recorded in 1986. Two of the seven American facility attacks were
directed against the media. The majority of the non-American
assassinations were directed against unknown civilians (26 per cent),
police and military (23 per cent), government (19 per cent) and political
parties (15 per cent).

Trends in Type of Incident

The data available also allow us to observe trends in type of incident
although, once again, different data bases provide different classifications.

The most exhaustive list of incident types comes from Mickolus (see Table 13). Some types, such as threat, theft/break in, conspiracy, hoax and arms smuggling clearly stretch the definitional limits of terrorism. Others, such as suicide car bombing, added for the 1980s, are clearly newly emerging tactics. Still others, like nuclear-related weapons attack, represent the fears/expectations of policy-makers rather than the inclination of specific terrorist groups.

TABLE 13

RELATIVE FREQUENCY DISTRIBUTION OF EVENT TYPES, 1968–1987

	Mickolus A (1968–1980)		CIA (1968–1978)		Mickolus B (1980–1987)		Change (B–A)
	No.	%	No	%	No.	%	
Kidnapping	401	6.0	243	8.0	335	9.0	+3.0
Hostage/barricade	139	2.1	60	2.0	57	1.5	−0.6
Hijacking	173	2.6	92	3.0	61	1.6	−1.0
Explosive bombing	2,371	35.3	1,473	48.4	1,364	35.4	+0.1
Incendiary bombing	753	11.2	162	5.3	238	6.2	−5.0
Letter bombing	470	7.0			42	1.1	−5.9
Armed attack	278	4.1	162	5.3	366	9.5	+5.4
Assassination	442	6.6	199	6.5	468	12.1	+5.5
Sabotage	24	0.4			15	0.4	0.0
Exotic pollution	22	0.3			0	0.0	−0.3
Threat	1,008	15.0			401	10.4	−4.6
Theft/break-in	107	1.6	76	2.5	9	0.2	−1.4
Conspiracy	121	1.8			54	1.4	−0.4
Hoax	58	0.9			120	3.1	+2.2
Sniping	152	2.3	63	2.1	24	0.6	−1.7
Shootout with police	16	0.2			16	0.6	+0.4
Arms smuggling	62	0.9			42	1.1	+0.2
Other actions	117	1.7	76	2.5	121	3.1	+0.4
Car bombing					72	1.9	+1.9
Suicide car bombing					10	0.3	+0.3
Nuclear-related weapons attack					0	0.0	0.0
Non-aerial hijacking					8	0.2	+0.2
Facility occupation					33	0.9	+0.9
TOTAL EVENTS	6,714		3,046		3,856		

Mickolus' data allow for a trend analysis over a longer period. A comparison of the relative frequency distributions for the 1970s and 1980s shows higher relative frequencies for 12 event types and lower relative frequencies for nine event types. For one event type, sabotage, no change in the relative frequency was found. The largest increases were found for assassinations (5.5 per cent), armed attacks (5.4 per cent) and kidnappings (3.0 per cent). The largest decreases were found for letter bombing (5.9 per cent), incendiary bombings (5.0 per cent) and threats

(4.6 per cent). In the 1980s Mickolus did not record any nuclear-related weapons attack or exotic pollution. For the 1980s, he introduced several new event types that were new phenomena, including car bombing (1.9 per cent) and suicide car bombing (0.3 per cent).

When one examines the relative frequencies for each year, from 1980 through 1987, one finds different trends for the various event types. The relative frequencies of threat and hoax show an upward trend in the 1980s. The relative frequencies of incendiary bombing, barricade/hostage, sniping and shoot out with police show a downward trend. The relative frequency of sabotage remains fairly constant. The relative frequencies for the remaining event types show a cyclical pattern.

TABLE 14

RELATIVE FREQUENCY DISTRIBUTION OF EVENT TYPES, 1987–1989

	US State Department %	%	Jaffe Center %	%	Risks International %	%
Skyjacking	0.1	1.1	0.2	0.5	0.2	0.2
Bombing	56.7	45.6	49.6	49.0	52.0	43.0
Arson	18.0					
Armed attack	15.9	28.9	28.2	35.0		
Kidnapping	6.4	14.3	7.8	5.9	3.0	0.6
Sabotage	0.7	1.3	2.5	0.7		
Other	2.2					
Specific threat		6.9	9.2	6.7	9.2	
Letter bomb		1.6	0.5	0.2		
Barricade/hostage		0.3	1.4	1.2		
Assassination					14.0	22.0
Facility attack					31.0	31.0
Poisoning			0.2	0.2		
Unknown			0.2	0.2		

Not all data collecting agencies use such a specific breakdown of event types as Mickolus. In Table 14, the relative frequency distribution for event types is presented according to various recent reports. It is clear that, regardless of source, the majority of incidents are bombings, approaching or surpassing one half the total number of incidents. In addition, the number of skyjackings has gone down considerably; the relative frequency decreased to less than 1 per cent. A comparison of the various sources shows differences for several event types. The Jaffee Center recorded a higher percentage of armed attacks, the US State Department a higher percentage for bombings and Risks International a higher percentage of facility attacks. It can be assumed that the facility attacks (Risks International) are included in the category armed attack (US State Dept., Jaffee Center). It is not clear why Risks International has such a high percentage for assassinations compared to the other two sources which list none. A possible explanation is that most assassinations are domestic incidents. These are only covered by Risks International. The US State Department has a separate category for arson and the Jaffee Center uses separate categories for specific threats and letter bombs. Probably the US State Department includes the letter bombs in the category bombing.

Trends in Western Europe

Trends in Incidents: It is very difficult to find a clear pattern of the total number of domestic and international terrorist incidents in Western Europe. Ted Robert Gurr collected data on domestic terrorist incidents in the 1960s (1961–70).[11] He recorded a total of 65 terrorist episodes and 40 terrorist campaigns for Western Europe plus the North American NATO countries, Canada and the United States. The majority of the episodes occurred in Italy (18), France (8), Greece (6), Britain (6), Turkey (6) and Ireland (5). The majority of the campaigns occurred in the United States (14), Italy (9) and France (9) and Canada (4). The Scandinavian countries of Denmark, Norway and Sweden had no terrorist episodes or campaigns during this period. Gurr's study was restricted to terrorist actions and campaigns carried out by internal groups; thus it does not include the international terrorist acts by various Palestinian groups that began in 1967.

The most complete breakdown of transnational terrorist incidents is presented by Edward Mickolus.[12] His data cover 1968–87. He recorded a total of 2,718 incidents in European countries during this period, of which 1,240 incidents took place in the 1970s and 1,478 in the 1980s. In the 1970s the most affected countries were the United Kingdom (212), Italy (178), France (176) and Greece (120), the Netherlands (112) and Turkey (97). Those least affected were Scandinavia, the Benelux except the Netherlands, Cyprus, Austria, Switzerland and Portugal. In the 1980s the most affected countries were France (308), the Federal Republic of Germany (205), Spain (163), Greece (156) and Italy (133). For the whole period, the most affected countries were France (17.8 per cent), the United Kingdom (11.8 per cent) Italy (11.4 per cent), the Federal Republic of Germany (11.2 per cent) and Greece (10.2 per cent). More than 60 per cent of the transnational incidents were recorded in these five countries.

There are considerable changes in the relative frequency distributions for the 1970s and 1980s. Fifteen European countries showed an increase, while nine countries showed a decrease during the 1980s. The highest increases in number of incidents from one decade to the next were recorded in France (+132), Spain (+121) and the Federal Republic of Germany (+106). The largest decreases were recorded in the United Kingdom (–102), the Netherlands (–92) and Turkey (–22).

Table 15 looks at the number of terrorist incidents in Western Europe during the 1980s using data from three different data bases. The data of Mickolus and the US State Department are based on a variety of sources, including diplomatic channels and information of the secret services, while the data collected by the COMT is based on one newspaper, the *International Herald Tribune*. The COMT data base includes domestic incidents as well as international ones.

TABLE 15

TERRORIST INCIDENTS IN WESTERN EUROPE
A COMPARISON OF THREE DATA BASES, 1980–1987

	80	81	82	83	84	85	86	87
Mickolus	186	198	189	122	174	231	168	140
US State Department	204	249	343	186	232	218	156	152
COMT	221	284	184	172	166	190		

Looking now at the five countries most affected by terrorism during the 1980s, the same three data bases provide the following picture (Table 16).

TABLE 16

THE FIVE MOST AFFECTED COUNTRIES IN EUROPE
A COMPARISON OF THREE DATA BASES, 1980–1985

Country	Source	1980	1981	1982	1983	1984	1985	Total
France	USSD	31	39	44	31	41	25	211
	MICK	45	36	49	45	42	23	240
	COMT	33	34	51	42	38	32	198
Fed. Rep. Germany	USSD	24	48	76	53	35	45	281
	MICK	19	40	46	11	19	33	168
	COMT	8	28	32	12	7	32	119
Spain	USSD	7	14	15	27	60	37	160
	MICK	13	14	10	10	25	29	101
	COMT	60	47	28	35	37	40	247
Greece	USSD	15	20	27	11	17	26	116
	MICK	31	22	20	14	17	30	134
	COMT	4	7	6	7	7	10	41
Italy	USSD	29	24	39	11	14	14	131
	MICK	24	22	26	5	13	19	109
	COMT	58	50	39	15	17	19	198

Source: USSD = US State Department, MICK = Mickolus, COMT = Centre for the Study of Social Conflicts, Leiden

The three data bases show similar trends for France although there are slight differences in the number of incidents for each year. Mickolus recorded the highest number of incidents (240) for the six-year period. The three data bases show similar trends for the Federal Republic of Germany, but there are considerable deviations in the number of incidents. For some years, the differences are 3–400 per cent. The US State Department recorded many more incidents in 1982, 1983 and 1984. For the whole period, it recorded more than twice the number recorded by COMT. The COMT recorded many more incidents for Spain. This might be explained by the fact that domestic incidents are also included, while the other two data bases concentrated on international incidents. The US State Department recorded 59 more incidents than Mickolus. COMT's data show a decrease until 1982, followed by an upward trend. Mickolus' data shows a similar pattern, despite the smaller annual figures. However, the data of the US State Department show a steady upward trend from 1980, peaking sharply in 1984. The two data bases on international incidents show more or less similar trends for Greece, except for 1980, where Mickolus recorded twice as many incidents as the US State Department. The COMT data base, despite including domestic incidents, records less than half as many incidents as the other two data bases. For Italy, however, COMT records many more incidents than the other two data bases for 1980 and 1981. Otherwise, all three data bases record fairly similar numbers.

The exclusion of domestic incidents by some data bases and not by others renders comparisons problematic. The most detailed, publicly available national breakdown of domestic incidents is the one reported by the North Atlantic Assembly. On the basis of a questionnaire sent to NATO member countries, a North Atlantic Assembly working group on terrorism constructed the following table (see Table 17).

In 1980–86, it recorded a total of 13,112 terrorist incidents in Western Europe, an average of 1,873 per year or five per day. The incidents caused the deaths of 2,585 people, an average of 369 per year or one per day. The most affected countries were Italy (34 per cent), Turkey (34 per cent) and Spain (19 per cent). Most of the deaths caused by the reported incidents occurred in Turkey (86 per cent), Spain (8 per cent) and Italy (4 per cent). Some reservations have to be made because the United Kingdom decided to exclude all data related to the conflict in Northern Ireland. West Germany did not answer the questionnaire. It can be concluded from the data that Turkey excluded all data relating to its conflict with the Kurds. It would seem that these countries consider their domestic terrorist incidents as internal problems which they do not wish to be discussed within NATO.

TABLE 17

TERRORIST INCIDENTS IN NATO COUNTRIES, 1980–1986

Country	No. of Incidents	%	No. of Deaths	%
(1) Italy	4,487	34	95	4
(2) Turkey	4,459	34	2,223	86
(3) Spain	2,450	19	203	8
(4) France	529	4	***	
(5) Portugal	335	3	10	<1
(6) Greece*	260	2	23	<1
(7) United States	190	2	5	<5
(8) Netherlands	165	1	7	<1
(9) Belgium	124	1	10	<1
(10) United Kingdom**	72	<1	6	<1
(11) Canada	21	<1	3	<1
(12) Denmark	9	<1	0	0
(13) Luxemburg	11	<1	0	0
(14) Iceland	0	0	0	0
(15) Norway	0	0	0	0
(16) Federal Rep. of Germany***				
TOTAL	13,112		2,585	

Notes:
*   Answer includes 1987 data
**   Excludes Northern Ireland
*** Not anwered

Source: J.L. Nunes, L.J. Smith, Final Report of the Sub-Committee on Terrorism, North Atlantic Assembly Papers, Jan. 1989, 59pp.

It is possible to construct a more complete table of the number of terrorist incidents in Western Europe, based on the various sources publicly available (see Table 18).

Several conclusions can be drawn from this table, although some reservations have to made: not all European countries are mentioned; the data cover different periods; the sources used included different event types. Nevertheless, it appears that, since 1969, more than 120,000 violent incidents have been reported in Western and Southern Europe, causing more than 10,000 deaths and more than 10,000 injuries. The most affected countries were the United Kingdom (Northern Ireland), Turkey, Italy and West Germany. Turkey accounts for more than half of the recorded deaths.

The majority of domestic terrorist incidents goes unreported in the international press. Furthermore, the international press concentrates on the major and the most lethal incidents. Even then, when a terrorist campaign reaches a certain level of violence, only a small number of incidents is covered. The normal day-to-day violence goes unreported and only the important qualitative developments will be covered. Social

TABLE 18

OVERALL NUMBER OF TERRORIST INCIDENTS IN WESTERN EUROPE

Country	Period	No. of Incidents	Deaths	Injured
Northern Ireland	1969–1988	43,777	2,672	11,906
Turkey	1978–1981	40,500	5,241	
	1984–1989		1,000–1,500	
Italy	1968–1985	14,589	419	Thousands
France	1975–1984	5,737	130	746
	1985–1987	2,426		
Federal Republic	1970s	1,493	99	404
of Germany	1980s	550	26 (right-wing)	
	1980s	11,660	7 (left wing)	
Spain	1968–1988		672	
Netherlands	1980s	249	7	20
TOTAL		120,981	10,273	

science research based on press and media reports alone will therefore automatically miss many terrorist incidents. That is why we have to be careful with any trend analysis based exclusively on press reports.

Distribution of Incident Type in Western Europe

For changes in the relative frequencies of event types, we have to rely on data of the US National Foreign Assessment Center for the 1970s and on data of the US Department of State for the first half of the 1980s. Table 19 shows the relative frequencies for event types in Western Europe for the two periods. They are also compared with the relative frequencies for event types for the whole world, during 1980–87, as presented by Mickolus.

Table 19 shows increases in the relative frequency of explosive bombing (11 per cent), armed attack (5.6 per cent), theft/break-in (4.3 per cent), hoax (1.5 per cent) and barricade/hostage (1 per cent). Decreases in the relative frequency are observed for incendiary bombing (9.2 per cent), threat (3.2 per cent) and kidnapping (1 per cent). Because letterbombing was not a separate category for the US Department of State and it was not possible to check whether such incidents were included in their category explosive bombing, the observed 11 per cent increase in explosive bombing may really be a mere 2 per cent. All other categories showed changes of less than one per cent. A comparison of the West European relative frequencies with those of the world total shows that, in the first part of the 1980s, Western Europe had higher (more than 1 per cent) relative frequencies for explosive bombing, incendiary bombing, barricade/hostage and theft/break-in and lower (more than –1 per cent) relative frequencies

TABLE 19

TERRORIST INCIDENTS IN EUROPE, 1968–1987

Type of Incident	1968–80 Europe[1] %	1980–85 Europe[2] %	1980–87 World[3] %
(1) Explosive bombing	39.0	50.0	35.4
(2) Incendiary bombing	18.0	8.8	6.2
(3) Threat	12.5	9.3	10.4
(4) Letter bombing	9.0	—	1.1
(5) Assassination	6.4	6.0	12.1
(6) Armed attack	2.4	8.0	9.7
(7) Kidnappings	2.0	1.0	9.0
(8) Other actions	1.8	1.8	3.1
(9) Barricade/hostage	1.7	2.7	1.5
(10) Conspiracy	1.6	0.06	1.4
(11) Hijacking	1.4	0.9	1.8
(12) Exotic pollution	1.0	0.06	0.0
(13) Arms smuggling	0.9	—	1.1
(14) Theft/break-in	0.9	5.2	0.2
(15) Sniping	0.7	0.6	0.6
(16) Hoax	0.5	2.0	3.1
(17) Sabotage	0.4	0.06	0.4
(18) Shoot-out with police	0.3	0.06	0.4
(19) Minor explosions	—	3.6	—

Sources:
1. US National Foreign Assessment Center, June 1981.
2. US Dept. of State, Office for Combatting Terrorism, Annual Reports.
3. Adapted from Mickolus 1989, Patterns of International Terrorism: 1980–1987, p.xvii.

for threat, assassination, armed attack, kidnapping and hoax. The other event types showed differences of less than one per cent.

If one looks at the US Department of State's annual breakdown of event types for Western Europe from 1980 through 1985, certain trends stand out. The peak year for explosive bombing was 1982 with 203 explosions or 28.5 per cent of the total number of bombings over the six-year period. The number of armed attacks shows a steep upward trend, jumping sharply from negligible numbers between 1980 and 1982 to 20 in 1983 and doubling again in 1984. Assassinations, hoaxes and threats were recorded mainly in the early 1980s and have not been recorded in Western Europe since 1982. The number of barricade/hostage incidents shows a downward trend from a peak of 12 in 1981 to negligible numbers in 1984 and 1985. The US Department of State recorded only two cases of arson in the early 1980s. From 1983 on, it became a favourite tactic of terrorists in Western Europe, averaging 32 incidents from 1983 through 1985.

International terrorist incidents in Western Europe have two important characteristics. A great number of them are directed against American targets or are related to a spillover from the problems in the Middle East.

Anti-American attacks: In the 1980s at least 460 anti-American attacks were reported in five major European countries. Nearly half of the number were reported in West Germany (46 per cent), followed by Spain (20 per cent), Greece (16 per cent), Italy (12 per cent) and France (6 per cent). These incidents caused 21 deaths and 259 injured. In the FRG, the number of anti-American attacks reached a peak in 1982 (58 incidents) and has since then steadily decreased to three in 1988 (January to September). American military presence is an important explanatory factor in the occurrence of anti-American attacks. Yet there have also been NATO countries with no attacks on American military personnel or facilities, for example, in the Netherlands. Overall, the total number for the five countries has decreased in recent years, from a peak of 120 incidents in 1982 to 14 incidents in 1988. In 1988 most anti-American attacks were reported in Spain (7).

Spill-Over from the Middle East: A great deal of international terrorist incidents in Western Europe is caused by a spill-over from the Middle East. The distribution of the incidents shows an increase up until 1985 and a decrease thereafter. The Mediterranean countries, Greece (37), Italy (32) and Cyprus (25), account for the highest number of incidents, along with France (35), Spain (21) and the United Kingdom (22).

In the past, victims were generally people caught in the crossfire, but in 1985 they increasingly became the specific target. In 1985 Middle Eastern terrorism spread to five West European countries, Belgium, Denmark, Malta, Sweden, and Switzerland, that had not experienced such attacks in 1984. All told, Middle Eastern terrorists operating in Western Europe killed 109 people and injured 540. Most victims were of Middle Eastern origin, in particular, Palestinians, Israelis, Jordanians, Syrians, Libyans and Iranians. Palestinian terrorists were the major contributors to the spill-over violence, conducting nearly 60 per cent of the incidents in 1985 and some 40 per cent of all Middle Eastern origin attacks in Western Europe during 1980–85. Much Palestinian terrorism in Western Europe continued to be carried out by anti-Arafat groups who opposed a negotiated settlement with Israel and refuse to recognize Israel's right to exist.

Middle Eastern terrorist groups have operated in Western Europe for several reasons. There are attempts to release jailed Middle Eastern terrorists in West European prisons. Numerous Middle Easterners, many in expatriate and student communities, live and travel in Western Europe and provide cover, shelter and potential recruits. There are few travel restrictions among Western European countries. Very many accessible targets exist in Western Europe, in contrast to the Middle East. Worldwide publicity accompanies international terrorist attacks in Western Europe. Some West European countries host exile groups and former leaders that are attractive targets for regimes. Certain Western European countries have offered support to terrorist groups or, by their rhetoric, have created environments that appear sympathetic to terrorists. Finally, in some cases, states apparently have struck deals with terrorists, making concessions in exchange for agreements that terrorists will refrain from conducting attacks on their territory.

Active organizations

What are the major domestic terrorist organizations in Western Europe? Most of the attacks were the work of a relatively small number of groups (see Table 20).

TABLE 20

DOMESTIC TERRORIST ORGANIZATIONS IN WESTERN EUROPE

Group	Formed	Hardcore Membership	Area of Operation
(1) ASALA	1975	?	Worldwide
(2) ETA	1959	200	Spain/France
(3) CCC	1984	?	Belgium
(4) DA	1979	?	France/Belgium
(5) GRAPO	1975	<25	Spain
(6) Iraultza	1982	<20	Basque provinces
(7) INLA	1975	<20	Urban areas Northern Ireland
(8) JCAG	1975	?	Worldwide
(9) FP-25	1980	6–10	Portugal
(10) PIRA	1970	200–400	Northern Ireland, occasionally England and continental Europe
(11) RAF	1968	20–30	West Germany
(12) RB	1970	50–75	Italy
(13) RZ	1973	100	West Germany
(14) RO 17 NOV	1975	20–25	Greece (Athens)
(15) ELA	1973	?	Greece (Athens)

Note: See text for full names of groups.
Source: Terrorist Group Profiles, US State Dept. (Washington, DC: US GPO), 1988, 131pp.

According to the US Department of State, at least 15 West European domestic terrorist organizations have been active in recent years. The most recent formed was the Communist Combatant Cells (CCC) in Belgium. Most of them were formed in the mid-1970s. Four organizations have operated in countries other than where they are located. The Armenian organizations, Justice Commandos of the Armenian Genocide (JCAG) and Armenian Secret Army for the Liberation of Armenia (ASALA) have operated worldwide. Most organizations have a hardcore membership of less than 100. At least six organizations have a hardcore membership of less than a few dozen.

Five of the mentioned organizations have been uprooted; namely the CCC, JCAG, ASALA, Popular Forces of 25 April (FP-25), Action Directe (DA). Most of the indigenous West European terrorists are 'urban terrorists'. The most notorious groups espouse a revolutionary philosophy, usually some form of Marxism-Leninism; they are dedicated to overthrowing the existing government and social order; but are inarticulate about their vision of a substitute system. Lethal terrorist acts usually are carried out by a small nucleus. Some groups are highly structured. All groups attack the state, its representatives and symbols of the established order, and some target the United States and NATO as representatives of 'imperialism'. According to the US State Department, eight of these organizations have been involved in lethal anti-American attacks. Targets are usually selected very deliberately rather than indiscriminately and involve consideration of the symbolic value of the target. Members of these indigenous groups are usually from the middle class and are not deprived members of society. Members are often well-educated and include doctors, lawyers and other professionals.

The 15 groups have different modes of operation (see Table 21). Twelve of the 15 groups have used the tactics of bomb attacks and eight have used the tactics of assassinations. The Belgian CCC, the Spanish Iraultza, the West German Revolutionary Cells and the Greek ELA have limited themselves to bomb attacks. The shadowy Greek November 17 Organization has limited itself to assassinations. Four organizations have used the tactics of kidnappings. The Provisional IRA and Portuguese FP-25 have staged mortar attacks. Table 22 identifies the favourite targets of the major terrorist organizations active in Western Europe.

TABLE 21

OPERATION MODES OF TERRORIST ORGANIZATIONS IN WESTERN EUROPE

(1) ASALA	Bomb attacks, assassinations
(2) ETA	Bomb attacks, assassinations, kidnappings
(3) CCC	Bomb attacks
(4) DA	Bomb attacks, assassinations
(5) GRAPO	Bomb attacks, assassinations, kidnappings
(6) Iraultza	Bomb attacks
(7) INLA	Bomb attacks, assassinations
(8) JCAG	Bomb attacks, assassinations
(9) FP-25	Assassinations, mortar attacks
(10) PIRA	Bomb attacks, assassinations, mortar attacks
(11) RAF	Bomb attacks, assassinations, kidnappings
(12) RB	Assassinations, kidnappings
(13) RZ	Bomb attacks
(14) RO 17 NOV	Assassinations
(15) ELA	Bomb attacks

TABLE 22

CHARACTERISTIC TARGETS OF MAIN TERRORIST GROUPS IN EUROPE

(1) ASALA	World Council of Churches, Turkish diplomats, Turkish airline offices, other international airline offices, Esenboga airport, Dashnag Armenian political party members.
(2) ETA	Spanish Prime Minister, security headquarters, Bilbao nuclear power-plant, tourist industry, industrialists, military officers and personnel, military petroleum pipeline, Civil Guard, French business interests, state-owned petrochemical plant, supermarkets, former members.
(3) CCC	Weapon factories, NATO fuel pipelines, telecommunication towers, support facilities, Belgian Employers Federation building, Belgian Police General Directorate for Logistics and Finance, Belgian gas company, steel company, Belgian Army information office, Bank of America offices.
(4) DA	National Council of French Employers, Orly airport, banks, Rolls Royce dealership, exclusive restaurant, clothing store, American school, European HQ of the World Bank, Jewish-owned hardware store and bank, Marseille Trade Fair, European Space Agency, Interpol HQ, Offices of the special anti-crime squad, Renault, National Immigration Offices, judge, former Justice Minister.
(5) GRAPO	Military personnel, US Cultural Center, cafes, Bank of America, Civil Guard, government offices, banks, French banks, consulate, business interests, real estate companies.
(6) Iraultza	Stock market, banks, Rank Xerox offices, General Motors affiliated company, IBM offices, movie theater showing an American film, Firestone offices, Hertz and Avis offices, 3M Company, Honeywell and Bull, NCR offices, Ford showroom, showrooms displaying French cars.
(7) INLA	British Conservative Party members, British consulate, government officials, congregation of the Mountain Lodge Gospel Hall, British Legion Hall, politicians, INLA members in an internal power struggle.
(8) JCAG	Turkish embassies and consulates, Turkish airlines offices, Turkish tourist offices, Turkish representatives in international organizations.
(9) FP-25	Minister of Finance, British Airways office, porcelain factory, US Embassy, NATO ships, cars belonging to West German Air Force personnel, Director General of the National Prison System, NATO's Iberian Atlantic Command.
(10) PIRA	British targets include the London Stock Exchange, the House of Commons, the Bank of England, the London subway and railway system, major shopping areas, British ambassadors, hotels, pubs and restaurants, member of the Royal family, Prime Minister, military personnel and barracks, Royal Courts of Justice, Whitehall.
(11) RAF	US Officers' Club, President of the German Supreme Court, German Federal Prosecutor, German businessmen, NATO commander, US Air Force HQ, department stores, NATO fuel pipelines, Foreign Ministry personnel.
(12) RB	Public Prosecutor, Chief Prosecutor, President of the Christian Democratic Party, Christian Democratic Party building, president of the Sicilian regional government, US Army personnel, banks, University of Rome economics professor, mayors, economic adviser to the Prime Minister, military personnel.

(13) RZ	US military facilities, construction companies, NATO fuel pipelines, mining and shipping offices, private businesses and institutions, Alien Welfare Office, chemical plant, military trains, vehicle depot, government facilities.
(14) RO 17 NOV	US Embassy personnel, US military personnel, Greek police officers, Greek industrialist, Greek minister, Turkish Embassy cars.
(15) ELA	US military personnel, US Information Agency, American Express Offices, foreign-owned vehicles, Hellenic-American Union, police stations, pubs, discotheques.

Conclusion

On the basis of the data discussed here, it is safe to say that terrorism will persist. However, it is hard to say whether it will increase. Recent years have shown several positive trends in Western Europe. The total number of international incidents shows a downward trend, with the US State Department recording a steady decrease from 1988 through 1990, with an upturn again in 1991 that approximates to the 1989 level. The number of anti-American attacks and the incidents caused by the Middle Eastern spill-over have also gone done. However, the London Institute for the Study of Terrorism, which includes both international and domestic incidents, records a doubling of incidents from 1990 to 1991.[13]

There is clearly no general trend for all European countries. For some countries, the situation has worsened, but for others, it has improved. Although international terrorist incidents are relatively few, some European countries, in particular Turkey and the United Kingdom (Northern Ireland) and, to a lesser extent, Italy and Greece have serious problems related to domestic terrorism. The most serious external threat in Western Europe comes from various Middle East terrorist groups, although it is not clear whether this will continue to be the case. With the geopolitical changes in the Eastern Europe and the former Soviet Union, it remains to be seen whether domestic conflict and national and ethnic rivalries will be the prime motor of future terrorism or whether transnational and international terrorism will continue to be as serious a problem as it has in the past.

Country Surveys

Austria

The majority of the terrorist incidents that occurred in Austria were a spill-over from the Middle East. There are no active domestic terrorist groups. Palestinian and Arab terrorists have targeted diplomatic missions (Israeli, French and Turkish embassies, British consulate), Jews and

Jewish facilities (houses, shops, synagogues). The most bloody attack was the armed attack on the Schwechat airport in December 1985, causing 3 deaths and 30 injured. In 1988 no international incidents were reported.

The most outstanding incident in 1989 was the assassination of the leader of the Democratic Party of Iranian Kurdistan, Abdul-Rahman Qassemlou, on 13 July. Gunmen broke into a meeting of Kurdish activists in an apartment in Vienna and killed Qassemlou and two other men, identified as Abdullah Ghaderi Azar and Fadel Mala Mahmoud Rasoul. A fourth person, a Kurd carrying an Iranian diplomatic passport, was seriously wounded. The three victims were living in Austria as political exiles. The wounded person was identified as Jafari Sahraroodi, an Iranian officer of the Revolutionary Guard. Although he was a crown witness and possibly one of the perpetrators, the Austrian authorities allowed him to leave the country after severe pressure from Iran. Press reports even mentioned retaliatory threats by Iran if the man was not allowed to leave the country.[14]

In February 1989 Israel's national airline, El Al, threatened the suspension of flights to Vienna to protest against new check-in procedures. Under the new procedures, El Al passengers would no longer check their baggage separately from other passengers but at multiple check-in counters. After one day the dispute was solved and security officials allowed El Al to check in baggage and passengers separately.[15] In April 1989 a discussion evening at the Technical University on *The Satanic Verses*, the controversial novel by British author Salman Rushdie, was postponed after participants received bomb and murder threats. The program was to have included a reading from the book and a discussion that included Iranians[16] On 20 April police in Braunau sealed off the border town where Hitler was born 100 years ago, after bomb warnings. In West Germany the police arrested 53 persons, seized weapons and stepped up protection of foreign residents against possible neo-Nazi violence. Almost all those arrested had been seeking fights with rightist extremists.[17]

Belgium

Belgium has several left-wing and right-wing organizations that engaged in terrorist activities in the 1980s. The Combatant Communist Cells (CCC) have received most attention. CCC started a campaign of bomb attacks directed against material targets in 1984; it lasted until December 1985. The main targets were NATO facilities, weapon factories, the general directorate of the police, several companies, banks and government facilities. It relied on bombings as its sole mode of operation. Two firemen were accidentally killed in one of the attacks that caused damage estimated at 25 million dollars. Four men and two women were arrested and tried in October 1988.

Much less publicized are the activities of several right-wing organizations, like the National Front (FN) for the Liberation of Belgium, the Flemish Militant Order, Westland New Post and the Youth Front. Members of some of these organizations engaged in terrorist activities, including murder. Press reports have revealed important links between these organizations and the Belgian secret service, which allegedly has been involved in some crimes, including the murder of the director of FN, Mr Mendez, and the theft of several NATO telex messages.[18] In June 1989 judicial authorities searched the homes of 16 employees of the People's Union (Volksunie), in an operation codenamed 'Salvador'. They were suspected of corruption and the hiding of terrorists. W. Kuipers, an MP, or one of his assistants was said to have been hiding members of the Spanish ETA and Kurds.[19]

A criminal gang, the Gang of Nijvel, has been responsible for bloody raids on supermarkets, restaurants, a taxi company and a textile firm in which a total of 20 people were killed. The group is allegedly led by a former policeman. Their activities have been described as traditional banditry. However, several authorities have suggested that the gang was a right-wing organization with an extreme right-wing ideology.[20] One of the main suspects, B. Beyer, a former policeman who was linked to the murder of a Lebanese businessman in Antwerp, was allowed to flee to Paraguay, via Madrid.[21]

In the 1980s several dozen international terrorist incidents took place. The major targets were embassies (Turkey, France, Yugoslavia), airline offices (Aeroflot, El Al, Air France, JAT), tourist offices, and Jewish facilities (school, synagogue). Individuals have also been targeted, including a PLO representative, an ANC representative, Yugoslav and Turkish groups, migrant workers, and ambassadors. In February 1988 bullets missed Godfrey Motsepe, the ANC representative, at the ANC office in Brussels. Later a bomb was defused in front of the office. South Africa was held responsible for the attack. In August 1988 the IRA claimed responsibility for the assassination of a British soldier in Ostend.

In January 1989 former Prime Minister Paul van den Boeynants was kidnapped. He was released after a large ransom had been paid, two million dollars according to press reports. It turned out that he had been kidnapped by ordinary criminals. However, some people suggested Mr Van den Boeynants had organized the kidnapping to circumvent corruption charges against him. The criminal gang of Patrick Haemers, that includes Basri Bajrami and Philippe Lacroix, was officially held responsible for the kidnapping.[22] Haemers was arrested on 28 May in

Brazil. He had organized the kidnapping because armed raids on money transports had become too risky.[23] The kidnapping was also claimed by the Socialist Revolutionary Brigade, the CCC and the CCPRP.[24]

The Socialist Revolutionary Brigade demanded 30 million Belgian francs for the hostage's release. It demanded that two-thirds of the ransom come from Mr Van den Boeynants' political and business partners and that it be given to charity organizations. The rest of the ransom would be for 'the group's participation in the effort to mobilize the people'. The group alleged that Mr Van den Boeynants had stolen public funds for his own profit and called for a people's tribunal to try him.[25] The CCC offered the release of the kidnap victim in exchange for the release of four imprisoned members.[26] In June 1989 the police prevented the kidnapping of the Belgian Minister of Justice, Mr Wathelet. Fifteen persons were arrested. The suspects had contacts with the gang that kidnapped Mr Van den Boeynants. They were said to have planned to trade Mr Wathelet for the release of Basri Bajrami.[27]

In 1989 several assassinations were reported. On 29 March the leader of the Belgian Muslims and an aide were shot and killed after one of them had received threats related to the novel *The Satanic Verses*. A Muslim group in Lebanon, the Soldiers of Truth, claimed responsibility for the assassination. In a statement it was said: 'Our organization declares its responsibility for executing God's judgement on the traitors Abdullah Ahdal and Salim Bahri in Brussels.' It said it killed the two because they had used an Islamic centre in Brussels as a front for anti-Islamic activities. The group had earlier claimed responsibility for kidnapping a Belgian doctor and assassinating Saudi Arabian diplomats.[28] The newly appointed spiritual leader of Muslims in Belgium, the Netherlands and Luxemburg, received death threats.[29]

On 3 October 1989, a gunman ambushed and killed Dr Joseph Wybran, the chairman of the Belgian Auschwitz Committee. He was shot in the head as he got into his car outside Brussels University Hospital, where he headed the immunology department. The organization of Jund al Haq, an offshoot of the Fatah-Revolutionary Council claimed responsibility for the killing. The group said the killing was carried out in revenge for 'Israel's escalatory measures against the Palestinian uprising in the West Bank' and 'in reaction to suspicious moves and gestures to normalise relations and coexistence with the Israeli enemy'.[30] Two other groups, Young Palestine and Proud and Free claimed responsibility in a letter sent to several newspapers. One group, the Soldiers of Justice, said it killed Dr Wybran, because he was a spy for Israel.[31]

On 11 May terrorist sympathizers seized offices of the European Community in Brussels. The police broke in and arrested 44 people, ending a four-hour take-over. The protesters demanded political prisoner status for convicted terrorists on a hunger strike in West German and French prisons.

Corsica

There have been few transnational incidents on Corsica; the main terrorist problem is a domestic one. The terrorist campaign of Corsican separatists still continues, although most activities are no longer reported in the international press. The French Polemological Institute estimates that 70 per cent of the bomb attacks go unreported. The separatists are responsible for hundreds of bomb attacks each year, mainly against property. In recent years, the total number of attacks has decreased from 608 in 1983 to 484 in 1987. (See also under France). The attacks on the continent reached a peak in 1984 with 47 incidents, and have since then decreased.

On the political level the FLNC appeared to moderate its demands when, at the end of 1983, it declared itself ready to accept 'association' of an independent Corsica with the French Republic. But in recent years it again stepped up its activities. In March 1988 a gendarme was shot to death hours after the separatists held a news conference in which they announced an intensification of activities on the island. In April the separatists used a booby-trapped car bomb for the first time.[32] On 20 October a journalist working for Radio Corse International, Jean Jacques Besri, was shot and killed in Bastia as he returned home from work. He had been a supporter of the Corsican independence movement. The police claimed that the slaying did not appear to have been politically motivated.[33]

Cyprus

For years, Arab terrorists and Israeli secret agents have been involved in an underground war on the island. Arab groups use the island for settling their internal disputes. It has been estimated that among the 15,000 Arabs in Cyprus there are at least 1,500 terrorists. In 1988, 700 Arabs were discreetly expelled and entrance of 500 others was prohibited.[34] In the same year, 500 Iranians moved to the island.

Since 1981 at least 26 terrorist attacks of foreign origin have been reported according to the West German magazine, *Der Spiegel*. Mickolus recorded a total of 54 incidents. At least five incidents were reported in 1988. They included three bomb attacks, a hijacking and the storming of the Israeli embassy. In February 1988 a ferryboat that was chartered to transport Palestinian deportees on a symbolic voyage to Israel was destroyed in a bomb attack. The PLO accused the Israeli secret service of having placed the explosives.[35] In April 1988 a hijacked Kuwaiti jetliner landed in Cyprus after Syrian troops prevented it from landing in Beirut. The hijackers, members of Hizbollah, demanded the release of 17 Iranian terrorists imprisoned in Kuwait. They killed two of the hostages and threatened to kill more if the plane was not refuelled. In the end the plane was flown to Algeria where the hijacking ended peacefully after negotiations with the Algerian government.[36] In May 1988 two people were killed and ten were injured in a car bomb attack near the Israeli embassy in Nicosia. The driver, who was killed in the attack, had tried to park the car in front of the embassy but he was driven away by security personnel.[37]

Domestic violence is related to the unresolved dispute between the Greek and Turkish communities on the island. A propaganda war has raged. Since the Turkish invasion in July 1974, which caused the death of 6,000 people, the island has been divided. The election of George Vassiliou, a Greek Cypriot millionaire businessman, as President of Cyprus opened the road to formal peace talks in September 1988. The parties disagreed over a timetable for the withdrawal of the 29,000 Turkish troops stationed in the Turkish sector as well as other provisions relating to freedom of movement, of property ownership and of settlement. During 1988 there were several shooting incidents and violent incidents. In May an Austrian soldier serving with the UN Force in Cyprus shot and killed a Turkish Cypriot man in the village of Pyla. It was the first fatal shooting involving the UN Force since it arrived on the island in 1964.[38] In November students tore down barbed wire fences and fought with UN peacekeeping forces.[39] In March 1989 new demonstrations organized by the 'Women walk home' were organized along the buffer zone.[40]

During 1989 at least two international terrorist attacks were reported. On 29 May Cypriot police arrested four men who were reportedly planning to kill Major General Michel Aoun by shooting down his helicopter with a surface-to-air missile over Larnaca airport. The discovery by two divers of a pair of SAM missiles led to the arrest of a total of six persons in a holiday apartment where automatic rifles and hand grenades were found.[41] On 28 August 1989 Bahman Javadi, a member of the central committee of the underground Iran Communist Party and its Komala Kurdish guerrilla forces, was killed by two young men firing silenced 7.65mm pistols and a companion was seriously wounded.

Denmark

Denmark has no domestic terrorist groups. However, there have been reports of violent activities by right-wing and left-wing groups. Right-wing groups have targeted immigrants. In 1985 a taxi-driver was killed and a right-wing group demanded that a message be broadcast on television that all immigrants must be expelled. Left-wing groups have targeted mainly business interests. Anti-apartheid groups caused several million dollars damage to Shell filling stations and banks that had links with South Africa. Four activists who were arrested in January 1989 were officially charged.[42]

The government has recorded nine major terrorist incidents in the 1980s. The targets were airline offices, travel agencies and Jewish interests (including a synagogue, a food store and a home for the elderly). Mickolus recorded a total of 15 transnational incidents. In 1989 no major international terrorist incidents were reported. During a trial in April five people, four men and a woman, were charged with organizing several bank robberies in 1982 and 1983 and a kidnapping in 1980. The robberies netted about two million dollars. Part of the money was transferred to the Popular Front for the Liberation of Palestine.[43] Renewed anti-apartheid activities were also reported in 1989. The group 'BZ' was held responsible for a series of attacks on Shell filling stations.[44] On 8 September anti-apartheid activists stormed and damaged the South African consulate in Copenhagen. The action was claimed by 'BZ' and by 'United Action against Apartheid'.[45]

Federal Republic of Germany

For many years before reunification the now defunct Federal Republic of Germany experienced activities of extreme right-wing and extreme left-wing terrorist groups. In the 1970s the Minister of Interior reported a total of 1,493 violent incidents, causing 99 deaths and 404 injured. Almost half of the attacks were attacks against property (44.8 per cent), followed by fire bombings (21.7 per cent) and attempted bombings (10.5 per cent). Less than ten per cent of the incidents (7.3 per cent) were attacks against persons. Forty per cent of the attacks against persons were directed against the police. The number of incidents reached peaks in 1972, 1977 and 1980. More than half of the number of injured were recorded in 1980. The Red Army Faction was responsible for 41 per cent of the attacks against persons, 2.2 per cent of the attacks against property and 23 per cent of the robberies.

In the 1980s the Ministry of Interior recorded a total of 13,073 violent incidents, 95.2 per cent caused by left-wing groups and 4.8 per cent caused by right-wing groups. The left-wing and right-wing groups show different violence profiles. More than three quarters of the left-wing violence consisted of arson attacks and property damage. In 1987 damage was estimated at 38 million Deutschmarks. Right-wing groups have been

more inclined to assassinate people. being responsible for 26 assassinations in the 1980s, compared with eight by left-wing groups. Left-wing
groups have used the tactic of assassination very selectively. During the
1980s the two types of groups showed opposite trends for assassinations.
Most right-wing assassinations occurred in the early 1980s. No assassinations were recorded after 1985. On the other hand, all left-wing assassinations were recorded in the later 1980s, with none recorded for the first
half.

About 12 per cent of the total number of violent incidents are related
to breaches of transport and other resistance activities. Some other
European governments do not consider these activities as terrorist but as
politically-motivated activism. For other European countries, there are
no data on this type of activity. German legislation is very strict in
comparison to other European countries. In 1987 it broadened Article
129a of the Penal Law Code and, since then, several forms of civil
disobedience are classified as terrorist activities.

Protest activities in West Germany have been massive and very
violent. The violence escalated in the late 1980s and in 1987 the police
were for the first time attacked with firearms during a demonstration.
Protest activities were in many cases linked to major events. In 1988 the
International Monetary Fund annual meeting at West Berlin was such an
event, a wide variety of peaceful and violent protest activities occurred
before, during and after it. Banking and money institutions were
specifically targeted. An attempt to assassinate a Finance Ministry
official, Hans Tietmeyer, failed. Minor and major arson attacks caused
extensive damage. Other violent attacks were related to anti-militarism,
high technology development, nuclear policies, animal protection and
immigration policies. There has also been a growing number of attacks
against migrant workers and refugees by right-wing groups that has
only become worse since reunification. Some violent incidents have
been linked with the internal political struggles within the migrant
communities.[46]

The number of anti-American attacks reached a peak in 1982 with 58
attacks and decreased to three in 1988. The number of international
incidents also reached a peak in 1982 with 76 decreasing to 18 in 1988,
according to the US State Department. Mickolus recorded a total of 205
transnational incidents. The most important attacks in 1988 were the two
attacks on British Army barracks in Duisburg and Dusseldorf claimed by
the IRA, and the two attempts to derail trains carrying American troops
by the Popular Front for the Liberation of Palestine – General Command
(PFLP–GC). American officials claimed that Ahmed Jebril's operatives
were responsible for placing bombs on a railway track near Hedemünden

on 31 August 1987 and on 26 April 1988.[47] On 14 October 1988 agents of the Jebril group, including Mr Jebril's top lieutenant, Hafez Kassem Dalkamoni, were arrested. Other international incidents were related to the stepped up activities of the IRA on the continent after two IRA suspects were charged with attempted murder in the bombing of two British Army bases at Mönchengladbach and Duisburg.[48]

France

The most detailed information on terrorist incidents in France is published by the French Senate and the French Polemological Institute in Paris. The French Senate recorded a total of 5,737 incidents during 1975–84. Almost three quarters of this number was caused by autonomist groups. The extreme left has been responsible for 12 per cent of the incidents. Right-wing and racist groups each were responsible for four per cent of the incidents. Only six per cent of the total number of incidents were international terrorist incidents. Mickolus, however, recorded a higher level of international incidents for the early 1980s.

The majority of the terrorist incidents were directed against property (93 per cent), only seven per cent being against persons. A total of 130 people were killed and 746 injured in terrorist incidents during 1975–84. An average of 540 incidents were reported annually, 500 directed against property and 40 against persons. On average, 13 people were killed and 75 injured annually. International terrorism has been the most lethal type of terrorism in France. Although it represents only six per cent of the total number of incidents, it represents 54 per cent of the dead and 55 per cent of the injured. The extreme left has caused only three per cent of the dead and five per cent of the injured. According to the French Senate statistics, international terrorism reached a peak in 1981 (51 incidents) and since then has decreased considerably. The highest death toll was recorded in 1982 (25 dead) and 1983 (32 dead). The number of injured reached a peak of 232 in 1982.

The French Polemological Institute (IFP) has published several reports on terrorism in France. Apparently, it uses another definition of terrorism because its data differ from those of the French Senate. According to the IFP, the total number of terrorist incidents in France has steadily decreased from a peak in 1983 of 948 incidents to 724 in 1987. Terrorism in the overseas areas reached a peak in 1985 with 83 attacks, ten per cent of total incidents. Basque terrorism has steadily declined to 19 attacks in 1987 since a peak of 45 in 1985. International terrorism in France peaked in 1984 and 1986, with 28 attacks in 1986. Anti-American attacks reached a peak in 1982 with eight attacks and have since then declined to zero in 1988, according to the US State Department.

In 1988 the international incidents were linked to South Africa and to immigrant problems. In March ANC representative Dulcie September was assassinated in Paris. Press reports identified a South African agent that was responsible for the attack. The attack caused some anti-South African incidents. Immigrant communities have been the target of right-wing groups. Magazines that have taken clear anti-racist stances have been targeted in bomb attacks. Immigrant hostels and organizations have suffered bomb and arson attacks.

France has experienced several terrorist campaigns in overseas areas. The conflict in New Caledonia reached new levels of intensity in 1988. Kanak separatists attempted to disturb local elections and held French hostages in an underground cave, including the head of the French anti-terrorism force. Military reinforcements were dispatched to the territory to restore order. When the military intervened in May, a total of 19 separatists and two commandos were killed in a seven-hour battle. Three Kanaks were reportedly executed after they surrendered, including Kanak leader, Alphonse Dianou, and his lieutenant, Wenceslas Lavelloi. On 4 May 1989 the leader of the separatist Melanesian population, Jean Marie Tjibaou, and his aide, Yeiwene Yeiwene, were assassinated by three gunmen headed by Djoubelly Wea, who heads a pro-independence Melanesian faction. Bodyguards of Mr Tjibaou then killed Mr Wea and wounded another gunman. The FULK, a hardline pro-independence faction, called the assassination a 'severe warning' to authorities in France.[49] The FULK has repeatedly condemned the Matignon accords, arguing that these did not recognize the Kanak people's innate right to sovereignty or guarantee them independence in their own land.[50]

Action Directe is the best-known left-wing terrorist group in France. It has been responsible for six assassinations and 80 bomb attacks. At least 36 members of the group have been imprisoned. In January 1989 four leaders were sentenced to life in prison for the assassination of George Besse in 1986.[51]

Terrorist incidents in 1989 were related to French-Iranian relations, rising problems with the Muslim community in France and the stepped up measures against foreign terrorists on French soil. The French government established a new Institute of Advanced Studies on International Security that began its activities in November 1989 with a major review of problems such as terrorism, delinquency, crime and drugs. The Institute will bring together judicial and civilian officials, senior police as well as outside experts to examine fresh approaches to security problems.[52]

During 1989 the authorities arrested terrorists of foreign groups, including the Red Brigades, the IRA and ETA. In January and April anti-terror teams in co-operation with Spanish authorities staged raids in

Southern France and arrested several leading figures of ETA, including José Antonio Urrutikoetxea, who is believed to head ETA's military wing, Sergio Yegorov Arantzeka and Maria Helena Belliko.[53] In July French counter-intelligence agents arrested three suspected members of the IRA near the West German border. One of them was linked to the October 1984 bomb attack on Prime Minister Margaret Thatcher. The three were identified as Patrick Murray, Donnogh O'Kane and Pauline Drums. They were charged with having ties to a terrorist organization, conspiring to commit a crime, explosives offenses and falsification of documents.[54] In September five Italians were arrested, three men and two women, who were believed to be members of the Italian Red Brigades. It was said that they were preparing new attacks.[55]

French-Iranian relations deteriorated as a result of the French refusal to release a Lebanese terrorist, Anis Naccache. Iranian leaders claimed that the French government had promised in May 1988 that the Lebanese would be pardoned in return for Tehran's help for freeing French hostages in Beirut. President François Mitterrand rejected this claim and declared that France had made no such commitment. When three French hostages, MM. Carton, Fontaine and Kaufman, returned home from Lebanon on 5 May 1988 several reports said that Naccache's pardon was part of the secret bargain negotiated by Interior Minister Charles Pasqua. Prime Minister Michel Rocard said that M. Pasqua had left no record of the deal and that the new government would carry out only the obligations it was aware of – renewed diplomatic and commercial ties. In June former Prime Minister Jacques Chirac made remarks that suggested that France struck a continuing, multi-faceted deal with Iranian and Lebanese terrorists in Beirut to get its hostages back from Lebanon and to end Iranian-sponsored acts of terrorism inside France. Another French official said that France had pledged to make several payments to Lebanese terrorists groups and that the current government continues to pay. France has also promised eventually to release Naccache, resume diplomatic ties with Iran and refrain from prosecuting Wahid Gordi, a former Iranian diplomat implicated as accomplice in several terrorist acts committed in France between 1985 and 1986.

The release of 3,091 prisoners to celebrate Bastille Day 1988 did not include terrorists, persons sentenced to life or escaped prisoners. In September French intelligence services and the French embassy in Lebanon reported that Lebanese pro-Iranian Shiite groups were preparing terrorist actions against French interests in Africa. French intelligence officers were in the process of dismantling a network of Lebanese Shiites in Africa. Meanwhile, Anis Naccache went on a hunger strike. He was transferred to a prison hospital on 10 October after a month-long fast. He had lost 15 kilograms and was said to be in serious condition. On 19 September a French DC-10 airliner exploded in mid air over the Sahara in Chad, killing the 171 people aboard in an attack claimed by Islamic Jihad. The explosive used to blow up the plane was reported to be of the same type used in the attack on a Pan American World Airways jumbo jet over Scotland, in December 1988. It was reported that investigators believed the blast was triggered by a suitcase coated with the explosive pentrite taken on board at the Congolese capital of Brazzaville.[56]

During 1989 an increasing number of violent incidents related to the Muslim community were reported. Other violent incidents were related to the death threat against the British writer Salman Rushdie. On 2 October 1989 an explosion shattered windows on the first and second floors of Fayard, a prestigious publishing house that co-published the French edition of *The Satanic Verses*.[57]

Greece

Both domestic and international terrorist groups have been active in Greece. The government has reported a total of 260 incidents during 1980–86 including 23 deaths. The majority of the incidents were anti-American attacks. They reached a peak in 1985 with 14 attacks and have declined since then to three reported incidents in 1988, according to the US State Department. There were at least eight international incidents in 1988. The most infamous incident was the armed attack on the Greek cruise ship, *City of Poros*. Masked attackers threw hand grenades and fired machine guns at the passengers, killing eight and injuring another 98 persons. The attack was carried out after an initial plan to seize the liner and take hostages went wrong. The plan reportedly was to take hostages aboard the ship and to stage a car bomb attack on an American military base in Greece. However, a premature explosion of the car near Athens caused the attackers of the liner to alter their plan.[58]

Other major incidents were the assassination of Captain W. E. Nordeen, the American military attaché, by the November 17 Revolutionary Organization,[59] and the assassination of Hagop Hagopian, founder and leader of ASALA, by two unidentified gunmen.[60] There was also an armed attack against PLO representative, Ismat Sabri.[61] At least six bomb attacks were reported in 1988. Targets included a bar frequented by American soldiers, government buildings and the Turkish embassy.[62] Greece has been severely criticized for its extradition policy on terrorists. A Greek law prevents extradition if the Greek government believes that the terrorist is fighting for freedom. In 1988 Greece refused to extradite a Palestinian terrorist to Italy.

He was deported to a country of his own choosing, reportedly Libya.[63]

In 1989 the most dangerous domestic terrorist organization in Greece, the November 17 Revolutionary Organization, targeted several public prosecutors for assassination. On 10 January gunmen shot and injured public prosecutor, Costas Androulidakis. He died from his wounds on 10 February.[64] On 18 January gunmen shot Panayotis Tarasouleas, a Greek officer of justice, three times in his legs.[65] On 23 January two gunmen pulled up on a motorcycle at the home of the Supreme Court deputy prosecutor, Anastasios Venarthos, and shot him five times. He later died in hospital.[66] The organization said that the judiciary was partly to blame for the current financial problems in Greece. It also started a wave of bomb attacks directed against empty apartment buildings to protest against the government housing policies.[67]

In protest against the attacks, the officers of justice went on strike for ten days. The government decided to step up its anti-terrorist activities. In January, it said that it would strengthen its maritime anti-terrorist squad with 150 divers and commandos to thwart terrorist attacks on cruise ships. The expanded unit has 185 members.[68] In September 1989 Public Order Minister, Yannis Kefaloyannis, announced that an anti-terrorism squad would be set up, that his ministry would be reorganized and that three million drachmas (17.6 million dollars) would be made available to modernize and equip police. A reward of 200 million drachmas (more than one million dollars) would be given for information leading to the arrest of November 17's members.[69] In September 1989 the terrorist organization assassinated an MP for the first time. On 26 September Pavlos Bakoyannis, spokesman for the New Democratic Party, was shot five times at close range by two men as he entered his office about ten blocks from the parliament building. He died in a nearby hospital. The organization accused Mr Bayokannis of being the 'main partner' in the early career of George Koskotas, a fugitive banker accused of organizing the Bank of Crete fraud in which former Prime Minister Andreas Papandreou was later implicated. It said: 'We decided to execute the swindler and robber of the people's money.'

In 1989 several other domestic groups were responsible for bomb attacks, some related to a decision concerning an American request to extradite Muhammed Rashid, a Palestinian terrorist, that was postponed several times. On 10 April the May First organization bombed the apartment building of the Greek judge, Samouil, and threatened to assassinate any judiciary officials who support extraditing Palestinian terrorists. Other bomb attacks during 1989 were claimed by the Revolutionary Popular Struggle.[70] These were largely directed at government buildings, causing extensive damage but no injuries.

Italy

Since 1968 a total of more than 14,589 terrorist incidents have been recorded by the government. A total of 419 persons were killed and thousands were injured. The years 1976–80 were the most violent and bloody in Italy. In the 1980s the number of incidents declined substantially from a peak of 1,278 in 1980 to 339 in 1984. The 1980s incidents caused a total of 95 deaths. The US State Department recorded a total of 198 international incidents in 1980–85. The annual number reached a peak in 1980 and declined to 15 in 1983. The more recent years show an upward trend. Mickolus recorded a total of 133 transnational incidents in the 1980s. His figures show no clear trend although the annual number of incidents has decreased since 1982. The major incident in 1988 was a bomb attack at a club for American servicemen in central Naples on 14 April. Five persons were killed and another 17 were injured. The attack was claimed by the Anti Imperialist Brigade, a group which is believed to be made up of members of the Japanese Red Army, Red Army Faction and Red Brigades.[71] Another international incident was the poisoning of grapefruit in a campaign apparently aimed at Israeli exports.[72]

Compared to other European countries, Italy has a high level of violence related to organized crime. Umberto Santino estimated the turnover of Italian crime at 150 trillion lira of which about 40 per cent (32–49 billion dollars) flows to the Mafia. The state-run statistical agency calculates Italian Mafia profits at close to 71 billion dollars a year. Other officials put Mafia-linked drug profits in Italy at 21–42 billion dollars. In the United States, the FBI estimates that the leading Mafia families make 142 billion dollars each year in the drug trade. Mafia profits come overwhelmingly from drugs, mostly heroin but increasingly cocaine. Extortion and kidnapping remain lucrative ventures, but the Mafia has also reached into a wide variety of legitimate businesses.[73] Pino Arlacchi, a sociologist whom many consider to be Italy's foremost expert on Mafia finances, has long warned about the growing sophistication of organized crime in business matters. He predicts that the fall of European barriers in 1992, combined with widespread confusion over the recent overhaul of the Italian justice system 'will open a new golden era for Mafia Inc'.[74]

In a five-year period the Mafia killed the highest representative of the state in Sicily, the head of the region, the prefect sent by Rome, the prosecutor of the Republic, two police chiefs, two commissaries, a judge, leaders of the Communist and Christian-Democratic party, tens of policemen.[75] In the last 20 years, 851 kidnappings have been reported, including 40 children. 'Ndrangheta alone kidnapped more than 500 people.[76] Most of these kidnappings had criminal motives. Organized crime activities by the Mafia are generally excluded from the political violence data. However, given the Mafia's strong political ties this is not warranted. In the Palermo area alone, the Mafia has killed 425 people in 1978–82 including magistrates, police investigators, and politicians. In 1987 the gang war within the Camorra resulted in 230 deaths.[77] In the Palermo area a total of 114 people were killed.

In a 1989 report Prime Minister De Mita underlined that the Mafia, 'Ndrangheta and Camorra activities are a major danger to the stability of Italy'.[78] He reported that the Mafia had killed 335 persons in the June–November 1988 period. In January 1989 the government cracked down on a network of right-wing extremists and Mafiosi involved in drug trade, arms smuggling and forgery of cheques. The network even attempted to sell Mirage jet fighters to the West African state of Guinea Bissau.[79] In February 1989 the police captured a Danish ship with 170 tons of weapons aboard. They were destined for violent movements in Bolivia and Colombia. The weapons (pistols, machine guns, rifles and ammunition), all of Czech origin, were packed in 5,200 crates with false documents. The police arrested 11 persons with Danish, Belgian and Italian nationalities.[80] The investigation showed the existence of a right-wing international political organization that financed itself by financial operations and links with organized crime. The Mafia supplied weapons to the extreme right-wing groups in exchange for support operations in the smuggling of cocaine and heroine.

In September 1989 the anti-terrorist police uncovered an arms trafficking racket involving the 'Ndrangheta and the PSF, a Palestinian guerrilla faction. Police said raids on 26 apartments and houses all over Italy had led to 30 Palestinians and 16 Italians being identified and implicated in the traffic.[81] All the Palestinians involved worked or studied legally in Italy. According to ANSA, the Italians wanted to buy part of a weapon delivery the Palestinians were expecting from a Middle Eastern country.[82] In its stepped up activities against the Mafia, Italy closely co-operates with the United States.[83]

The Italian government has been more successful in coping with the Red Brigades than with the Mafia. In 1988, 83 suspected members of the Red Brigades were arrested.[84] The government is still looking for 200 identified left-wing terrorists of which 100 have been located. But there are still active members of the Red Brigades. A group of Red Brigade guerrillas announced in December 1988 that they had formed a new fighting cell and declared war on NATO and the Italian state. A document sent to the Italian news agency said the '14th of December Brigade' would be active throughout Italy. The document called for the renewal of the Fighting Communist Party.[85] In 1988 the Fighting Communist Party claimed responsibility for the assassination of Roberto Ruffili, a Christian Democratic senator, in Forli on 16 April. Signor Ruffili was a close adviser of Prime Minister Mita on plans for reforming Italian political institutions.[86] With the arrest of 11 persons in France and Italy, the police said that it had definitely dismantled the Red Brigades. One of the 11 arrested turned out to be a Jordanian of the Abu Nidal group, Biravi Thamer Khalid Hassan Hussein.[87] On the other hand, in October 1989, an Italian court acquitted 253 members of the Red Brigades of armed insurrection and civil war.

During 1988 a new wave of bomb attacks was reported in Alto Adige (South Tirol). Since 1956 a total of 356 bomb attacks have been recorded in the area. The 21 attacks that were reported in 1988 were mainly directed against property, including the Brenner Pass railway, cars, buildings, apartments, a broadcasting company, power pylons. They caused damage estimated at eight million dollars. No casualties were reported. The German-speaking separatist group Ein Tirol has claimed the majority of the attacks.[88]

Luxemburg

There are no terrorist groups active in Luxemburg. However, in 1985 the country was struck by a wave of bomb attacks that caused extensive damage. No organization has claimed responsibility. Targets included a natural gas plant, a swimming pool complex and a building where European leaders held a meeting. In February 1985 half a metric ton of explosives, one kilometre of fuse wire and 465 detonators were stolen from three quarries. It was feared that the material could fall into the hand of anti-NATO terrorists.

Malta

There are no active terrorist groups on Malta. However, because of its location near the Middle East, it has been troubled by a spill-over from Middle Eastern terrorism. In 1985 an Egypt Air Boeing 737 was forced to land on Malta. It was stormed by Egyptian commandos causing the death of 59 persons. Most of them died from smoke inhalation.

The Netherlands

In the 1970s a total of 48 international terrorist incidents were reported in the Netherlands. The Dutch government recorded a total of 165 terrorist incidents in 1980–86 that caused the death of seven persons. The Center for the Study of Social Conflict of Leiden University has collected data on terrorist incidents based on a definition used by the US State Department.

Between 1969 and 1988, 61 significant international incidents and 52 significant domestic incidents were recorded.

Three of the incidents recorded in 1988 were international incidents: two assassinations and one bomb attack. In May, a gunman fired into a car containing three Royal Air Force men as they sat in a parking lot in the town of Roermond, killing one and wounding the others. Thirty minutes later, in the village of Nieuw Bergen, two more Britons were killed and a third was seriously injured when their car blew up after they left a discotheque. In a statement to the BBC, the IRA claimed responsibility. In June 1988 Nihat Karaman, leader of the Turkish Workers Association in the Netherlands (HTIB) was assassinated in his home in Amsterdam. No one claimed responsibility for the attack and Dutch authorities were not able to determine who was responsible for the murder. An anonymous letter claimed that the attack was organized by two Turkish brothers who were supporters of Alpaslan Turkes, the leader of the Turkish right-wing group, the Grey Wolves.[89] There were other murders in 1988 but it is difficult to determine from press reports whether the attacks had political, criminal or racist motives.

International terrorist incidents recorded in 1989 included an assassination attempt on Hüseyin Yildirim, a lawyer and one of the leaders of the People's Party of Kurdistan, in the town of Retranchement and a handful of bomb attacks on Spanish facilities in The Hague, attributed to ETA. During 1989 many domestic violent incidents were related to the activities of single issue organizations. The issues include anti-militarism, anti-apartheid, animal rights, the environment and religious freedom.

Northern Ireland

In Western and Southern Europe, only Turkey has been more affected by terrorism than Northern Ireland in the last two decades. By early 1989 the conflict caused the death of 2,762 people (including 1,904 civilians) and another 12,000 have been injured.[90] The majority of the victims, including terrorists, were civilians. An estimated 400 British soldiers have also been killed. On average, every three days somebody is killed, while four people are wounded every day. The violence reached a peak in 1972 when 467 people were killed and nearly 5,000 were injured. Since then the violence has steadily decreased until 1987, when the violence rose again. In 1988, 93 people were killed.[91] In 1989, 60 people were killed.

In the 1969–85 period, an estimated 30,424 shootings, 11,829 bombings and 43,777 incendiary attacks have been recorded. On average this means seven incidents per day, five shootings, two bombings and every fifth day an incendiary attack.[92] More than 700 security forces had been killed by

Republicans. More than 400 Catholics had been assassinated by Loyalists while more than 265 Protestants fell to Republican assassins. The total number of casualties is more or less equally distributed among Protestants (51 per cent) and Catholics (49 per cent).

In 1988 the IRA stepped up its activities on the continent. It attacked British Army targets in the Netherlands, West Germany, Belgium and allegedly planned an attack in Gibraltar. The attacks on the continent continued in 1989, particularly in West Germany. In summer 1989 the IRA extended its list of 'legitimate targets' to include judges, officials, prison guards, informers, businessmen and construction workers that are linked with government projects.[93]

The security situation in Northern Ireland is costing Britain an annual total of 1.6 billion pounds excluding the costs related to the Army and the Police. According to the government, the unrest justifies the deployment of 10,500 troops, 6,500 reserve troops (UDR), 8,300 RUC policemen and 4,000 police reserves. The government admits that it cannot win with purely military means.[94] In the Irish Republic extra costs in 1988 relating to the security situation in Northern Ireland amounted to 172 million pounds. Since 1969, when border patrols became necessary, the Irish Army increased from 4,000 to 12,500 and the Garda (police) from 3,000 to 10,600.[95]

Portugal

The terrorist movement Popular Forces of 15 April (FP 25) still exists and from time to time carries out attacks. The group is anti-American and anti-NATO and has committed a series of assassinations, bombings, and rocket attacks against Portuguese government and economic targets. Its leader, Lieutenant Colonel Otelo Saraiva de Carvalho, is currently serving a 15-year sentence. In 1988 no incidents by this group were reported. However, one international terrorist incident was reported in 1988: in April, the former secretary-general of the Mozambican guerrilla organization RENAMO, Evo Fernandez, was kidnapped and murdered.

Spain

Terrorism in Spain is closely linked to the separatist struggle in the Basque province. The Freedom for the Basque Homeland (ETA) organization has been responsible for the majority of the casualties in recent years. ETA violence caused 479 deaths (including 206 civilians) and 758 other casualties (including 375 civilians) between 1968 and December 1985. According to a more recent estimate, ETA has killed 672 people. The violence reached a peak in 1980 with almost 120 deaths. Since then the annual death toll has varied between 30 and 60. In 1988 a slight increase was reported with a death toll of 73. More than 500 ETA members have been imprisoned. Several members accepted an amnesty and many former members went one step further, openly denouncing the continuation of the violence.[96] It is estimated that 83 per cent of the Basque population want ETA to put down their weapons.[97]

Some other right-wing and left-wing terrorist organizations have been active in Spain. In February 1989 the Guerrilla Army of the Free Galician People, a separatist group in Galicia, claimed responsibility for its first killing and threatened more attacks.[98] In Catalonia the organization Terra Lliure has been responsible for bomb attacks.[99] Since 1980 this Catalonian organization has claimed responsibility for about 160 attacks that claimed one death and tens of injured. In 1989 it was reported that it had started negotiations with the government about a truce.[100] The left-wing organization First of October Anti-Fascist Resistance Group (GRAPO) has been responsible for a number of assassinations. It targeted the police and businessmen in 1988.[101]

Anti-American attacks in Spain reached a peak in 1983 and decreased to seven in 1988. In 1980–88, 292 international terrorist incidents were recorded by the US Department of State. The annual number reached a peak in 1984 (60 incidents). Since then, the number has steadily decreased to 36 incidents in 1988. Mickolus recorded a much lower total number of transnational incidents. His data show a cyclical pattern with a high peak of 35 incidents in 1986.

Major incidents during 1988 were a failed attack by suspected West German terrorists against a NATO delegation in Cadiz, bomb attacks on the American embassy claimed by the Anti-Imperialist International Brigades, on the British consulate and on French interests in the Basque province.[102] Two members of the Red Brigades were arrested for involvement in bank robberies.[103]

Turkey

Mickolus recorded a relatively low number of international terrorist incidents in Turkey. The main terrorist problem in Turkey is an internal one. The most bloody conflict in Europe today is the Kurdish guerrilla campaign in Turkey and its suppression by the Turkish government. The struggle of the Kurdish minority (8.5 million, 19 per cent of the population) is characterized by periods of increased repression and intensified violence. After the declaration of martial law in 1979, government repression intensified in the south-eastern provinces as a reaction to the establishment of so-called liberated zones by the guerrillas. The most militant faction of the Kurds, the Kurdish Workers Party (PKK), moved from Ankara to the south-east of the country and declared an armed struggle against feudalism and colonialism. It started a terrorist campaign directed against traditional local leaders. Although large sectors of the local population agreed with the idea of abolishing the power of the local landowners, they considered PKK tactics too brutal and irresponsible. The conflict has become more and more militarized as the government tries to apply a military solution to the problem.

Violence in Turkey reached a peak in 1980. After the military takeover in September 1980 a decrease in the violence was reported but, since 1984, the level of violence has gone up again. In the 80 days before the military coup of 25 September 1980 the government recorded a total of 1,609 attacks and shootings and another 704 incidents. In the first 80 days after the coup these numbers decreased to 305 attacks and shootings and another 238 incidents.[104]

There are varying estimates of the number of incidents and casualties in the more recent period. After the September 1980 military coup the government announced that 5,241 Turks had lost their lives.[105] By early 1981 some 30,000 persons were in detention for suspected terrorist activities, the majority of them being members of some 40 different groups. By the end of 1981 it was officially declared that most terrorist groups in Turkey had been dismantled. On the other hand, *Devrimci Sol* (Dev-Sol), a left-wing organization declared illegal by the military government, reported in November 1982 that 122,600 people had been detained, including 81,634 Kurds. It also said that 68,300 persons were still being sought by the government.[106]

In response to a 1987 North Atlantic Assembly questionnaire, the Turkish government reported 4,459 terrorist incidents that caused 2,223 deaths in 1980–86.[107] Government repression was severe after the military coup. The newspaper *Demokrat Turkiye* reported in September 1982 that since September 1980, 170,000 people had been arrested, 593 people were killed during raids, 125 people were tortured to death, 21 persons were 'officially' executed and in 4,522 cases the death penalty was demanded.[108] The newspaper *Turkei Infodienst* reported in February 1983 that the death penalty was demanded in 5,265 cases. About 170 people actually received the death penalty and 41 persons were hanged. Another 665 persons were extra-judicially executed.[109] In July 1987 Amnesty International reported that in 1980–87 a total of 250,000 people had been arrested for political reasons. Many of them were tortured. The actual number of political prisoners varies from 3,000 to 18,000.

Since 1984 the PKK has stepped up its activities again. The casualty reports show large variations. According to one estimate, 700 civilians and troops and 700 guerrillas have been killed in the conflict since 1984.[110] Another report places the death toll at 1,300. According to official figures,

130 Kurds were killed and another 100 imprisoned since January 1988. In the same period, 45 soldiers and 100 civilians were killed. Well-informed sources in Diyarbakir, the south-eastern regional capital, estimated the number of insurgents at 400.[111] Foreign journalists have been banned from visiting the area.[112] At least 42 Turkish journalists and editors are currently in prison for what they have written. Since 1981 about 150,000 troops have been stationed in the south-eastern provinces.

In June 1988 a former member of the right-wing organization, the Grey Wolves, attempted to assassinate President Turgut Ozal. At least two international terrorist incidents were reported in 1989. On 2 April five bombs exploded at British and Turkish targets. In Ankara the car of the British vice-consul and the British cultural centre were damaged. Dev-Sol claimed responsibility for the attacks. In Istanbul, the buildings of two Turkish companies, Enka and Sabanci, were the target of bomb attacks. No one claimed responsibility for the attacks. On 10 October Abdurrahman Shrewi, a Saudi Arabian military attaché was seriously wounded when a bomb exploded in his car near his office in Ankara. There were no immediate claims of responsibility.[113] During summer 1989 the level of violence rose again in the Kurdish guerrilla war.

United Kingdom

The United Kingdom has a domestic and an international terrorist problem. The conflict in Northern Ireland has already been dealt with. The IRA has also been active in Britain, including attempts to murder Prime Ministers Margaret Thatcher and John Major and their Cabinets. The IRA also stepped up attacks against the British Army. On 22 September 1989 an explosion caused by a bomb planted in a British military barracks by the IRA killed at least 11 Royal Marines and injured 22 others in the town of Deal. This made it one of the bloodiest attacks on the British mainland.[114]

Other domestic terrorist incidents have been linked with separatism in Wales. In the last decade about 150 attacks have been directed at British interests, mainly related to the tourist industry, causing extensive damage. The Sons of Glendower have been responsible for most of the attacks. During 1989 several letter bombs were sent to real estate offices.[115] The most important international incident in 1988 was the mid-air bombing of a Pan American World Airways Boeing 747 that crashed in Lockerbie, Scotland on 21 December, causing 270 deaths.[116] American intelligence officials initially believed that the PFLP-GC of Ahmed Jebril was responsible for the attack and that Iran had helped the terrorists plan and execute the operation. After intensive investigation over several years, officials implicated two Libyan agents in the preparation and planting of the bomb.

NOTES

1. *Etudes Polémologiques*, Vol.37 (1986), p.20; Vol.47 (1989), p.85. On the basis of recent data for France, the researchers concluded that no parallel developments exist between delinquency, general criminality and terrorism. In France, the number of terrorist bomb explosions account for .029 per cent (1984), .021 per cent (1985), .024 per cent (1986) and .025 per cent (1987) of the total number of criminal offences. On material damage, see Eugene Mastrangelo, 'International Terrorism: a Regional and Global Overview, 1970–1986', in Y. Alexander, H. Foxman and E. Mastrangelo (eds.), *The 1986 Annual of Terrorism* (Dordrecht: Martinus Nijhoff Publishers, 1987), pp.7–59.
2. Statistics on the overall level of incidents in 1975 showed a brief drop in the level of international terrorism. Yet in the eyes of the media and the public it became known as 'the year of the terrorist' because of the impact of certain dramatic incidents, such as the seizure of the OPEC oil ministers in Vienna, the seizure of the embassies in Stockholm, Kuala Lumpur and Madrid, and the hijacking of a train in the Netherlands. Paul Wilkinson, *Terrorism and the Liberal State*, 2nd ed. (London: Macmillan, 1986), p.46.
3. See, e.g., Risks International (Alexandria, Virginia), 'Regional and Entity Analysis by Target and Statistical Overview, 1986', in Alexander, Foxman and Mastrangelo (eds.), pp.205–8.
4. Bruce George (rapporteur), *Final Report of the Working Group on Terrorism: North Atlantic Assembly Papers* (Brussels: North Atlantic Assembly, 1987); José Luis Nunes and Lawrence J. Smith (co-rapporteurs), *Final Report of the Sub-Committee on Terrorism: North Atlantic Assembly Papers* (Brussels: North Atlantic Assembly, 1989).
5. Ted Robert Gurr, 'Empirical Research on Political Terrorism: The State of the Art and How It Might Be Improved', in Robert O. Slater and Michael Stohl (eds.), *Current Perspectives on International Terrorism* (London: Macmillan, 1988), pp.115–154, at pp.144–5.
6. US State Dept., *Patterns of Global Terrorism*, (Washington, DC: US Dept. of State, 1987), p.v.
7. E.F. Mickolus, *Patterns of International Terrorism: 1980* (1989), p.xiii.
8. Jaffee Center, *Inter 1988*, pp.2–3.
9. Ted Robert Gurr, 'Some Characteristics of Political Terrorism in the 1960s', in: M. Stohl (ed.) *The Politics of Terrorism* (NY: M. Dekker, 1979), p.25.
10. *Etudes Polémologiques* (1986), p.12.
11. Gurr (note 9), p.46.
12. Edward F. Mickolus, *Transnational Terrorism. A Chronology of Events, 1968–1979* (London: Aldwych Press, 1980); Mickolus, 1989.
13. Ian Geldard. *Chronology of Terrorism 1990* (London: Intel Publishing, 1991), 86pp.; idem, *Chronology of Terrorism 1991* (London: Intel Publishing, 1992), 144pp.
14. *International Herald Tribune*, 15 July 1989. *NRC Handelsblad*, 1 Aug. 1989.
15. *International Herald Tribune*, 8 and 9 Feb. 1989.
16. Ibid, 25 April 1989.
17. Ibid, 21 April 1989.
18. Volkskrant, 7 Jan. 1988.
19. Ibid., 3 June 1988.
20. NRC Handelsblad, 4 Nov. 1988.
21. Volkskrant, 22 Sept. 1989.
22. *International Herald Tribune*, 15 Feb. 1989.
23. *Volksrant*, 28 May 1989.
24. Ibid., 16 Jan. 1989.
25. *International Herald Tribune*, 18 Jan. 1989.
26. *NRC Handelsblad*, 18 Jan. 1989.
27. *Volksrant*, 26 June 1989.
28. *International Herald Tribune*, 1 April 1989.
29. Ibid., 7 April 1989.
30. Ibid., 6 Oct. 1989.

31. Ibid., 7 Oct. 1989.
32. Ibid., 9 March and 25 April 1989.
33. Ibid., 21 Oct. 1989.
34. *Der Spiegel*, nr.27, 1988.
35. *NRC Handelsblad*, 15 Feb. 1988. *International Herald Tribune*, 16 Feb. 1988.
36. *International Herald Tribune*, 9, 11, 12 and 13 April 1988.
37. *NRC Handelsblad*, 11 May 1988.
38. *International Herald Tribune*, 23 May 1988.
39. J. Bruce, 'New Hopes for a Cyprus Settlement', *Jane's Defence Weekly*; C.F. Foss, Cypriot re-armament completed', ibid., 12 March 1988; *International Herald Tribune*, 27 Sept. and 16 Nov. 1988.
40. *NRC Handelsblad*, 20 March 1989. *International Herald Tribune*, 7 April 1989.
41. *International Herald Tribune* and *NRC Handelsblad*, 30 May 1989.
42. *Volkskrant*, 10 Jan. 1989. *Rotterdamsch Nieuwsblad*, 17 Jan. 1989.
43. *NRC Handelsblad*, 15 April 1989.
44. *Volkskrant*, 11 Sept. 1989.
45. Ibid.
46. *Der Spiegel*, 23 Jan. 1989.
47. *International Herald Tribune*, 6 Feb. 1989.
48. Ibid., 15 June 1989.
49. Ibid., 5, 8, 10 May 1989.
50. Ibid., 11 May 1989.
51. *NRC Handelsblad*, 10 Jan. 1989. *International Herald Tribune*, 16 Jan. 1989.
52. *International Herald Tribune*, 3 Nov. 1989. The Institute's official name is *L'Institut des Hautes Etudes sur la Sécurité Intérieure* [RDC].
53. *International Herald Tribune* and *Volkskrant*, 13 Jan. 1989. *NRC Handelsblad*, 26 April 1989.
54. *International Herald Tribune*, 19 July 1989.
55. *Volkskrant*, 6 Sept. 1989.
56. Ibid., 3 Oct. 1989.
58. *International Herald Tribune*, 13, 14, 21, 27 July and *Volkskrant*, 12 and 18 July 1988.
59. *International Herald Tribune*, 30 June 1988.
60. Ibid., 29 and 30 April 1988.
61. *NRC Handelsblad*, 30 April 1988.
62. *Volkskrant*, 21 March, 6 July 1988, *NRC Handelsblad*, 6 July 1988, *International Herald Tribune*, 24 May, 3 Dec. 1988.
63. *International Herald Tribune*, 7 Dec. 1988.
64. *Volkskrant*, 20 Jan. 1989.
65. Ibid.
66. *International Herald Tribune*, 24 Jan. 1989.
67. *NRC Handelsblad*, 23 Feb. 1989.
68. *International Herald Tribune*, 19 Jan. 1989.
69. Ibid., 28 Sept. 1989.
70. Ibid., 27 May 1989.
71. *Volkskrant*, 15 April 1988. *Knipselkrant*, May 1988.
72. *International Herald Tribune*, 27 April 1988.
73. Ibid., 20 May 1989.
74. Ibid.
75. *Volkskrant*, 6 Feb. 1988.
76. *International Herald Tribune*, 22 June 1989.
77. *Der Spiegel*, 14 Feb. 1988.
78. *Volkskrant*, 21 Jan. 1989.
79. *NRC Handelsblad*, 31 Jan. 1989.
80. Ibid., 10 Feb. 1989.
81. *International Herald Tribune*, 14 Sept. 1989.
82. *NRC Handelsblad*, 14 Sept. 1988.

83. *International Herald Tribune*, 2 Dec. 1988.
84. *Volkskrant*, Jan. 1989.
85. *International Herald Tribune*, 15 Dec. 1988.
86. Ibid., 18 April 1988.
87. *Volkskrant*, 8 Sept. 1989.
88. *Trouw*, 27 Aug. 1988, *Der Spiegel*, 31 Oct. 1988, *Volksrant*, 19 Nov. 1988.
89. *NRC Handelsblad*, 28 June 1988. *Volkskrant*, 13 July 1988.
90. *NRC Handelsblad*, 24 Feb. 1989. *International Herald Tribune*, 14 Aug. 1989.
91. Home Secretary's Speech at the Instituto Superiore Di Polizia, Rome, 12 Jan. 1989.
92. RUC Chief Constable's Annual Report 1985, p.68.
93. *NRC Handelsblad*, 2 Aug. 1989.
94. Ibid.
95. *Volkskrant*, 13 Sept. 1989.
96. Ibid., 8 Nov. 1988.
97. Ibid., 14 Jan. 1989.
98. *International Herald Tribune*, 4 Feb. 1989.
99. *Volkskrant*, 3 May 1988. *NRC Handelsblad*, 3 June, 18 Aug. 1988. *International Herald Tribune*, 29 March and 28 July 1988.
100. *Volkskrant*, 30 Sept. 1989.
101. *International Herald Tribune*, 5 and 6 Oct. 1988. *NRC Handelsblad*, 5 Oct. 1988.
102. *NRC Handelsblad*, 20 June 1988. *International Herald Tribune*, 18 March and 5 July 1988.
103. *Volkskrant*, 1 April 1988.
104. *International Herald Tribune*, 8 Dec. 1980.
105. *Newsweek*, 22 Sept. 1980.
106. *Tageszeitung*, 5 Nov. 1982.
107. Nunes and Smith, Working Group on Terrorism, 1989 Final Report, p.7.
108. Quoted in *Turkijkrant*, April 1983.
109. Ibid.
110. *NRC Handelsblad*, 2 April 1988.
111. *Volkskrant*, 28 Feb. 1989.
112. *NRC Handelsblad*, 3 Feb. 1989.
113. *International Herald Tribune*, 17 Oct. 1989.
114. Ibid., 23 Sept. 1989.
115. *Volkskrant*, 4 Feb. 1989. *International Herald Tribune*, 12 March 1988. *NRC Handelsblad*, 29 Nov. 1988.
116. *International Herald Tribune*, 22 Dec. 1988.

PART II
EUROPEAN NATIONAL EXPERIENCES

Countering Terrorism in the Netherlands

ALEX P. SCHMID

This essay contends that there is something called the 'Dutch approach' to anti-terrorism. The great degree of tolerance in Dutch society has absorbed many protests and, with few exceptions, prevented them from evolving beyond material destruction. Most protest groups were co-opted even before they reached this stage. The authorities have combined pragmatism with strict adherence to the rule of law. Downright repression has been exceptional and negotiation with terrorists during incidents or with leaders from their constituency afterwards has been the rule. No fully-grown terrorist underground organization has ever evolved. International terrorists have found few local sympathizers. Both local militants and foreign terrorists have received fair trials and have sometimes been set free when legal procedures were not strictly followed or evidence could not stand up in court. Imprisoned extremists have not been successful in mobilizing sympathizers from the outside who could be recruited to form new generations of extremists, as happened in Germany. Yet it was not only Dutch civil culture and governmental pragmatism and restraint but also luck that played a role in sparing the Netherlands the tribulation of patterned and persistent terrorism.

'Every country has the criminality it deserves.'

J.A. Lacassagne

'And the effect of righteousness will be peace and the result of righteousness, quietness and trust for ever.'

Book of the Prophet Isaiah 32:17

'The best politics is to do the right thing.'

E.M. House

In 1977 nine years before the American raid on Libya, the Dutch government sent in the air force to end a 'trainjacking'. The six F-104 Starfighter jets were only brought in for the roar, not for the bang. Yet when the ground attack under the thunder of the planes was over – with all the terrorists caught or killed and two hostages dead – the Dutch Prime Minister, Joop den Uyl, announced the raid with these words:

That violence was necessary to end the hostage situation we experience as a defeat. Yet we had to use it to prevent a worse outcome. Violence by itself does not solve anything, yet sometimes violence is necessary to prevent a worse outcome.[1]

The American raid on Libya in 1986, accompanied by triumphant policy statements, and the modest Dutch domestic air operation of 1977 are, of course, not really comparable. By the mid-1970s the Netherlands was no longer a colonial power with vital overseas interests to defend. The statement of Joop den Uyl, however, is typical of the Dutch attitude towards terrorism that I shall try to dissect.

Dutch Exceptionalism: Why?

Of the countries examined by this volume, the Dutch case is exceptional: while there have been a fair number of incidents which can be labelled 'terrorist', there has never been a full-grown domestic terrorist movement. Acts of international terrorism have also less frequent in the Netherlands than in surrounding countries (see Jongman, this volume, pp.68–9). While American soldiers and NATO installations have been attacked in Belgium, France, West Germany, Turkey, Italy, Greece, Portugal and Spain, nothing matching this has been recorded here. This near absence of major attacks of terrorism has been explained in terms of a conspiracy theory. This theory holds that 'International terrorism' uses the Netherlands as a rest place and sanctuary from where new attacks are planned. Such thinking is not uncommon in American and German anti-terrorist establishments; occasionally even a Dutch journalist accepts this line of reasoning despite the absence of more than the faintest circumstantial evidence.[2]

If it is not a conspiracy, there are only two other possibilities: either it is sheer good luck, in which case science cannot detect why, or there must be an explanation that has to do with Dutch society and the Dutch government's preventive policy in this field. If it is the latter, there are, perhaps, some Dutch lessons for other Western democracies. This question will be addressed later. First, some general traits of Dutch society are given as background to the point-by-point discussion.

Historical Roots of Dutch Peacefulness

An outstanding feature of Dutch society is the absence of a strong central government. When the Dutch nation came into existence through the Union of Utrecht in 1579, the seven provinces which formed this union remained sovereign and this decentralization was maintained until Napoleon tried to reorder things in the image of France. Right from the beginning, the Dutch nation was divided between the Catholic south below the big rivers (including Belgium which split off in 1830) and a Protestant north. There was a second divide within the Protestant camp, between orthodox Calvinists and less rigorous Protestants who were economically and politically dominant. The result of these divisions was religious tolerance. Later, a secular tendency began to develop. Each of the three tendencies, the liberal (or 'neutral'), the Calvinist and Catholic one, – 'pillars', as they are called – developed its own political parties, education system and cultural and recreational facilities, trade unions, and media. Dutch society was thus vertically divided, rather than along horizontal class lines. In the late nineteenth century, the socialist movement was co-opted into this system rather than breaking the pillars along class lines.

This division of Dutch society meant also that no political party could ever reign alone; it always had to find a coalition of political forces and these coalitions have been changing regularly until the present time. Political compromise between the elites of the different pillars is a necessity. To this legacy of tolerance in matters of belief, and compromise and pragmatism in matters of domestic politics, a third tradition linked to foreign policy has to be added: a position of neutrality between the larger powers, combined with a policy of mediating between the great European powers.

The 1960s: Change and the Challenge of the New Social Movements

These three traditional roots of Dutch peacefulness were strengthened, and in part, superseded, by a social learning process that occurred in the 1960s. The traditional roots of Dutch peacefulness were beginning to change. Neutrality had already been abandoned with the experience of the Second World War. In its wake, the Netherlands became a trusted member of the North Atlantic Treaty Alliance, with public support for NATO rarely falling below the 70 per cent range of public opinion. In domestic politics, the 'pillars' also began to change. Since the 1960s, 'depillarization' has been noticeable. The churches' influence on socialization and education declined with secularization.[3]

New political parties emerged on the left of the Social Democrats and on the right of the Liberals. The Catholic and Protestant alliance found its expression in the Christian Democrats (acronymed CDA – *Christen Democratisch Appel*, 1977). The Social-Democrats (PvdA) had begun to make political inroads even in the Catholic southern provinces. In the political center where the CDA is dominant, the left-liberal non-confessional Democrats gained 66 votes and became a coalition party next to the Liberals (VVD), the PvdA and CDA. This depillarization occurred quite rapidly in 1966–75, by the end of which time a certain stabilization was achieved.[4]

A major catalyst of this process was the public media, and television in particular. The broadcasting media freed themselves in varying degrees from their pillars and, with the new technology that made live broadcasting possible, magnified political conflicts by highlighting new issues brought into the public discussion by the new social movements: youth, students squatters, peace, the women's movement, ecology, and the Third World movement, to name but the most important ones.

The rise of the social movements was not an expression of social misery, great injustice, sharp social stratification, or systematic repression. Rather, it was made possible by the welfare brought about by the expanding postwar economy and the huge natural gas reserves found under Dutch soil. These were not revolutionary movements whose aim it was to overthrow the government; rather, they were mostly single issue movements. For a revolution, these movements lacked the support of the masses who enjoyed the fruits of a postwar economic boom and were materially satisfied; at least there was no crying material poverty in the exemplary Dutch social and economic welfare state. These movements were manned to a considerable degree by the postwar youth which entered the universities and other institutes of higher learning in massive numbers since the 1960s.

When the Amsterdam-based youth movement around the anarchist journal *Provo* constituted itself from elements of the 'Ban-the-Bomb-movement', the emerging ecological movement and the reaction against the consumer society, it was a clearly non-violent but provocative movement. It utilized playful happenings to bring home its political points and also offered creative proposals to society's problems. In the spring of 1966 *Provo* also gained considerable sympathy with its articulation of protest against the wedding of the heir to the throne with a German aristocrat who had marched in Hitler's army. The police at that time clearly overreacted to minor non-violent provocative happenings (with high news value) and its heavy-handed baton charges created new sympathizers and portrayed the police as oppressors. The Provos' anarchistic and often apolitical happenings became so numerous that eventually the available manpower of the Amsterdam police could not repress these disturbances of the public order. It therefore had to tolerate these manifestations which became part of the street culture.

The absence of repression not only meant an absence of news coverage of police operations. It also meant that fewer people felt a need to empathize with the victims of police charges. Consequently, since the mid-1960s there has been a profound change in the way the police are used in the capital. Before this period, riots and other disturbances of public order were solved in a technical manner by the police, with little or no consultation with the political authorities, a kind of reflex reaction to each challenge.[5] After 1966 the police response became more flexible.[6] The former director of the Dutch police academy, P. van Reenen, put it this way:

> The 'official' monopoly of physical force came to an end in the sixties. The clearness and the simplicity of both structure and action appeared unable to solve the new problems that arose at this time. On the contrary, official force made things worse. It especially worsened problems of legitimation of authority that had mushroomed overnight. Massive voluntary submission to political power was no longer self-evident. Legitimation was to be a central problem for both political authority and public officials. Goal-rationality and differentiation break through the fixed pattern that we knew of the official monopoly. Force no longer is a predictable reaction to a challenge. Much more it becomes a choice as to whether or not force will be used, and to what extent, and whether or not other means of control will be combined with that force.[7]

By 1967 the anti-authoritarian Provo movement was already disappearing and was replaced by the student movement which, in turn, declined three years later. The student movement was in many countries (Germany, Italy, France and others), the parent organization which, when declining, gave rise to terrorist groups. In the Netherlands, the police had already learned the lesson that heavy-handed repression was likely to produce radicalization, and thus the police reaction to it was milder than in neighbouring countries. This was, arguably, an important factor for the near-absence of major domestic native political violence (see Table 1).

The political violence that the Netherlands experienced since the late 1960s is, to some degree, linked to the colonial heritage. Three contexts have been significant. On the one hand, there have been a series of incidents linked to South Moluccan immigrants. On the other hand, political violence has been brought over from the birth pangs of one of the last Dutch colonies becoming independent, Surinam. Five years after independence (1975), the ex-colony was plagued by a sergeants' coup which in turn made the Netherlands a side-show of the civil war in Surinam. Finally, the fact that Afrikaans-speaking Boers still have cultural and commercial links with the Netherlands, has led to a taking of sides in the South African conflict by part of Dutch society. This has led

TABLE 1

POLITICAL PROTEST IN WESTERN EUROPE, 1948–77

	FR	DE	UK	GFR	BE	NE	IT	GR	SP	PR
Protest demonstrations	378	38	691	300	76	19	230	158	358	246
Regime support demonstrations	94	3	34	84	9	3	44	28	42	43
Political strikes	154	4	142	22	51	1	173	21	173	35
Riots	207	7	372	143	60	9	444	127	265	187
Armed attacks	827	6	3,931	157	42	28	544	670	313	117
Assassinations	4	0	50	4	1	0	6	2	7	1
Death from political violence	164	14	1,463	61	81	13	259	9,341	216	66

Key: FR = France, DE = Denmark, UK = United Kingdom, GFR = Federal Republic of Germany, BE = Belgium, NE = The Netherlands, IT = Italy, GR = Greece, SP = Spain, PR = Portugal

Source: Ch.L. Taylor and D.A. Jodice, *World Handbook of Political and Social Indicators*, 3rd ed. Vol.2: *Political Protest and Government Changes* (New Haven, CT: Yale UP, 1983), pp.24–51.

to pro- and anti-apartheid political violence in the Netherlands.

While these are specifically Dutch features of international terrorism and other forms of political violence, there are elements the Dutch share with other West European countries. These include: political violence among immigrants and between immigrants and Dutch people as well as by foreign governments against immigrants in the Netherlands; the fact that Middle Eastern terrorism uses Western Europe as one of its principal stages; the fact that some secessionist movements in Europe at times stage incidents in the Netherlands as well, in particular, groups from the Basque country, Northern Ireland and the Armenian diaspora; the fact that its large eastern neighbour, the former Federal Republic of Germany, had a terrorist problem; the fact that, geographically, the Netherlands are situated at the crossroads in Europe.

Main Terrorist Groups Active in the 1970s and 1980s

Since this study deals mainly with the response problem, the activities of foreign and domestic groups will not be covered in detail here. As far as domestic terrorism is concerned, there were only three groups that ever came close to being full-blown terrorist actors:

1. Red Youth/Red Help, a Maoist group active in the early 1970s;
2. South Moluccan militants active in the mid-1970s;
3. Revolutionary Anti-Racist Action (RARA) *fl*. late 1980s.

The following lists the main incidents of South Moluccan terrorism:

1. Occupation of the Residency of the Indonesian ambassador in Wassenaar, 31 August / 1 September 1970. Thirty-three South Moluccan

Youth stormed the place, killing a policeman and taking 30–35 hostages, but the Indonesian ambassador managed to escape. Manusama and another South Moluccan leader, Metiary, negotiated with the terrorists and managed to bring about their surrender. They received prison sentences ranging from four months to three years;

2. On 2 December 1975 a train running from Groningen to Zwolle was hijacked near Beilen by seven young South Moluccans who took 75 passengers hostage in an incident lasting 12 days and costing the lives of three Dutch people. They demanded that the Dutch government confess its past injustice towards the Moluccans and bring their cause to the attention of the United Nations, a committee of which had to establish contacts between the Badan Persatuan (their political organization) and Indonesia;

3. On 4 December 1975 another group of seven South Moluccans spontaneously occupied the Indonesian consulate in Amsterdam, taking 41 hostages (of whom one died after jumping out of a window). Like their fellow terrorists in the train they surrendered after 15 days. They received a prison sentence of seven years, half as much as their colleagues in the train;

4. On 23 May 1977 another train was hijacked near De Punt by nine South Moluccans who took 54 hostages. The incidents ended on 11 June 1977, with an assault costing the lives of eight people (6 terrorists, 2 hostages), wounding another nine (1 terrorist, 6 hostages, 2 men from the marine unit);

5. On 23 May 1977, in a co-ordinated move, 110 people, all but five of them children, were taken hostage at a school in Bovensmilde by four terrorists. The incident ended simultaneously with incident number four, without loss of lives or wounded;

6. On 13 March 1978 three members of a 'South Moluccan Suicide Squad' occupied the administrative center of the province of Drente in Assen, killing one person. The incident, lasting 28 hours, involved 69 hostages. One of them subsequently died from a bullet from the terrorists and five were wounded while the security forces stormed the place. The three received a prison sentence of 15 years.[8]

The following is a list of the major anti-apartheid sabotage incidents attributed to RARA:

1. On 17 September 1985 a Makro supermarket in Duivendrecht was burnt down, causing material damage valued at 48 million guilders (hfl.);

2. On 9 July 1986 RARA caused arson at the Royal Packing Industry

(*Koninklijke Emballage Industrie*) Van Leer, Inc. in Amstelveen. Damage: hfl. 750,000;

3. On 18 December 1986 a Makro supermarket in Duiven (near Arnhem) burnt down. Damage: hfl. 49 million; a renewed nightly attack on the rebuilt Duivendrecht Makro failed. Damage: hfl. 100,000;
4. On 10 January 1987 a Makro supermarket in Nuth (Limburg) was burnt down, causing hfl. 39 million worth of damage. [This incident was not claimed by RARA and it is likely that the perpetrators were not RARA.]
5. On 19 June 1987 Shell petrol stations in Nieuwegein and Zaandam were burned down, causing hfl. 39,000 in damage at the site;
6. On 26 June 1987 a Shell-owned storage house Boot Olie/van Staveren Marion Gas in Alphen a.d. Rijn was burnt down, causing damage amounting to hfl. 550,000.

Neither RARA, the South Moluccan extremists nor the Red Youth/ Red Help developed into real underground terrorist organizations, with sufficient task differentiation, cell structure, charismatic leadership, discipline, organizational skills, counter-intelligence measures, justifying ideology, safehouses, weapons, false identity papers, foreign contacts, weapons and ammunition, training, adequate finances and cars, members prepared to take high risks, and a pool of political desperados ready to be recruited. True, some of these elements were at one time or another present in all three groups, but not enough or for long enough to form the critical mass necessary to take off into a terrorist campaign. Add to this the fact that the Dutch authorities' reaction was not escalatory, did not create martyrs, and was not inhumane. This meant that the terrorists could not portray themselves as victims, thereby generating enough empathy for attracting new recruits. A Red Youth member, Lucien van Hoesel, reviewing his career, observed:

> If you situate my case in Germany, I would have been dead, or imprisoned for life or would still be a fugitive. It is very strange to realize this. In the Netherlands you get so much freedom that the motivation to take action dissolves. A rather strange effect if you notice it in your own behaviour. The liberal climate in the Netherlands has called a halt to terrorism; in Germany reactionary forces have kept terrorism artificially alive for ten years.[9]

The near-absence of a fully developed domestic terrorist movement has made it difficult for foreign terrorists to conduct operations in and from the Netherlands. Without local safehouses, know-how, and weapons, it is more risky to launch successful operations there. This is not to say that the Netherlands has not had a moderate number of international terrorist and quasi-terrorist incidents. Among the international organizations, the following groups were implicated in terrorist incidents on Dutch soil or targeting Dutch persons and assets abroad:

1. Palestinian groups: PFLP, Fatah, Black September Organization, Al Saiqa, and the Japanese Red Army, collaborating with the Palestinians;
2. Armenian groups: Justice Commandos of the Armenian Genocide (JCAG);
3. Northern Irish Groups: Provisional IRA;
4. German Groups: RAF (only in the form of unplanned shootouts);
5. Grey Wolves ['Bozkurtlar'] (Turkey);
6. Pan Turkish Organization;
7. Kurdish Workers Party (PKK);
8. Jewish Defense League;
9. Surinam Flying Brigade;
10. Basque ETA.

Given the fact that there were on average less than ten major incidents per year and given the diversity of actors responsible, the volume of political violence has never reached the critical threshold necessary for creating terror and panic. There were, however, brief periods of public apprehension (Eindhoven 1972, the South Moluccan double incidents of 1975 and 1977, The Makro fires of 1985–87). It is significant that actions of domestic groups caused the greatest concern.

For the same reason, it is also difficult to establish patterns. The fact that domestic groups targeted property rather than people constitutes a clear pattern. This is the main thing that distinguishes them from practitioners of political violence in some other countries of Western Europe. Incidents involving loss of Dutch lives have gone down, as have acts of hostage-taking and political (not criminal) kidnappings. Hijackings of aircraft have gone down, in line with an international trend. There has been an increase in the frequency and destructiveness of political violence in recent years, especially in the area of arson and firebombings. The level of Middle East-related incidents has gone down. The level of incidents related to Northern Ireland has gone up, while incidents related to the German Red Army Faction have gone down. South Moluccan terrorism has stopped, while incidents involving other immigrant groups have gone up.

The Threat Posed to the Country

There has never been a serious threat to the country as a whole. Terrorist acts did not find any positive resonance in significant sectors of the public.

The demands of the terrorists were – except within the South Moluccan community – not perceived as justified. Given the pacific state of Dutch society, terrorism discredits itself and the government does not have to struggle with the terrorists for the favour of the people. There is no legitimacy problem involved. In parliament, there was no major controversy over the security forces' deadly assault that ended the incident at De Punt in 1977. Only the radical parties in parliament felt a need to criticize the handling of the incidents by the Government.

The Dutch people gave their government good grades for both the 1975 and the 1977 incidents, despite their different outcomes (peaceful capitulation in 1975, assault in 1977). In 1975 a NIPO survey found that 69 per cent of the public were pleased with the outcome. In 1977, 90 per cent of those interviewed held that the government had dealt with the situation as well as possible.[10] With such solid backing, there was no major threat to the country at any time. There is at present, in Dutch society, no clear and present threat of domestic terrorism and the threat perceived to emanate from international terrorism is not judged to be particularly high, although there are regular alerts issued on the basis of confidential information obtained from abroad.

The Political Setting in Which Responses Were Developed

Since the end of the nineteenth century (if not earlier), Dutch society has been pacified. Social conflicts between labour and capital did not occur with the same ferocity as in some other industrializing countries – thanks to the 'pillar system' discussed earlier. The idea of a strong centralized state in the Hegelian sense is alien to the Dutch. Rather, the government was and is seen as a 'corporationist distribution center of money and other instruments of power'.[11] Dissident groups in Dutch society are generally treated with tolerance and, wherever possible, co-opted and integrated into Dutch society rather than left at the margin. This applies to both criminal and political marginal groups and individuals.

A 1987 policy paper by the Ministry of Justice on ways of dealing with *crime*, in general, puts great emphasis on social welfare policy as an instrument to bind groups to society. In particular, it stresses the role of general youth assistance, which includes providing facilities for those unemployed for a long period and leisure time measures. Then there is also a volunteer work policy, a housing policy and a minority policy. There are also programs for individuals, who through personal or social circumstances, have encountered problems. The goal is to enable these people – often alcoholics and drug addicts – to regain control over their lives.[12]

The political integration of dissident minorities is facilitated in the

Netherlands by the fact that, unlike in Germany, there is no five per cent threshold (of the total vote cast during an election) which discourages political newcomers from entering parliament. For most of the postwar period, there were several political homes to choose from on the left. First, there was the Communist Party (CPN). Then there was the Pacifist-Socialist Party (PSP) which fulfilled an integrative function even for those who were less than pacifist in terms of political violence. Finally, there was the Political Party of Radicals (PPR) which in the mid-1970s was part of a coalition cabinet.

There has, in recent years, however, been a trend away from the small parties, which is unfortunate as they have served as a parliamentary voice for basically extra-parliamentary social movements and action groups. They have contributed to preventing dissidents from becoming criminalized and dealt with only by the law enforcement machinery. In 1989 four small parties on the left (CPN, PSP, PPR and the Evangelic People's Party EVP) formed a 'Green Bloc' to fight the European elections. They managed to gain seven per cent of the total vote.[13] The term 'terrorist' has rarely been applied to Dutch violent action groups, except during the heyday of South Moluccan terrorism in the mid-1970s. Rather, the term 'politically-motivated violent activists' was and still is used. Nevertheless, the authorities chose a crime approach for dealing with terrorism.

General Legislative and Legal Framework

Basically, there are three ways a political system conceptualizes acts of terrorism. These can be defined, as happens in Israel, as warlike acts. Terrorism can also be defined as disturbances of the public order, an approach apparently favoured in France. The third possibility is to treat acts of terrorism as criminal activities. This is the Dutch government's approach. However, when this choice was made in the early 1970s, it did not represent a denial of the political content of terrorism, which is central to it. Rather, it was the peculiarities of Dutch police organization that favoured this choice. If terrorism had been defined primarily in terms of a public order problem, then the local burgomaster (mayor) of one of the 800 municipalities in the Netherlands would have had much say in the handling of a local incident. Since mayors are appointed directly by the Queen, they enjoy considerable autonomy. The conceptualization of terrorism as crime allowed the use of the more centralized lines of command of the juridical apparatus. Crisis situations tend to produce decision-making at the highest possible level and the channels of authority of the Dutch legal machinery lend themselves better to this organizational imperative.

The police – not the military or some special unit – was the institution chosen to deal with terrorism in the first instance. Due to the dual authority system, the police fall both under the Minister of the Interior, responsible for public order, and the Minister of Justice, which controls the penal system. In the set-up chosen in the early 1970s, the Minister of Justice was given priority while the burgomaster is consulted.[14]

While the criminal route was chosen to manage counter-terrorism efforts, the Dutch authorities nevertheless did not attempt to define terrorism in the 1970s. It was not until 1987 that the Minister of Justice volunteered a definition, along the lines of the TREVI definition:

> An organized crime of a terrorist nature is understood to be the use of, or the threat with the use of violence by a coherent group of persons for the purpose of achieving political goals, excluding the waging of war. Included in these crimes are also punishable facts which in themselves are not violent but which are serious due to the circumstances that they are perpetrated in the same framework for the achievement of said goals (so-called connected crimes).[15]

This is not a very good definition, the more so since there is no definition of 'organized crime' in Dutch penal law or any other body of relevant legal thought. Some characteristics of terrorist acts, such as their preference for unarmed civilian targets, the disrespect for prisoners, the lack of moral restraint, the instrumental nature of the victims of violence for manipulating third parties, are not addressed in this definition. Yet what the Dutch policy makers had in mind was clear; hijackings, kidnappings and other acts of hostage-taking stood out in everybody's mind as terroristic, certainly after the attack on Israeli athletes during the Olympic Games in Munich in 1972.

In juridical terms such incidents amounted to unlawful deprivation of freedom, sometimes combined with murder. The so-called 'Terror-letter' of the Prime Minister, dated 22 February 1973, stated that 'the actual fight against acts of terror is a form of combating crime and as such the task of the police.'[16] No special domestic legislation was therefore sought by Dutch policy-makers for dealing with terrorism.

General Social, Political and Law Enforcement Policies and Practices

Crisis Management and the Use of Force

The organizational structure for dealing with land-based acts of hostage-taking was first established in 1972 in the so-called 'Hostage Circular' (*Gijzelingscirculaire*) and the 'Terror Letter' mentioned above. When such a terrorist incident takes place, a Crisis Centre is set up at the Ministry of Justice in The Hague. This serves as the decision-making body and is chaired by the Minister of Justice who also consults with some of his fellow ministers, in particular, the Prime Minister, the Minister of the Interior, the Minister of Defence, and, if necessary, one or more of the other ministers, depending on the incident.

In the municipality where the incident takes place a Policy Centre is established. It is headed by an Attorney-General, who is assisted by the Chief Commissioner of the local police and the District Commissioner of the State Police as well as the regional Public Prosecutor. Also part of this Policy Centre (the name is misleading as it does not make policy but provides information to the policy-making Crisis Centre and executes orders received from there) are the Queen's Commissioner (who governs the province), the local mayor, and several other officials. The following arrangements then have to be made:

1. The place of action has to be isolated by the police;
2. Specially trained units (marksmen and close combat fighters) have to be mobilized;
3. A negotiator has to be selected who is not the same person as the decision-making authority;
4. Arrangements for the provision of information have to be made;
5. Communication lines have to be installed rapidly and effectively.[17]

In 1973 the government also created an Official Steering Group, Terroristic Actions (ASTA – *Ambtelijke Stuurgroep Terroristische Acties*). The idea of creating a special organization charged exclusively with the prevention of and the fight against terrorism was dismissed in the early 1970s not only because it would take too much time to set up a whole new organization but mainly because the danger was envisaged that such a body would isolate itself from society. The 'Terror-letter' of 22 February 1972 stated 'According to the view of the government, the combating [of terrorism] shall not be allowed to take place in a form which could do harm to the open character of our society.'[18]

The task of fighting terrorism was therefore to be a police task. If stronger means were necessary, the assistance of the Royal Constabulary (*Koninklijke Marechaussee*) and the Armed Forces could be called upon, but these too would fall under the authority of the Minister of Justice. The 'Terror-letter' announced the formation of two armed units, one from the police and one from the military. Both would consist of long-distance sharpshooters (the mistakes of the security forces at Munich in 1972 was still fresh in the memory). In addition, a number of military men were to undergo special close combat training, while another detachment was prepared for cordoning-off the site of a terrorist incident. The 'Terror-letter' stated that these units should be formed from volunteers and fulfil these tasks in addition to the irregular police or military duties. It was also specified that they should be brought to the scene only after a decision by the Minister of Justice to that effect had been explicitly made.

The use of the police in the fight against terrorism falls, like other police uses, under the regulations of the Police Code (*Politiewet*). If military units assist the police they also fall under this code. Article 28 of the Police Code describes the task of the police as follows:

> the actual maintenance of the legal order in subordination to the appropriate authority [either the Public Prosecutor or the Mayor] and in accordance with the valid rules of law and the giving of help to those who need help.[19]

The rules of engagement of the Dutch police for implementing this have been summarized as follows:

1. The use of armed violence has to be necessary. 'The police may not take recourse to a more powerful instrument as long as it can achieve the result with a less powerful one';
2. There can be no disproportion between the threatened legal good (*rechtsgoed*) and the violence to be used (the so-called symmetry or proportionality principle);
3. Each use of violence by the police has to be preceded by a warning and order (warning shot or oral), which can be excluded only in cases of necessary self-defence;
4. Force may never be used against helpless persons and persons surrendering (the helpless are, according to most instructions for officials, women, handicapped, senior citizens and children; the self-defence exception also applies here);
5. Each use of arms has to be protocolized. The reason for this prescription is that in this manner 'the possibility of complaint, responsibility and recompensation is assured.'[20]

In 1987 a governmental commission studying the use of arms by the police, added another set of considerations which takes a more strategic view of the context:

> The regulation of the use of violence [the Dutch term *geweld* covers both 'force' and 'violence'] by the police has to strive, even more than has been done in the past, to prevent a hardening [of the conflict situation]. Violence, including legitimate force, is a socially disruptive factor, which may never be brought into play easily and

disproportionally. The conditions and the degree wherein violence is to be used have to be a constant concern for the government. For this, the right balance between the reduction of the private use of violence on the one hand, and the reduction of the use of force by the government has to be maintained.[21]

These are rather severe restrictions. The killing of terrorists who have been disarmed after hostage liberation – as happened after the 1980 SAS storming of the Iranian embassy in London – would not be acceptable in the Dutch context.

These guidelines are characteristic of the Dutch political culture. This is also reflected in the Dutch rating for its human rights performance. The World Human Rights Guide places the Netherlands, on the basis of weighed factors, among the top five nations when it comes to observing human rights, on the same level as Denmark, Finland, New Zealand and Sweden.[22] All told, the Netherlands is a remarkably civilized country. Corruption by public officials is minimal, governmental response to public grievances is high, public access to the media is probably unsurpassed and the reaction of the government to political violence is measured and proportional.

Legal Measures

The terrorist threat to the Netherlands has not been of such a serious nature that the State of Emergency Law (*Wet Buitengewone Bevoegdheden Burgerlijk Gezag* – WBBBG) was ever invoked. This Law on Extraordinary Powers of the Civil Authority was created in 1952 (partly in reaction to the 1948 Communist coup in Czechoslovakia). When this Law was revised in 1976, at the time of South Moluccan terrorism, no extra provisions were included which would have made it suitable for combating terrorism. Nor was recourse made at that time to the War Law for the Netherlands (*Oorlogwet voor Nederland*) of 1964, which grants the authorities even stronger powers. While Canada invoked its War Measures Act in October 1970 to deal with multiple kidnappings by the *Front de Libération du Québec* (FLQ), Dutch authorities did not take this road. The challenge facing the Dutch was, of course, much smaller than in the case of Canada, where violent incidents had been going on since 1963.[23] The reasoning behind this reluctance has been given by a public official, F.J. Kranenburg:

Yet it was right to operate without a state of emergency. It would have meant a clear triumph for the terrorists if the Netherlands had declared quasi-war and thereby recognized the gentlemen as a war-waging power. The Dutch public, too, would not have appreciated the notion that our normal legal and administrative system could not cope with the situation. Some action *contra legem* and *praeter legem* for a good purpose is pardonable.[24]

In the last sentence the writer indicates, however, a problem posed by the use of normal legislation for extra normal violence. There have been a few occasions when activities in the field of anti-terrorism were not covered by normal law, but would have been acceptable under either the Law of War or the Emergency Law. In 1970 when President Suharto of Indonesia visited the Dutch capital, shortly after a terrorist incident at the Indonesian residency in nearby Wassenaar, the authorities expected further attacks. A police cordon was therefore laid around The Hague during the visit on 3 September 1970. The police were instructed to stop and return all cars with dark-skinned passengers. The explanation given by the Minister of the Interior to Parliament was that the government

> . . . felt justified and obliged to give these orders in order to live up to the duties of international law with regard to the security of the Head of State of Indonesia, as well as for the maintenance of the public order and security. The measures taken by it were proportional to the apparent dangers.[25]

This appeal to 'international law' can hardly be taken seriously. One author commented that 'This decision . . . lacked any basis in Dutch law'.[26]

Other incidents when anti-terrorist activities were not adequately covered by law occurred in 1970 and 1977 in the South Moluccan neighbourhoods of Ijsseloord and Assen. State Police and Royal Constabulary, with hundreds of men and armoured personnel carriers, systematically searched South Moluccan houses for weapons. Article 97 of the Dutch Code of Criminal Procedure (*Wetboek van Strafvordering*) allows a house search only in cases of 'serious suspicion' which did not exist for every one of the South Moluccan families living there.[27] Subsequently, the Dutch government introduced legislation for an Arms and Ammunition Law which gave the government the power to conduct searches where reasonable suspicion existed that weapons were possessed illegally.[28] Prior to that, a traffic law had been used for searching cars for explosives and weapons, but that was a use not in the spirit of that particular law. By creating this new Law on Arms and Ammunition, the government implicitly acknowledged that it had on these occasions acted outside the law (*praeter legem*).

After an aborted attempt to take Queen Juliana hostage in 1975, the question of the desirability of a law against terrorist planning and conspiracy was discussed. The Minister of Justice announced in October 1976 that he was considering a law that would make it punishable to 'conspire for performing terroristic acts'.[29] However, this particular conspiracy – against the Royal Family – was already covered by an ancient law and no legislation in this regard was introduced.[30] The absence of a conspiracy law comparable to Paragraph 129a in Germany is welcomed (Article 140 refers to membership in a criminal organisation). However, this misuse has apparently been abandoned again, as it tended to drive dissidents underground.

In the eyes of some officials, there is a need for a law enabling authorities to raise charges against persons preparing acts of hostage-taking and armed assaults. In 1988 the Minister of Justice, F. Korthals Altes, established a working group to study the feasibility of such a law, but by 1992 it was still not introduced. Beyond the Law on Arms and Ammunition (which took force only in September 1989) there does not seem to be any legislation which can be considered as flowing from exigencies of counter-terrorism. The authorities the author consulted do not envisage major legislation. The only new law desired is one which makes the issuing of false bomb threats a criminal act. At present, a terrorist telephone threat costs only a dime and goes unpunished. Due to their frequency and disruptiveness these have become a nuisance, but it is doubtful whether legal measures alone can have a major impact.

The individual freedom of Dutch citizens has not been affected by either emergency legislation or the extension of security forces powers. The press has not been muzzled during terrorist incidents, but there have been a few partly successful appeals to the editorial responsibility of media gatekeepers. In the mid-1970s a consultative body 'Justice-Police-Press' (*Overleg-orgaan Justitie-Politie-Pers*) was created, but this has not led to a press code or a media council comparable to the practices in Great Britain and Germany. The Dutch law does not permit prevention of publication, only the taking of legal measures after publication. The government has utilized, however, an information 'blackout', especially in cases of criminal kidnappings. Yet journalists are free to gather information from unofficial sources and from officials who wish to 'leak' information.[31]

The freedom of the press is utilized to the fullest not only by journalists hunting for scoops but also by terrorist sympathizers. In the late 1970s some persons formerly associated with the Red Help formed a Red Resistance Front (*Rood Verzet Front*), which in August 1978 began to issue a Clipping Journal (*Knipselkrant*). It produced about 35 issues a year. This alternative press service regularly published communiqués and strategy papers from terrorist organizations, such as the RAF, the CCC, the French Action Directe, the Italian Red Brigades, the PIRA and the Basque ETA. In West Germany, this activity would be prohibited under Article 129a, section 3 of the Penal Law, which prohibits advertising and recruiting for a terrorist association, but there is no equivalent Dutch law against publications advocating political violence. In summer 1986 Paul Moussault, the Communist editor of *Knipselkrant*, was briefly detained by the Dutch authorities in connection with a suspicion of a violation of the Law on Explosives but he was released after two weeks for lack of evidence.

There is one piece of legislation which is likely to be introduced during 1993. The opening of the European borders (in 1990 between Germany, France and the Benelux countries and after 1992 with the other EEC states) has led to pressure to make the carrying of a personal identification paper mandatory on certain occasions (such as when using public transportation). This will marginally contribute to the fight against terrorism.

Since there have been no serious terrorist campaigns and few convictions of terrorists in the Netherlands, there have not been any modifications of trial, detention and sentencing procedures. However, prison sentences for terrorist offenses (unlawful deprivation of liberty in the case of acts of hostage-taking, murder in the case of assassinations) have become longer, at least for the South Moluccan terrorists. With regard to foreign terrorists, there is (or was) a certain reluctance to sentence apprehended perpetrators for long terms or even to keep them in Dutch prisons at all. The fear exists that their colleagues still at large will attempt to free them by an exchange against hostages.

The fear of being blackmailed in such a way probably influenced the decision-making of the Dutch Minister of Justice in 1974. Two Palestinian terrorists, Adnan Ahmad Nuri and Sami Houssin Tamimah, who had hijacked a British VC-10 passenger aircraft and subsequently destroyed it at Schiphol airport (Amsterdam), were sentenced to five years imprisonment each. According to a Dutch weekly, the Minister of Justice (Van Agt) and his Secretary-General (Mulder) ordered, in a most unusual way, that the Officer of Justice of Harlem (under whose jurisdiction Schiphol falls) should not pass a sentence higher than five years of imprisonment.[32] To make matters even worse, the Dutch authorities subsequently released the two in exchange for the passengers of a British VC-10 which had been hijacked and brought to Tunisia. According to the author's sources, the Dutch authorities made it known that there were Arab freedom fighters whose release they would consider favourably if demanded. This actually happened, and Nuri and Tamimah departed for Tunisia where they were handed over to the PLO, which promised to punish them.[33] However, there have been no cases where jurors have been threatened. Nor have there been reports of harsher prison conditions for terrorists than for non-political prisoners.

Negotiation with Terrorist Groups

The Government of the Netherlands, in line with the defeatist mood prior to the July 1976 Entebbe raid which turned the tide for other nations as well, repeatedly made concessions.[34] Perhaps the worst incident in this regard took place on 13 September 1974, when three terrorists from the Japanese Red Army (*Sekigun-Ha*) seized the French embassy in The Hague, taking 11 hostages, including the Ambassador. The terrorists made several demands on the French government, including the release of an imprisoned Japanese terrorist named Furuya (a pseudonym). Remembering a previous incident at the Israeli Lod Airport in 1972, where Japanese terrorists killed 27 people and wounded 78, the Dutch authorities favoured concessions.[35] Prime Minister Den Uyl personally flew to Paris on the second day of the four-day long occupation.[36] The French authorities were prepared to release Furuya, but were not prepared to offer a French aircraft with a French crew for the free exit. In the end, the terrorists were allowed to leave in a French aircraft, with a Dutch team of pilots, their friend Furuya, several weapons and 300,000 dollars provided by the Dutch government.[37]

This outcome was strongly criticized, especially the fact that the terrorists were given new hostages (the aircrew) and allowed to keep some of their weapons. From the sources available, it is not clear whether the French or the Dutch government were more willing to grant such concessions. It is, however, known that the French flew their 'gorillas' to Amsterdam airport, apparently with a view to storming the embassy.

The year before, a domestic incident raised a perennial problem surrounding negotiation with terrorists. It was a simple criminal incident in which two hostage-takers, in exchange for releasing their hostages, were allowed to go home to their house in The Hague. The police promised not to arrest them before late at night next day. This promise was apparently broken; the police smoked the two out of their house with tear gas before the agreed-upon deadline. The question arises as to whether the Hague police acted correctly or not in arresting the hostage-takers ahead of the agreed-upon time. Breaking promises made under duress is easily advocated, but it reduces future credibility and options.

This probably played a role on 26 October 1974, in another hostage-taking at Scheveningen prison, when the Dutch authorities decided to break a promise of safe passage and chose instead to launch a surprise attack. In all likelihood, the broken promise of the previous incident must have played a role in favouring this alternative, as the other one was 'discredited'.[38] Since the assault was successful and nobody was killed, the 'iffy' question became irrelevant. It did recur, however, in 1977 in one of the Moluccan incidents, when another promise was broken by the authorities.

As the Dutch authorities gained experience with hostage negotiations, the position they took became clearer. It consisted of three elements: saving the lives of the hostages, but not at any price; maintaining a hard line *vis-à-vis* the hostage-takers with regard to giving in on substantial matters (like not allowing the terrorists to depart with their hostages); and maintaining a security forces' presence to bring pressure to bear on the terrorists and to make it clear to them that there is no alternative to negotiation.

The dilemma of hostage situations is often one between sacrificing principles (the rule of law) or the lives of hostages. Principles are abstract and lives are concrete, so the temptation exists to favour the latter over the former. Yet this is short-sighted. A society can live without some of its citizens (the hostages), yet it cannot survive for long without an intact system of the rule of law. The fact that there is a rule-based public order means that people experience a sense of security, that they are certain that they will be protected against arbitrariness, abuse of power and violent aggression. To give in to terrorist extortion means to suspend temporarily the rule of law. Any advantage conceded to the terrorist side lessens public respect for the authorities and gives rise to feelings of anger, fear, revenge and disrespect for the law of the land. Any successful act of hostage-taking resulting in political rewards for the perpetrators is likely to invite repetition by others. Deterrence of future acts of hostage-taking is more likely to be achieved by a hard-line, no-concessions stand by the authorities in previous tests of strength with the terrorists.

The Dutch policy has generally been to give the maintenance of the rule of law priority, although the impression that the lives of the hostages have priority is deliberately created. In practice, however, concessions have been made. The pursuit of both goals – saving the rule of law and the lives of hostages – is served by playing for time, time to persuade the hostage-takers to give in, and/or time to neutralize them, if necessary, by a surprise assault. An important element in gaining time is to make sure that the negotiator is not somebody with the authority to make binding concessions and decisions. Concessions on non- or less-substantive matters (facilities, food, money, even a free exit) are made or brought into the discussion but these are linked to conditions which the hostage-takers have to fulfil before they get what they want. Essential in this strategy of gaining time is a good assessment of the state of mind and the likely response of the terrorists. In the beginning, negotiations were carried out by untrained persons. Yet, as early as 1973, two psychiatrists were consulted, and in subsequent incidents the use of behavioral scientists became a prominent feature.[39]

Playing for time wears down terrorists, especially when lack of sleep takes effect. The long waiting can increase despair, but also the willingness to compromise. It can also increase the inhibition to kill hostages due to the fact that terrorists and hostages interact and perceive themselves as sharing the same hardships. In 1975 during the first train incident, these features played an important role in terminating the incident. The psychological war of nerves waged against the terrorists depended, however, on an accurate assessment of the state of mind of the hostage-takers. Information about this could be obtained from released hostages, South Moluccan intermediaries sent to the train, and from listening devices placed under the train.[40]

Methods of talking to terrorists were first developed systematically in the New York Police Department by Frank Bolz and Harvey Schlossberg. These experts were brought to the Netherlands where a domestic negotiator, the psychiatrist Dr Dick Mulder, adapted their approach to political terrorists (most of the hostage situations in New York were purely criminal affairs). Mulder, who worked for the Ministry of Justice (and is now retired) has been credited with the 'Dutch approach' which is, in fact, a New York approach. However, Mulder added some features, pertaining to the different phases.[41] He identified three specific phases in a hostage situation:

1. In the first phase, the terrorists are nervous and aggressive, anxious and alert. They want to enforce respect by aggressive behaviour in order to prove that they mean business. This requires calmness from the negotiator. He has to satisfy the hostage-takers' desire for publicity as much as possible, by passing messages to others, letting them talk to journalists, appear on television or whatever they want. In the meantime, he assures them that the government requires time and that there is no chance of a fast solution;

2. When, after the first period in which the captors are predominantly unstable, the status quo has been attained, phase two begins. The negotiator observes carefully how the hostage-takers structure their day. In addition, they are placed in a subordinate position by the imposition of all sorts of rules. This is done by regulating the schedule for bringing food, by establishing sleeping hours and arranging the moment when the next contact is made.

3. The third phase is the most dangerous one, as the hostage-takers begin to feel that they are going to lose. They want to go back to phase one; they sharpen their demands and words and become aggressive again. The negotiator must keep them calm and create the impression that their wishes are being met. If that impression has been successfully created, the time for resolution has arrived.[42]

Negotiation, in this sense, becomes negotiated surrender or, if surrender is beyond reach, a prelude to a sudden, forceful solution. In the first South Moluccan incident in 1970, surrender did not take the form of capitulating to the Dutch authorities directly. A more face-saving solution was found, after South Moluccan intermediaries were brought in. The terrorists surrendered to a South Moluccan churchman, who subsequently handed them over to the police.[43]

In the last two South Moluccan incidents, however, negotiations were not leading to a peaceful solution. Playing for time, as Mulder and his colleagues did in 1975, works only if the opponent is not fully aware of the game being played. However, Max Papilaya, the leader of the 1977 terrorists had (as a Dutch government employee) an opportunity to study the policy evaluations of the 1975 incidents. He therefore took some countermeasures. One thing he wanted to avoid was the 'Stockholm syndrome' and so he prohibited all contacts with the hostages of the De Punt hijacking. After 19 days, in phase three of Mulder's 'periodization', he and his colleagues suddenly became very dangerous, and it was feared that they would kill hostages since they had not developed enough empathy with them. In 1978, at the provincial administrative centre in Assen, the 'South Moluccan Suicide Commando' refused to enter into bargaining for small concessions.[44] They thought that sticking to their full catalogue of demands would be their best strategy. However, given the fact that they had already killed a hostage right at the beginning, there was no room for concessions which the Dutch government could have 'sold' to the public.[45] It had become an unwritten principle of the Dutch authorities that, once blood had flowed, a free exit out of the country was no longer possible.[46]

In the 1980s there were no major hostage incidents comparable to the South Moluccan ones. The government still has a team of 15 trained negotiators who speak Spanish, English, French, German and Dutch (but not Arabic or Japanese), should the need arise. There have also been no major foreign kidnappings which required negotiations. Kidnappings of Dutch citizens took place in Colombia in the early 1990s. Yet these were 'commercial' rather than 'political' and did not lead to policy crises.

Target Hardening

In contrast to the military, the terrorist is not constrained in his choice of targets. He can either choose a random target and link an explanation to the accidental victims; he can select a representative target which brings home his message to all members represented by this person, or, he can choose a symbolic target. The last kind of targets are the most worthwhile in terms of publicity and demoralization.[47] Presidents, royalty, celebrities and religious leaders are the most priceless targets for insurgent terrorists.

When Pope John Paul II came to visit the Netherlands in the 1980s he was a potential prime target. The Dutch security forces launched their biggest security operation this country had ever seen. More than 12,000 men from the State Police, the Municipal Police and the Royal Constabulary and other units were mobilized to prevent a repetition of the 1981 tragedy in Saint Peter's Square. However, when the Pope drove along the Peace Palace in his special vehicle, his car was hit by an empty bottle thrown from a tree where a young boy had climbed up.[48] It could just as easily have been a bomb.

There is no absolute protection against a determined opponent in an open society. In the Netherlands only the members of the (extended) Royal Family receive permanent and substantial protection from a special team of the police security service. This measure was taken in the wake of a controversial South Moluccan plan to take Queen Juliana hostage in April 1975.[49] The Dutch Prime Minister, on the other hand, is not permanently guarded. The present Prime Minister, Ruud Lubbers, moves unescorted about the parliament building in The Hague. On 6 May 1987 a firebomb was thrown by unknown persons through the living-room window at his home in Rotterdam but he managed to throw the projectile into the garden and extinguished the fire. His house is apparently still not permanently protected and has been burglarized once in his absence. However, in early 1988 steps were finally taken to create a bodyguard system for Dutch ministers. Yet it is not expected that the team of bodyguards will be used on a permanent basis by ministers. They would not tolerate such an intrusion on their privacy.

In the 1970s some foreign embassies in the Netherlands became targets of terrorists. Since then, security measures have been taken by the Dutch authorities in addition to those taken by the embassies themselves. There is electronic surveillance of high-risk installations and there are heavy gates in places like the US Ambassador's residence. In 1976 the Royal Constabulary formed a Brigade for Special Protection Tasks (BSE – *Brigade Speciale Beveiligingsopdrachten*), which has automatic weapons and armoured cars. These teams (a commando group of four and six groups of five men) have been trained by the German GSG-9 and the British SAS. For regular duties there are more than 80 men of the Royal Constabulary. The Municipal Police of The Hague also provides protection for embassies and ambassadorial residences in The Hague and Wassenaar.[50] These often mobile teams are co-ordinated by the city's special bureau 'Protection and Guarding' (*Bescherming en Bewaking*).

Permanent protection is reserved to a few such as the Israeli, American, British and German embassies. In the past, Indonesia and Turkey were also on this list, but have now been dropped.[51] In 1988 India felt that its embassy was threatened by Sikh terrorists, but the Dutch government cannot honour all requests for permanent protection by a observation team stationed in an elevated bullet-proof steel and glass booth in front of the embassy. Lately such protection was given to Spanish diplomatic sites, but one rocket attack in late 1989 occurred right in front of such a surveillance booth. It was not manned at the time of the attack.

The single biggest security concern of the Netherlands is Schiphol, Amsterdam's international airport. More than 14 million people pass through it every year and more than 35,000 persons work there every day in one of the 500 businesses on the 1750 hectare site. Sixty-five different airlines fly from and to Schiphol, making it one of the top five airports in Europe. Until a recent reorganization took place, there were 13 different local security and protection services attempting to make Amsterdam airport safe.[52] Body-searches and screening of hand baggage, for instance, require 350 personnel from a private security firm. The costs of this screening is paid by the Dutch Ministry of Justice. Recently the government advanced the idea that the airport users, rather than the taxpayers, should pay for this service.[53] Some airlines do additional discrete screening of passengers but the costs involved are substantial. A level of security as is maintained by Israel's state airline El Al is impossible for a commercial enterprise the size of Royal Dutch Air Lines (KLM). El Al spends no less than 30 per cent of its budget on security while maintaining a traffic volume of only one fifth of KLM. In the past 26 years KLM has faced five hijackings, all without loss of lives.

Military and Paramilitary Measures

Military intelligence is charged with monitoring terrorist threats to military installations. NATO members regularly inform each other about terrorist activities but NATO itself has, as far as it is known, no special authority to deal with terrorist activities in NATO member countries. That, at least, was the situation in the mid-1970s.[54] While policy documents from the early 1970s assign the Minister of Defence a role in the Crisis Centre, it has not been a prominent one. However, the military has assigned certain units for anti-terrorist assistance and keeps them on an 'around-the-clock' alert scheme. One of them is BBM, a 70-man special assistance unit from the Royal Dutch Marines unit trained in close combat. The Marines also have another special unit, comparable to the US Navy Seals, for protecting the North Sea oil platforms. Another unit of 50 sharpshooters (recently reduced to 30) belongs to the paramilitary Royal Constabulary. Then there is the Explosives Disposal Service (EOD – *Explosieven Opruimingsdienst*) which receives some 4,000 bomb reports per year. The police receive about 10,000 per year, a figure considered on the low side as many enterprises and foreign missions have given up of reporting each hoax call to the police.[55] During hostage incidents, the military has been drawn upon to a considerable degree, mainly for cordoning off sites of terrorism.

Conflict Resolution and Modifications of Foreign/Domestic Policies in Response to Terrorist Pressures

Of the three terrorist and violent domestic threats to Dutch society – from the Red Youth, the South Moluccans and from RARA – only the second led to a determined conflict resolution process involving the Dutch government. The other groups represented only themselves, and their problems – the Greek dictatorship, the South African Apartheid system – were not open to resolution by the Netherlands. The South Moluccan problem, on the other hand, was the problem of 35,000 immigrants and not just that of a few dozen terrorists.

In December 1975, after the first double incident, Prime Minister Den Uyl announced the government's intention to talk with the South Moluccan community. What the Dutch government could do for them, of course, fell short of their dreams. Clearly, the Royal Dutch Navy could not reconquer the thousand islands of the South Moluccas 7,500 miles away and resurrect the defunct South Moluccan Republic. These were, as Den Uyl put it, 'illusions that the Netherlands cannot satisfy'. He and some of his colleagues met a South Moluccan delegation on 17 January 1976, and the decision was then made to create a permanent forum for their grievances and for the search for solutions. The task of this mixed South Moluccan-Dutch Commission was to deal with the problems arising from the fact that 'in the South Moluccan community in the Netherlands, political ideals are being pursued which the Netherlands government cannot support but whose existence and gravity it recognized.'[56]

The Köbben-Mantouw Commission (so named for the two chairmen) tried to sort out the conflict by looking, *inter alia*, at the historical roots of

the South Moluccan Republic (RMS) and the decision-making underlying the arrival of 12,500 South Moluccans in the Netherlands during
the early 1950s. The commission was active from 25 May 1976 to 1
December 1978. It was enlarged after the second double incidents of 1977
to include young representatives of the South Moluccans. Some of its
work appeared only after the dissolution of the commission. This
included a historical study, based on hitherto secret government archive
materials. This analysis, 'Dossier Ambon 1950, the Attitude of the
Netherlands with regard to Ambon and the RMS', revealed that –
contrary to South Moluccan accusations and myths – the Dutch had not
left their colonial South Moluccan soldiers in the lurch. Rather, the
record revealed the Dutch authorities had, in 1949–50, even sacrificed
their own long-term interests for the sake of doing everything that was
possible to accommodate the political goals of the Ambonese. The record
revealed that the Dutch government had gone out of its way to secure
some political guarantees from the new rulers of Indonesia, as well as
from the United Nations' Commission for Indonesia for the short-lived
RMS. This was all in vain because the RMS was conquered by Indonesian
troops in November 1950 although resistance continued on a declining
scale well into the 1960s.[57]

While this effort to set the historical record straight was not published
until 1981, other studies of the Köbben-Mantouw Commission were
published earlier, while the danger of renewed South Moluccan acts of
hostage taking had not yet subsided. One study of the Commission dealt
with the climate of political opinion in the South Moluccas in 1978.[58] It
indicated that political support for the RMS was minimal. This finding
was shocking to the 'world view' of South Moluccan Liberation fighters in
the Netherlands and most of them, if they read it at all, were not prepared
to believe it. At this stage, a high official of the Ministry of Culture, Social
Affairs and Leisure (CRM) had the brilliant idea of sending young
militant South Moluccans with leadership potential to Ambon to see for
themselves. Between 100 and 200 South Moluccans were offered free
round-trips to Ambon and the surrounding islands of the South
Moluccas. Practically all who were offered such 'orientation travels'
accepted them, despite the fact that the Indonesian Embassy was a co-
sponsor of this initiative.

When the young South Moluccans from the Netherlands arrived in the
promised land, some of them wore the RMS colours, but the local people
did not even recognize 'their' national flag's colour. Many illusions were
shattered when they were confronted by reality. There was no
nationalism worth speaking of in the South Moluccas. There was no
desire for separation from Indonesia, only a certain animosity against

Javanese immigration and the central authority in Djakarta in general. These South Moluccan visitors found that their tropical islands were less than heavenly; the smells, the dirtiness, the boredom of the place struck them. They were actually looking at Ambon through Dutch eyes. They had become more Dutch than Ambonese, and, without openly acknowledging it, most of the visitors realized that this was not the place they would want to live in, let alone fight and die for.[59]

This realization, more than any other counter-measure against terrorism in the Netherlands, brought a halt to the chain of terrorist episodes which had plagued the Netherlands between 1970 and 1978. The 'orientation travels' were a psychological move that was penetrating the 'group think' of the South Moluccan community in the Netherlands. More than the military operations against the terrorists, it was this subtle process of changing attitudes which solved the South Moluccan terrorist problem. From then on, the Dutch and the South Moluccans were able to break down their polarization.

In addition to this initiative, numerous other measures were taken by the Dutch government to pacify the South Moluccan Community. Pension schemes for old South Moluccan soldiers were revised, special educational programmes introduced and measures were taken facilitating gainful employment for young South Moluccans. This was supplemented with a generous housing scheme which foresaw the construction of up to 6,000 houses. This created a certain envy in other minorities. A Surinam spokesman once jokingly advocated terrorism to obtain the same benefits and, in a way, terrorism did obtain them. The measures taken for the South Moluccans were the spearhead of a broad political program for all minorities, a program now costing close to 800 million Dutch guilders per year. The conflict between the South Moluccans in the Netherlands and the Dutch government was officially buried in 1986, on the 35th anniversary of the arrival of South Moluccans in the Netherlands. The Dutch government and the political body representing the South Moluccans, Badan Persatuan, issued a joint declaration and concluded, in the presence of the Queen, a kind of peace treaty.[60] This reconciliation was not in any way seen as a concession to terrorism. With regard to foreign policy, there has been no modification of Dutch policy stances due to terrorist pressures.

Conclusion

Is there something like a 'Dutch approach' or a Dutch lesson to be learned for other countries? This study suggests that there is. It has to do with the way political activists and terrorists are treated. This Dutch approach can

best be characterized by two quotes, one from an anonymous official of
the Central Investigation Information Service (CRI) and the other from
one of the most respected elderly statesmen in the Netherlands. The CRI
official gave this advice on how to deal with politically-motivated violent
activists:

> If you react too strongly as a government with your monopoly of
> violence, you run the risk that a hard core of an activist group finds a
> motive to detach itself and to develop into a cell of terrorists. It pays
> to keep on trying with all your energy to forestall that a number of
> frustrated people become isolated. For this reason it is a good thing
> that we leave ample room in our society for extraparliamentary
> actions. This is not a plea for passively watching how our public
> order is eroded. (. . .) Tolerance has its limits and to turn a blind eye
> to the course of events is dangerous. The Netherlands cannot be
> allowed to become a launching pad for terrorism. That is why we
> carefully monitor the moves of sympathizers who are in contact with
> terrorist groups.[61]

The former Minister of Justice, De Gaay Fortman, had this advice:

> The leading principle with regard to combating terrorism has to be
> that the Constitutional State has to act according to its own norms: it
> remains bound to the rules which have been set for countering
> infringements on the legal order.

> Tactically this is a disadvantage for the State. The government is
> . . . not allowed to fight the terrorist in the same manner he fights.
> To take two striking examples. The government has to go to the
> utmost limit of its responsibility in order to prevent the loss of
> human lives, including those of the terrorists. It may never resort to
> maltreatment and torture to obtain information.

> The ultimate goal of the action of the government has to be the
> restoration of the legal order. The duty to spare as many human
> lives as possible can seemingly impair this goal, since the
> government will at times have to agree to the free departure of
> hijackers and occupiers. However, a legal order that invariably
> demands in such cases that the terrorists not depart without
> punishment, without consideration for the hostage, becomes an
> abstract goal in itself rather than a means to advance a peaceful life.
> Therefore, choices have to be made each time. In this, however, it is
> a fundamental point of departure that the concern for the hostages
> has more weight than that which is also fitting with regard to the life
> of terrorists.

The approach towards the terrorist laid down here can also be described in these terms: the terrorist too should be allowed to profit from the legal order. (. . .) This may be asked since the legal order is for all men, for better and for worse.[62]

With this recipe from the anonymous CRI terror-fighter and the legal philosophy of an old anti-revolutionary Christian Democrat, the terrorist problem in the Netherlands has been contained and the democratic character of Dutch society preserved. The balance between effective security and democratic openness (acceptability) has been reached. Yet luck also played a big role. It is by no means certain that the 'Dutch approach' could have withstood the 'test' of a higher level of violence.

NOTES

1. J. den Uyl, 11 June 1977, quoted in Uriel Rosenthal, *Rampen, rellen, gijzelingen. Crisisbesluitvorming in Nederland* (Amsterdam: De Bataafsche Leeuw, 1984), p.467.
2. J.A. Emerson Vermaat, 'Terrorist Sympathizers in the Netherlands', *Terrorism: An International Journal* 10/4 (1987), pp.329–335.
3. Within little more than a decade, for instance, the belief in a personal god declined from 48 per cent of the population in 1966 to 34 per cent in 1979. W. Goddijn, H. Smets, and G. van Tillo, *Opnieuw: God in Nederland* (Amsterdam, 1979), p.46; quoted in Martin Moerings, 'Niederlande: Der subventionierte Protest', in Henner Hess *et al.* (eds.), *Angriff auf das Herz des Staates* (Frankfurt, A.M.: Suhrkamp, 1988), p.291.
4. Moerings, 'Niederlande: Der subventionierte Protest', p.292: the discussion above is based mainly on Moerings, pp.283–92.
5. Ibid., pp.294–99, 302.
6. Ibid., p.330.
7. P. van Reenen, *Overheidsgeweld: Een sociologische studie van de dynamiek van het geweldsmonopolie* (Alphen a.d. Rijn: Samsom, 1979), p.354.
8. A.P. Schmid *et al.*, *Zuidmoluks terrorisme, de media en de publieke opinie* (Amsterdam: Intermediair, 1982), pp.37–60; Joke Cuperus and Rineke Klijnsma, *Onderhandelen of bestormen: Het beleid van de overheid inzake terroristische akties* (Groningen: Polemologisch Instituut, 1980), pp.4–42.
9. Lucien van Hoesel, quoted in *De Groene Amsterdammer*, 13 Feb. 1985.
10. NIPO, Bericht no.1851, 24 June 1977.
11. Hubert Smeets, 'In Nederlandse luwte is geweld niet bon ton', *NRC Handelsblad*, 13 April 1988.
12. Ministerie van Justitie, *Actieplan voor de aanpak van veel voorkomende criminaliteit* (Den Haag: Ministry of Justice, 29 Jan. 1987), p.15.
13. *Volkskrant*, 19 June 1989, p.3.
14. Cuperus and Klijnsma, 'The set-up and functioning of crisis- and policy-centres during "terrorist actions" in Holland from 1970–78', paper presented at AFK/VVK Conference on Peace and Security, Brussels, 17–19 May 1979, p.6.
15. F. Korthals Altes, quoted in J.H.M. Bol, 'Politiek terrorisme als crimineel verschijnsel' in *Beveiligingsjaarboek* (Arnhem: Noorduijn, 1988) p.26. The TREVI definition is: 'Terrorism is defined as the use, or the threatened use, by a cohesive group of persons of violence (short of warfare) to effect political aims'. Quoted by F. Korthals Altes, 22 Jan. 1987, in House of Parliament, *Handelingen II, 1986/87, Bijlagen 197000 Hoofdstuk IV*, no.30, p.5, as quoted in Peter Klerks. *Terreur Bestrijding in Nederland, 1970–1988* (Amsterdam: Ravign, 1989), p.22.

16. Letter, Prime Minister to the Chairman of Parliament, dated 22 Feb. 1973, *Handelingen Tweede Kamer der Staaten Generaal, Zitting 197201973 – 12000, VI*, pp.11–12. ('Terror-letter'.)
17. Cuperus and Klijnsma, 'set-up and functioning of crisis- and policy-centers', p.8, n.4 [see note 14].
18. Letter, Prime Minister to the Chairman of Parliament (1973), pp.11–12.
19. Ibid., p.11, n.7.
20. Quoted in W.F.K.J.F. Frackers, 'Terrorismebestrijding, een taak voor de politie?', in J.S. van der Meulen (ed.), *De bestrijding van terrorisme* (Den Haag: Stichting Volk en Verdediging, 1979), p.36.
21. Quoted in A.R. Haakmat, 'De bestrijding van terreurakties (Juridische en polemologische visies vergeleken)', in Meulen (ed.), *De bestrijding van terrorisme*, p.8.
22. Charles Humana (comp.), *The World Human Rights Guide* (London, Pan Books, 1986), pp.xiv–xvi.
23. See Ronald D. Crelinsten, 'The Internal Dynamics of the FLQ During the October Crisis of 1970', in David C. Rapoport (ed.), *Inside Terrorist Organizations* (London/NY: Frank Cass/Columbia UP, 1988), pp.59–89.
24. F.J. Kranenburg, 'Een verstoorde samenleving', *Nederlandse Gemeente*, No.10 (1976), p.111.
25. Quoted in F.G.B. Grotenhuis and J.J. Schat, *Terreurbestrijding: De bestrijding van gijzelingsacties in juridisch perspectief* (Zoetermeer: MS, 1979), pp.45–6.
26. R.G.C. Bik, *De Europese Conventie tot bestrijding van het terrorisme* (Apeldoorn: Nederlandse Politie Akademie, 1979), pp.66–7.
27. Bik, *De Europese Conventie*; also van Reenen, *Overheidsgeweld* [see note 7], pp.293–4.
28. Valentine Hermans and Robert van der Laan Bouma, 'Nationalists without a Nation: South Moluccan Terrorism in the Netherlands', in Juliet Lodge (ed.), *Terrorism: A Challenge to the State* (Oxford: Martin Robertson, 1981), pp.140–1.
29. *Handelingen Tweede Kamer*, 21 Oct. 1976, as quoted in Uri Rosenthal, 'Terreurbestrijding in Nederland: vijf thema's ter discussie gesteld', *Tijdschrift voor de Politie*, No.5 (May 1979), p.253.
30. Bol, 'Politiek terrorisme als crimineel verschijnsel' [see note 15], p.28.
31. A.P. Schmid *et al.*, *Zuidmoluks terrorisme, de media en de publieke opinie* (Amsterdam: Intermediair, 1982), pp.121–41.
32. *De Nieuwe Linie*, 27 Nov. 1974, as quoted in Cuperus and Klijnsma, *Overhandelen of bestormen* [see note 8], pp.13n–14n.
33. Private information; see also Cuperus and Klijnsma, *Overhandelen*, p.19 [note 8].
34. See Richard Clutterbuck, 'Negotiating with Terrorists', this volume p.270, for a more detailed history.
35. J. Bowyer Bell, *A Time of Terror: How Democratic Societies Respond to Revolutionary Violence* (NY, Basic Books, 1978), p.174.
36. Cuperus and Klijnsma, *Overhandelen*, p.17–18 [note 8].
37. The money, it turned out later, was not taken by the Syrian government, as had been suspected, but was stolen by the Dutch Transavia crew who had volunteered to fly them to Damascus.
38. Cuperus and Klijnsma, *Overhandelen*, pp.17–18 [note 8].
39. van Reenen, *Overheidsgeweld*, p.299 [note 7]; Rosenthal, *Rampen, rellen, gijzelingen*, p.422 [note 1].
40. See Dick Mulder, 'Terrorisme', in J. Bastiaans *et al.*, *Mensen bij Gijzelingen* (Alphen aan den Rijn: A.W. Sijthoff, 1981), pp.81–185.
41. Mulder, 'Terrorisme'.
42. Edwin Oostmeijer, 'Zonder een traumaatje kom je het leven niet door', *Hervormd Nederland*, 2 July 1984, p.12.
43. van Reenen, *Overheidsgeweld*, pp.283–4 [note 7].
44. Rosenthal, *Rampen, rellen, gijzelingen*, pp.292–3 [note 1].
45. Cuperus and Klijnsma, *Overhandelen*, pp.40–1 [note 8].
46. Rosenthal, *Rampen, rellen, gijzelen*, p.401 [note 1].

47. See also Ronald D. Crelinsten, 'The Victims' Perspective', in David L. Paletz and Alex P. Schmid (eds.), *Perspectives on Terrorism and the Media* (Beverly Hills: Sage, 1992), pp.208–38, esp. pp.212–14.
48. *Trouw*, 18 Jan. 1986, p.5.
49. Cuperus and Klijnsma, *Overhandelen*, pp.21–2 [note 8].
50. *Die Welt*, 30 April 1983; Perrick, 'Politie en Bijstand. Een Terugblik', *Tijdschrift voor de Politie*, (1983), p.127.
51. Hans Smits, 'Verkeerde Code', *Vrij Nederland* 47, 1 Feb. 1986; private information.
52. *NRC Handelsblad*, 16 Jan. 1986.
53. *Het Financiele Dagblad*, 5 Sept. 1986.
54. *Handelingen, Tweede Kamer, Zitting 75/76, 12 February 1976*, 'Gijzelingszaken en bestrijding van terreurakties', Cuperus and Klijnsma, *Overhandelen*, p.91 [note 8].
55. *Trouw*, 16 Dec. 1985.
56. Quoted in Herman and van der Laan Bouma, 'Nationalists without a Nation', in, Lodge (ed.), *Terrorism: Challenge to the State* (1981), pp.137–8 [note 28].
57. E.I. van der Meulen, *Dossier Ambon 1950, de houding van Nederland ten opzichte van Ambon en de RMS* (The Hague: Staatsuitgeverij, 1981); see also the review of J.J.P. de Jong, 'Regering gokte steeds verkeerd in Ambon', *Volkskrant*, 3 July 1981, p.6.
58. *Commissie van Overleg Zuid-Molukkers-Nederland. De politieke stemming in het gebied der Zuid-Molukken anno 1978* (The Hague: Staatsuitgeverij, 1978).
59. Private Information.
60. Herman and van der Laan Bouma, 'Nationalists Without a Nation', p.138; *Marinjo* (informatiebulletin van het Inspraakorgaan Welzijn Molukkers) 86/12, pp.8–9.
61. Quoted in Schmid, 'Politically-Motivated Violent Activists in the Netherlands in the 1980s', in Juliet Lodge, (ed.), *The Threat of Terrorism* (Brighton: Wheatsheaf, 1988), p.174.
62. W.F.F. de Gaay Fortman, *Rechtsstaat en terrorisme* (Alphen a.d. Rijn: Samsom, 1979), p.15.

Spain: The Terrorist Challenge and the Government's Response

FERNANDO JIMÉNEZ

This essay briefly surveys political violence in Spain since 1968 and describes the principal domestic groups engaged in terrorism, including their history, political objectives and principal actions. A selected chronology of Middle Eastern terrorism in Spain and a brief description of Galician terrorism are also provided. Governmental and societal responses to terrorism are then discussed. A history of the political measures taken towards solving the Basque problem is coupled with ETA's responses in order to highlight the persistence of terrorism despite significant concessions and reform. The strengths and weaknesses of various counter-terrorist measures are assessed and the principal anti-terrorist organizations are described. Finally, the contribution provides five general principles that should guide democratic governments in their fight against terrorism: a well-defined political aim; a clear, centralized chain of command; adherence to the rule of law; a strong and centralized intelligence capability; and long-term planning.

A young boy on crutches hobbles across a dusty road, apparently oblivious to an onrushing army truck. The truck brakes and comes to a halt, barely missing the boy. As the truck stops, a large group of boys appears and begins pelting the soldiers in the truck with stones and bottles. When struck by a stone, one angry soldier fires his weapon into the crowd, wounding a young boy. A large crowd quickly forms, which results in more soldiers and police being called in to restore order. Thus is created a confrontation between the government forces and the civilian populace. It is interesting to note that, when the shot was fired by the angry soldier, the little boy with the crutch dashed down a side street *leaving his crutch behind*.

An incident such as that described could have taken place recently in the Basque Country of Spain, in the Philippines, South America or even in Israel. It did not. It took place in South Vietnam over 20 years ago. The point is that the tactics used by terrorists then are still valid today: procedures have become standardized. Through the use of threats, intimidation and murder, those in positions of influence in a community are induced to leave the community or otherwise relinquish their powers to the terrorists. Incidents designed to turn the populace's sentiments against the current government authorities are an important part of this process and are easily staged, as in the above example.

If an assessment of future terrorist trends is to have any validity, it must take into account the events of the past to glean lessons which may provide insights into which patterns of activity remain relatively constant. In this perspective, terrorist tactics seem to remain basically the same. We know that terrorists, contrary to popular belief that they are all suicidal, do pay close attention to risk factors when planning an operation. If the risk is too high, they generally avoid the target. The terrorist's objective is to undermine confidence in the ability of the national government to provide basic security. The aim is to create economic and political dislocation that will ultimately render the target government incapable of governing. In such situations, a power vacuum is created which those challenging the government attempt to fill.

National and International Challenges in the Field of Political Violence and Terrorism

Active Groups

A. BASQUE FATHERLAND AND LIBERTY (ETA)
Date formed: 1959
Estimated membership: Basque provinces of Spain: Viscaya, Alava, Guipuzcoa, Navarra; and Basque provinces of France.
Area of operations: Spain and France.
Leadership: The 1989 arrest in Bayona (Bayonne) of José Antonio Urrutikoutxea Bengoetxea, 'Josu Ternera', veteran ETA leader considered the most opposed to the dialogue with the government, places the historic Francisco Múgica Garmedia, 'Paquito' or 'Artapalo', in total control of the organization.
Other names: Euzkadi ta Askatasuma (original language).
Political objectives/target audiences: To establish an independent and probably Marxist Basque nation, Euzkadi, through terrorism against Spanish interests to pressure Madrid into making desired concessions; to create an economic crisis in the Basque provinces by terrorizing businesses in the region.
Background: ETA is one of the oldest West European terrorist groups currently operating. Although the leadership of the ETA generally espouses a Marxist-Leninist ideology, the primary motivation for many of its members is Basque nationalism. The group is actually composed of several factions that established a loose alliance but still maintain separate identities. The more vehemently aggressive faction is known as the ETA-Military Wing (ETA-M). It advocates a relentless campaign of terrorist violence directed at the Spanish government. Another faction,

the ETA-Political-Military Front (ETA-PM), now largely inactive, pursued a course of terrorism but tried to blend it with grassroots political agitation to broaden the base of revolution. The ETA-M does have political connections through the Herri Batasuna (HB) political party.

ETA regularly targets Spanish government officials, members of the military and security forces, and moderate Basques for assassination. In addition, the group has carried out numerous bombings against government facilities and economic targets, including seasonal campaigns against tourist resorts. ETA is believed to be responsible for over 500 deaths since 1968, and can claim to be one of the most violent groups in Europe. Funds for ETA terror are generated by kidnappings, armed robberies, and extortion of 'revolutionary taxes'. Millions of dollars have been 'liberated' through large ransoms and bank robberies. ETA has, on occasion, obtained ransoms of more than one million dollars.

The organizational structure of ETA is very sophisticated. The majority of the members (commandos) are organized into three- or four-member cells. Most commandos are 'legal' ETA-members, not known to the police, who live open lives without suspicion. They carry out operations and then disappear into their surroundings. A smaller number of commandos are 'illegals', who are known to the authorities and live and operate entirely underground. There is also a large group that provides information, communications, and the other support needed to maintain ETA's infrastructure. Resources for a wide-ranging program of terrorism are available not only in the Spanish Basque provinces, but in the French Basque areas along the border, although recent actions by the French government may have the effect of denying sanctuary there.

The international connections of the ETA are quite extensive. It has reported ties with the Provisional Irish Republican Army, with which it has numerous common characteristics. Its other connections may be based on a common Marxist orientation. In the past, ETA members have trained at Middle Eastern terrorist training camps. The Cuban government has provided safe haven and training for ETA militants. There are also ETA members in Nicaragua, some of whom have been implicated in attacks against opponents of the Sandinista government. Most of the ETA presence in the region results from transfer agreements between the Spanish government and the government of the receiving country. Thus, activity associated with ETA members probably involves individuals acting on their own rather than being directed by ETA leaders in Europe.

In autumn 1987 a series of complementary arrests in France and Spain resulted from documentation seized by the French during the October 1987 capture of 'Santi Potros'. Police operations against ETA have been continuous and often successful. For example, French police arrested

José Antonio Urrutikoutxea Bengoetxea ('José Ternera', one leader of the terrorist organization) on 11 January 1989 (another leader was arrested in France in April 1992 and a major arms factory was uncovered there in February 1993 [eds.]). Nonetheless, ETA seems able to rebound from even the most successful counter-terrorist operations. Because of the group's sizeable support base and the high level of nationalist sentiment among the Basques, ETA violence is expected to continue to plague Spain for the foreseeable future.

B. FIRST OF OCTOBER ANTI-FASCIST RESISTANCE GROUP (GRAPO)

Date formed: 1975.

Estimated membership: Probably less than 25.

Area of operations: Spain.

Leadership: Manuel Perez Martínez ('Camarada Arenas').

Other names: Grupo de Resistencia Antifascista, Primero de Octubre (original language).

Political objectives/target audiences: To overthrow violently the Spanish government and establish a Marxist state; to oppose Spain's participation in NATO and US presence in Spain.

Background: GRAPO was established as the 'military' arm of the outlawed Communist Party of Spain Reconstituted (PCE-R), which is a splinter group of the officially recognized Communist Party of Spain (PCE). An urban-oriented group, GRAPO has committed assassinations, bombings, and kidnappings against Spanish personnel and facilities. On occasion it also attacked American interests. The group has preferred ambushes using automatic weapons. Like ETA, the GRAPO has financed its operations through kidnap ransoms, bank robberies, and extorting 'revolutionary taxes' from individuals and businesses. These sources of funds have proved adequate for financing its range of operations and for procuring weapons and explosives.

Direct ties between the GRAPO and foreign terrorist groups or state sponsors have not been established. The GRAPO, however, has made public statements supporting other terrorist groups, including the German Red Army Faction and the Italian Red Brigades. GRAPO's structure has been based on a cellular concept for maximum internal security. These cells are probably quite small in view of the group's very limited numbers. GRAPO members are either 'legal commandos' or 'liberated commandos'. The legal commandos, unknown to police, lead apparently normal lives and periodically carry out terrorist actions. The liberated commandos are full-time members who are known to the authorities and live underground.

Successful Spanish police operations led to the arrests of the most significant known GRAPO members in January 1985. Although the GRAPO has not committed any significant act of terrorism since December 1984, it has demonstrated the capability to rebuild and to conduct minor operations, such as a series of robberies that took place in southern Spain in 1987.

C. IRAULTZA
Date formed: 1982.
Estimated membership: Less than 20.
Headquarters: Unknown.
Area of operations: Basque provinces of Spain: Vizcaya, Alava, Guipuzcoa, and Navarra.
Leadership: Unknown.
Other names: Basque Armed Revolutionary Workers' Organization.
Political objectives/target audiences: To establish an independent, Marxist Basque nation; to end foreign, particularly American, investment in the Basque region; to protest against American foreign policy, particularly in Latin America, expressing solidarity with radical leftists there.
Background: Little is known about the Basque terrorist group, Iraultza, and its origins are obscure. Marxist and strongly anti-American, Iraultza, although believed to consist of fewer than 20 members, has committed numerous bombings against American and French economic interests in the Basque region. The group has probably committed more bombings against American business interests than any other European terrorist group, causing thousands of dollars in damage. Anonymous callers claiming responsibility for Iraultza bombings (written communiqués are not known to exist) have voiced opposition to American aid to the Nicaraguan resistance, American actions in Grenada and Lebanon, and Spain's participation in NATO. Attacks against French interests have been prompted by the arrest and expulsion of Basque terrorists from France. Iraultza, however, has not directly attacked US government personnel or facilities.

Iraultza members leave small, unsophisticated bombs on the pavement or in the street outside the intended target, late at night. Although an anonymous caller then warns the police, there is usually not enough time for the police to react before the bomb explodes. Intending only to cause property damage, Iraultza's 'midnight' bombs have injured several people and killed a construction worker when one of the bombs malfunctioned.

D. FREE LAND (TERRA LLIURE)
Headquarters: Cataluña Region of Spain: Provinces of Barcelona, Tarragona, Lerida and Gerona.

Area of operations: Cataluña and Valencia.

Political objectives/target audiences: To establish an independent and probably Marxist Catalonian Nation, 'Paysos Catalans', through terrorism against Spanish interests to pressure Madrid into making desired concessions.

Background: Terra Lliure had started to form towards the end of 1978. Several isolated groups among which was the *Partit Socialists d'Allibera-ment Nacional Provisional*(PSANp), created the Comité Catalá against the Spanish Constitution as a first step toward the formation of the revolutionary independence movement in the Paysos Catalans. The creation of a military organization was the second step. Since 1979 Terra Lliure gave its political representation to the *Independentistes dels Paysos Catalans* (IPC) movement, formed by the union of the PSANp and the French Catalan group OSAN. At the present time, this relationship has broken up and the *Moviment de Defensa de la Terra* (MDT) is the one that groups the sectors closest to Terra Lliure and wants to act as a Catalan *Herri Batasuna* (Basque political party).

Terra Lliure is going through a deep internal crisis and a progressive dismemberment process, since several of its principal leaders have left the group and others have been expelled. The group has carried out attacks with firearms and explosives and have perpetrated robberies at gunpoint.

E. INTERNATIONAL (MIDDLE EASTERN) TERRORISM
Selected incident chronology:

26 Jan. 1973 – An Israeli is assassinated in Madrid. Attributed to the Fatah-Black September group.

15 Sept. 1975 – Four terrorists occupy the Egyptian Embassy in Madrid, take diplomats hostage whom they threaten to kill if Egypt does not halt the Geneva talks and condemn the provisional agreement with Israel. The terrorists escape with the hostages to Algeria where they free them. This attack was attributed to the Fatah group.

3 March 1980 – A terrorist murders a lawyer and his daughter in Madrid. It was a mistake; his intent was to assassinate the Honourary President of the Jewish community. Attributed to Abu Nidal, Black June.

16 Sept. 1982 – A Kuwaiti diplomat is assassinated in Madrid. Not attributed to any group.

1 Oct. 1982 – Two explosive devices are discovered in front of the Israeli Diplomatic Delegation in Madrid. Not attributed to any group.

29 Dec. 1983 – A terrorist attempt against two employees of the Jordanian Embassy in Madrid, killing one and injuring the other. Attributed to Abu Nidal.

17 Aug. 1984 – Attempt against a Palestinian in Madrid.

21 Sept. 1984 – Two terrorists shoot and injure a Libyan diplomat. Attributed to Amal.

2 Nov. 1984 – Lebanese citizen Elias Joseph Awad is injured in an attempt. Attributed to Abu Abbas.

2 Nov. 1984 – Several Abu Nidal terrorists are arrested with information about future attempts against Israelis in Spain.

27 Feb. 1985 – A bomb explodes in a Madrid travel agency linked to Israel. Five persons injured. Not attributed to any group.

13 April 1985 – A high potency bomb explodes in El Descanso restaurant, Madrid, patronized by North American military personnel. Attributed to Islamic Jihad.

1 July 1985 – The offices of the Jordanian Airline Alia are attacked. Attributed to Abu Nidal.

1 July 1985 – A bomb explodes in the building where TWA and British Airways offices are located. Attributed to Rosm-Black September.

12 July 1985 – Two terrorists carrying explosives and false identifications are arrested. They were engaged in an attack against the Syrian Ambassador in Madrid. Attributed to Fatah.

5–6 Oct. 1985 – Two Israeli soldiers are kidnapped and assassinated in Barcelona. Attributed to Fatah. Also, according to other sources, it is attributed to Group 17, the intelligence arm of the PLO.

May 1986 – Several members of an Arab terrorist group with links to Libya are arrested in Madrid. (Mossad sources claim the action for themselves.) Apparently Spanish intelligence also participated.

26 June 1986 – A briefcase-bomb explodes on the counter of the Israeli airlines El Al, in the Barajas airport, Madrid, injuring 13 persons, including an El Al security agent.

1987 – An objective of Abu Nidal's terrorist organization was the assassination of the Spanish Prime Minister, Felipe González, according to the declarations of the Palestinian terrorist Khaled Ibrahim Mahmood, who was wounded in the attempt carried out at Fumicino Airport in Rome, where 13 persons were killed and another 80 were injured. The wounded terrorist's declaration appears in the official minutes and literally states that, within Abu Nidal's terrorist group, 'Several judged Felipe González, and considered him the person to be most punished because of the contacts he had established with the Government of Israel.'

F. GALICIAN TERRORISM – *Exercito Guerrilleiro do Pobo Galego Ceibe*
Political Arm: Frente Popular Galego (FPG)
Galician terrorism caused its first mortal victim in the Coruña locality of Vilarboy, in an ambush set up by the FPG against the civil police, where

one policeman was killed and another was seriously injured. The terrorists were later apprehended. The FPG started its actions in Galicia in 1986 and since then has carried out some 50 attempts against high tension towers, banks, state administration buildings and the statue of General Franco in El Ferrol.

The Response of the Government and Society

Legislative and Procedural Changes

The last legislation passed by the previous non-democratic regime was reflected in Decree-Law no.10/1975 of 26 August on Prevention of Terrorism. Between 1978 and 1979 the democratic government's serious resolve to combat terrorism resulted in the introduction of anti-terrorist laws which include:

a. Speeding up trial of terrorist crimes by 'emergency' procedures;

b. Providing *Audiencia Nacional* (Law courts) greater scope to intervene in a wider range of crimes;

c. Allowing judges to retain in custody those charged with terrorist crimes until necessary additional information is obtained;

d. Facilitating access of the Ministry of Internal Affairs to information on people renting flats and offices;

e. Imposing legal obligations upon businesses to comply with government security standards;

f. Authorizing police to carry out postal intercept and wiretapping of persons suspected of terrorist involvement.

The continuous attacks against the Democratic State made it necessary for the Spanish parliament in December 1984 to approve an Organic Law Against the Actions of Armed Groups, putting in motion the system established by the Constitution itself. Consequently, the parliament approved Organic Law no.8 on 28 December 1984, known as the 'Anti-terrorist Law'. The deadlines established by this law and the constant pressure from social and political parties to avoid excessive limitations to individual freedom led to modifications in this law and the new articles have become part of the Common Spanish Criminal Law and its supplementary Process Law. Therefore, the present legislation is essentially based in two Organic Laws: Organic Law 3/1988 of 25 May 25 for the Reform of the Penal Code; and Organic Law 4/1988 of 25 May for the Reform of Criminal Process Law.

Extradition and Expulsion Policies

The internationalization of the terrorist phenomenon and the ever increasing cooperation with French justice is allowing the policy of extradition with France to work efficiently, in spite of the difficulties that still exist. France has stopped being a logistic sanctuary for ETA members, thanks to the judicial co-operation established. The Spanish government has publicly expressed its appreciation to France for its understanding and solidarity (6 November 1986). The French government, in turn, believes that the solidarity of the French and Spanish democracies is a natural occurrence. Since 1987 the French government has been delivering ETA members to Spanish police, without the need for an extradition request. As soon as the Spanish border is crossed, they are delivered to the authorities.

Special mention should be made of the extradition by Costa Rica of the ETA member Gregorio Jiménez Morada, 'El Pistolas' (May 1986). The arrest of El Pistolas in that country, where he was contributing to the attempted attack against anti-Sandinista leader Edén Pastora, revealed ETA's presence in Central America, especially in Nicaragua.

Freezing of Assets

The terrorist organization ETA has an annual budget of more than 700 million pesetas ($6.6 million at 1992 rates). ETA collects an annual amount of approximately 150 million pesetas from 'revolutionary taxes'. A Ministry of Internal Affairs report puts the average amount obtained from each kidnapping at about 100 million, although in some cases, up to 340 million has been collected.

International action needs to be taken to cut the flow of funds to terrorist groups. It becomes essential to investigate financial resources of these groups. Treaties must be signed between Spain, the United States, Britain, Switzerland, Australia, and offshore tax havens such as the Cayman Islands and the Turks and Caicos Islands, which will allow access to personal and corporate bank accounts of any person or company in those countries suspected of being involved in laundering illegal cash.

Financial Rewards

The need to deactivate ETA commandos responsible for assassinations and kidnappings, especially in the urban areas, and the need to halt new terrorist actions, have prompted the authorities to establish a rewards programme aimed at citizens that collaborate by providing information leading to the arrest of terrorists. The collaboration works through special phone numbers and, in any event, the informers are guaranteed total confidentiality and anonymity.

Political Measures

In this section, each measure taken towards the solution of the Basque Problem will be paired with ETA's response.

A. PACIFYING MEASURES

I. BANISHMENTS

On 20 May 1977 a partial pardon is granted together with the penalty of banishment, which affects 19 ETA members (3 with death penalty already pardoned and 19 *preventivos*).

Only one month later, on 22 June, ETA assassinates Javier Ibarra in Baraza.

II. AMNESTY

On 15 October 1977 amnesty is granted for all political insurrection acts committed prior to 15 December 1976 up to 15 June 1977, as long as those acts were directed towards the restoration of political rights or the recovery of autonomy.

On 17 October Civil Guard Idelfonso Sánchez Arnil is injured in an ETA attempt at Lasarte, and on 26 November Commander Imaz is assassinated in Imaz.

III. ABOLITION OF THE DEATH PENALTY

This is established in Article 15 of the Constitution, approved by national referendum on 6 December 1978.

On 9 December ETA assassinates Municipal Policeman (for Civil Guard) Juan Jiménez Gómez, in Pasajes.

B. IMPORTANT STEPS IN THE POLITICAL SOLUTION OF THE BASQUE COUNTRY

I. FIRST LEGISLATIVE ELECTIONS (CONSTITUENT COURTS)

They take place on 15 June 1977 and *Euskadico Ezkerra*, derived from ETA-PM, is present.

On 22 June Javier Ibarra is assassinated, as previously stated, and ETA claims the assassination.

II. SECOND LEGISLATIVE ELECTIONS

They take place on 1 March 1979 and *Euskadico Eskerra* and *Herri Batasuna*, both political branches of ETA, are present.

On 9 March the Chief of the Municipal Police of Beazaín, Miguel Chavarri Irasa, is assassinated.

III. REFERENDUM FOR THE APPROVAL OF THE AUTONOMY STATUTE

It takes place on 25 October 1979. *Euzkadiko Ezkerra* and ETA-PM support the affirmative vote, while *Herri Batasuna* and ETA-M abstain.

On 27 October builder Germán González López is assassinated in San

Sebastián, and on the 30th, the Civil Guard Manuel Fuentes Fontán is assassinated in Portugalete.

IV. FIRST ELECTIONS TO THE BASQUE PARLIAMENT

They take place on 9 March 1980.

On 18 March there is an attempt against General Esquivias in Madrid, and on the 24th, jeweller Dámaso Santos and sculptor José Artera are assassinated in Durango and Escoriaza.

V. TRANSFERS APPROVAL

On 26 September 1980 the Council of Ministers approves the first Transfer package. On 29 September Retolaza and Rosón have interviews in Madrid, and the next negotiations between Suárez and Garaicoches are officially announced.

On 29 September José Igancio Ustarán, UCD leader, is assassinated in Vitoria.

On 3 October a deputy chief of police and an inspector of the Special Police Corps as well as a national policeman, are assassinated in Durango.

On 4 October, in a clear escalation effort, three Civil Traffic Guards are assassinated in Salvatierra.

C. CONSEQUENCES OF THE ABOVE

It can easily be seen from the above that there has been no positive response from either branch of ETA to the pacifying measures undertaken by the Spanish government. The pacification or normalization of the post-Franco regime has followed one path, and the war has followed another.

D. NEGOTIATIONS

In spite of the foregoing, in spring 1989 the government held high-level talks with the leaders of the terrorist organizations in Algiers. A unilateral, so-called 'credibility truce' maintained by these leaders allowed the restart of conversations that had been interrupted for many months as a consequence of the crimes and constant attacks carried out by ETA.

In Algiers the Spanish government proposed to ETA a peace plan for the Basque Country which is basically the same that was delivered to ETA leader Domingo Iturbe in 1984. The peace plan consists of six phases. The first is to stop the violence and the second includes the preparation of a political document agreed upon by the social forces, in order to ready a referendum on the possible integration of Navarra into Euskadi, as well as a possible pardon for the terrorists jailed. Other phases refer to the call for elections in the Basque Country, from which a new parliament and an autonomous government would emerge; a process of *reuskaldinizacion*, the graded substitution of police forces by autonomous police; and the creation of a Basque department with a civil servant upon whom the armed forces for this community would depend. The President of the Basque Parliament, socialist Jesus Eguiguren, has stated that, in the Algiers talks, 'the Government cannot go beyond a generous offer of readmission. To do so, would be to establish a precedent incompatible with democracy'. The talks ultimately failed, despite the signing of an eight-point agreement by both sides.

E. INTERNATIONAL COOPERATION

The TREVI Group

The European Community (EC) countries' main objective is to eliminate terrorism in their territories. With that purpose in mind, in 1976, they created the TREVI (Terrorism, Radicalism, Extremism and political Violence) Group, formed by the Ministers of Internal Affairs of 'the twelve', who periodically meet in order to exchange information and take new measures. In 1983 Portugal and Spain were added as observers and in 1985 they became full members. The TREVI Group is the only police co-operation structure against terrorism that exists among all the community countries. It has three working levels. First, there are the people responsible for the internal affairs of each country; second, the police groups that carry out the agreements and exchange the information; third, those in charge of the fight against drug trafficking. In each national capital, there is a liaison office.

On 25 September 1986 it was decided to create a 'red phone' for fast and efficient communication among the community capitals about activities of terrorist organizations. It was also decided to review the procedures in order to obtain visas and exclusion systems. The European Community was no longer a sanctuary for terrorists. After that meeting, the community countries adopted a no-flaw policy with the objective of ending terrorism. The new policy allows an ample exchange of information and the analysis of possible operations that the terrorists might be planning. Likewise, Spain will promote the establishment of a European police force. The model for the community police under study proposes that the TREVI Group's activity be co-ordinated through a permanent central office, whose main objectives would be terrorism repression, both national and international, as well as illegal immigration. This office would be formed by selected agents in each country, experts in the above mentioned matters.

Blockade of Iran and Libya

In December 1987 the TREVI Group decided to adopt economic measures against countries that protect and finance terrorist movements, such as

Libya and Iran. In addition, data on terrorists was updated in order to improve the search for, as well as information exchange on, explosives and firearms thefts.

An anti-terrorist summit meeting was held in Paris towards the end of May 1987, at the initiative of the interior ministers of France and West Germany. Belgium, Canada, Denmark, the United States, Italy, Japan and Great Britain also participated. There is also a French-German Joint Anti-terrorist Committee and several bilateral agreements of co-operation, such as those signed by Spain and France, West Germany and Italy, which have given positive results in the anti-terrorist fight. The Spanish government also favours the creation of a central office in the TREVI Group that will reinforce and co-ordinate the fight against crime and terrorism.

F. INTERNATIONAL ORGANIZATIONS

The Council of Europe has sponsored several international conferences to discuss international terrorism, of which most countries have been a victim, and which is considered a destabilizing element in democratic societies.

Already in 1979 the Council of Europe, through Maltese representative Vicent Tabone, suggested a series of recommendations, including the reinforcement of police action – both preventive and repressive – by means of information exchange. Of great help in this task has been the data bank installed in Wiesbaden, Germany, which has more than ten million items of data on terrorists. Other preventive measures included an increase in security police forces in ports and airports, an increase in the control of visitors and the reinforcement of protection to VIPs and military and industrial installations. In 1984 the 21 countries that form the Council of Europe unanimously approved a proposal to carry out joint action against terrorist activities, including the elimination of diplo-matic immunity that certain countries abuse.

In 1970 the United Nations joined the fight against terrorism as a result of the rise in hijackings. In 1972 the UN created a special commission on international terrorism that studies its causes and the measures to fight it.

G. EDUCATION (STUDENTS AND TERRORISM)

ETA has increasing problems recruiting new members. The median age for ETA members has increased and the commandos are the same ones of years past. The traditional talent depository of the terrorist organization, which was *Herri Batasuna*'s youth organization called JARRAI, does not produce as many activists as before due to police pressures and the isolation that begins to be felt in the pro-ETA youth sectors. JARRAI is the organization that groups the youth among the leadership block of KAS (*Coordinadora Abertzale Socialista*). ETA officially forms part of KAS and in practice dictates its beliefs. JARRAI, which is defined as 'the political vanguard of *Euskalherria* youth', has always been a source of recruits for ETA.

Police studies demonstrate that the median age of ETA militants is now around 30 years, when a few years ago it was 25, with some older leaders. Today, those leaders have left or gone over to other political activities and the militants have grown older in ETA, where they are slowly replaced, but with increasing difficulty. There are two factors which have forced the terrorist organization to revise its recruitment strategy. On the one hand, the hasty recruitment of very young militants caused accidents in preparing terrorist attacks and these deaths were criticized by other organizations. On the other hand, the attention and vigilance of police in the more radical sectors among *Herri Batasuna*'s youth allowed the tracking and the dismantling of several commandos.

Surveillance and Infiltration

According to police sources, it is JARRAI members who attack super-markets supposedly linked to French interests or stone policemen during pro-amnesty marches. ETA has recruited members from these groups and surveillance and infiltration has therefore led to some success against ETA commandos. The police strategy has forced JARRAI to cover up some of its activities with names of other groups created for specific actions and later disbanded. But police pressure has also succeeded in blocking ETA recruitment, forcing ETA to resort to clandestine groups that were in reserve to carry out more recent actions.

H. IMPACT OF PUBLIC OPINION

Overall the effectiveness of ETA, and particularly ETA-M, cannot be denied, and can be considered the best organized, most dedicated and extreme of the groups. The cellular structure of the organization and its leadership have also contributed to the continued success of this small and violent group. In the final analysis, the success or failure of all terrorist organizations largely depends on the public's attitude. If the people are behind the organization, even in a small percentage, or apathetic or neutral in their view of the terrorists, then the chances of terrorist success are substantially increased.

There are weak links in the chain, however. An inherent weakness, for example, lies in the terrorists' credibility with the public *vis-à-vis* money collection. Is the organization using the sums that have been extorted through kidnapping and the 'revolutionary tax' for personal gain, or is the money used to achieve the stated revolutionary aims? The collection of funds by terrorists is almost always suspect in the eyes of the public and thus presents an ideal target for the government. The fact that thus far it appears that none of the terrorist organizations have used the funds they have gained by any of the stated methods for personal use and 'high living' is beside the point. If the public can be convinced that the terrorists are little more than common extortionists, then their credibility is seriously weakened and popular support declines.

Despite its obvious strengths, there are actual or potential weaknesses within the organization that are open to counteraction by government security forces aimed at disrupting and discrediting ETA. These include:

1. Lack of a strong ongoing propaganda apparatus;
2. A vulnerability to psychological warfare operations;
3. A vulnerability to clandestine operations;
4. A lack of co-operation between the various terrorist groups, particularly in the field of operations;
5. A vulnerability in the terrorist's method of financing operations;
6. A hard-working Roman Catholic population in the Basque region that is not interested in becoming separate from Spain;
7. An appeal that is racist and therefore finds little, or no support, within the remainder of Spain.

I. INFORMATION SERVICES AND PROPAGANDA

Under the Franco regime the Ministry of Information played a powerful role and a strong and persistent propaganda line was pursued in support of government policies. It would appear that over a prolonged period this approach produced a strong antipathy on the part of the general public towards propaganda. Since the process of democratization began, the use of propaganda has largely been discontinued. Although an infrastructure of Information Services remains, its role is largely confined to the straightforward reporting of government matters.

By far the most powerful medium for mass communication is television. Television has been used with considerably good results by government to counter terrorist campaigns in some countries, notably in Germany. In countries with a free press, television can be a double-edged weapon, but the government should make maximum use of its opportunity to exploit this medium. Television and broadcasting in Spain are under government control, but a much greater freedom of reporting and discussion has been introduced. Television coverage extends throughout the country and is accessible to the vast majority of the population, either through their own sets or television facilities in bars and other public places.

Strengths and Weaknesses

The strengths of the government's and the security forces's position with regard to the pursuit of successful counter-terrorist measures would appear to include the following:

a. Government's firm resolve to suppress terrorism and provide essential resources to do this;
b. Government's determination to operate within the law and to respect democratic institutions and procedures;
c. Government's determination to consolidate a degree of autonomy to the Basque people compatible with legitimate historical claims;
d. The dedication and discipline of the security forces involved in counter-terrorist operations;
e. The professional status of those forces and the core of experience possessed in operational units.

There are possible weaknesses in the following areas:

a. Shortcomings hitherto in the machinery for the central direction and co-ordination of the counter-terrorist campaign at the national level;
b. Absence of a centrally directed and co-ordinated intelligence organization;
c. Political restraints on the use of military manpower and resources;
d. As yet insufficiently developed intelligence resources and coverage;
e. Over-commitment of manpower to static and defensive tasks;
f. Shortcomings in adequate scales and types of specialist equipment;
g. Shortcomings in low-level and specialist training;
h. Restrictions on exploitation of propaganda resources.

Administrative Anti-Terrorist Organizations

National Level of Government

The main responsibility for the direction of the campaign against ETA and other terrorist and subversive groups lies with the Ministry of the Interior. Now established with the Ministry and answerable to the Minister is a Secretary of State Security with a Director General in charge of all police forces and all Chief Commissariats of the *Cuerpo Nacional de Policía.* The *Guardia Civil* are administratively part of the Army, but are placed in the Ministry of the Interior chain of command for operational purposes.

The principal police forces available to the Minister of the Interior for the purposes of counter-terrorist operations and for the general maintenance of public order are noted below with their general responsibilities:

1. *Guardia Civil* (GC). This is a paramilitary force that is responsible for policing in country areas and in towns under 20,000 population, frontier control, highway patrols and security of certain government buildings (e.g., in Madrid);
2. *Cuerpo Policía Nacional*. This force is divided into (I) Secret Police, a plainclothes force with Special Branch duties that include criminal investigation, drug control, passport control, records and staffing of police stations; and (II) Uniformed Police, a paramilitary force responsible for mobile patrols and riot control (*anti-disturbios*);
3. *Policía Municipal* (PM). These are uniformed police responsible for local maintenance of public order (towns of over 20,000 population).

There are two operational police units: (I) *Grupo Especial de Operaciones* – GEO (Special Operations Group) in charge of special counter-terrorist operations, anti-hijacking, etc.; and (II) GAR (Counter-terrorist Civil Guard, rural areas). There are also Basque police forces that are responsible for maintenance of public order in the Basque provinces. These are independent forces that answer to the Basque administration established under arrangements for autonomy.

The Army has not been committed to the counter-terrorist role as a deliberate government policy of avoiding 'militarisation' of the situation. It is assumed that this policy applies equally to the Air Force and the Navy. Units and headquarters of military forces remain responsible for the security of their establishments and equipment against terrorist threat.

Since July 1987 a diplomat has been in charge of centralizing and co-ordinating anti-terrorist external policy. His performance has made it possible to get better results on the diplomatic side of negotiations of the anti-terrorist war. He coordinates the actions of the TREVI Group (police co-operation), the European Council (judicial co-operation) and bilateral and multilateral relations of Spain. He has participated in the dialogue with France and Algeria, countries which are actively co-operating with Spain in the fight against ETA. He also co-ordinates the group of the External Policy Secretariat that meets every six weeks with their European counterparts at EC headquarters. At these meetings, they examine the national and international terrorism situation and policies to be followed are established. The EC has elaborated confidential documents about the countries that protect terrorist groups and the measures that the community should take in extreme cases.

Provincial Level Government/Security Force Organization

Provincial administration is headed by an appointed civilian provincial governor answering to the Ministry of the Interior, which has overall responsibility for security operations in the province. Each province also has a military governor commanding the armed forces within the area and who is answerable in the military chain of command to the military regions.

Recommendations and General Principles

Political Aim

The first principle is that the government must have a clearly stated political aim, both in the long-term and with regard to intermediate phases of the development of that aim. It is only with such direction that the complex variety of measures covering not only purely military action, but also economic, social and cultural policies can be elaborated, co-ordinated and put into effect. One may take the British 1948–60 campaign against communist insurgency in Malaya as an example of a successfully completed campaign where the establishment of a clear overall policy contributed largely to government success.

For an example of the lack of a clear and consistent political aim inhibiting a military solution to an insurgency or terrorist campaign, we have to look no further than Northern Ireland. It has not been possible to date for the British government to elaborate a constitutional solution which would gain the support of both main communities in the population. This has meant that the security forces are engaged in a campaign of containment and attrition of terrorism, which has not itself, despite short-term successes, succeeded in eliminating the terrorist threat posed by the Provisional IRA and other terrorist organizations.

Another aspect of the application of this principle relates to the morale of the population in general, and of the security forces in particular. Acceptance of the inconvenience and expense to the population, in terms of human suffering and financial loss involved in the pursuit of an anti-terrorist campaign, will be considerably affected by the government's degree of resolve and the clarity of its stated aims. A corollary is that the development of effective policies in the important fields of propaganda will largely depend upon the existence of clear long- and short-term political aims.

Direction and Co-ordination of Countermeasures

The second principle is that government measures to defeat terrorism must cover the entire spectrum of the existing and potential threat posed by the terrorist organization and that these measures must be centrally directed and closely co-ordinated at all levels, from the national one down to the local administrative or operational area. The terrorist threat itself will be posed not only in terms of armed action against security forces, but also will seek to exploit advantages through subversion or physical violence directed towards political, economic, social, psychological and cultural targets. Government measures must seek to defeat these efforts in their respective fields as part of a comprehensive, close-knit and co-ordinated overall plan. Thus, for example, while the security forces are engaged in identifying and eliminating terrorist cells, government information services and the propaganda organization should be pursuing the psychological battle to win the support of the mass of the population for the measures being taken, and to discredit the ideology, aim and methods of the terrorist organization. Similarly, efforts by the terrorist organization to exploit such cultural issues and the language grievances of groups should be countered by appropriate government policies, co-ordinated with overall political aims; indeed, it should be the government's aim to gain the initiative in this field.

The necessity of close co-ordination between the civil and the military operational effort at the national level is obvious, but the need is as great at the lower level. Military or police officers are required to initiate proposals for wearing down and defeating terrorists, but representatives of other government departments will have to scrutinize these in order to ensure that they do not conflict with long-term government aims. Conversely, security force commanders and staffs will have to ensure that action proposed by civil departments does not inhibit the operational effort. At the grassroots level, police, military and local government officials will need to work extremely closely in the devising and implementation of such measures as imposition of curfews, restrictions on movement of population, vehicles, etc. The conduct of a counter-terrorist campaign is an immensely complex task. A clear chain of command must be established and provided with the necessary machinery to formulate and execute policies, to decide upon priorities and allocation of resources and to react promptly to changes in the threat.

The Rule of Law

The third principle is that the government should function in accordance with the law. There is a very strong temptation for government forces, in dealing with terrorist actions, to act outside the rule of law, the excuses being that the processes of law are too cumbersome, that the normal safeguards in the law for the individual are not designed for an emergency and that, given the often indiscriminate violence perpetrated, the terrorist deserves to be treated outside normal law. This temptation is fuelled by the manner in which terrorist organizations often seek ruthlessly to exploit national and international law to further their aims and to inhibit action by the government and the security forces. Action outside the law puts at stake the government's moral authority. However, there are also practical considerations which make it very much more in the government interest to remain within the law in pursuing terrorism than going outside it.

First, there is the government's standing within the country. If the government does not adhere to the law then it loses respect and fails to fulfil its contractual obligations to the people as a government. If its officers and officials cease to be responsible for their actions, then the government forces may seem no better than the terrorists whom they are seeking to eliminate. Action outside the law also provides a focus for propaganda exploitation by the terrorist organization, not only within the country but also in an international forum. The spheres of detention and interrogation are particularly sensitive in this respect.

Intelligence

The fourth principle is that priority must be given to the establishment of a centrally directed and co-ordinated Intelligence organization. There is probably no factor more essential to completing a campaign against terrorism and subversion successfully than the provision of accurate and timely intelligence. All too often this factor is grossly neglected in the period leading up to the outbreak of terrorism and in a campaign's initial stages, whereas the early development of an intelligence infrastructure might have enabled the subversive or terrorist organization to be identified and eliminated before it could properly take root.

Good intelligence not only enables the general capabilities and intentions of the terrorist enemy to be accurately assessed (an essential prerequisite to the devising of effective counter-measures), but, and this is of primary importance, enables these measures to be applied selectively. A main objective of the terrorist organization (as in the case of ETA) is, through their actions, to force the government into a draconian and indiscriminate response which will affect the population as a whole and thus produce a backlash of unfavourable reaction. The intelligence requirement is to identity those individuals and deal with them through carefully targeted operations and other measures which impose the minimum hardship, danger or inconvenience upon the population as a whole. Selectivity of action is the key in counter-terrorist operations and only intelligence can provide this.

To be effective, intelligence operations require unified direction, close control and detailed co-ordination at all levels. Conversely, the presence of a variety of uncoordinated intelligence agencies, each pursuing its own aims and targets, can prove a disaster not only to the effective direction of operations against the enemy but also to the security of tactical units and of the intelligence organizations themselves.

The Time Factor

The point has been made earlier that the government should seek to meet the terrorist and subversive threat across the whole range of potential attack. The other dimension of action, the time factor, merits comment. In a democratic society, terrorism and subversion are unlikely to be eliminated in the short-term once they have seriously established themselves, unless there is a radical change of government and policies. Even when successful attack and attrition have substantially reduced the seriousness and the scale of the threat, providing a nucleus of determined and professional terrorists remains, a residual level of violence is likely. This situation may be maintained over many years, perhaps slipping gradually from ideologically motivated attacks into activity for purely criminal purposes. In determining its counter-terrorist policies, government must accordingly think in the long-term – not in terms of one or two years, but planning, say, ten years ahead. (ETA has, after all, been operating for a third of a century already.) Plans and investments made for the long term are in this way much more likely to be effective and economical than a piecemeal approach, although the initial investment may be heavy.

France and the Fight Against Terrorism

GILBERT GUILLAUME

This essay briefly examines the kinds of terrorism that have occurred in France in the past 20 years and the recent domestic and international measures taken to combat them. Domestically, countermeasures include legislative and procedural changes and reorganization of police structures and operations. On the international level, increased co-operation has taken place in the areas of legal conventions, diplomatic initiatives and policing.

In the course of the past twenty years France has encountered three types of terrorism, not all of equal gravity. In the first place, there have been violent actions which have their roots in the demands of advocates of regionalism in Brittany, Corsica and the Basque country. In the second place, there has been terrorism inspired by a revolutionary ideology analogous to the one which motivated the 'Red Army Faction' in the Federal Republic of Germany, the 'Red Brigades' in Italy or the 'Combatant Communist Cells' in Belgium. Within this type of terrorism, there developed a national wing and an international wing of 'Direct Action' (*Action Directe*). Finally, France, like other West European countries, has been the scene and, at times, the target of terrorist movements of foreign origin, mainly from the Middle East.

These last two types of terrorism turned out to be more active and certainly more dangerous in the 1980s than they had been in the preceding decades. The annual number of assaults, which was 754 in 1979, reached more than 1,000 in 1982, 1983 and 1984. The internationalist wing of the *Action Directe* group progressed from nightly bombings and machine gun attacks on prominent buildings to minutely prepared assassinations (those of General René Audran in 1985 and of M. George Besse, the General Director of Renault, in 1987). In addition, terrorism of foreign origin manifested itself from 1980 onwards in acts no longer directed against individuals for the official roles they fulfilled, but turned against various segments of the population (the assault on the synagogue in the Rue Copernic in 1980; the *Le Capitole* train and the Goldberg restaurant in Paris in 1982; the railway station of Marseille and the TGV [High-Speed Train] in 1983; big department stores and public buildings in 1985 and 1986). This evolution has forced successive French cabinets to conduct a more active fight against terrorism both in the domestic and in the international field.

The Domestic Field

In the domestic field police action has been accompanied by the adoption of new legislative and administrative measures. The Amnesty Law of 4 August 1981 was very broad, covering also certain acts of terrorism. Its application made it possible to bring to a halt the violent expression of the autonomist movement in Brittany and led to important changes within the Corsican autonomist movement. The other side of the coin was that certain persons who benefited from this law, Régis Schleicher, Jean-Marc Rouillan or Nathalie Ménigon, were among those who organized the assassinations which were subsequently committed by *Action Directe*. As a consequence, the Amnesty Law passed seven years later, on 20 July 1988, showed more restrictive features.

In the meantime, a law relating to the struggle against terrorism and attacks on the security of the State was adopted on 9 September 1986. It was not the purpose of this piece of legislation to create new terrorist offenses; rather it establishes new rules regarding the jurisdiction of the courts and the procedures to be applied for those offenses which 'are related to individual or collective attacks aiming at disturbing the public order by means of intimidation or terror'.

First, the investigation of these offenses is centralized in the office of the 'Parquet General' of Paris and the passing of verdicts is in the hands of a jury which no longer consists of ordinary jury members but of seven professional magistrates. Second, if the questioning or the investigation make it necessary, the period of arrest of adult suspects can be the subject of a supplementary prolongation of 48 hours if the president of the court or the investigating judge decides so. This means that it can be extended from two to four days. Beyond that, the judge can, in the course of questioning, decide to order the search of premises and homes or confiscate pieces of evidence which might be instrumental in obtaining a conviction. For this, the consent of the person whose place is being searched is no longer necessary. Third, the law permits the exclusion from punishment of all persons who, having passed information to the authorities, have made it possible to prevent the occurrence of an offense. In addition, it allows the reduction of those penalties for acts which the perpetrator or their helpers committed if they have brought about or facilitated the identification or the arrest of others who are guilty. Finally, a system of compensation for the victims of acts of terrorism was established after the creation of a guarantee fund financed by a tax on property insurance contracts.

These legislative measures are accompanied by an improvement in the structures and methods of policing. In 1983 the Ministry of the Interior created a special database named VAT: violence, assassinations, terrorism. In 1984 a co-ordinating body for combating terrorism was installed within the same ministry, the goal being to increase the effectiveness of the various services operating in this area. Furthermore, the police tried to improve operating methods (for instance by displaying posters of wanted persons and by calls to the public for assistance to locate their whereabouts).

The International Field

These different measures, while useful, were clearly not sufficient and had to be accompanied by an improvement in international co-operation. This co-operation took place in three areas: the juridical, the diplomatic and the police. While participating in the first two areas, France always considered the third as the crucial one.

The *juridical co-operation* between states manifested itself predominantly in the elaboration of international conventions which aimed at extending the jurisdiction of national courts with regard to certain offences, and to facilitate the extradition of delinquents as well as to proceed more frequently to prosecutions. To this end, France has signed and ratified the conventions which were elaborated within the International Civil Aviation Organization (ICAO), that is, the Tokyo Convention of 14 September 1963, the Hague Convention of 16 December 1970, and the Montreal Convention of 23 September 1971. In addition, France has signed and ratified the protocol to the Montreal Convention of 24 February 1988, which deals with offences committed within the perimeter of airports and she signed the Convention for the Suppression of Unlawful Acts against the Safety of maritime Navigation which was adopted by the International Maritime Organization (IMO) in autumn 1988, following the *Achille Lauro* incident.

France is also a party to the regional conventions elaborated within the Council of Europe, that is, the European extradition convention of 13 December 1957, the European Convention on the Suppression of Terrorism (ECST) of 27 January 1977, as well as the Dublin agreement of 4 December 1979, concerning the application within the European Community of the ECST. On the other hand, France is neither a party to the United Nations' Convention on the protection of diplomats of 12 December 1973, nor the UN Convention against acts of hostage-taking of 17 December 1979. According to the French point of view, these two instruments make unjustified distinctions between acts of terrorism based on the motives which can inspire such acts.

In the *diplomatic area* France participates in the Economic Summit

Conferences of the seven most industrialized countries (G-7) as well as in the European Political Cooperation. She has always given special attention to the latter and fully subscribes to the conclusions which the European Council arrived at on 5 and 6 December 1986. It is therefore appropriate to recall the wording of these, in particular:

> The Council of Europe has agreed that the fight against terrorism and those who support acts of terrorism ought to be based on the following principles:
>
> – no concessions to the coercion of terrorists and those who support them;
> – solidarity among the member states in their efforts to prevent acts of terrorism and to bring those guilty to justice;
> – concerted action in response to terrorist attacks on the territory of a member state and in response to proofs of foreign participation in such attacks.

Nevertheless, it is clear that the opening of the borders between the members in 1993 will, in this regard, lead to new problems. The European Council of the European Community (EC) specified these on 5 December 1988, in these terms: 'The realization of the objectives of the community, and in particular a space without frontiers, is linked to the progress of international cooperation in the fight against terrorism, international crime, narcotics and the trafficking of all sorts.'

It is clear that combating terrorism belongs to the domain of the police and from this perspective *police co-operation* is absolutely essential. On the global level, this co-operation is unquestioningly organized by Interpol, whose status has been construed in 1984 in a direction which allows it to play a role in this area. Yet the main co-operation takes place on the regional and bilateral level. In the framework of Europe, France participates in the Club of Berne, the Club of Vienna and, above all, in the TREVI group which was installed in 1976. Since 1985 this particular group brings together, at least twice a year, the EC ministers who are in charge of the police. TREVI has created several working groups of which the one on terrorism has adopted various measures, mostly confidential. Furthermore, France holds that bilateral co-operation is of utmost usefulness. This can remain informal without becoming fruitless, as the information exchanges with the *Bundeskriminalamt* (German Criminal Office) have proven. It can also be formalized: such co-operation agreements have recently been signed with Germany, Spain, Great Britain and Italy.

Conclusion

Taken together, this pragmatic policy at home and abroad has brought a certain measure of success. The violent actions claimed by regionalists have ceased in Brittany, and have decreased in the Basque country and on the island of Corsica. The *Action Directe* group has been dismantled and its principal members were recently convicted. As far as foreign-based terrorism is concerned, there have been ups and downs in France as there have also been in other West European countries. In all these countries, this has been a latent problem whose solution requires a strong political will and effective international co-operation.

The German Federal Republic's Response and Civil Liberties

KURT GROENEWOLD

This study examines the measures taken by the Federal Republic of Germany* to deal with captured members of the Red Army Faction. As such, it focuses mainly on legal proceedings, trials and conditions in prison rather than on measures to combat active members. It is argued that the proceedings against captured Red Army Faction members were primarily political rather than ordinary criminal proceedings. To put this case, the author highlights the special conditions in prison, for example, solitary confinement, the legal prohibition of a joint defence, government attempts to influence public opinion, legal and administrative measures such as the monitoring of defence lawyers' mail or the forced feeding of Red Army Faction prisoners on hunger strikes, publicity during the trial that criticized the government, and the extension of criminal proceedings to so-called sympathisers. In drawing lessons for a unified Europe, the conclusion highlights the need to protect prisoners' rights and to avoid the use of criminal prosecution to suppress nonviolent dissent.

I distinguish, along with Alex P. Schmid,[1] between groups which refer to national aims and others which refer to socio-revolutionary ideas. The only form of fighting groups which have existed in the past in West Germany and still exist today are those which justify their actions on the basis of socio-revolutionary ideas. I am not concerned with the problem of how such groups have been or are to be combated by the government, the holder of state authority. I am concerned with the question of whether or not the measures taken by the Federal government to combat captured members of urban guerrilla groups and to bring them to trial, plus any supporting measures, are acceptable from the point of view of civil liberties and the self-image of the Western constitutional democracies.

An urban guerrilla group was first set up in the Federal Republic of Germany in 1970. It published its political aims in many publications.[2] It also made so-called commando statements about individual actions. The Red Army Faction based itself on the model of the Tupamaros in Latin America. In its writings, it listed the social injustices which it found in the Federal Republic of Germany.[3] However, it defined itself first and foremost by its struggle against American imperialism. It saw itself on the side of the peoples of the Third World, who were exploited and oppressed by American imperialism. Its models were the struggle of the Vietnamese against the USA and that of the Palestinians against Israel. The Federal

Republic was seen as one of the satellites or sub-centres of American imperialism within the Western system. Consequently, some of the first campaigns were directed at American military installations on West German territory. It was claimed, for example, that these installations were used in connection with the bombing of Cambodia in 1972. I am not going to examine here which of these observations on which the terrorists' actions are founded correspond with reality and which do not. The description of the group's political identity reveals that it justifies its actions on the basis of socio-revolutionary aims.

The leading members of the Red Army Faction were arrested in 1972 – Andreas Baader, Gudrun Ensslin, Ulrike Marie Meinhof, Holger Meins, Jan Carl Raspe. The arrests of other members had already begun in 1970 and 1971. Criminal proceedings against the leading members were not initiated until three years after their arrest, however, in 1975, before the Higher Regional Court in Stuttgart (Stuttgart-Stammheim). One of the leading members, Holger Meins, had already died in December 1974, during a hunger strike. The case ended with four members of the group being sentenced to life imprisonment.

In 1977 the industrialist Martin Schleyer was kidnapped, in order to blackmail the government into releasing the imprisoned members of the group. This campaign also included the hijacking of a Lufthansa aircraft, whose passengers and crew were freed by the military commando action of a special police unit at Mogadishu airport (Somalia). During the night following this action, the convicted members of the Red Army Faction were found dead at Stuttgart-Stammheim prison. The convictions of the leading members Andreas Baader, Gudrun Ensslin and Jan Carl Raspe never became final and absolute, because the accused had lodged an appeal against the sentence prior to their deaths.

Criminals or Political Prisoners?

I repeat: I am concerned not with the combating of active groups, but with trials and conditions in prison. The trials of the Red Army Faction members were political trials. I base this assertion on Otto Kircheimer's definition:

> The subject matter of a trial is a period in history, its standard of values is provided by the law and the judgement provides a guide for the future. In order to understand the subject matter of the trial, the selected period must be reconstructed. For the purpose of the decision to be reached by the court it is essential that an individual is charged on the basis of the role which he has played in a specific

historic context. Only under this condition can the judge become the person competent to judge a political conflict. If he were to deal with the conflict in a form which extended beyond the specific historic constellation, on the basis of a programme or a matter of basic principle, for example, he would not be competent to pass judgement.[4]

Two options were available to the Federal government for the trials against the arrested Faction members:

1. They could treat them as criminals in the customary sense of the word. This means that the customary law and the customary procedures would be applied to which criminals are generally subjected or to which they are generally entitled to have recourse. The customary procedure includes the right of the accused to be defended, to submit statements and to present his own view of the events concerned. Such a presentation may also be propaganda, in cases concerning a political trial. In a Western constitutional democracy the accused may determine the manner in which he defends himself, which arguments he uses and which strategies. His right to defend himself cannot be restricted either by his own well-understood interest or by a right on the part of the government to determine the aspects on which the accused is permitted to comment. The accused is presumed innocent until found guilty. Neither the acts nor the views of the accused may be treated as having been established prior to judgement being passed;

2. On the other hand, the Federal government could regard the accused as enemies of the state and, in this context, as political prisoners. The Federal government could have attempted to establish a right to simply take them to court on the basis of this. The accused would then not have been independent subjects of the trial, but simply objects of the strategy for attaining convictions. They would then not have had the customary rights, but only the right to be present and to reply to questions with a yes or a no. They would not have been permitted to submit undesired explanations and statements. This is the form taken by mock trials.

In a political trial, namely a trial concerning the legitimation of actions by the state or even the existence of the state, a legal defence can incriminate a government. In contrast, there are cases in which a government uses a trial to present its own views and to show the crimes or the anti-government group itself. Ben Gurion stated that the 1960 Adolf Eichmann trial served not only the purpose of convicting a criminal, but also of reminding the generation living today of the crimes committed by the National Socialists.[5] The trials of the Quislings, Hitler's allies in the occupied states, that is, Norway, France, the Netherlands, served the purpose of further discrediting these persons, who were regarded as traitors, and of showing the illegality of their co-operation with Hitler in a public trial. The trials held in France of the former Vichy state president, Marshal Pétain, and the former prime minister, Pierre Laval, are examples of such intentions.[6]

In 1976 Federal Public Prosecutor Buback justified the delay in the commencement of the trial at Stuttgart-Stammheim with such tactical considerations when he stated: 'We had to put on trial a greater subject matter because it was about the leading members of the Baader-Meinhof gang. It was therefore necessary to present a representative cross-section of their deeds'.[7] The Federal government attempted to implement both options outlined above. It did not wish to decide between the two alternatives. It prepared the trial as normal proceedings against criminals. At the same time, in the context of these criminal proceedings, it attempted to divest the accused of their statutory rights and the statutory possibilities available to them. Richard Schmidt, one of the judges who was active in proceedings after 1945, and who was himself imprisoned by the Nazis, criticised this approach on the *Süddeutscher Rundfunk* radio broadcasting station in 1975:

> In so doing, it (the judiciary) wishes on the one hand to stir up public opinion against the accused without, on the other hand, refraining from presenting the accused as dangerous anarchists and persons who are attempting to overthrow our society, which is obviously a political aim.[8]

Federal Chancellor Helmut Schmidt provided an indication of these measures in his statement in the German Bundestag (Lower House) in 1975, when he declared that 'They therefore even represent violent criminals outside of the rules set by our democratic constitutional state'.[9] The Federal government and the judicial organs justified their standpoint by referring to the fact that the accused retained their political convictions and in this way continued the existence of the group. For this reason, they stated, the prisoners were not to be treated as normal prisoners under the control of the state and prisoners of the judiciary system, but as persons who continued to belong to the group. Concessions could and can still be expected only by persons who renounce their convictions.

Conditions in Prison

The prisoners were subjected to special conditions of imprisonment from the outset. The concept for their imprisonment was developed not by the judicial authorities but centrally, by the Federal Office of Criminal

Investigation.[10] The special aspect of their imprisonment was that they were isolated from all social contact within the prisons. At times they were accommodated in so-called dead sections, in which hardly any sounds could be heard. Such concepts as solitary confinement and sensory deprivation had been developed not only in the Federal Republic of Germany, but also in other states as well.

The manner in which the prisoners were treated was suitable for destroying their personality and identity. The treatment was also degrading. Lights were often left on the entire night or the light was switched on or off every hour. If the prisoners spoke to other persons during their walk in the prison compound they were put into detention cells. Persons who spoke to the prisoners were prevented from conversing by force or were put into a calming-down cell and subjected to disciplinary action.

The psychiatrist whom the Stuttgart Higher Regional Court had appointed as a consultant, Professor Wilfried Rasch, published the effects of these measures and described them to the court. He assessed the prisoners as being unfit for trial due to the psychological and physical consequences of the isolation. He described the isolation measures as follows:

> Based on a much higher zero line, security measures were devised and implemented, the aim of which was totality, complete control of all manifestations of life, including shrewd insulation . . . . Acumen and imagination were employed to eliminate every risk. The perfected procedure had to be content with the designation solitary confinement.[11]

In his written report Rasch stated: 'The reference of the accused was completely channelled. They lived outside the normal infra-structure by means of which a prisoner normally obtains a certain degree of psychological support.'[12]

Not only the judicial bodies, but also the Federal government was aware of the psychological consequences of solitary confinement. For this reason, a new legal regulation (231 a, Code of Criminal Procedure – StPO) was adopted for the forthcoming trial at Stuttgart-Stammheim on 21 December 1974, permitting criminal proceedings to be held without the accused, when the accused had made himself unfit for trial. On the basis of this legislation, the Higher Regional Court in Stuttgart decided to conduct the legal proceedings without the accused. The Court stated that the accused themselves were to be blamed for their conditions of imprisonment:

... They must be considered responsible for the circumstances which impair their ability to appear at the proceedings. Their dangerousness left the authorities with no other choice. The prisoners and their lawyers have continually described this form of imprisonment as destructive torture. Therefore, they have evidently been able to observe the effects of the conditions of imprisonment. They doubtless possess special intelligence which has enabled them to identify the consequences. They have nevertheless continued their behaviour over a period of years, which has compelled the state authorities to impose these conditions of imprisonment on them, the nature of which was suitable to constitute a risk to their ability to stand trial. This is sufficient to constitute suspected intent in accordance with Art. 321, Para. 1, StPO.[13]

In the Court's decision, the prisoners are described as dangerous, because '. . . as the imprisoned members of an armed group which is fighting against the existence of the State, they do not accept the law as binding and hold the judicial structures in contempt.'[14] It is further stated that they are also dangerous '. . . because they exercise their right to silence in preparing their defence'. The argument of the Court in 1975 shows that the words of Federal Chancellor Schmidt had by then had a decisive effect. Destructive conditions of imprisonment were not only legitimised, the imprisoned Red Army Faction members themselves were even made responsible for such conditions, because they refused to renounce their political views.

Statements during Proceedings

The central element of the defence was to be the statements made during the trial. The accused had prepared for this during their period in custody. The Federal Republic was afraid of these statements. It believed that the accused intended to turn their statements and subsequently the entire proceedings into a 'propaganda operation'. This is how the *Stuttgarter Nachrichten* newspaper put it in 1974, with reference to the Federal Public Prosecutor's Office:

The judicial authorities now possess comprehensive material which reveals that the Baader-Meinhof people intend to transform the forthcoming trial into a political demonstration. The entire system in the Federal Republic is to be put in the dock.[15]

The accused had decided to carry out a joint defence, in other words, to present their political concept. For this reason, they had chosen lawyers who were to defend them jointly. There was talk of a block defence. Each lawyer was to represent each of the accused at the main trial.

Up to 1975 this was practised in many criminal proceedings. For the proceedings at Stuttgart-Stammheim, the German Bundestag adopted a law on the motion of the Federal government which prohibited the joint defence of several accused persons by one lawyer. This law, which came into effect in December 1974, that is prior to the beginning of the trial, was already under discussion in March 1974. That is why the article from the *Stuttgarter Nachrichten* states that this law will result in a collapse of the block defence. It is indicated that the judicial organs hoped that the Federal government would work swiftly.

The Federal government was not content to sit in fear of the trial statements. It had already gained an impression of the way in which the accused intended to present their defence and the statements which they intended to submit by means of numerous searches of the prisoners' cells and the confiscation of defence documents. The courts approved the cell searches and the confiscation of defence documents due to the rigorous and unfamiliar character of the language employed by the accused. Consequently, not only did the state authorities acquire knowledge of the defence strategy, but the accused were also deprived of the written material which they required to prepare their trial statements. The confiscations were a continuation of the policy of social isolation.

Public Opinion and the Media

These measures were supplemented by an attempt to generate hostile public opinion. Otto Schilly, one of the defending counsel, presented the Federal government's strategy in an application for dismissal of the criminal proceedings, in which he based his argument on a violation of the principle of fair trial. The Federal government had expressed its views not only on the concept of the urban guerrilla, but also, in extremely concrete terms, on the accused persons. In 1975 Federal Public Prosecutor Buback, who acted on behalf of the Federal government, expressly admitted having provided the public with injurious information on the accused. A newspaper published this admission as follows:

> Federal Public Prosecutor Buback expressed his support for a campaign of providing the public with offensive information on the Baader-Meinhof gang. He stated, however, that the important factors were how, when and which information was passed on.[16]

Certain elements of the press argued that 'any humanizing portrayal of the terrorists was irresponsible and unintelligent'.[17]

In order to win over the public and stir it up against the accused, the Federal government published a so-called 'Documentation on the activities of violent anarchists', which contained excerpts from the investigation files, defending counsel's letters and other material relating to the proceedings. The Minister of the Interior, Werner Maihofer, stated on behalf of the Federal government:

> Every line of this published material will have been the subject of consultation between the Federal Public Prosecutor and the Federal Office of Criminal Investigation, which means that informing the public in this manner will result only in benefits, and in no damage whatsoever.[18]

A complaint which was lodged on the basis of the prohibition of the publication of files as stipulated in the law was dismissed by the judicial authorities on the grounds that this case constituted a state of emergency which took priority over this law, as a result of which the Federal government had the right to create a certain image of the accused by means of a specific publication.

Measures and Laws against Defendants

The measures taken by the Federal government were of both an administrative and legal nature. The laws concerning the conditions of imprisonment, the capability of the accused to take part in the trial and their preparations for the trial have already been mentioned. All these laws came into effect after charges had been brought against the leading members of the group, when the trial was imminent. The measures adopted by the Federal Government became law in December 1974. On the basis of these laws, the three best-prepared defending counsel of the accused, who had fought for many years against the conditions of imprisonment and against the Federal government's administrative measures, were excluded from the proceedings.

They were accused not of criminal activities or participation in criminal acts, but of having ensured, by means of their manner of defending, that the self-image of the accused as urban guerrillas remained intact.[19] The Federal government and the judicial organs thereby admitted to their aim of breaking the self-image of the imprisoned Red Army Faction members as urban guerrillas in custody prior to commencement of the trial. Such an aim in a state in which the Western constitutional system applies, a state which has placed human rights and basic rights at the head of its constitution, is equivalent to the establishment of emergency law.

The Federal government also appears to have understood this measure in this light, as the then Federal Minister of Justice, Jochen Vogel (SPD), advocated a time limit for the so-called anti-terror laws: 'Vogel advocated a time limit for the more stringent measures which have been introduced into criminal law and criminal proceedings, and which are currently necessary, due to the Baader-Meinhof trials.'[20] The Federal government's measures were centred on the defending counsel as these were the people who had broken the imposed silence by informing the public, by press statements and press conferences. They had not only complained of the Federal government's measures at the open trial, but had also pointed out the contradiction between the principles of a constitutional state on the one hand and the measures of the Federal government on the other. In order to eliminate these lawyers, the Federal government attempted to identify them with their clients' intentions. In the campaign against the defending counsel, false assertions were made – that they had transported weapons or news for the groups outside of the prisons. The complaints lodged by the defending counsel for defamation were not pursued.

It is not my intention to present the Federal government's campaign here – a comprehensive description has been provided by Frank Rühmann.[21] The administrative measures consisted of confiscating the defending counsel's mail, subjecting the defending counsel to extreme controls, which involved, for example, compelling them to remove some of their clothing or, at times, even all of their clothing, before they were allowed to speak to their clients. The Federal government also published details of their social contacts and relationships.

The anti-terror law introduced at the end of 1974 allowed the following:

1. Defending counsel could be excluded from defending accused persons on the basis of mere suspicion. Joint defence was prohibited. While the public prosecutors were required to read out their bill of indictment at the beginning of a trial, lawyers were not allowed to make any opening statements. The monitoring of defending counsel's mail was introduced in political proceedings, and in political proceedings only. Finally, a separating panel was used in meetings between defending counsel and clients suspected of terrorism. The right of the accused to summon witnesses or specialists was restricted and placed at the discretion of the court. Later, the law on the cutting-off of detainees from contact with the outside allowed the government to prohibit any visits by and correspondence with the defending counsel whatsoever for a certain period of time.

2. One administrative measure aimed directly at the imprisoned members of the urban guerrilla group was forced feeding. The Federal government and the judiciary assumed that the prisoners had no right to

carry out hunger strikes. Even at the time, this view was not undisputed, however. The hunger strike was understood primarily as being a political means of blackmailing the Federal government into improving the conditions of imprisonment. Upon close consideration of this matter, it must be admitted that the prisoners did use their hunger strikes to improve their situation, but that they also saw them as a political fighting instrument, a measure which could strengthen the members' feeling of solidarity. This aspect should not be ignored.

On the other hand, there is a centuries-old traditional view which grants prisoners the right to use their own bodies to improve their conditions. This is illustrated not only by the examples of the Russian anarchists or Gandhi, but also by many hunger strikes carried out by both political and non-political prisoners. Heribert Ostendorf, professor of criminal law and presently chief public prosecutor for the Federal State of Schleswig-Holstein, wrote a monograph on this subject in 1983, and reached the conclusion that the right to carry out a hunger strike is a human right, even if it is connected with political aims.[22]

Nevertheless, the Federal government not only accused defending counsels of supporting a hunger strike by their clients, it also treated prisoners on hunger strike like rabble-rousers. It ordered coercive measures to be carried out, namely the forced feeding of such prisoners. They were tied up, their heads were held in a fixed position, and liquid food was administered to them in a more or less painful manner.[23] These measures were carried out by doctors. Many doctors and doctors' organisations have consequently protested against employing prison doctors for such coercive measures. One prisoner, Ronald Augustin, a Dutch citizen, was even moved from his normal prison in Hanover, because the doctors there refused to carry out such measures. He was transferred to a different prison and prison hospital. There he was deprived of water in order to force him to start eating again in the face of the danger that he would die of thirst. Beer and food were also placed in his cell. *Maître* Roland Houver, the French lawyer of a defending counsel, commented that this scene reminded him of the thirst strike of Vicar Kolbe at the Auschwitz concentration camp. As a result, he was not only rebuked by the Federal Public Prosecutor's Office, but an application was even lodged for him to be forbidden from defending the accused lawyer on the grounds of his having disparaged the Federal government.[24]

Critical Publicity

The measures taken by the Federal government did not receive a positive response from the public. This was due to the fact that the disregard of laws of procedure revived memories of a time in which no laws of procedure whatsoever had existed. It could not be overlooked that the Federal government had, in order to enable it to carry out the proceedings in accordance with its desires, introduced new laws only a few months prior to the beginning of the proceedings, which had a decisive effect on the structure of the entire system of criminal procedure, as they reinforced the rights of the state while severely weakening the rights of the accused and the defending counsel. The international public was also unable to understand how the courts could accept these new laws without further ado and dismiss the defending counsel who had been working on the cases only days before the commencement of the proceedings.

By treating the imprisoned accused as if they had no procedural rights, as if it were not their deeds which formed the subject matter of criminal proceedings but they themselves who were the objects of a police-state trial, the government disregarded the principle of an independent judiciary. The government turned the courts into a tool – and the courts allowed themselves to be turned into a tool.

The government was nevertheless unsuccessful in its attempt to blur over the difference between imprisoned accused persons and group members who were at large. Not only the public,[25] but the government itself has recognised this.[26] The measures taken by the Federal government have been investigated and criticised by the Third International [Bertrand] Russell Tribunal,[27] the subject of which was the violation of human rights in the Federal Republic of Germany. Public interest was directed more towards the measures taken by the Federal government against the rights of the accused than towards the charges brought against these accused persons.

Only gradually did the public begin to adopt a disapproving attitude towards the Red Army Faction. This was due primarily to the actions of the urban guerrillas themselves, the assassinations of individuals, in particular industrialists, which filled the public with abhorrence. However, the Federal government did not use this development as an opportunity to alter its rigorous policies with regard to the imprisoned defendants. The severe conditions imposed on prisoners and accused persons and the refusal to normalise conditions of imprisonment will continue to bring the Federal government criticism – not only on humanitarian grounds – and will continue to antagonise public opinion.

The Concept of Support of a Criminal Association

The Federal government intensified its measures against terrorist groups and detainees by extending criminal proceedings to include proceedings against so-called sympathizers. This was an attempt to prevent critical intellectuals from questioning the government's actions by means of defamation. Members of the Federal government openly stated this aim at the time. The Federal Minister of Justice, Jochen Vogel stated, for example: 'It is cause for concern that it has not yet been possible to achieve a uniform public view of the Baader-Meinhof complex.'[28]

The Federal Minister of the Interior at the time, Werner Maihöfer, stated:

> Yes, we are now in a situation in which the population's awareness must really be promoted, in which it is the act which must be the prime object of attention, while the motive is of secondary importance (. . .) The prime factor is always the act, the motive is always of secondary significance. Anyone who argues differently makes himself an accomplice.[29]

The juridical construct of support of a criminal association (conspiracy) was expanded in such a manner that any form of support could be regarded as an offence. In some cases, it was sufficient to distribute a leaflet or to show a banner bearing the slogan 'Unite the prisoners from the RAF'. This was the demand made by the prisoners themselves, and it was now argued that the feeling of solidarity between the prisoners was strengthened when such slogans appeared outside the prisons. It was further claimed that these slogans were clearly propagandistic in character. The assertion by the leaflet distributor that he had been demonstrating for better conditions in prison did not prevent him from being convicted. The court deemed the decisive factor to be the fact that this demand was known as a slogan of the detainees, as a result of which it was to be judged as a profession of support for Red Army Faction aims. The courts did not distinguish between imprisoned members and members who were at large, but represented the view that the prisoners were to be regarded as members of a criminal group, as they had not renounced their political aims. In this way, numerous persons were involved in criminal proceedings or were deterred from committing themselves to an improvement in the conditions of imprisonment.

Those who are acquainted with the proceedings against members of the Communist Party of the USA in accordance with the Smith Act will know that the Supreme Court was very late in making a ruling restricting the extended form of criminal proceedings which were also practised there. The ruling was formulated by Judge Robert H. Jackson, the former chief prosecutor in the Nuremberg Trials against the major war criminals.

Since then, a person can only be convicted of conspiracy if it is proven that he himself has been involved in criminal offence. Mere intellectual support of ideas is not an offence. These basic regulations also apply in principle in the Federal Republic of Germany, but they are implemented for 'normal' criminal cases only, and not in proceedings concerning associations which are political in character.

The government accompanied its measures relating to criminal law with a campaign against critics. It also described as sympathizers with terrorism anyone who criticised its measures, who demanded a change in the conditions of imprisonment or who sought explanations for Red Army Faction actions. In this way, the impression was created that merely sympathizing was punishable as a criminal offence. The intention was to blur over the difference between a criminal offence and the expression of an opinion, if not to eliminate this difference altogether. The aim was not only to prevent public criticism. The individual was to be left uncertain as to whether he must expect his house to be searched, his telephone to be monitored or other police measures.

These ideas explain how intellectuals, in particular, such as Adorno, Horkheimer, Marcuse or Habermas could be described as 'fathers of the urban guerrillas'. Heinrich Böll, holder of the 1972 Nobel Prize for Literature, was subject to the same accusation. In an article entitled 'Violence through Information', Böll had analyzed the reporting of the tabloid newspaper, BILD-Zeitung and accused it of passing off assumptions and suspicions as facts. In the campaign against him, Richard Löwenthal, for example, the moderator of a current affairs programme, stated on the second German television channel (ZDF): 'The sympathizers with this left-wing fascism, the Bölls and Bruckners, and all the other intellectuals, are not one bit better than the intellectuals who led the way for the Nazis.'[30] The publicist Hans Habe wrote the 'Fascism would be [rampant] if PEN president Böll were to remain in his post'.[31] The intellectual climate in the Federal Republic in these years was all too similar to that which prevailed in the USA during the McCarthy era.

European Outlook

What does the 'German model' mean for a future Europe? In this connection I have not concerned myself with the question of what methods of investigation have been developed or whether the institutional structure and these methods would be suitable for application in other countries. I have concerned myself with the legal and socio-political conflict which arises when a government regards political trials as a continuation of investigations, namely, disregards legitimate rights of the individual (civil rights) which are established in the law.

With regard to the question of whether the measures carried out in the Federal Republic of Germany are applicable in other countries, the answer must depend on two principles: First, it must be asked whether these measures are reconcilable with the political culture of Western European nations and their commitment to human rights. The institution of the European Court of Human Rights and recognition of the International Human Rights Policy with the pacts adopted by the United Nations are not only an integral element of current legal policy but also an ideal for every future state organisation. It should be emphasised, therefore, that at present no measures below the legal standard must be applied against imprisoned persons who belong to an urban guerrilla force or another terrorist organisation. The fundamental principle that imprisoned persons retain inalienable rights must not be annulled in a united Europe.

Second, it should be pointed out that the measures taken by the government of the time were calculated not only to destroy human identity and also to deny the need for social dissent, both of which concepts are great cultural achievements of mankind. The nature of these measures also casts doubt on the fundamental credibility of this form of politics. For this is a form of politics based on a paranoid approach to security, the politics of 'internal security', which provides the necessary conditions for the prosecution of actions other than those which involve violence as criminal offenses, for the prosecution of political groups other than those which take the form of guerrillas/urban guerrillas.

It is furthermore a form of politics which, as a result of the attempt to condemn views and convictions, itself becomes an instrument of suppression. Polarisation and incapacitation of the population by means of the specific defamation of individuals was also practised in the Federal Republic of Germany. The comparison with McCarthyism or the practices of totalitarian states demonstrates the poor extent to which the Federal government has managed to master this problem – without actually continually reviving the problem itself.

To summarise: The separation between the area of police prosecution and that of the judiciary must be clearly maintained. Civil liberties are not available for arbitrary use. When a government disregards this separation, it not only violates the principles of international human rights, it also loses its justification and its credibility and will therefore experience failures.

NOTES

*This article was written before the reunification of Germany [eds.]

1. A.P. Schmid, 'Force or Conciliation. An overview of some problems associated with current anti-terrorist response strategies', *Violence, Aggression and Terrorism* 12/2 (1988), pp.149–78.
2. Red Army Faction, *Texte* (Malmo, 1977).
3. RAF, *Texte*.
4. Otto Kirchheimer, *Political Justice* (Princeton, NJ: Princeton UP, 1961).
5. Hannah Arendt, *Eichmann in Jerusalem* (Munich, 1974).
6. Margret Boveri, *Verrat im 20. Jahrhundert* (Hamburg: Reinbek, Rowohlt, 1956).
7. Bakker-Schut, Enzensberger, Ferron, Groenewold, Hosbroek, Wielek, *Deutschland, Deutschland. Straatschutz und Berufsverbote* (Hamburg, 1977).
8. Richard Schmid, *Suddeutsche Zeitung*, 2 July 1975.
9. Minutes of the German Bundestag, 13 March 1975.
10. Ulf Stuberger, *In der Strafsache gegen Andreas Baader u.a. wegen Mordes Documente aus dem Prozess* (Frankfurt: Syndicat, 1977).
11. Cited in Stuberger, *In der Strafsache*.
12. Ibid.
13. *Bundesgerichtshof*, 22 Oct. 1975, BGH St 26, p.228ff.
14. Ibid.
15. *Stuttgarter Nachrichten*, 14 March 1974.
16. *Frankfurter Allgemeine Zeitung*, 25 Feb. 1975.
17. *Die Welt*, 13 March 1975.
18. Bundesminister des innern, *Dokumentation über Aktivitäten anarchistischer Gewalttäter in der Bundesrepublik Deutschland* (Bonn: Bundesministerium des Innern, 1974).
19. Kurt Groenewold, *The Charge of the Federal Prosecution against Kurt Groenewold as Defence Counsel of the Red Army Faction (RAF) Prisoners* (Hamburg, 1976).
20. *Süddeutsche Zeitung*, 9 May 1975.
21. Frank Rühmann, *Anwaltsverfolgung in der Bundesrepublik 1971–1976* (Hamburg: Neue Politik, 1977).
22. Heribert Ostendorf, *Das Recht zum Hungerstreik* (Frankfurt, 1983).
23. Kurt Groenewold, *Angeklagt als Verteidiger* (Hamburg: Attica, 1978).
24. Ibid.
25. Werner Birkenmeier, *Deutsches Allgemeines Sonntagsblatt*, 8 March 1977; Guenther Graffenberger, *Frankfurter Rundschau*, 12 March 1977; Foreign Press Opinions of *Le Monde*, *Neue Zuericher Zeitung*, *Baseler Nationalzeitung*, quoted in *Deutsches Allgemeines Sonntagsblatt* 13 July 1975.
26. Federal Minister of Interior Baum, in a public discussion with the poet Erich Fried, Hamburg, 3 March 1987.
27. International Russell Tribunal, *Zur Situation der Menschenrechte in der Bundesrepublik Deutschland*. Vol.4: *Einschränkung von Verteidigungsrechten* (Berlin, 1979).
28. Cited in Bakker-Schut *et al.*, *Staatsschutz und Berufsverbote* (note 7).
29. In a televised discussion, ZDF, 17 Dec. 1974.
30. Cited in Klaus Wagenbach and Michael Krueger, *Tintenfisch: Zehn Jahrbuecher zur Deutschen Literatur von 1967–1976* (Berlin, 1981), p.40.
31. Ibid.

Institutional Responses to Terrorism: The Italian Case

DONATELLA DELLA PORTA

This study analyzes the main trends in the Italian response to terrorism for the effectiveness of specific policies and their impact on civil liberties. Four periods are highlighted. The first (1970–74) is characterized as 'immobilist'; while left-wing terrorism was not recognized as a threat, right-wing terrorism, which was much more serious at that time, was protected by the Italian secret service. The second period (1974–76) is characterized by a decline in right-wing terrorism and a more serious attack on left-wing terrorism within a wider repression of organized and violent crime. The third period (1977–82), called the Emergency period, is characterized by a new wave of left-wing terrorism and increased repression that ultimately promoted terrorist recruitment. The fourth period (1982–89) represents the defeat of left-wing terrorism through new anti-terrorism policies, such as amnesty and repentance laws. The conclusion draws three lessons for Europe: the possible implication of secret services in right-wing terrorism; the inefficacy of emergency legislation that treats terrorism like organized crime; and the importance of reintegrating former terrorists into society.

Terrorism and the State in Italy: a Presentation

For the average Italian citizen, terrorism probably is the single most important political phenomenon in his or her memory of the 1970s. In this decade similar forms of political violence also emerged in other Western democracies. Only in Italy, however, did they reach such an intensity and a persistence in time as to be considered a serious challenge to the regime. A few figures can help to recall the climate of that period. Between 1969 and 1982, 4,362 events of political violence have been counted as well as 6,153 unclaimed bombings against property; 2,712 attacks whose responsibility was claimed by terrorist groups; 324 of which were directed against people, with 768 injured and 351 killed.[1]

Several dozen underground organizations used 657 different names to take responsibility for their attacks. Six thousand people were charged with the offenses of subversive association and constituting an armed band; 1,427 people for participation in left-wing underground groups between 1978 and 1988 (643 in the Red Brigades; 239 in Front line; 545 in other organizations); in summer 1989, 464 people were in prison serving sentences for politically motivated crimes; 60 of them were serving life sentences.[2]

To deal with such a wave of political violence, the Italian State implemented several quite different policies. Anti-terrorism policies are usually valued first of all in terms of their effectiveness in combating political violence. A 'normal' cycle of state action against terrorist groups should be characterized by limited attention in the beginning, when the terrorist organizations are still weak and their potential danger difficult to detect. The stronger – and therefore more visible – they become, the more the state should concentrate its efforts to defeat them. The specialization of the security forces in the fight against terrorism should therefore produce a series of defeats for the underground organizations – arrests of their members, discovery of their headquarters – until their dissolution. This process can be longer or shorter according to the relative strength of the opponents, the effectiveness of the state repression, the degree of external support for the underground organizations. Unless a revolutionary process is considered as a possibility in today's democratic societies, however, the state is much stronger in military and legitimation resources.

When did the state response start to be effective against Italian terrorism? As far as right-wing terrorism is concerned, it is enough to recall that only very few neo-fascists responsible for terrorist massacres and their protectors have been discovered. Given its connection with organized crime gangs and secret services, right-wing terrorism should be considered a continuing threat. For left-wing terrorism, though official statistics on arrests of terrorists have never been published, I can quote some figures from a data bank on 1,124 members of left-wing underground organizations, which I constructed using trial records as source.[3] I used the same source for the data on terrorist events. The number of terrorist events can be taken as an indicator of the strength of terrorist organizations; the number of arrests as an indicator of state success. If we compare the curve of arrests with the curve of events, we notice that, oddly enough, the decline in terrorist activities preceded the wave of arrests of terrorist militants. The number of left-wing terrorism actions increased rapidly in 1977, with 197 events, and peaked in 1978, with 240 events. The decline in the number of terrorist actions started in 1979, with 179 events, and continued in the next years (with 131 events in 1980; 63 in 1981; and 49 in 1982). It should be noted that 64 per cent of terrorist actions occurred before 1979 and almost 80 per cent before 1980. The data on arrests indicate that only 12.3 per cent (173 in my sample) of the militants were arrested before 1979; another 63 were arrested in that year (7.6 per cent). Magistrates and police started, however, to achieve significant results only from 1980 on, with 345 arrests in that year (42 per cent of the sample). Various explanations have been given for this long period of ineffectiveness, which will be discussed in the following sections of this study.

Together with effectiveness, a second set of questions will be addressed: the problem of the side-effects of anti-terrorism state policies on citizens' rights. It has often been emphasized that responses to terrorism can be more dangerous for a democratic regime than terrorism itself. This problem is summarized by Martha Crenshaw: 'No policy toward terrorism is free of social and political costs. All policies toward terrorism can be analyzed in terms of negative side effects for civil liberties.'[4] In fact, most of the anti-terrorism policies implemented in Italy in the period of the so-called *emergenza* (emergency) have been criticized for their side-effects on citizens' rights. In the 1980s the need was indeed expressed to repair the damage produced during the *anni di piombo* (years of lead).

1970–1974: The Protection of Right-Wing Terrorism by the Italian Secret Service

Between the end of the 1960s and the early 1970s Italy experienced the most intense wave of right-wing violence. The massacres perpetrated by neo-fascist groups – 17 people killed by a bomb in the Bank of Agriculture, on 12 December 1969, in Milan; 6 killed on a train in July 1970; 8 killed during a union meeting in Brescia and 12 killed on the train Italicus, near Bologna in 1974 – had been, indeed, the most brutal forms of political violence at a time when it came mainly from the radical right. The repression of right-wing terrorism was so ineffective that – as already recalled – instigators and executants of those crimes are still unknown.

This inefficacy is explained, above all, by the protection that right-wing extremism received from the Italian secret services.[5] The Italian secret services after the Second World War have been described as characterized 'first by lack of accountability to Parliament, second by dependence on the policy decisions and resources of Italy's NATO allies, in particular the United States, and third by a vigorous anti-communism'.[6] In 1964 General De Lorenzo, the head of the military intelligence service, *Servizio Informazioni delle Forze Armata*/SIFAR, was accused of planning a coup d'état and had to resign.

Although reforms were made, the quality of the intelligence services did not improve. Their strategy between the end of the 1960s and the beginning of the 1970s was the so-called 'strategy of tension', that is, the use of the threat of the violent 'opposed extremisms' to induce public demand for 'law and order'. This strategy was carried out mainly by means of a protection of the right-wing groups. According to a study written by a member of the Italian Parliament on the basis of parliamentary acts:

More or less relevant signs of direct action or involvement by the secret services can be singled out in all the trial records referring especially to the most serious crimes of right-wing terrorism, such as the massacre of Piazza Fontana, of Piazza della Loggia, on the train Italicus, at the Bologna railway station, the attempted coup of the Rosa dei venti and Golpe Borghese.[7]

As far as left-wing terrorism is concerned, the Red Brigades – the only left-wing terrorist group active in that period – were still very weak. Until 1974 they were very similar to those dozens of small radical groups, active at the margins of the mass movement of the late 1960s and early 1970s. A report from the Prefect of Milan to the Ministry of the Interior testifies that, already in the year of their foundation, the existence of the Red Brigades was known by the police, but the potential threat they represented was not realized. This report told, in fact, about 'another group, present only in Milan . . . called *Collettivo Politico Metropolitano*. Founded in 1969 by some militants of the extra-parliamentary Left, . . . the group has announced the formation of some nuclei called Red Brigades, to intervene in the big factories'.[8] Until 1974 state reaction against the Red Brigades consisted only of the infiltration of an *agent provocateur* which had brought about, in May 1972, the arrest of two leaders of the organisation. It was indeed in 1974 that the word 'terrorism' appeared for the first time in an official statement of a prime minister to the parliament.[9]

An adequate comment on 1970–74 Italian anti-terrorism policies is that: 'It took the Italian political classes at least five years to alert themselves seriously to the problem of terrorism, in the sense that their initial reactions to it were immobilist, using the events for short term political gains and leaving their sources untouched.'[10] Moreover, the major party derived several advantages from the existence of both right- and left-wing terrorism:

> Since the PCI [Communist Party] was not acceptable (as a legitimate governmental partner) either internally to the DC [Christian Democrats] or externally to Italy's NATO allies, the threat of the authoritarian solution in the shape of neo-fascist terrorism and attempted coups d'état served the purpose of impressing on the minor parties the urgency of not depriving the country of a government at certain times as well as of reinforcing the centrality of the DC. At the same time, the existence of left-wing terrorists, described by themselves as 'communist', 'red' and 'Marxist', enabled the DC to lay suspicion on the attachment of the PCI to liberal democracy, and therefore its suitability for government.[11]

1974–1976: The Creation of Anti-Terrorism Police Units and the First Defeats for Left-Wing Terrorism

This period is characterised by serious defeats for a first wave of terrorist organisations. After 1974 there was a sudden and long decline of right-wing terrorism. Moreover, if the Red Brigades could survive initially because they were too weak to attract a specific response by the state, in 1974 the growing danger they posed became evident with the kidnapping of the judge Sossi, who was kept in a 'people's prison' for 35 days. This action gave a national notoriety to the underground group, and – at the same time – pushed the state to increase its repressive efforts. Two types of state response can be singled out.

On one hand, the response to left-wing terrorism was included in a wider strategy of repression of organized crime. During the 1960s the reformist Centre-left governments had enacted a series of new laws in defence of individual rights. In the same vein, in the early 1970s, a maximum period for incarceration before trial was fixed by the Law of 1 July 1970 n.406; and the possibilities for a judge to parole a defendant (even for those crimes for which arrest was compulsory) were increased by the Law of 15 December 1972 n.773. The improvements in individual rights introduced by late 1960s and early 1970s legislation, however, vanished with the new legislation on organized crime and public order. In 1974 two new laws were approved as a reaction to the growth of organized and violent crimes. The *provedimenti urgenti sulla giustizia penale* ('Urgent measures on criminal law'; decree of 11 April 1974 n.99) increased to eight years the maximum period of preventive detention. The *Nuove norme contro la criminalità* ('New regulation against criminality'; Law of 7 June 1974 n.220) established a *rito per direttissima* – namely, a faster procedure – and increased the sentences for such crimes as armed robbery, extortion, and kidnapping.

The police were given the right to interrogate a defendant, a right which a law of 1969 had reserved for the judges. Two laws passed in 1975 – Law of 18 April 1975 n.110; and Law of 22 May 1975 n.152 (art. 6) – sharpened the legislation on control of arms, munitions, and explosives. The most important law on public order – the Law of 22 May 1975 n.152 (*Disposizioni a tutela dell'ordine pubblico*, or *Legge Reale*) – limited the ability to obtain bail; provided for the search and arrest of suspects without a warrant; allowed suspects to be held for 48 hours without charge; and introduced a sort of preferential treatment for crimes committed by on-duty policemen.

A widely shared comment upon these laws is that they were *norme di facciata* – 'façade norms' – that is, that they aimed merely to reassure public opinion about the growth of violent crime.[12] They did not have any direct effect in the fight against terrorism and, on the contrary, undermined confidence in the security forces.

Positive results in the repression of terrorism were achieved by two specialized structures, founded in 1974: the General Inspectorate for Action against Terrorism (*Ispettorato generale per la lotta contro il terrorismo*) and the Special Group of Judiciary Police (*Nucleo Speciale di Polizia Giudiziaria*) in Turin. In only two years, their activity brought about the dissolution of the Armed Proletarian Nuclei, and the arrest of most leaders of the Red Brigades. According to the testimony by some Red Brigades members, in 1976 fewer than a dozen regular members of the organisation were outside prison.[13] No other underground left-wing group was active in that year.

1977–1982: The 'Emergency' Policies and their Outcomes

Different causes brought about a new wave of left-wing terrorism, only a few months after what seemed to be its final defeat. During this 'second cycle' of left-wing terrorism, state intervention evolved quite atypically. While the dangers posed by the underground organizations were realized from the very beginning, only rare successes followed until the end of the decade. What were the characteristics of the state response in those years? Three aspects will be analyzed: the changes in legislation; the policy of the police apparatus; and the activities of the security forces and the courts.

The 'Emergency' Legislation

As far as legislation is concerned, it was in this period that many specific laws on terrorism were passed. The body of these laws forms the so-called 'Emergency Legislation'. To cope with increasing public order problems, the Law of 8 April 1977 n.533 introduced the prohibition of adopting disguise in public places and the seizure of the headquarters of political groups where arms or explosives were found.[14] Court procedures were also modified in order to respond to several crimes committed by the Red Brigades to intimidate members of juries and defense attorneys. The Law of 7 June 1977 n.296 abolished the maximum limit for preventive detention when a trial was suspended because it was impossible to form the jury or to exercise the defense rights. In the same direction, the Law of 24 March 1978 n.74 modified some rules for the formation of juries.

Special prisons were created with another set of 'emergency' laws. The escape of several terrorists from prison provoked two laws – the Law of 12 January 1977 n.1; and the Law of 20 February 1977 n.450 – which stiffened prison legislation on special permissions to prisoners and measures for surveillance. According to these laws, on 4 May 1977, a decree – signed by the Ministers of the Interior, Defense, and Justice – entrusted a General Office of the Carabinieri with the task of co-ordinating the external and internal security of the penitentiaries. The outcome was the implementation – confirmed on 25 November 1980 – of the so-called *carceri di massima sicurezza* (high-security prisons), where the rules for the treatment of prisoners introduced by the Penitentiary Law of 1975 were suspended. Art. 90 of the same law allowed, in fact, for the suspension of prisoners' rights 'for serious and exceptional motives of order and security'. It was observed, however, that its generalized use for such a long period was a clear breach of the limitation of the application of this article to only 'exceptional' circumstances and short periods.

Moreover, the effectiveness of the special prison system in the fight against terrorism can be questioned. On the one hand, escapes from prisons were prevented. On the other hand, the high security prisons worked – to quote a former member of a terrorist organization – as a '*respirazione bocca a bocca*' ('mouth to mouth resuscitation') for terrorist organizations; 'that is, they gave terrorist organizations, which were in throes of death, the kiss of life.[15] The solidarity produced among the prisoners of the high security system in fact helped a terrorism in crisis to survive.

Increased sentences for terrorist crimes were introduced by two other 'emergency' laws, in 1978 and 1980. Until the kidnapping of the President of the Christian Democratic Party, Aldo Moro, the only law in this direction had been the Law of 10 May 1976 n.342, called 'Repression for offenses against the security of air navigation'. A few weeks after the kidnapping, the Law of 18 May 1978 n.191 introduced the crime of 'kidnapping for terrorist or subversive aims' (art. 289-bis c.p.).

A new 'anti-terrorism' law was approved at the end of 1979, a few days after the left-wing group Front Line had assaulted a school of management and wounded five students and five professors, after a so-called 'proletarian trial'. The Law of 6 February 1980 n.15 introduced the two specific crimes of 'association with the aims of terrorism and subversion of democratic order' (art. 270-bis c.p.) and of 'attack with terrorist or subversive aims' (art 280 c.p.).[16] The aggravating circumstance of 'terrorist or subversive aims' brought about an increase in the sentences of up to 50 per cent of the normal sentences; exclusion from extenuating circumstances and parole; extension up to one third of the maximum time of preventive detention. Preventive detention could in some cases be extended up to ten years and eight months.

Both laws limited citizens' rights. The Law of 1978 lessened the restrictions on searches and telephone tapping and allowed the police to interrogate a suspect without the presence of a defence attorney (art. 225-bis c.p.p.). As far as trials were concerned, the Law stated that a defendant who had been expelled twice from the courtroom could not be admitted again until the end of the trial. Moreover, it became compulsory for landlords to report any guest to the police within 48 hours.

The Anti-Terrorist Law of 1980 introduced the so-called *fermo preventivo* (preventive arrest) allowing police to detain in custody a person who had not committed any crime, if the suspicion existed that he/she might commit one. The Law stated, in fact, that the police could detain in custody persons 'against whom, for their attitudes and in relation with time and place, it appears necessary to verify the existence of behaviours and acts which, even if they do not imply any attempted crime, could nevertheless be oriented to commit such crimes as . . .'.

In general, the a-posteriori judgment on these articles of the two 'anti-terrorism' laws was that the degeneration of citizens' rights was not compensated by any efficiency in the repression of terrorism.

> On one hand, they relied upon the perspective of a consistent sharpening of the sanctions for the socially more stigmatized crimes . . . On the other hand, they relied upon a wider use of the trial for aims of social defence, counting on an increasing limitation of the protection of the defendant's rights, both *vis-à-vis* the judge and, especially, the police.[17]

It was also noticed that the aim of the increase in the possible time period of preventive detention was to *tranquillizzare gli animi* (to tranquillize the mind), 'to satisfy not a desire for "justice" or for "truth", but a need for a scapegoat'.[18]

The decision to increase the sentences was criticized because it aimed at reassuring public opinion, instead of defeating terrorism. The tortuosity and vagueness of the definition of 'police arrest' was criticized as an encouragement for unacceptable activities of inquisition, as opposed to the most fundamental human rights'.[19] Moreover, it was very dubious that increased sentences for terrorist crimes could have any deterrent effect on people with such a high ideological dedication and who had accepted greater risks than long imprisonment. The bimonthly reports by the Minister of the Interior to Parliament about the use of the *'fermo di polizia'* showed in fact that it was useless against terrorism.[20]

Together with repressive measures, the Law of 1980 provided some 'compensations' for the members of underground organizations who collaborated with the judges. These ranged from 'not liable for punishment' to reduced jail sentences of up to 50 per cent with non-application of aggravating circumstances. They were expanded by a new anti-terrorism law in 1982, which provoked praise as well as criticism. Advantages and shortcomings of the 1980 'compensation laws' will be discussed in more detail in the next section.

The Lack of a 'Policy of the Police Apparatus'

Police reactions were also inadequate for a long time. Italian security forces were structurally quite weak. Most Italian prisons were old and overcrowded. The internal police (*guardie di custodia*) were underpaid and very much underqualified. Throughout the 1970s escapes by terrorists were numerous. In 1979 only 10 per cent of the programme for the building of new prisons had been implemented.

Some data about the police will show some reasons for their inefficiency. In 1978 only 11,000 members of a staff of 69,000 people were assigned to the fight against organized crime; 15,000 places were not filled; 50 per cent of all policemen had not gone beyond elementary school (i.e., the first five years of the educational system); training structures were almost non-existent. These conditions were the result of deliberate policy choices:

> The refusal of DC ministers in 1949 to demilitarize the police reflected the view that the major function of the police was that of internal security of the State – the preservation of public order – rather than the prevention and investigation of crime and in these latter fields the police corps (*Corpo delle guardie di pubblica sicurezza*) has remained underdeveloped, lacking both expertise and equipment.[21]

No computerized system of information was available for either the police or the magistrature. The appropriations for the 'technological potentiation and modernization of security forces' was implemented only in 1979.

Moreover, there was a chronic lack of co-ordination both between and within the different police units. The weakness of the Italian police was, in fact, singled out in the 'difficulty of realizing a real co-ordination in the activities of the different units . . .; the difficulty of producing professional expertise outside the logic of special powers.'[22] The two already mentioned police branches built in 1974 to fight terrorism were dissolved in 1976, for reasons unexplained. Some of their functions were later on taken over by the *Ufficio centrale per le investigazioni e le operazioni speciali* (UCIGOS; Central Office for Special Investigations and Operations). When it was created in 1978, however, a lot of the knowledge acquired two years before had already been lost. The same can be said for a new *'Nucleo speciale'*, built by the Carabinieri in the same year.

Only two years later, the basis for a co-ordination of anti-terrorism activities was introduced by the Law of 14 February 1980 n.23, which entrusted the Ministry of the Interior with the co-ordination and unitary direction of police forces as far as order and security were concerned. A year later, the *Nuovo ordinamento per l'amministrazione della pubblica sicurezza* ('New regulation for the management of public security'; Law of 1 April 1981 n.121) set up a Centre for Computerized Information at the Ministry of the Interior. All the information and the data relevant to the protection of order, public security, and prevention and repression of crimes had to be collected, classified and archived there.

It has already been mentioned that the secret services also passed through quite a turbulent period, and the Defense Intelligence Service (*Servizio Informazioni della Difesa*/SID) was dissolved because of the protection given to right-wing terrorism. Only in 1977 were the new services organized, namely the Military Security Information Service (*Servizio informazioni sicurezza militare*, SISMI) for external and military security; and the Democratic Security Information Service (*Servizio informazioni sicurezza democratica*, SISDE) for internal security.

Police and Court Activities during the 'Emergency Period'

One explanation for the state's inefficacy in finding an adequate response to internal terrorism stresses the structural 'unpreparedness' of the Italian police apparatus, and – therefore – its difficulties in coping with a phenomenon which had assumed such dimensions. According to the declaration of Francesco Cossiga – Minister of the Interior during the kidnapping of Aldo Moro – to a parliamentary committee: 'the police could face a few sporadic terrorist episodes, but the State was altogether unprepared for facing terrorist phenomena such as those involved in the Moro case, from the point of view of both the legal system and the repressive apparata.'

This explanation is, however, not satisfactory at explaining the secret services' activities. According to an alternative explanation, in fact, the structural weaknesses had been 'piloted' in order to hamper the repression against the terrorist groups. Those who support this hypothesis point to some national or international groups, which were 'objectively' interested in the survival of terrorism. This hypothesis is supported by evidence and indications of 'deviations' in Italian secret service activities.

A 'deviation' of the newly organized secret services is also more than likely if we take into account the participation of their highest officers, such as the General-in-Chief of the SISMI, Santoviti, and the General-in-

Chief of the SISDE, Grassini, in the Masonic Lodge 'Propaganda 2'.[23] Another three members of the Technical and Operational Committee entrusted with the co-ordination of security force activities during the Moro kidnapping belonged to the same Lodge: the head of the Joint Chiefs of the Defence Staff, Admiral Torrisi; the Chief of the *Guardia di Finanza*, General Giudice; and the Chief of the Joint Chiefs of Staff of the *Guardia di Finanza*, General Lo Prete.

About the ties between 'Propaganda 2' and right-wing terrorism V. Rognoni, Minister of the Interior 1978–82, declared in a recent interview:

> There was an Investigatory Committee of the Parliament, and there were statements by the judges. From the knowledge thus acquired, there is proof of connections between the P2 and black terrorism, in terms of support, protection and instrumental use to reach goals of power and control . . . in order to influence and correct the political process.[24]

More than one book has been written on the many obscure episodes in security force activities during the kidnapping of Aldo Moro, which neither the judges, nor a special parliamentary commission were able to clarify. For instance, many questions remained unanswered about a long series of 'disappearances' of evidence: one of Moro's bags with top secret documents; the records of the 'trial' of Moro conducted by the Red Brigades; some tapes with telephone interceptions made by the police; a film shot by an amateur photographer; the records of some of the meetings of the Technical and Operational Committee of the Ministry of the Interior. No explanation emerged about why the competent authorities did not search some terrorist headquarters – Via Montalcini and Via Gradoli – about which they had been informed before the hostage was killed.

Another episode about which evidence of misconduct of the secret services emerged was the kidnapping of the Christian Democrat (DC) member of the Regional Government of Campania, Ciro Cirillo. According to the investigating judge, a ransom was paid by members of the DC, with the mediation of the secret services and organized crime. One part of the ransom was paid to the Red Brigades and another to the Neapolitan Camorra. In an official report, the President of the Parliamentary Commission for the control of the intelligence services condemned the cases of secret service misconduct during the Cirillo kidnapping.[25]

It would be difficult to deny that 'there is a clear need to inquire into the secret services on the basis of the realistic consideration that these apparata, at least as far as some of their members and sectors were concerned, offered protection for or were directly involved in terrorism'.[26] It has further been suggested that the action of the secret services was engineered by groups acting also within the political parties.[27] Although no evidence supported this hypothesis, until now, it should not be forgotten that the masonic lodge 'Propaganda 2' had important ramifications inside many parties.

The deviation from democratic goals involved only the secret services. The activities of the police forces and the judges remained, everything considered, within their constitutional limits. Nevertheless, in a few cases, there was suspicion of misconduct in the police apparatus. On 28 March 1980 the police killed four members of the Red Brigades, during an attempted arrest in a terrorist headquarters on Via Fracchia, which was judged as at least 'awkward'. In 1984 some members of a special police unit, active during the investigations surrounding the kidnapping of US and NATO Brigadier General James D. Dozier, were charged with torture against a Red Brigades' prisoner and were convicted.

Finally, the jurisprudence of the 'emergency period' also underwent severe criticism. An analysis of the court decisions in trials for terrorism in those years singled out several new trends.[28] Several trials carried out in those years were called *processi indiziari*; that is, based on circumstantial evidence. First of all, extensive use was made of 'collective responsibility' and the 'crime of association'. It was often justified by the difficulties in presenting evidence for individual crimes, but was also criticized as disrespectful of the constitutional principle of a defendant's individual responsibility. Individual responsibility for a crime was often inferred from just one testimony or, in the worst cases, from the ideology of the legal groups an individual had belonged to. The most typical example of a *processo indiziario* is the so-called 7th of April trial, involving more than 200 people coming from various 'autonomous' groups, most of whom were acquitted after several years.[29] After the 'emergency period' was over, concern was also expressed for the often disproportionate increase in the sentences, produced first of all by the vague definition of some crimes (such as, for instance, subversive association, *banda armata*, armed insurrection against the power of the state).

The increasing repression of the legal radical groups, which started after the decline of a wave of youth protest in 1977, produced contradictory results. Conducted to isolate the terrorist organizations, the wave of arrests of the 'autonomous', radical but legal groups produced new recruits for terrorism instead. Many new members of the terrorist organizations were, in fact, members of radical groups who joined a terrorist organization in order to have logistic support while escaping arrest. My data on the evolution of recruitment in left-wing terrorist organizations indicates a big jump in 1979, that is, just when the judiciary and police apparata increased the repression against the semi-legal groups of the so-called 'autonomia', which had survived the decline of the 1977 movement. The following comment on the risks of generalized repression fits the Italian case very well:

> Governments may fail to limit punitive measures to the appropriate target. . . . Ignorant of who the terrorists are – and they are typically a small number – the government is tempted to arrest the opponents it knows and to arrest indiscriminately. Suspects from familiar opposition movements are arrested, interrogated, even held in preventive detention. Few of those caught off guard are terrorists (who are the only ones prepared for repression). The net effect is to promote recruitment into the terrorist organization.[30]

1982–1989: New Anti-Terrorism Policies and the Defeat of the Underground Groups

According to several judgements, terrorism as a political phenomenon was defeated in Italy in the early 1980s. In the already cited interview, former Interior Minister Rognoni recalls: 'I quit [the Ministry] in 1983, after five years, leaving an already concluded experience. Terrorism had been politically defeated.'[31] In this last section, I will try to explain this sudden success of the Italian state, by looking at the characteristics of anti-terrorism policy in the 'post-emergency' period.

The first factor in explaining the defeat of Italian terrorism is the changes in the party system.[32] During the 1970s the level of cohesion inside the government and in the party system was very low. Several indicators of a high degree of conflict within the party system can be given. The 1960s had been the decade of the Centre-left government. The 1970s were the decade of its crisis: 13 governments followed in succession with a wide variety of different formulas, with the participation, the abstention, or the opposition of one or the other of the small laic parties or of the PSI (Italian Socialist Party).

The 1970s were also the decade of premature elections: the first premature closure of the legislature in the history of the Republic was in 1972. The following two legislatures also ended before their normal termination. Early elections were therefore held in 1972, 1976 and 1979. The period of lower efficacy in the action against terrorism coincided with the highest degree of instability in the Italian party system in the entire history of the Republic.

The parties were often divided on the response to be given to the terrorist organizations. For instance, during the kidnapping of Aldo

Moro, bitter controversy developed between the so-called *Fronte della fermezza* ('Front for firmness') – including the Communist Party (PCI) and almost all the DC, against any pact with the 'enemies of democracy' – and the *Fronte della trattativa* ('Front for bargaining') – including mainly the PSI, in favour of a compromise to save the life of the hostage. It was often observed that these different strategies were based on 'selfish' interests of the various parties: the PSI's humanitarian position reflected the smaller party's need to differentiate itself from the two bigger ones; the PCI's position was explained by its search for democratic legitimacy; and the DC position was considered the result of internal conflicts among the different factions.

The kidnapping of Judge D'Urso also risked precipitating a crisis in the government. On this occasion, the request for closure of a special prison was granted to the terrorists after a statement in this sense by one governing party leadership, that of the PSI, against the advice of the DC Minister of the Interior.[33] The climate of that period has been summarized this way:

> The major failings in the response to terrorism have been the deliberate manipulation of organized political violence to satisfy short-term goals – goals that have been predominantly electoral but that have also been concerned with the formation of alliances within and between the parties.[34]

Only in the early 1980s did the party system find a new point of equilibrium, with a retrenched DC, a legitimized PCI, and a PSI more autonomous and with a major power of coalition. It reflected the changes in the electoral strength of the different parties in the second half of the 1970s, when the left-wing parties jumped from 40 per cent in 1972 (with more than 50 per cent for the Centre) to 47.7 per cent in 1976 (with 44.6 per cent for the Centre), results which were confirmed in the following elections of 1979 and 1983. The new situation was reflected in a new stability of government, with laic Prime Ministers, Giovanni Spadolini, PRI, between 1981 and 1982; and Bettino Craxi, PSI from 1983. This new stability favoured the search for an efficient strategy to fight terrorism.

Another explanation for the inefficacy of the state response until 1980 should, however, be added to those already given: most laws passed during the 'emergency' years treated terrorism as organized crime. The peculiarities of terrorism as a political phenomenon were not taken into account. The organizational dynamics and motivational processes going on in an underground group with political aims were not understood.

After the 'emergency' declined, new laws were passed that were able to take advantage of the terrorist organizations' internal crisis.

The first of these laws is the Law of 29 May 1982, n.304, which referred to crimes committed by 31 January 1981.[35] This law expanded the number of cases in which the 1980 law's norms about collaboration could be applied and stated that the 'compensation' had to be proportional to the 'amount' of collaboration and its outcome. In a collaboration that yielded evidence identifying one or more accomplices, sentences between 10 and 12 years substituted for life sentences. Other sentences were reduced by one third and could not exceed 10 years. A further reduction by one third was applied to those who had offered an exceptional contribution leading to the dissolution of a whole terrorist structure. Moreover, those who had already served half of their sentence could be paroled.

The reductions were also extended to those who had not collaborated with the investigations, but had fully confessed their own crimes. In this case, the life sentence was substituted with sentences from 15 to 21 years. Other punishments were reduced by one third and could not exceed 15 years. Merely belonging to a terrorist organization, the aiding and abetting of non-punishable members, and minor crimes related to arms and explosives were declared non-punishable when the defendant abandoned the underground group.

These provisions were criticized as 'anti-constitutional' because they introduced different treatments for the same crimes, with the risk that fake confessions were given in order to improve one's own position or to take revenge against someone else.[36] It was acknowledged, however, that the 'compensations' introduced by this law hastened the crisis within the terrorist organizations. According to former Interior Minister Rognoni, the law was in fact highly recommended by 'many judges, on the basis of a personal professional experience, which gave to them, more than to others, the possibility of observing the increasing crisis of the terrorist in prison, his acknowledgment of the failure of the armed struggle'.[37] According to the data provided by the Minister of Justice, the members of terrorist organizations who took advantage of the 1982 law – within the deadline of 120 days from the publication of the law (a deadline which was extended another 120 days) – have been 389: 78 classified as '*grandi pentiti*' or major repentant; 134 as repentant; and 177 as dissociated.

The 1982 law was, therefore, able to take into account organizational and group dynamics. It was observed that the efficacy of the 'recompense laws' came from their being able to exploit the ongoing crisis of the terrorist organizations. Most of the 30 former members of left-wing terrorist organizations interviewed during a research project of the *Instituto Cattaneo*[38] assessed that there was a widespread awareness of the impending defeat of 'armed struggle' by 1979. Many militants started to feel isolated and to criticize the terrorist organizations they belonged to: 'This organization which is lacerated because it cannot solve its problems, which is at an impasse (. . .) All the people I knew were in prison, those with whom I had started were not there anymore; nobody was there, nothing was there'.[39]

The growing brutality of the terrorist crimes upset the same militants and disgusted many of the members of terrorist organizations, especially some acts of retaliation: for example, the assassination in prison of a very young member accused of being a traitor; or the assassination of two private guards with the sole aim of 'denouncing' the suspected treason of another militant. The temptation to take advantage of the 'repentance' law therefore became stronger and stronger:

> You cannot think that a person who, in the perspective of the building of communist society was ready to undergo long periods of imprisonment or even to die, when he/she realizes that . . . the political defeat is there, can freely and easily accept paying such a high price . . .. When the old ideological categories are abandoned, the indispensable need to start again, to believe, to hope, to work for something new and different arises.[40]

The 'recompense' law of 1979 had been able to exploit the discontent of some of the members and to inflict military defeat on the terrorist organizations. Nevertheless, it also produced unforeseen and undesired side-effects. Many militants in the process of quitting terrorism were in fact compelled to react to the 'treasons' of some of their fellow-comrades by remaining loyal to the organization. As one former militant said: 'No matter how many criticisms there were, on one side there was solidarity, friendship and the necessity of creating a common front in prison, on the other side the lack of a possibility for a political exit from the organization'.[41] These solidarity bonds were, therefore, often strengthened when the only choice was between a complete collaboration with the state – with a corresponding loss of political identity – and loyalty to the friends-comrades. The climate of violence and intimidation inside the 'special prisons' also hampered these processes of quitting the terrorist organizations.

A second characteristic of the anti-terrorism policies of the late 1980s has to be singled out. When the defeat of terrorism became evident, anti-terrorism legislation started to be influenced by a different logic. From 1982 on, there was in fact an increasing awareness that the military defeats of terrorist organizations had to be followed by what was called the 'exit from the emergency'. A very widespread judgment upon the 'emergency laws' was that: 'It became clear that such a continuous erosion of individual rights could not be pursued without breaking the constitutional boundaries'.[42] An attempt was therefore made in the 1980s to repair the considerable damage produced by the 1970s laws, in terms of individual freedom as well as citizen rights *vis-à-vis* the state apparata.

On the other hand, there was the problem of re-integration into society of the hundreds of young people who had been involved in terrorist organizations. In recent years, in fact, a political awareness has grown of the importance of a 'reconciliation'. The institution of the so-called *aree omogenee*, where – on the basis of their own requests – former terrorists could serve their sentence together, created the possibility for this 'political exit' from terrorism. In June 1986 a new law – *Nuove proposte per la difesa dell'ordinamento costituzionale attraverso la dissociazione* (New proposals for the defence of the Constitution through dissociation) – reduced sentences for those who had abandoned the armed struggle without any collaboration or confession.

The implementation of prison reform created the preconditions for re-integrating former terrorists into society, through professional training and, above all, through the use of alternatives to imprisonment, such as home arrest, controlled custody, permission to work outside prisons. Very recently, representatives of many different parties – including some DC members of parliament – are elaborating a proposal for a pardon.

To conclude, it is important to note that, at different times and in different ways – but with only very few exceptions, as far as left-wing terrorism is concerned – most of the former militants of terrorist organizations have acknowledged the failure of their political project and have expressed a new confidence in democracy. I think this should be considered one of the most important lessons from the Italian experience.

Italian Lessons for Europe

Three main lessons emerge from the analysis of the state response to terrorism in the Italian experience:

a) ROLE OF THE SECRET SERVICES. It is usually assumed that a peculiarity of the relations between the democratic state and terrorist organizations is that, because the terrorist organizations, by definition, refuse the rules of the democratic game, the state is – as the main guarantor of these rules – their enemy. The relation between the state and underground groups should, therefore, be a 'zero-sum conflict': the terrorist groups aim to overthrow the democratic institutions; the state acts to defeat terrorism. The Italian experience, especially as far as right-wing terrorism is concerned, shows that it is misleading to consider the state as a unitary body fighting against terrorism. Under certain circumstances, parts of the state apparatus may attempt to exploit the presence of terrorism for their own aims.

This 'objective' interest in the survival of terrorism can produce 'active' support for some terrorist organizations. By their very nature, the secret services are, among the state apparata, the most exposed to infiltration by groups with such 'objective' interests in the survival of terrorist organizations. In this case, the secret services will protect terrorist organizations instead of fighting them. This is more likely to happen with right-wing terrorism, which usually has a very small constituency and uses forms of action – such as massacres with random targets – which are more apt to spread terror. Moreover, protection of terrorist organizations by the internal secret services is more likely to happen in periods of social and political changes, when the élites are divided about the strategies to be implemented in order to control these changes.

b) ANTI-TERRORISM EMERGENCY LEGISLATION. The Italian case has demonstrated that an efficient strategy against terrorism cannot be implemented without a profound knowledge of the way in which terrorist organizations work. The fight against terrorism was not aided, for instance, by those laws which treated terrorism as organized crime. Special powers to police and investigators were not only inefficient as far as the 'military' defeat of terrorism was concerned, but were even dangerous because they reduced the legitimacy of the state and extended the environment in which terrorist organizations could find 'logistic' support. It is also dubious whether increased sentences had deterrent effects for individuals who, like the terrorists, have strong ideological motivations. Better results can be expected instead from those laws which aim to increase knowledge about terrorist organizations and by those laws which exploit this knowledge in order to accelerate a crisis within them. The internal organizational problems of terrorist groups are increased by laws which make it easier for members to quit.

c) THE PROBLEM OF 'RECONCILIATION'. An important lesson to be drawn from the Italian experience is that the fight against terrorism does not end with the military defeat of the terrorist organizations. After the military defeat, the reinsertion into society of those who were involved in the terrorist organizations requires special attention. Reintegration of those who quit underground organizations is aided by interventions which allow former members to maintain a collective identity and to continue to share their bonds of solidarity outside the terrorist organization.

NOTES

1. D. della Porta and M. Rossi, *Cifre crudeli. Bilancio dei terrorismi italiani* (Bologna: Instituto Cattaneo, 1984); idem, 'Il Terrorismi in Italia tra il 1969 e il 1982', in G. Pasquino (ed.), *Il sistema politico italiano* (Bari: La Terza, 1985), pp.418–56.
2. *Il Manifesto*, 5 July 1989.
3. Donatella della Porta, *Il terrorismo in Italia. Le organizzazioni clandestine di sinistra* (Bologna: Il Mulino, 1989).
4. Martha Crenshaw, 'Introduction: Reflections on the effect of terrorism', in Martha Crenshaw (ed.), *Terrorism, Legitimacy and Power: The Consequences of Political Violence* (Middletown, CT: Wesleyan UP, 1982), p.13.
5. On the Italian secret services, see G. De Lutiis, *Storia dei servizi segreti* (Rome: Editori Riuniti, 1984); on secret services and Italian terrorism, see L. Violante, 'Politica della sicurezza, relazioni internationali e terrorismo', in G. Pasquino (ed.), *La prova delle armi* (Bologna: Il Mulino, 1984).
6. Paul Furlong, 'Political Terrorism in Italy: Responses, Reactions and Immobilism', in Juliet Lodge (ed.), *Terrorism: a Challenge to the State* (Oxford: Martin Robertson, 1981), p.83.
7. S. Rodota, 'La risposta dello stato al terrorismo: gli apparati', in Pasquino (ed.), *La prova delle armi*, p.83.
8. Report of the Prefect, Libero Mazza, to the Minister of the Interior, Restivo, Dec. 1970.
9. G. Pasquino, *I soliti ignoti: Gli opposti estremismi nelle analisi dei presidenti del consiglio*. Working paper (Bologna: Instituto Cattaneo, 1988), p.11.
10. Furlong, 'Political Terrorism in Italy', p.77 (note 6).
11. Ibid., p.79.
12. F. Bricola, 'Politica criminale e politica dell'ordine pubblico (a proposit della 1. 22 maggio 1975, no.152, *La questione criminale* 1975; V. Grevi, 'La procedura speciale per i reati commessi in servizio dagli appartenenti alla polizia. Un privilegio non conforme al principio d'equaglianza', *Giurisprudenza costituzionale*, vol.1 (1976); V. Grevi, 'Sistema penale e leggi dell'emergenza: la risposta legislativa al terrorismo', in Pasquino (ed.), *La prova delle armi* (note 5).
13. G.C. Caselli and D. della Porta, 'La storia della Brigate rosse. Strutture organizzative e strategie d'azione', in D. della Porta (ed.), *Terrorismi in Italia* (Bologna: Il Mulino, 1984).
14. For a comment, see L. Ferrajoli, '1977: Ordine pubblico e legislazione eccezionale', *La questione criminale* (1977).
15. Cited in V. Rognoni, *Intervista sul terrorismo*, a cura di G. De Carli (Bari: Laterza, 1989).
16. G.C. Caselli and A. Perduca, 'Terrorismo e reati associativi. Problemi e soluzione giurisprudenziali', *Giurisprudenza italiana*, vol.4 (1982); S. Giambruno, 'Considerazione sulle ultime misure urgenti per la tutela dell'ordine democratico e dellea sicurezza pubblica', *Giustizia penale*, vol.1 (1980); D. Pulitano, 'Misure antiterrorismo. Un primo bilancio', *Democrazia e diritto*, No.1–2 (1981).
17. Grevi, 'Sistema penale e leggi dell'emergenza', p.49 [cited in note 12].
18. Magistratura Democratica, 'Osservazioni sul decreto legge 15 dicembre 1979 n.625 concernente misure urgenti per la tutela dell'ordine democratico e della sicurezza pubblica', *Foro italiano*, vol.5 (1980), p.101.
19. Ibid., p.98.
20. For instance, M. Chiavario, 'Un anno di fermo di polizia nella relazione del Ministro dell'Interno', *La legislazione penale* (1981).
21. Furlong, 'Political Terrorism in Italy', p.81 (note 6).
22. Rodota, p.87 (note 7).
23. Flamigni, *La tela di ragno. Il delitto Moro* (Rome: Edizione associate, 1988).
24. Rognoni, p.51 (note 15).
25. Quoted in ibid., p.127.
26. Rodota, p.83 (note 7).

27. G. Galli, *Storia del partito armato* (Milan: Rizzoli, 1986).
28. See L. De Ruggiero, 'I problemi posti dai processi di terrorismo', in Magistratura Democratica (ed.), *La magistratura di fronte al terrorismo e all'eversione di sinistra* (Milan: F. Angeli, 1982); P. Onorato, 'Processi di terrorismo e inquinamento della giurisdizione', in ibid.
29. See L. Ferrajoli, 'Il caso "7 aprile". Lineamenti di un processo inquisitorio', *Dei delitti e delle pene*, No.1 (1983); G. Palombarini, *7 aprile: Il processo e la storia* (Venice: Arsenale, 1982); G. Scarpari, 'Processo a mezzo stampa: il "7 aprile"', *Quale giustizia*, No.51 (1979); idem. 'La vicenda del "7 aprile"', *Questione giustizia*, No.3 (1982).
30. Crenshaw, 'Introduction', p.19 (note 4).
31. Rognoni, p.174 (note 15).
32. On terrorism and the party system in Italy, see D. della Porta and G. Pasquino, 'Interpretations on Italian left-wing terrorism', in Peter H. Merkl (ed.), *Political Violence and Terrorism: Motifs and Motivations* (Berkeley, CA: Univ. of California Press, 1986), pp.169–90.
33. Rognoni, pp.114–15 (note 15).
34. Furlong, p.86. (note 6)
35. For a comment, see Magistratura democratica, 'Osservazioni sul disegno di legge'.
36. For the scientific debate on 'compensation laws', see A. Bernardi, 'Dissociazione e collaborazione nei delitti con finalita di terrorismo', *Questione Giustizia* (1982); R. Bertoni, 'La legge sui "pentiti". Una prima valutazione d'insieme', *Giustizia Penale*, Vol.2 (1982); G.C. Caselli, 'La questione dei pentiti', *Quaderni della giustizia*, No.4 (1981); G. Chelazzi, *La dissociazione dal terrorismo* (Milan: Giuffre, 1981); D. Croce, 'La legge sui pentiti', *Quaderni della giustizia*, No.8 (1982); G. Mosconi, 'Lo sterotipo del terrorista pentito. Natura e funzione in relazione al decorso legislativo', *Critica del diritto*, No.25–26 (1982); G. Salvini, 'Riflessioni su gestione dei processi per reati di terrorismo e sulle nuovi disposizioni in tema di dissociazione dalla lotta armata', *Giustizia penale*, Vol.3 (1982); G. Salvini, *La legge sui terroristi pentiti. Un primo bilancio* (Milan: Unicopli, 1983).
37. Rognoni, p.96 (note 15).
38. See D. della Porta, 'Recruitment Processes in Clandestine Political Organizations. Italian Left-Wing Terrorism', in S. Tarrow, B. Klandermans and H. Kriesi (eds.), *From Structure to Action* (NY: John Jay Press, 1988); G. De Lutiis, *Moventi e motivazioni della dissociazione*. Working paper (Bologna: Instituto Cattaneo, 1988).
39. Interview with A.S., p.54.
40. Interview with I.R., pp.59–60.
41. Interview with A.B., p.120.
42. Grevi, 'Sistema penale e leggi dell'emergenza', p.50 [cited in note 12].

United Kingdom: The United Kingdom Response to Terrorism

DAVID BONNER

This essay examines, from a lawyer's perspective, the United Kingdom's response to terrorism, particularly in respect of security legislation, policy, and anti-terrorist personnel. Most contemporary British experience with terrorism has been connected with Northern Ireland and it is this that has shaped most significantly the government response. The primary legal measures taken have been to increase investigative and coercive powers of the security forces, to modify judicial procedure in Northern Ireland, to create new criminal offences, to enable UK courts to try certain offences committed abroad, and to limit the scope of the 'political offence' exception to extradition. Resort has also been made to extra-judicial, executive processes. The article also describes measures taken in the economic, political, security and intelligence, prison and media spheres, as well as the organisation of specialized anti-terrorist units and the anti-terrorist bureaucracy in Great Britain and Northern Ireland. Finally, the article assesses both the acceptability and the effectiveness of the anti-terrorist measures surveyed and draws three lessons for Europe after 1992: the importance of the rule of law, a preference for the criminal process in dealing with suspected terrorists, and the need for closer co-operation between nations.

To set matters in proper context, it is appropriate first to set out some key characteristics of the constitutional and legal orders of the entity under study. The United Kingdom (UK) consists of the mainland, known as Great Britain (consisting of England, Wales and Scotland), and of Northern Ireland, consisting of the six counties in the north-eastern corner of the island of Ireland. Until 1922 the whole island formed part of the United Kingdom, but the remaining 26 counties now form the Republic of Ireland, one of the United Kingdom's partners in the European Community. The Republic's constitution lays claim to Northern Ireland as part of its national territory, but its government has often recognised, most recently in the Anglo-Irish Agreement (1985),[1] that such unity can only be attained by peaceful persuasion and with the consent of a majority of the people of Northern Ireland, a majority at present being in favour of continued union with Great Britain as an integral part of the United Kingdom.

The United Kingdom is a unitary state with a parliament whose legislative power is, legally speaking, unfettered, since there is no over-riding, written constitution limiting its powers, and no power in the courts to invalidate an Act of parliament. In practice, a government with a majority in the House of Commons is able to dominate the legislative output of parliament. Executive dominance (an 'elective dictatorship') is a central feature of the constitutional order. Power is limited by public opinion in this liberal democracy so that values considered fundamental by the polity are respected, and the United Kingdom is party to such international human rights instruments as the European Convention on Human Rights and the United Nations' International Covenant on Civil and Political Rights. These constitute yardsticks against which to measure the acceptability in a liberal democracy of anti-terrorist laws and policies.

Although a unitary rather than a federal state, the law and legal system are not uniform across the United Kingdom. Scotland has its own legal system, and for many years, Northern Ireland had its own devolved parliament, and its laws are somewhat different from those in England and Wales and those in Scotland. However, for the purpose of the security legislation examined in this article, the real division is between Great Britain, on the one hand, and Northern Ireland, on the other, with the more extreme departures from the norm applying only in Northern Ireland, reflecting the greater terrorist threat there. Within Great Britain, the various police forces (43 in England and Wales alone), some with special units, constitute the anti-terrorist personnel. Within Northern Ireland, its police force, the Royal Ulster Constabulary (RUC), with paramilitary equipment and special units, is in charge of operations, assisted particularly in border areas (e.g., the so-called 'bandit country' of South Armagh) by British Army units (e.g., the Special Air Service or SAS), some of which are themselves accused of perpetrating a form of terrorism.[2]

National and International Challenges in the Field of Terrorism

Since 1968 the United Kingdom has experienced several terrorist challenges which have prompted and moulded its response. In responding, it has also been able to draw on its experience with 'terrorist' emergencies in its withdrawal from colonial empire and with earlier violent manifestations of the troubled relationship between Britain and Ireland.

International Terrorism

'International terrorism' is here taken to cover political terrorism which is '(i) directed at foreigners or foreign targets; (ii) concerted by governments or factions of more than one state; or (iii) aimed at influencing the policies of a foreign government'.[3] Like its European partners, the United

Kingdom has been victim of acts of international terrorism, involving the
hijacking and destruction of its aircraft abroad, the kidnapping and killing
of its nationals abroad, and bombings and assassinations and attempted
assassinations in the United Kingdom by foreign terrorist groups, mostly
connected with the Middle East.[4] Some of this terrorism has been state-
sponsored (e.g., by Syria). In other cases, foreign governments (e.g.,
Libya, Iran) have liquidated or sought to liquidate expatriate opponents
of the regime living in the United Kingdom. Certain ethnic groups settled
in the United Kingdom (e.g., Sikhs) have used terrorist methods to
promote attention for causes in their homeland. Much of this terrorism
has been combated by the police, albeit with special units, deploying the
ordinary law of the land, although since 1984 special powers of arrest and
extended detention without charge, once applicable only to terrorism
connected with Northern Ireland affairs, have also been deployed. Some
international terrorist suspects have been tried in the United Kingdom for
criminal offences. Others have been deported under the security powers
in the Immigration Act 1971. In legislative terms, the main result of
international terrorism has been seen in the realm of aviation security and
legislative implementation of international agreements designed to deal
with hijacking and interference with aircraft, in the provisions with
respect to the taking of hostages and in the narrowing of the 'political
offence' exception to extradition.

Domestic Terrorism Not Concerned With Northern Ireland Affairs

There have also been terrorist acts perpetrated by Scottish and Welsh
nationalists, by ultra-right, racist, neo-Fascist groups, by anarchists such
as the Angry Brigade, and in the form of bombings, particularly
incendiary bombings of stores, and food contamination, by extreme
fringe elements among campaigners for animal welfare. Apart from the
creation of a specific 'food terrorism' offence in the Public Order Act
1986,[5] all such terrorism has been met using the ordinary law. In
particular, it should be noted that the special anti-terrorist powers of
arrest and extended detention without charge are expressly stated not to
apply in respect of acts of terrorism connected solely with the affairs of the
United Kingdom or any part thereof other than Northern Ireland.[6]

Terrorism Connected With Northern Ireland

The principal terrorist threat which has shaped the United Kingdom
response since 1968 has been terrorism connected with Northern Ireland
affairs, that is to say, connected with the question whether Northern
Ireland should remain part of the United Kingdom or should rather be
detached to form part of an all-Ireland socialist republic. As the most

significant shaping force, this threat needs to be examined in more detail so that any limitations of the United Kingdom experience in terms of national lessons for Europe can properly be appreciated.

This terrorism is perpetrated by paramilitary groups on both sides of a sectarian divide, in a context in which religious affiliation and political loyalties coincide: by Republicans/Nationalists (Catholics), on the one side, and by Loyalists/Unionists (Protestants) on the other. The Republican terrorist campaign has manifested itself in bombings on the mainland since 1972, the most spectacular being the Brighton bombing in October 1984, designed to eliminate the Prime Minister and many of her Cabinet, and in attacks on British diplomats, service personnel and military installations on the Continent. The February 1991 missile attack on 10 Downing Street while John Major's Cabinet was in session at the height of the Gulf War appears to have been a variant on the theme of targeting the highest level of government on the mainland. Loyalist mainland activity has primarily been confined to the acquisition of weaponry from sympathisers in Scotland. Protestant paramilitaries have crossed the border and perpetrated several terrorist attacks in the Republic of Ireland. Northern Ireland, however, has borne the brunt of the violence. Some 3,000 people have been killed there in the troubles since 1969.

It should be recalled that the population of Northern Ireland is only some 1.5 million. An equivalent impact for other countries can be gauged by the simple device of multiplying the deaths figure by the multiple obtained by dividing the particular country's population by that of Northern Ireland. The violence in Northern Ireland is a complex of insurgent guerrilla warfare (some of it irredentist), sectarian killings and attacks, inter- and intra-factional conflicts within both communities, knee-cappings, punishment-shootings and other modes of enforcing discipline both amongst members of the paramilitary groups and against deviants (e.g., drug dealers, petty criminals or sex offenders) in the communities dominated by the paramilitaries, and activity of more traditional criminal provenance (e.g., bank robberies, kidnappings and protection rackets).

On the Republican/Nationalist side, the main terrorist group is the Irish Republican Army (IRA), which can trace a history of political violence aimed at severing the link with Britain back into the mid-nineteenth century.[7] Practically moribund militarily in 1969, following the abject failure of its 1956-62 armed campaign to drive the British from Ulster, it re-emerged in the sectarian violence accompanying the political upheaval set in train by the Civil Rights movement, principally as a defender of Catholics against sectarian attacks. It split, late in 1969, into two 'wings': the Official IRA, favouring primarily a non-sectarian political approach to the status of the Province, and the Provisional IRA, firmly dedicated to the traditional physical force approach. But both groups have used violence for political ends.

Since 1972, however, apart from feuds in the mid-1970s with the Provisionals and the Irish National Liberation Army (INLA), another breakaway group, the Official IRA moved away from physical force into an apparently exclusively political approach, recognising Northern Ireland institutions and contesting elections, finding expression first in Republican Clubs (Official Sinn Fein), later in the Workers Party. Nevertheless, the Official IRA, as such, remains a proscribed organisation.

The main Republican/Nationalist group, the Provisional IRA (PIRA), has proved the most significant threat to the stability of the United Kingdom. Its violence, sometimes apparently mindless or gratuitous, is clearly aimed at producing a 'war weariness' among electorate and government in Great Britain, enhancing support for a British withdrawal from Northern Ireland. In seeking ultimately an all-Ireland socialist republic of Gaelic hue, unitary rather than federal, it also threatens the constitutional and governmental structure of the Republic of Ireland, whose government it perceives as illegitimate. In 1975 it became dominated by a Northern Ireland leadership and, since 1983, it has operated, with its political 'front', Provisional Sinn Fein (hereinafter 'Sinn Fein'), a dual strategy of seeking its all-Ireland socialist republic through 'armed struggle' (the Armalite in one hand), contesting elections, taking seats at local government level in both parts of Ireland, and being willing to take seats at parliamentary level in the Republic but not in the United Kingdom (the ballot box in the other hand). Dropping the traditional policy of abstentionism in relation to the Republic's Parliament, the Dail, provoked a further split between traditional and modernist Republicanism, with the formation of a minor political group of traditionalists, Republican Sinn Fein, which so far appears to have no military wing.

Militarily, PIRA is well armed and equipped to carry on its 'war of national liberation'. It is an experienced terrorist organisation. Some 1,000 strong in the 1970s, in the mid-1980s its strength is estimated at some 250–300 strong, but it is able to call on a wider range of support of varying degrees (e.g., turning a blind eye), some willing, some intimidated. It was initially organised along conventional army lines of brigades and companies, but changes were made as this proved increasingly cumbersome and insecure, and it now appears to be a mixture of 'Companies' and so-called Active Service Units (ASUs). 'Company' work consists mainly of 'policing' operations in the ghettoes dominated by PIRA. The trained ASUs carry out operations and attacks in Northern Ireland, in Great Britain and on the Continent. Conscious of the need for security, the ASUs operate a cell system, to minimise damage if operatives are caught. PIRA also trains its activists in techniques of resisting interrogation. It deploys a security unit to search out and execute informers, and has successfully operated an amnesty system for those informers who voluntarily disclose their activities.

Financially, PIRA has a strong base. Although it may not possess as many Swiss bank accounts as the Palestinian Liberation Organisation, whose financial status and impact has been compared to that of a multinational corporation, PIRA does have protection rackets and sophisticated money laundering operations more reminiscent of the Mafia than an avowedly Marxist organisation.[8] Its annual income is variously estimated at between £3 and £7 million Sterling, generated, mainly in Northern Ireland, from robbery, extortion, defrauding government and the European Community, from direct collections and subscriptions, and from a variety of business operations (cheap fare taxis in West Belfast, social clubs, video shops) of varying degrees of legitimacy, which also offer opportunities for 'laundering' money. 'Laundering' is here used to denote the process whereby proceeds and profits from criminal enterprises are converted through business and financial institutions into respectable funds, properties and accounts. Some money and materials have come from Libya. Irish-American groups are another source of finance and weaponry, now reduced because of inter-governmental co-operation and a strong line from the appropriate federal authorities and agencies.

The resources are used to support PIRA's ASUs and their dependents, and to fund the operations of Sinn Fein.[9] The latter is said now to take the lion's share of resources. One British Army assessment is that PIRA can be damaged but not defeated militarily: there is no purely military solution.

A smaller Republican/Nationalist terrorist group has already been mentioned: the Irish National Liberation Army (INLA), a proscribed organisation since it burst upon the world stage with its assassination of the Conservative Party spokesman on Northern Ireland, Airey Neave MP, at the House of Commons in 1979. INLA, and its political support, the Irish Republican Socialist Party (IRSP), broke away from the Official IRA. Their firm commitment to violent struggle also attracted from the Provisionals recruits more committed to physical force than to the political approach. The group has been much weakened by the 'supergrass' system and the murderous internal feuding that followed it.[10]

Several terrorist paramilitary groups exist on the Unionist/Loyalist side of the politico-religious divide. The term, Loyalist, may seem a strange one for groups, some of which are prepared to use violence to resist the policies of the elected government. The loyalty of such groups is not to the United Kingdom government *per se*, but only to such governments and policies as maintain the status of Protestant Ulster as part of the United Kingdom, and the term has thus 'been associated with Protestants who have opposed concessions to the Catholic minority, condemned links between Northern Ireland and the Irish Republic, and resisted Westminster's attempts to enforce political change'.[11]

The Ulster Volunteer Force (UVF), sometimes known as the 'secret protestant army',[12] is an illegal, paramilitary organisation, briefly engaged also in political activity in the mid-1970s, which violently opposed concessions by a moderate Ulster government to Catholics, and which, over the course of the troubles since 1968, has carried out sectarian murders (so-called anti-IRA action) and committed robberies and bombings, including one in Scotland. The Red Hand Commando is apparently a violent offshoot of the UVF.

The Ulster Freedom Fighters (UFF) similarly carry out sectarian attacks as anti-IRA measures. The UFF is either an offshoot of or a 'flag of convenience' for the legal [proscribed in N. Ireland since Aug. 1992, eds.] paramilitary group, the Ulster Defence Association (UDA), enabling it to be involved in but to disown terrorist activity. The UDA, a predominantly working-class movement, began in 1971 as 'a co-ordinating body for the great variety of loyalist vigilante groups' set up to defend Protestant areas against attack.[13] Politically it has expressed interest in an independent Northern Ireland as well as more traditional calls for devolved government within the United Kingdom. It played a part in some politically motivated strikes, one of which brought down the Northern Ireland Executive, wherein power was shared between Catholics and Protestants. It has facets of a political organisation but also those of a Protestant counter-terror body, ready to take the war to the terrorists.

Although there have been violent clashes with the security forces, Loyalist violence has rather been directed against Catholics. Loyalist groups seem well equipped in terms of weaponry. They raise finance through protection rackets, some involving apparently *bona fide* security firms, the operation of cheap fare taxis in working class, Protestant areas of Belfast, and a variety of tax frauds connected with the construction industry. There is some evidence of collusion between Republican and Loyalist groups over demarcating their respective spheres of influence and of cash transactions between them.[14]

There is recent evidence of subsidised Loyalist arms purchases from abroad, in terms of a South African connection, involving Ulster Resistance, an extreme loyalist group set up to oppose the Anglo-Irish Agreement.[15] Fears are sometimes expressed of links between paramilitary groups and some members of the predominantly Protestant security forces, particularly the Ulster Defence Regiment [renamed in 1992 the Royal Irish Regiment, eds.], but clearly the authorities have not been slow to crack down hard on the activities of Loyalist paramilitaries.

In 1978 the European Court of Human Rights rejected a claim of a policy of politico-religious discrimination in the operation of internment without trial; the disparity in treatment resulted from the then inability of the police to operate in certain Republican areas.[16] Although there may be shadowy contacts between members of Protestant paramilitary groups and members of legitimate Unionist political parties, there is no analogue of the relationship between Sinn Fein and PIRA.[17]

While obviously important, the amount of money produced for paramilitary groups in Northern Ireland and the scale of money laundering involved are not the only points of concern. There is also their socio-economic involvement in the community (as employer, purveyor of cheap transport or leisure facilities, a vigilante force dealing with other criminal elements), which may make them a more acceptable part of the society they have set out to destabilise,[18] perhaps being seen as more efficient or legitimate than the agencies of the state which ostensibly governs the areas concerned. Each group is rooted in its respective community and shares its traditional fears, concerns and political aspirations. They have a permanence transcending the membership at any given time, and there seems a cultural permanence with little shortage of new recruits or leaders to replace those imprisoned.[19]

This suggests that only a political settlement acceptable to the vast majority of both communities in Northern Ireland can hope to bring lasting peace and stability. Security laws and policies can only assist in holding the ring, in containing violence at the minimum level possible. It is important to ensure that, so far as is possible, the existence and application of such laws and policies does not retard the attainment of a political solution by exacerbating tension between the security forces and the community, increasing suspicion of government and authority, and increasing political or material support for the terrorists. Possible short-term effectiveness of a policy (e.g., internment without trial) may have to be traded off against acceptability or longer-term damage to the overall political strategy. Moreover, one must remember that one does not save the liberal state from terrorism by trampling roughshod on its most precious values and postulates; that may be to change the nature of the state for the worse.

Since PIRA is the most significant group, it will be used throughout as an example of how particular powers and policies work. But that is not to imply that Loyalist terrorism is any less evil or that the powers are not used against Loyalist groups.

The Response of the Government and Society

The Legal Measures Taken

Since 1968 a legislative response to the problems posed by terrorism has been to enhance the security forces' investigative and coercive powers (inevitably at some cost to civil liberties), to modify the criminal trial process in Northern Ireland, to create new criminal offences, to enable United Kingdom courts to try certain offences committed abroad, and, in certain respects, to limit the scope of the 'political offence' exception to extradition.

The key anti-terrorist powers are found in the Prevention of Terrorism (Temporary Provisions) legislation, which is applicable (generally speaking) throughout the UK. First enacted in 1974, and subject initially to six-monthly, later annual renewal by Parliament, the 1989 version (hereinafter 'PTA') came into force on 22 March of that year.[20] The more extreme measures applicable to Northern Ireland are now found in the Northern Ireland (Emergency Provisions) Act 1991 (hereinafter 'NIEPA 1991').[21] Note two key features of this security legislation: (i) a wider definition of terrorism than that deployed by Alex Schmid (in this legislation, terrorism means the use of violence for political ends, including any use of violence for the purpose of putting the public or a section thereof in fear); (ii) that the main thrust of the response is to treat terrorist acts purely as another species of crime, its perpetrators as criminals rather than political offenders/'freedom fighters'/soldiers/prisoners of war.

The aim is to deal with such acts so far as possible through a criminal justice process, albeit a process somewhat modified to make it respond better to problems posed for it by the secret nature of terrorist groups and their ability to intimidate the community, witnesses or jurors. However, where it is perceived that a criminal process cannot work – for example, because certain evidence cannot be disclosed in court for fear of prejudicing intelligence networks, agents or informers – resort has been had to a variety of extra-judicial, non-court-oriented executive processes (deportation, exclusion from all or part of the UK, internment without trial). At this point in particular in the security response, especially with respect to terrorism connected with Northern Ireland affairs, there is an increasing danger of marked conflict between the political response and the security measures.

Key facets of the anti-terrorist legislation, which operate in addition to public awareness measures and intelligence gathering and analysis, warrant closer examination.

(a) Proscription: Certain groups, including the IRA, are proscribed/ banned organisations. Membership or professed membership are serious criminal offences. So are professions of support, for instance, organising a meeting in support of the IRA or parading in public to show support for it.[22] The rationale of these measures is largely presentational rather than practical: to enshrine in law public abhorrence at the methods used by such groups to achieve political ends in a liberal democracy. Neither members nor supporters of such groups can be directly heard on the broadcasting media, although their words can be reported there as well as in the press. This is an odd, arguably counter-productive and unjustifiable restriction on the public's right to know its enemy, on the polity's 'oxygen of information'. When tested in British courts as an unlawful interference with the broacasters' legal duty of impartiality, it was held valid.[23] A challenge in Northern Ireland, that it was void because of unconstitutional political discrimination also failed. It may well not breach the guarantee of freedom of expression in the European Convention on Human Rights.[24]

(b) Stop, Question and Search in Northern Ireland: The security forces may stop any person or vehicle and question any person with respect to his identity and movements and what he knows about any recent explosion or other life-endangering incident.[25] There are powers of random search of persons and vehicles in public places for munitions. Searches of houses for munitions require reasonable suspicion, other property not even suspicion and neither need prior judicial approval.[26]

(c) Attacking Terrorist Finances and Material Assistance for Terrorism: Steps have been taken to hamper the financing of terrorism. The steps somewhat parallel those with respect to drug trafficking, thereby emphasising by association the evil criminality of terrorism and aid to it. Much of PIRA's money is laundered through banks, at home and abroad, and through legitimate/quasi-legitimate businesses, so the steps go beyond penalising simple fundraising or supply. These steps include: requiring security firms in Northern Ireland to be licensed by the Secretary of State;[27] releasing persons (e.g., bank officials, accountants) from their legal obligation of confidence where money is thought to be for terrorist groups/purposes;[28] creating several offences in connection with possession of or dealing with terrorist money;[29] so structuring these

offences as to encourage the giving of information to the authorities about money handled that a person believes may be terrorist money, and so as to facilitate entrapment exercises or 'follow the chain' investigative operations.[30]

No doubt in order to encourage such co-operation, as well as to deter offenders by making conviction more likely, the threshold of criminal liability, as compared with comparable offences under the Drug Trafficking Act 1986,[31] is lower, and, with respect to some offences, the onus of proof with respect to a 'guilty mind' is passed to the defence.[32] The authorities can also use the new powers of terrorist investigation examined below. In addition to the usual criminal penalties, the courts can order the forfeiture of money or other property held for prohibited purposes, and can restrain dealing in it when proceedings are imminent, so as, for example, to prevent it being moved out of the country.[33] The government also hopes to conclude reciprocal agreement so that courts abroad can enforce UK orders against monies in the foreign jurisdiction, and so that orders of foreign courts can be enforced in the UK against terrorist monies/properties in the UK.[34]

(d) New Powers of Terrorist Investigation: The police have new powers to carry out a terrorist investigation which enable access to material relevant to the investigation held even by innocent third parties, for example, banks, accountants, lawyers or journalists.[35] 'Terrorist investigation' is defined widely so as to embrace not only the financial aspect of terrorism, although that is likely to be a prime target of these powers, but also its political support, physical force or operational dimensions. The material sought may well be confidential material or have been acquired to further another public interest (e.g., journalistic material and the public's right to know). Access to it usually involves a judge deciding whether it is in the public interest that confidentiality be overridden and material (e.g., details of bank accounts or financial transactions) be produced. In emergency, a senior police officer can authorise access.[36] In Northern Ireland, for investigations into a financial/material assistance offence, access may instead be authorised by the Secretary of State when an application to a judicial authority would be likely to prejudice the capability of RUC members to investigate financial assistance offences or otherwise prejudice the safety of, or of persons in, Northern Ireland.[37] It is to be hoped that use of such a power to bypass the safeguard of independent judicial scrutiny of applications to interfere with privacy and confidentiality will be rare. For terrorism connected with Northern Ireland affairs, the police have been able to use the threat of liability for the offence of failing to disclose information about terrorism, as a means

to 'persuade' the media to hand over untransmitted film without recourse to this judicial process.[38]

(e) Wider Powers of Arrest and Extended Detention Without a Criminal Charge Being Brought Against the Suspect: By 'wider' is here meant wider than the powers applicable to investigating other serious non-terrorist criminal offences.[39] Persons can come into police detention in two ways: (i) through an arrest anywhere in the UK on reasonable cause to suspect that the person is or has been concerned in the commission, preparation or instigation of acts of terrorism;[40] (ii) after being stopped at a port/ airport, generally when travelling to Great Britain from any part of Ireland or leaving Britain to go there.[41] There is no immigration control because the UK and Ireland form a Common Travel Area, which predates and is independent of the EC regime of free movement. Until 1974 there were no border/frontier controls on the movement of people between the UK and Ireland. Police at the port/airport have a power of random examination of travellers to see if any might be terrorists.[42]

The powers apply to terrorism connected with Northern Ireland affairs and to terrorism of any other description except acts connected solely with the affairs of the United Kingdom or any part thereof other than Northern Ireland, the second category commonly (but perhaps mistakenly) taken to confine the powers to 'international terrorism'.[43] In Great Britain the powers are still more extensively used in respect of Northern Irish than international terrorism, and in Northern Ireland appear exclusively used against that former category.[44] A person arrested or who is stopped and examined can be held for up to 48 hours on police authorisation.[45] That detention can be extended by up to a further five days (i.e., maximum of seven in all) with the approval of a Secretary of State.[46]

The European Court of Human Rights held in *Brogan v. United Kingdom*[47] that detention in excess of four days without the person being brought before a judicial officer breached Art.5(3). That Article demands that detained persons be brought 'promptly' before such an officer. Compliance with the Convention could be achieved simply by transferring the decision to extend detention to a High Court Judge, subject to procedures designed to prevent the disclosure to the suspect of information prejudicial to the safety or security of intelligence operatives, networks or informants. However, the Government has instead derogated from its obligations under the Convention because of a public emergency, that is, has made a public admission that a public emergency prevents compliance with the Convention.[48] A public emergency within the meaning of the Convention no doubt exists, but it is difficult to see that its exigencies require exclusion of the judiciary. The Government should have taken the judicial route to ensure compliance and inject an element of independence into a process which deprives terrorist suspects of their liberty to a greater extent than persons suspected of other serious criminal offences. Moreover, the power of arrest, and that of examination at the ports beyond one hour, should require reasonable suspicion linking the person with a specific and serious terrorist type offence.[49]

Extended detention serves several purposes: holding a suspect in safe custody pending the checking of alibis, the result of forensic tests, the translation of documents, communicating with other police forces. A prime purpose of extended detention is to enable proper questioning of the suspect in order to gain evidence of involvement in terrorism, sufficient to prefer a criminal charge.[50] The vast majority of persons detained are released without further proceedings, although the 'success rate' for the authorities is significantly higher in Northern Ireland.[51] The power is especially important there, because of local difficulties of gathering evidence by normal police methods. Witnesses able to point to the guilt of particular persons will not appear in court for fear of the consequences for themselves and their families. So in Northern Ireland there is a heavy reliance on the obtaining of confessions from suspects to be the only or the main evidence against them at their criminal trial.[52] There has been much concern about interrogation practices there in the period under study, with the European Court of Human Rights condemning practices of the British Army in 1971 as inhuman and degrading treatment violative of Art.3 of the Convention,[53] and evidence of serious physical abuse of suspects by RUC detectives later in the 1970s.[54] Enhanced supervision and other changes initially reduced the incidence of allegations of abuse, but they have recently increased.[55]

(f) A Choice of Process to Deploy Against a Terrorist Suspect: Criminal Charge or Some Extra-Judicial Executive Process: 1. *Criminal Charge*. There is no specific offence 'terrorism'. Rather, terrorists commit ordinary, serious criminal offences like murder or causing explosions. As we have seen, there are various special offences of support of such groups and handling their property. In Great Britain terrorists are tried in the ordinary criminal trial process, although there will be extra security arrangements in and around the court building. In Northern Ireland terrorist trials take place without a jury – trial by a single judge in so-called 'Diplock Courts'.[56] This is done for fear of intimidation of jurors and because partisan jurors might produce perverse acquittals. It has been established that a prime purpose of arrest and detention was to secure confessions. These are more readily admissible in terrorist trials in

Northern Ireland than elsewhere in the UK, but only if the prosecution establishes that no torture, inhuman or degrading treatment and no violence or threat of violence was used to obtain the confession.[57] The trial judge also has a discretion to exclude evidence not so obtained if he considers it would be in the interests of justice to do so.[58] Diplock trials have relied heavily on confessions for convictions; often the real trial is about what happened in the police interrogation centre to produce the confession.

In the early 1980s significant use was also made of accomplice/'supergrass'/converted terrorist testimony (cf. Italy). That strategy was initially successful with many convictions and undoubtedly hurt terrorist organisations. Later trials saw judges less happy with the quality of the evidence. Neither the Appeal Court nor the Government, through legislation, have altered the rule that permits the conviction of the accused on the uncorroborated testimony of an accomplice. The traditional rule, that the arbiter of fact must be warned that to do so may be dangerous, applies in Northern Ireland as in England and Wales, but in Northern Ireland this in effect merely requires the trial judge to warn himself to take the utmost care in assessing the evidence and drawing inferences from it.

The 'supergrass' strategy, now apparently at an end, may ultimately have been detrimental, further eroding public confidence in the administration of justice in Northern Ireland.[59] Dissatisfaction with trial by judge alone is quite evident in many quarters, and some responsible bodies and commentators would prefer to see collegiate (preferably three-judge) trial to increase public confidence and make for better decision-making.[60] The burdens involved are too great for one man, however much a man of integrity and devotion to duty. There have also been calls for a return to jury trial, with safeguards to protect jurors against intimidation.[61] It has been doubted whether the proposed measures would provide sufficient protection.[62]

Executive, non-court-oriented, extrajudicial processes. One can identify four processes used in the last two decades, not all of which are currently available:

A.   with respect to aliens, refusal of entry to the United Kingdom or deportation from it under the immigration laws on national security grounds, a process used mainly against international terrorist suspects (e.g., Iranians in the wake of Ayatollah Khomeini's 'sentence' on Salman Rushdie),[63] although it could be used against some Irish citizens suspected of IRA terrorism;

B.   exclusion from the UK of Irish citizens under the anti-terrorist
     legislation as suspected IRA terrorists.[64]
C.   exclusion from Great Britain under that legislation of British
     citizens connected with Northern Ireland as suspected IRA/
     Loyalist terrorists, a form of internal exile;[65]
D.   the internment without trial of terrorist suspects, a process
     only used in Northern Ireland (1971–75) and now in abeyance.
     In the absence of a public emergency threatening the life of
     the nation within the meaning of Art.15, internment without
     trial violates Art.5 of the European Human Rights Conven-
     tion.[56]

These processes can clearly be effective in removing terrorists from
circulation in a particular community. So too can summary executions,
which would clearly be abhorrent and inappropriate in a liberal
democracy. But while less drastic and more acceptable than that
draconian alternative, all of these processes are less satisfactory than a
criminal justice process because they involve varying degrees of
interference with an individual without being seen to prove anything
against him. Even when decisions are based on good intelligence from the
police and security forces, that may well fall short of establishing proof of
that person's guilt of a serious criminal offence. Nonetheless, particularly
in straitened times, the state may well feel it better to be safe than sorry.
The processes might be better perceived were they subject to binding
review by a judicial body, rather than merely to reference to an adviser or
advisers. But it is surely arguable that exclusion of citizens from one part
of a *United Kingdom* is counter-productive by emphasising Northern
Ireland as a place apart to which the Government is less committed than it
is to Great Britain; in other words, that the solution has become part of
the problem, contributing further to the suspicion and division that fuels
the conflict. That this was the case with internment without trial (which
had been used in a 'political' manner)[67] was eventually conceded and that
process was abandoned in 1975.[68] Calls for its reintroduction on a
selective, limited basis have been resisted on the grounds that it would
alienate a significant sector of the community in Northern Ireland and
that any further appearance of repression might increase the flow of funds
from sympathisers abroad.

*(g) Extradition Arrangements and Extraterritorial Jurisdiction of United
Kingdom Courts*: United Kingdom extradition law is complicated in that
it is governed by legislative, judicial and administrative arrangements
differing according to whether the state seeking the return of the fugitive

offender is the Republic of Ireland (in theory a relatively simple procedure, although recently dogged by practical problems), a fellow member of the Commonwealth or some other state with which the United Kingdom has some form of extradition treaty. Recently, steps have been taken to streamline arrangements in the third category so as to make extradition easier, for example, by enabling the removal of the prima facie case requirement which caused problems with some states (e.g., Spain) whose system of criminal justice is inquisitorial in nature. The steps should enable ratification of the European Convention on Extradition 1957.[69]

All the extradition arrangements preclude surrender of the fugitive where the offence in question is one of a political character. The regimes also strive to prevent his surrender where he would, for example, be prejudiced at his trial on account of his political opinion or punished as for an offence of a political character. The 'political offence' exception could prove a barrier to the extradition of terrorists on the basis that one man's terrorist is another man's freedom fighter, and there still remains, even in western Europe, some degree of chauvinism about differing legal and political systems. Steps, some judicial but mostly legislative implementation of international agreements, have been taken in the United Kingdom to reduce the possibility of the fugitive escaping punishment for his crimes, by removing the 'political offence' barrier for certain crimes and/or by enabling his prosecution before a United Kingdom court for certain offences committed elsewhere.

In the judicial realm the House of Lords (the highest court in the UK) introduced a remoteness test into the concept of an 'offence of a political character'. This means that while an assassination of a head of state by a political opponent of the regime in order to change it or its policies would bar extradition to the state with which the offender was politically in dispute (although not to a non-dispute state in which the act was perpetrated), a bank robbery would not qualify so as to bar extradition, the offence being too far removed from the political object to qualify as one of a political character.[70] On that view, terrorist acts killing innocent civilians probably would not rank as ones of a political character.[71]

In the legislative sphere, the Criminal Jurisdiction Act 1975 enables certain serious offences (e.g., murder) committed in the Republic of Ireland to be tried in the United Kingdom, should the UK authorities sanction the prosecution.[72] The Suppression of Terrorism Act 1978,[73] implementing obligations under the European Convention on the Suppression of Terrorism, but extending to more offences than that Convention requires, provides that a range of offences of a type commonly committed by terrorists are not to be regarded for extradition purposes as ones of a political character in relation to requests for surrender made by a state to which the Act applies (that is, another party to the Convention or some other state specified by government and approved by parliament, for example, the USA[74]). The Act specifies, however, that extradition can nevertheless be refused if the offender would be prejudiced at his trial, for example, because of his political opinion, and it gives UK courts jurisdiction to try the offence, regardless of the fact that it was committed outside the United Kingdom, thereby enabling the proper fulfilment of the Convention obligation to submit the case to the United Kingdom's prosecuting authorities where extradition is refused.

The Civil Aviation Act 1982,[75] replacing earlier legislation implementing the Tokyo Convention 1963, extends UK criminal jurisdiction to British-controlled aircraft, and gives jurisdiction to try offences committed on board to the courts of that part of the United Kingdom in which the offender is found. For extradition purposes, a crime on board an aircraft in flight is deemed to be within the jurisdiction of the state of registration. The Aviation Security Act 1982, consolidating earlier legislation implementing the Hague Convention for the Suppression of the Unlawful Seizure of Aircraft 1970 and the Montreal Convention for the Suppression of Unlawful Acts against the Safety of Civil Aviation 1971, gives UK courts extra-territorial jurisdiction over hijacking, destroying, damaging or endangering the safety of, civil aircraft (all punishable with life imprisonment). Thus, if the offender were not extradited to some other state in respect of the offence, the UK prosecuting authorities could decide to prosecute him for it in the United Kingdom.[76] The Internationally Protected Persons Act 1978,[77] the Taking of Hostages Act 1982[78] and the Nuclear Material (Offences) Act 1983[79] similarly implement international obligations of the 'extradite or submit to prosecuting authorities' model, by conferring on UK courts power to try offenders for relevant offences committed abroad. These arrangements enable the specific scheme to be used as an extradition treaty for the offences covered by the particular arrangement, even in the absence of a more general extradition treaty between another state party and the United Kingdom.

The Economic Measures Taken

The United Kingdom, sometimes in conjunction with its European partners, has applied sanctions against states supporting terrorism. It is party to the Bonn Summit Declaration 1978 which resolved that, in cases where a country refuses the extradition or prosecution of those who have hijacked an aircraft, the governments will take immediate action to cease all flights to that country and will initiate action to halt all incoming flights from that country, by the airlines of the country concerned. Giving effect to that declaration, the United Kingdom renounced its air agreement with Afghanistan when that state, contrary to its obligations under the Hague Convention 1970, released the hijackers of a Pakistan International Airlines aircraft in 1981.[80] It deployed some limited economic sanctions, but not the freezing of assets, against Iran in the wake of the US Embassy hostage seizure,[81] and diplomatic relations with that state were broken over the Ayatollah Khomeini's February 1989 death sentence on Salman Rushdie. The Libyan People's Bureau in London was closed after the shooting of Woman Police Constable Yvonne Fletcher in April 1984. Relations with Syria were broken in the wake of the 1986 attempt by Al-Hindawi to blow up an El Al flight by placing a bomb in his innocent girlfriend's suitcase. Three South African diplomats were expelled from London after the 1989 discovery of South African arms supply operations to loyalist paramilitaries, but economic sanctions were not applied.[82] Nor have they been applied against China after its 1989 state terror against the democracy movement. Of course, like most nations in an economically competitive world, the United Kingdom is reluctant to deploy sanctions which mean that UK nationals will lose business to their foreign competitors.

The new powers of the police to search out terrorist assets and have them frozen, pending the outcome of criminal proceedings, which, if successful, could result in their seizure, have already been noted as valuable, since an effective attack on the resources of terrorism is as important as combating the bomber and the assassin.[83] The powers will be rendered more effective when reciprocal international agreements on the freezing and seizure of assets are concluded, limiting the 'safe havens' for terrorist funds and property.

It appears that the government has never publicly proclaimed financial rewards for information on terrorists and terrorism, although money may well change hands between the police/intelligence services and a variety of informers/agents/operatives, and there were financial arrangements made for the benefit of those terrorists who gave evidence against their erstwhile accomplices as part of the so-called 'supergrass' strategy, although the amounts involved, the reasons for their payment and the elements covered remain a matter of acute controversy.[84] There has been general encouragement, including through television and newspaper advertising, of the public in Northern Ireland, to supply information to the police by way of the confidential telephone system. This produces information but not witnesses.[85]

A person commits a criminal offence in the United Kingdom if, having information which he knows or believes might be of material assistance in preventing the commission by any other person of an act of terrorism connected with Northern Ireland affairs, or in securing the apprehension, prosecution or conviction of any other person for an offence involving the commission, preparation or instigation of such an act, he then fails without reasonable excuse to disclose that information as soon as is reasonably practicable to the authorities.[86] The main role of this offence is as a pressure point during interrogation, although it does have implications for the activities of those involved in investigative journalism. A private individual, Ross McWhirter, was murdered in 1975 by the IRA after offering a £50,000 reward for information to help the police 'beat the bombers' who were plaguing the mainland.[87]

On the positive side, as part of a wider 'hearts and minds' campaign, various socio-economic measures have been taken since 1970, involving a massive inflow of governmental money to improve Northern Ireland's beleaguered economy and stimulate investment and employment, and to provide social security. But the economy remains depressed and unemployment high, particularly in Catholic areas.[88]

The Political Measures Taken

The main public stance of successive governments has been that terrorists are criminals, not freedom fighters, and that there are to be no negotiations with them, concessions to them, or amnesties for them. Government will not give in to terrorist blackmail since this only serves to increase terrorism and terrorist demands. This governmental stance is reflected in ministerial refusal to deal with Sinn Fein's elected representatives and, formerly in the bleak position of British hostages in the Lebanon. (Since the time of this writing, all British hostages have been released from Lebanon, more as a result of the changing alliances in the Middle East after the 1991 Gulf War than any concessions made by the UK [eds.]). This firm approach, however, has not been consistently applied over the last two decades. In 1970, following the hijacking at Dawson's Field in Jordan, one of the hijackers, Leila Khaled, was arrested when the aircraft returned to London, but she was later released when another British aircraft was hijacked, in part in order to secure her release.[89] In the 1970s truces were agreed in Northern Ireland with the IRA, and in 1972 IRA leaders, including Gerry Adams and Martin McGuinness, were flown to London for a secret meeting with the Heath administration's Northern Ireland Secretary, William Whitelaw, who had earlier conceded special category status to terrorist prisoners following a hunger strike.[90] There is also some indication that, as part of the 'political approach', internees were used by government almost in the manner of political hostages to guarantee the paramilitaries' good behaviour.[91]

Discussions with 'terrorists' might be one way of characterising the talks which led to the Lancaster House Agreement and the independence of Zimbabwe (S. Rhodesia). The government accords a degree of protection to officers and members of the ANC in London, despite having described them as terrorist and there have been intermittent contacts between Foreign Office ministers and the ANC.[92] Recent discussions with the PLO, after Chairman Yasser Arafat's renunciation of terrorism and recognition of Israel, however, fit squarely with the general stance.

It has always been recognised that combating terrorism not only has a security dimension but also political, economic, social and psychological dimensions, the so-called 'hearts and minds' aspects. The UK's part in promoting conflict resolution of disputes that generate terrorism (e.g., the Palestinian/Israeli problem, divisions in Northern Ireland, southern Africa) is inevitably greater in its own domestic sphere, although its colonial past connection with some of the areas involved and its Commonwealth and EC membership may give it a degree of influence elsewhere. Its political response to Northern Ireland terrorism is aimed at achieving a political solution to the divisions of Northern Ireland. This is to come in the form of governmental structures to reconcile the mutually inconsistent and conflicting traditions, aspirations and identities of divided communities, while according a consultative role to the Irish government, in order to provide stable, accountable government in the hope that this will help reduce the 'water' of grievance-generated community support in which the terrorist 'fish' swim. Steps to the same end have also been taken to try to meet legitimate grievances with reforms in voting and the electoral boundary system, housing allocation, public sector complaints and discrimination monitoring mechanisms, and by providing 'fair employment' legislation to try to combat politico-religious discrimination in employment.[93] That some of these have been singularly unsuccessful in part testifies to the intractability of the problem: concessions to one side tend to alienate or antagonise the other; despairingly, the problem may be that there is no solution.[94]

International Diplomatic Initiatives

The United Kingdom is party to multilateral treaties of the 'extradite or submit to prosecution' model, as discussed previously. It also has concluded bilateral arrangements with the USA and with the Republic of Ireland, in the former case to ease extradition with respect to terrorist type offences which are not to be regarded as ones of a political character,[95] and in the latter case to do that and also to create an extraterritorial jurisdiction whereby certain offenders can be tried in the one state for offences committed in the other. The role of the 1985 Anglo-Irish Agreement, giving the Republic a consultative role in certain Northern Ireland affairs and enhancing co-operation on security, has already been noted. Within the EC, the United Kingdom has sought to promote sanctions against states sponsoring terrorism. In the Political Declaration by the Governments of the Member States on the Free Movement of Persons, attached to the 1986 Single European Act, the UK has agreed to co-operate with its European partners to combat terrorism.[96] In the International Civil Aviation Organisation (ICAO) Britain tried unsuccessfully to secure a regime of sanctions against states which did not fulfil their obligations under the Hague and Montreal Conventions, although its proposals did not go as far as those proposed by the USA and Canada.[97] In the ICAO forum, at a special meeting in Montreal after the 1988 Lockerbie disaster, both the United Kingdom and the USA sought to tighten security at international airports, including updated internationally-agreed standards for the electronic scanning of baggage and detection of explosives and for stricter control of access to airports.[98] As one of the seven major economic nations, the UK supported and has given practical effect to the Bonn Economic Summit Declaration, noted earlier, and supported the London Summit Declaration 1984 which considered the problems of state-sponsored terrorism. At that summit it unsuccessfully proposed an international blacklist of diplomats guilty of involvement in terrorism, a proposal later accepted by the EC foreign ministers.[99] At the United Nations the United Kingdom has recently promoted an international obligation of states to take steps to ensure the proper marking of explosives and steps to assist in their detection. It has already agreed with Czechoslovakia that that country will add something to Semtex to make it detectable by smell.

The Military and Police Measures Taken

The response to terrorism has seen 'target hardening' of government offices and military installations, and protection for key personnel. Within Northern Ireland, the economic centre of several towns and cities, most markedly, Belfast, constitutes a security zone with restrictions on vehicular entry and sometimes searching of pedestrians and baggage.

Security at airports is a mixture of state-required provision and demands imposed by the carriers, those imposed by El Al being most restrictive and arguably most effective. Under the Aviation Security Act 1982 the British government has always had powers to demand information about protective measures from both airline operators and airline managers. It can require both operators and managers to guard aircraft.

In the post-Lockerbie era the original governmental power to require airport managers to use 'best endeavours' to ensure that security searches are conducted was extended, in a 1990 amendment to the Act, also to cover airline operators.[100] Some key airports are policed by the relevant local police force, reducing problems of inter-force liaison, and with the ability in certain spheres to override the airport managers.[101]

Research suggests that in Northern Ireland, especially, powers of arrest and detention conferred on the security forces have been used to build up an intelligence/security profile (of the population in which the terrorists operate) as part of counter-insurgency tactics developed by such military theoreticians as General Sir Frank Kitson. There is said to have been an increase in army 'undercover intelligence and surveillance operations' employing 'new technological devices such as concealed cameras, telephone-tapping and a computerised data bank on the bulk of the population'.[102] Certainly intelligence collation is increasingly computerised. Sophisticated surveillance devices, as well as painstaking physical observation, cover the border area and West Belfast.

Helicopter film surveillance, as well as untransmitted film obtained from the media, were recently used to secure the conviction of two men for their part in the 1989 murder of two army corporals who had strayed into a Republican funeral in West Belfast.[103] Much intelligence work inevitably remains secret, but it is clear that informants and intelligence operatives are an important part of successfully combating terrorism, and from the Stalker affair, that their protection from discovery is of overriding concern to the authorities.[104] That concern also partly explains a resort to executive processes rather than pure reliance on the criminal process.

Siege and assault techniques, and techniques of negotiation, are occasionally brought into public view, as with the 1975 Balcombe Street siege (involving the police and the threat of SAS deployment) and the 1980 Iranian Embassy siege (involving a dramatic assault by the SAS). SAS expertise in assault techniques is valued throughout the world.[105]

Prison Measures Against Terrorists

A firm current policy is to treat terrorist criminals like other prisoners convicted of serious criminal offences, notwithstanding that the terrorist claims political motivation for his acts, that research on Northern Ireland suggests that many terrorist prisoners would not be criminals but for the political cause,[106] or that those convicted in Northern Ireland have been convicted in a different criminal trial process from the normal.

In Great Britain this means that terrorist prisoners are treated like any other Category A (maximum security) prisoner in terms of the type of prison in which and the regime under which they are held, the eligibility for remission of one third of a determinate sentence for good behaviour, and their *prima facie* eligibility for parole, release on licence (subject to recall by the Home Secretary, advised by the Parole Board). For life sentence prisoners this involves the Home Secretary consulting with the Lord Chief Justice and the trial judge if available.[107] Current policy is that certain categories of life sentence prisoners, including terrorist murderers, 'can normally expect to serve at least 20 years in custody; and there will be cases where the gravity of the offence requires a still longer period'. Similarly, persons sentenced to more than five years for crimes of violence, a category covering many terrorists, 'will be granted parole only where release under supervision for a few months before the end of a sentence is likely to reduce the long term risk to the public, or in circumstances which are genuinely exceptional'.[108]

In Northern Ireland terrorist prisoners enjoy the same benefits as other prisoners, particularly a more generous remission allowance (one-half rather than one-third of sentence) for prisoners serving a determinate rather than a 'life' sentence. This is intended to compensate for the lack of a parole system in Northern Ireland. However, for terrorist offences committed after 15 March 1989, sentences of five years or more will only attract a maximum one-third remission.[109] Moreover, those sentenced to more than a year for a terrorist offence, whenever committed, who commit another scheduled offence after 15 March 1989 during a period of remission, will have to serve the remainder of the original sentence before starting the new sentence of imprisonment for the offence committed during the remission period. This provision is designed to deter those released from returning to terrorism.[110]

This general equality of status between terrorist and other prisoners has not always been the policy in Northern Ireland. In 1972 convicted terrorist prisoners and those persons interned without trial were housed in the main in compounds (with segregation of Republican and Loyalist prisoners), rather than in traditional cellular accommodation. In June 1972, after a hunger strike, the government introduced a special category status for convicted terrorists which set them apart from other convicted prisoners. It was in practice available to those who claimed political motivation for their crime and were acceptable to the appropriate compound leader. Special category status was not portrayed by government as political status – it meant merely a more liberal regime (e.g., no work, wearing their own clothes, more frequent visits) for such prisoners – but in practice many regarded it as such. Such prisoners saw themselves in the same light as internees and confidently expected an amnesty. The Gardiner Committee deplored the propaganda advantage which special category status handed to the terrorists and the weakening of the deterrent effect of long sentences handed down by the courts.[111]

Special category status has since been phased out: from 1976 it did not apply to anyone convicted of an offence committed after February 1976; then no person charged after April 1980 with an offence, no matter when committed, could claim special category status in respect of it. Thus the number of special category prisoners has declined.

The so-called 'dirty' or 'blanket' protest, followed by two hunger strikes, the first for political status, the second for a range of demands for a more liberal prison regime, secured some beneficial changes for all prisoners, not just terrorist ones, but no concession on political status.[112] Other controversial issues in Northern Ireland have been strip-searching of prisoners, especially women prisoners,[113] and the reluctance of the authorities to transfer Northern Ireland terrorists convicted in Great Britain to Northern Ireland prisons, where they would be closer to families who have significant problems in visiting them on the mainland, but would then be subject to more generous remission if serving a determinate sentence, and perhaps be more amenable to paramilitary influence. It has been argued that this reluctance in fact confers on such prisoners a detrimental special category status.[114]

Psychological Measures, including the Role of the Media

The role of the media in providing information, disinformation or propaganda to the public about terrorism in general and the Northern Ireland problem in particular, is controversial and can barely be touched on here. Impartial reporting is clearly difficult where key actors consider that one is in effect at war with the terrorist, and various measures have been taken by government to influence reporting, of which the broadcasting restrictions noted earlier are merely the most public part. The measures and influences brought to bear are canvassed in Curtis (1984).

Much information to the public from government has been concerned to assure the public that the 'battle' with the terrorist, though long and difficult, is slowly being won. There have also been many warnings on the need to take care and be vigilant, to be wary of unaccompanied luggage in airports, railway stations and the like, to report, rather than to tamper with, suspicious packages, and not to approach dangerous suspects identified by the police in the media.

Public opinion is itself a vague term, since it is not always clear whether it refers to the public as a whole, or rather to the opinion of key interest groups to which terrorists or governments look for support or response. But it seems clear that the opinion of various groups and the 'public' reaction to various acts and policies has impacted on and affected the actions and behaviour of terrorists and government. A few examples will have to suffice. One reason for PIRA's switch away from bombings in which innocent civilians were likely to be injured has been the need to win the support of a wider range of people than its 'hard core' supporters, especially given its electoral strategy.[115] It may be easier to keep that support, once won, by attacking only so-called 'legitimate' targets: security force personnel and property, persons involved in and aiding the 'British war machine'. On the other hand, killing off-duty RUC Reservists and part-time UDR personnel may have relatively little impact on British public opinion. Paradoxically, the worldwide wave of revulsion at the very public murder of the two army corporals in West Belfast in 1989 is said to have encouraged PIRA to once again target British soldiers to try to enhance public support in Britain for a withdrawal of British troops from Northern Ireland.[116] It may be of course that such actions merely reinforce public support for governmental determination not to give in to their demands. Public reaction is cited as one reason why government is reluctant to transfer terrorist prisoners from British to Northern Ireland jails.[117] The likely reaction of the Catholic community in Northern Ireland and the impact on influential Irish American opinion seem factors behind governmental refusal to reintroduce even selective internment without trial.

Government attempts to counter terrorist propaganda are described in Curtis (1984), noted above. The attempts to do so in the United States so as to limit fundraising there, appear to have had a degree of success.[118]

The Organisation of Anti-Terrorist Units and Bureaucracy

Under this topic, Great Britain and Northern Ireland need to be considered separately, because of different constitutional arrangements and the fact that a more intensive threat in Northern Ireland, at times akin to guerrilla war rather than combating crime, has necessitated the military's involvement in aid of the civil power.

Great Britain

Overall political responsibility for anti-terrorist legislation and policy rests mainly with the Home Secretary, although the Secretary of State for Scotland speaks for affairs there. Some key actions have to be performed by them, after they have been duly briefed by senior officials in their ministries. Extensions of detention under the PTA are given both by the Home Secretary (for England and Wales) and by the Scottish Secretary (for Scotland). Exclusion orders, with respect to persons in or who are or may be seeking to enter Great Britain, are solely the province of the Home Secretary, who is also responsible for refusal of entry to and deportation from the United Kingdom on security grounds. Whilst the Home Secretary has important responsibilities for the capital city's Metropolitan Police, and some role in maintaining an efficient police service, the day-to-day operational deployment of anti-terrorist measures rests with the heads of the various provincial police forces (43 in England and Wales alone): that is to say in London, in the hands of the appropriate Commissioner of Police for the Metropolis or the smaller City of London Force, and, outside London, in the hands of the appropriate Chief Constable. The constitutional position stresses the complete independence of Commissioner or Chief Constable in operational matters. However, powers of appointment, financial control and inspection do enable central government to exert influence through circulars and administrative directions, for example, on the proper use of the PTA.[119]

There is no single police force with overall control of any policing matter in Great Britain. Policing is spread among independent provincial forces, necessitating co-ordination and co-operation between them, but also raising the obstacle or difficulty of inter-force rivalry and distrust. Forces which have the greatest experience with the powers under the PTA are the Metropolitan Police and, because of the location of the so-called 'Irish' ports, the forces of Merseyside and Dumfries and Galloway.

In each force, a prime responsibility for combating subversion and terrorism, and gathering and evaluating intelligence on threats to public order, rests with the Special Branch of each force. That of the Metropolitan Police has responsibilities throughout the kingdom for dealing with Irish Republican extremism and terrorist groups, but there is no such thing as a special branch in a national sense. Each Special Branch acts to assist the internal Security Service (MI5) in its task of defending the realm against espionage, sabotage and subversion, including terrorism. Special Branch also provides armed protection for persons at risk. In May 1992 MI5 was given the lead role in anti-terrorist intelligence.

The Metropolitan Police also maintains Royalty and Diplomatic Protection Departments. Some inter-force units have been set up to provide a degree of co-ordination. The National Joint Unit at Scotland Yard, staffed by officers from Metropolitan and provincial Special Branches

> co-ordinates enquiries and applications from police forces in Great Britain concerning people held under the prevention of terrorism legislation. The Unit processes for onward transmission to the Home Office or the Scottish Home and Health Department as the

case may be, applications for extension of detention and exclusion orders under the legislation and co-ordinates the preparation of up-to-date assessments in connection with review of exclusion cases (since exclusion orders only have a three-year life but new orders can be issued). The National Ports Office, based at Heathrow Airport, provides a liaison and advisory service for port units in other force areas.[120]

Some forces maintain special firearms units, and the Metropolitan Police maintains an Anti-Terrorist Squad (replacing the Bomb Squad). *In extremis*, the police, with the approval of the Home Secretary, can call on the military to provide aid to the civil power,[121] for example, by calling in the SAS to storm a building in which persons are held hostage. Usually, specially trained police officers will try to bring it to an end through negotiations and establishing a rapport with the kidnappers or hijackers.

Northern Ireland

Here, there is only one police force, the Royal Ulster Constabulary (RUC), but the doctrine of the operational independence of the Chief Constable also prevails here. In 1969 the British Army was deployed in aid of the RUC when police could not cope with the sectarian rioting. For a while in the early 1970s the RUC were unable to operate in Republican areas, which were, therefore, 'policed' by the Army. One result of this differential approach to policing was that more Republicans were interned whilst Protestant paramilitaries were processed through the ordinary courts by the police using the more familiar criminal prosecution approach. Since 1976 the policy has been one of 'police primacy', with the RUC as the dominant security force, something that fits with the associated policy of 'criminalisation'. The Army, in much reduced numbers, plays a supportive role, but has a higher profile in border areas like the so-called 'bandit country' of South Armagh. This policy of 'police primacy' is sometimes referred to more pejoratively as 'Ulsterisation', since the main brunt of anti-terrorist action was to be borne by provincial Ulster forces, the RUC, supported by the locally recruited Army unit, the Ulster Defence Regiment (UDR), with the Regular Army taking a much lower profile. 'Policy primacy', of course, has only been possible because the RUC has to some extent become a well-trained, well equipped anti-terrorist force – a militarised police force.[122]

Overall political responsibility for policy rests with the Northern Ireland Secretary. He has regular security meetings with the Chief Constable and with the General Officer Commanding (GOC) Northern Ireland, responsible for the Army. The Anglo-Irish Agreement gives the

Republic of Ireland a consultative role, and there have been enhanced efforts at cross-border security liaison.

The RUC has developed special units. Its Special Branch plays a key role in gathering and collating intelligence, operating undercover agents and 'running' informers. One concern of the Stalker enquiry was that it was becoming almost a force within a force.[123] Another unit (E4A) was established to complement the Special Branch and act as the RUC's covert intelligence gathering arm. It too was complemented by the Special Support Unit (SSU) or Headquarters Mobile Support Unit, as a heavy fire-power 'armed measures' unit, trained by the SAS. Some of its operations gave cause for concern about a 'shoot to kill' policy, the subject of the Stalker investigation.[124] The RUC has specialised interrogation centres, including one at Castlereagh in Belfast. Interrogation there is now elaborately regulated and supervised to obviate abuse of suspects.[125]

The Security Service (MI5) has also been involved in intelligence gathering in Northern Ireland. MI6, whose province is abroad rather than at home, has had some role in matters too, generating a degree of damaging rivalry. Various Army intelligence units have also been deployed in the period (e.g., 14th Int., the Intelligence and Security Group). The activities of some of these in the early 1970s, as the Army pursued an undercover 'war' with the IRA, have wrongly been attributed to the SAS, which was not deployed in Ulster until 1976. The SAS's firepower and painstaking intelligence and observation work may be one reason for PIRA's late 1980s switch in operations to easier targets on the Continent.[126]

International Co-operation in the Field of Prevention and Prosecution

The United Kingdom plays an important role in Interpol, in the TREVI (Terrorism, Radicalism, Extremism and political Violence) group of Home Affairs Ministers of the European Community, and is committed under a Declaration attached to the Single European Act to co-operation with its partners. A co-operation and intelligence sharing agreement has recently been concluded with France. In international fora, the British government pressed for tighter standards of aviation security. Its commitment to and implementation of various international agreements of the 'extradite or prosecute' model has already been noted.

Criteria and Methods for Evaluating Acceptability and Effectiveness of Anti-Terrorist Measures

Acceptability in Terms of Human Rights and Liberal Democratic Values

The various international human rights conventions to which the United Kingdom is a party constitute yardsticks against which one can assess the acceptability of anti-terrorist legislation and policy. With its enforcement machinery and right of individual petition, the European Convention on Human Rights represents the most pertinent and practical yardstick, the impact of which has been seen at various points in this chapter. Since the Convention inevitably has gaps (e.g., it is silent on the value of jury trial, and does not apply its fair trial standards to public law matters between state and citizen other than in the criminal law field), one must also take account of other values thought fundamental by the polity. Bearing in mind the facets of a liberal democracy, it is suggested that the following principles should govern one's attitude to the invocation, formulation and use of special powers (i.e., powers over and above those applicable in respect of non-terrorist criminal activity) to combat terrorism:

(a) There should be resort to special powers only where it can be shown to be absolutely necessary. It must be abundantly clear, both in terms of the general situation and their application to individual cases, that the powers in the ordinary law are inadequate to deal with the threat;

(b) The measures should not go beyond what is demanded by the exigencies of the situation. There should be the minimum derogation necessary from existing civil rights and freedoms in domestic and international law, and absolute respect for those rights and freedoms which are non-derogable under international obligations or the domestic legal order;

(c) Resort to special powers should not be prolonged further than is absolutely necessary;

(d) The measures taken must have a democratic aim and be subject to effective, periodic parliamentary supervision of their invocation, use and continuation, and to oversight by an independent judiciary;

(e) The measures should be clearly and precisely formulated in statutory rules so that all concerned are able to make an adequate assessment of their respective powers, rights and obligations;

(f) The introduction and exercise of each measure should be accompanied by adequate safeguards against abuse, if necessary by the provision of special remedies and mechanisms over and above those available under the general law. Where there is doubt about whether such safeguards can be provided, careful consideration must be given to whether it is better to refuse to grant the power rather than run the risk of abuse, or whether, in terms of the threat to be met, the power is so vital that the risk of abuse must be run.

Of course, even were all to agree that these were appropriate principles to apply, their very generality means that there will be disagreements on their applicability to particular contexts. Rather than being able to resolve controversies (and the powers examined in this chapter are controversial), the principles are a framework in which rational discussion can take place. Respect for such principles, however, may reduce the danger of arbitrary exercise of power.

Effectiveness in Terms of Threat Reduction

The relationship between an anti-terrorist measure and a reduction in terrorist threat – indeed the very question whether there has in fact been a reduction – is a highly complex and controversial issue, perhaps clouded by the politicians' and the tacticians' need to present their policies as successful. One might look to an increase in the rate of prosecution, but these rates may fluctuate according to a complex of circumstances, some fortuitous (e.g., the emergence of a 'supergrass'), some the product of a change in personnel and approach within the framework of the same anti-terrorist measure (e.g., a greater willingness to chance a prosecution). Otherwise, one might look to the overall level of terrorist incidents or to the death toll as a result of terrorism. On that basis the reduction both in the number of incidents and of deaths in Northern Ireland since the peak of 1972–75[127] would appear to give some cause for congratulation among the framers and operators of the measures. Moreover, life in Belfast, for instance, is far more 'normal' than before.

However, the decline in incidents and in deaths serves to mask a more chilling effectiveness of terrorist action in terms of the number of deaths related to the number of incidents. While anti-terrorist measures may play some role, another variable, which the changes may reflect, is an alteration in terrorist tactics as PIRA pursues its electoral strategy in tandem with armed struggle, and a switch to easier targets on the Continent as surveillance and security forces' pressure renders actions in Northern Ireland rather more risky. In short, while there are some grounds for optimism, that is only because the recent past was much worse. Anti-terrorist measures are likely to be with us for the foreseeable future and must continue to be strictly scrutinised.

National Lessons for Europe in 1992

The UK experience may be exceptional because it is dealing not with sporadic terrorism from isolated groups with little support, but with well-organised groups with significant support – some willing, some the product of intimidation – both in the community in Northern Ireland and in Irish groups, as well as some political groups in the USA. Some of the limitations imposed on the UK government by the nature and intractability of the Northern Ireland problem will be absent elsewhere, and, of course, different constitutional, institutional and legal structures and traditions may necessitate different specific reactions to apparently similar problems. Nonetheless some general points of importance can be made with respect to lessons for a European response to terrorism.

1.   One must act within the rule of law, in that not only must legal authority exist for what is done but the law itself should comply so far as possible with the dictates of such human rights instruments as the European Convention on Human Rights. Otherwise the liberal state, in dealing with terrorism, is not remaining true to its own ideals, to its own fundamental values. The further it moves away from those values the more it risks losing support and aiding the terrorists' cause, which involves portraying government as repressive, nasty and illegitimate, with themselves as protectors of the community. There is also the danger that any victory achieved over terrorism by neglecting or overriding those values will be a hollow one, achieved at the cost of fundamentally altering the nature of the state from liberal to authoritarian, changing it to a regime which may threaten the civil liberties of us all.

2.   It is accordingly preferable to deal with suspected terrorists in a proper criminal process, as little modified as possible, since then they can be seen to be proved guilty of a specific criminal offence and can challenge the evidence against them. An alternative such as internment without trial, apparently attractive in terms of effectiveness and expediency, confines terrorists without that advantage of it being clearly demonstrated to the public that they are terrorists, and makes it easier to paint them as martyrs. Using a criminal justice process may result in less community support for the terrorists.

3.   There is a need for much closer co-operation between nations, particularly European nations, in the realms of an agreed definition of terrorism, investigation/intelligence sharing, fugitive offenders, and, for Europe after 1992, the issue of border controls. Secure external borders of the EC may serve to keep out non-EC citizen terrorists, but how will European nations cope with the exploitation of open frontiers by EC citizen terrorist groups such as the Provisional IRA or ETA? The opening of internal frontiers will demand even closer co-operation than that achieved so far. If like-minded Euro-

pean partners cannot achieve this, the public danger from terrorist action will not diminish. And friction between states over this issue is likely to influence other spheres of co-operation and further hinder full achievement of the European ideal.

NOTES

1. Command Paper (hereafter Cmnd.) 9657 (1985).
2. K.J. Kelley, *The Longest War: Northern Ireland and the IRA* (London: ZED books, 1988), pp.189–92, 248–9, 275. The anti-terrorist legislation is also said to have a 'terrorising' effect: see, A.McC. Lee, *Terrorism in Northern Ireland* (NY: General Hall, 1983), p.173.
3. P. Wilkinson, *Terrorism and the Liberal State*, 2nd ed. (London: Macmillan, 1986), p.182.
4. See for a more detailed list of acts: Review of the Operation of the Prevention of Terrorism (Temporary Provisions) Act 1976 by the Rt. Hon. Earl Jellicoe, DSC, MC, Cmnd. 8803 (1983), pp.8–9 (hereinafter cited as 'Jellicoe'); Review of the Operation of the Prevention of Terrorism (Temporary Provisions) Act 1984 by the Viscount Colville of Culross QC, Cmnd. 264 (1987), pp.3–4 (hereinafter cited as 'Colville'); C. Walker, *The Prevention of Terrorism in British Law*, 2nd ed. (Manchester: Manchester UP, 1992), pp.22–4.
5. 1986, c.64, s.38; see R. Card, *Public Order: The New Law* (London: Butterworths, 1987), pp.194–8.
6. Prevention of Terrorism (Temporary Provisions) Act 1989 (c.4) (hereinafter cited as 'PTA'), s.14 (2).
7. See P. Bishop and E. Mallie, *The Provisional IRA* (London: Corgi Books, 1988), Ch.2; T.P. Coogan, *The IRA*, rev. ed. (London: Fontana, 1987), Ch.1. Material in this section on the Republican movement predominantly comes from these two fascinating works.
8. J. Adams, *The Financing of Terror* (Sevenoaks, UK: NEL, 1986), p.5.
9. House of Commons Debates [hereafter HC Deb.], Vol.143, cols.212–13 (Mr D. Hurd MP, Home Secretary); J. Adams, R. Morgan and A. Bambridge, *Ambush: The War Between the SAS and the IRA* (London: Pan, 1988), pp.38–40.
10. K. Toolis, 'An Anatomy of INLA's Blood Feuds', *The Observer Colour Magazine*, 31 May 1987, p.36. The Irish People's Liberation Organisation is a recent offshoot.
11. S. Nelson, *Ulster's Uncertain Defenders* (Belfast: Appletree Press, 1984), p.9.
12. W.D. Flackes, *Northern Ireland: A Political Directory* (London: Ariel, BBC, 1983), p.243.
13. Flackes, *Northern Ireland*, p.229; P. O'Malley, *The Uncivil Wars: Ireland Today* (Belfast: Blackstaff Press, 1983), Ch.8.
14. Adams, *Financing of Terror*, (note 8), pp.207–8, 213.
15. See *The Independent*, 6 May 1989, pp.1, 2.
16. *Ireland v. United Kingdom* (1978) 2 E.H.R.R. 25, at pp.98–100.
17. See generally, Nelson, *Ulster's Uncertain Defenders*; E. Moloney and A. Pollack, *Paisley* (1986), Chs.3, 6, 12.
18. Adams, *Financing of Terror*, (note 8), p.216.
19. K. Boyle, T. Hadden and P. Hillyard, *Ten Years On In Northern Ireland: The Legal Control of Political Violence*, (London: Cobden Trust, 1980), p.23.
20. Prevention of Terrorism (Temporary Provisions) Act 1989 (c.4). For detailed analysis see D. Bonner, 'Combating Terrorism in the 1990s: The Role of the Prevention of Terrorism (Temporary Provisions) Act 1989', *Public Law* (Autumn 1989).

21. 1991 c.24, replacing Northern Ireland (Emergency Provisions) Act 1978 (c.5), as amended by the Northern Ireland (Emergency Provisions) Act 1987 (c.30). See generally D. Bonner, *Emergency Powers in Peacetime* (London: Sweet & Maxwell, 1985), pp.ix–x, Ch.3; J. Jackson, 'The Northern Ireland (Emergency Provisions) Act 1987', *Northern Ireland Law Quarterly* 39 (1988), p.235.
22. PTA, ss.2, 3; NIEPA 1978, s.21. The list of proscribed organisations is wider in Northern Ireland, embracing both Republican and Loyalist groups, whereas that in Great Britain merely catches the IRA and INLA.
23. *Brind v. Secretary of State for the Home Department*, [1991] 1 AU ER 720.
24. See M. Robinson, 'Paying lip-service to freedom of speech', *The Independent*, 2 June 1989, p.13. Cf. *Purcell v. Ireland* (1991) 12 HRLJ 254, rejecting a challenge to Ireland's more stringent restrictions.
25. NIEPA 1991, s.23.
26. NIEPA 1991, ss.19–21.
27. NIEPA 1991, Part V.
28. PTA, s.12 (1).
29. PTA, ss.9–13.
30. PTA, s.12 (2), (3).
31. 1986, c.32.
32. PTA, ss.10 (1) (b), (c), (2), 11 (1), (2).
33. PTA, s.13, Sched.4. Wider powers of confiscation apply in Northern Ireland (NIEPA 1991, Part VII).
34. HC Deb., Vol.143, col.214.
35. PTA, s.17, Sched.7. Extra powers are conferred by NIEPA 1991, s.57 and Sched.5.
36. PTA, Sched.7, para.7.
37. PTA, Sched.7, para.8.
38. See *Independent*, 28 June 1989, p.2, 30 June 1989, p.2.
39. Under the Police and Criminal Evidence Act 1984 (c.60), persons can only be arrested on reasonable suspicion of a specific criminal offence. Those so suspected of a serious offence may be held without charge for up to 36 hours, extendible up to 96 hours with the approval of a Magistrates' Court in an *inter partes* hearing.
40. PTA, s.14 (1).
41. PTA, Sched.5.
42. PTA, Sched.5, para.2.
43. PTA, s.14 (2) (b).
44. Colville, cited above n.4, pp.68–9, Tables 1–3.
45. PTA, s.14 (4).
46. PTA, s.14 (5).
47. (1988) 9 H.R.L.J. 293.
48. Council of Europe Document DH (89) 1, App. VI, pp.10–11.
49. Standing Advisory Commission on Human Rights (hereinafter 'SACHR'), Annual Report For 1986–87, H.C. 298 (1988), p.60 (para.26).
50. Colville, cited above n.4, pp.13–14.
51. Ibid., p.15.
52. Bonner, *Emergency Powers in Peacetime*, p.142 and sources cited there (nn.51, 52).
53. *Ireland v. United Kingdom* (1978) 2 EHRR 25, at pp.81–2, 107.
54. P. Taylor, *Beating the Terrorists? Interrogation in Omagh, Gough and Castlereagh* (Harmondsworth: Penguin Books, 1980).
55. Review of the Operation of the Northern Ireland (Emergency Provisions) Act 1978 by the Rt. Hon. Sir George Baker OBE, Cmnd. 9222 (1984) (hereinafter cited as 'Baker'), paras.308–14; *Guardian*, 29 Oct. 1991, p.3.
56. Technically Diplock Courts try 'scheduled offences'. On this concept see Bonner, *Emergency Powers in Peacetime*, pp.103–6. The concept is such that ordinary crimes, mostly armed robberies carried out for non-terrorist/non-political motives, can end up in the Diplock system: see D.P.J. Walsh, *The Use and Abuse of Emergency Legislation in Northern Ireland* (London: Cobden Trust, 1983), p.60.

57. NIEPA 1991, s.11 (1).
58. NIEPA 1991, s.11 (3).
59. D. Bonner, 'Combating Terrorism: Supergrass Trials in Northern Ireland' (1987) 51 M.L.R. 23; S. Greer, 'Supergrasses and the Legal System in Britain and Northern Ireland', (1986) 102 L.Q.R. 189.
60. SACHR, Annual Report for 1985–86, H.C. 151 (1986–87), pp.61–2, 63–75; Bonner, 'Combating Terrorism' (note 20).
61. S.C. Greer & A. White, *Abolishing the Diplock Courts: The Case for Restoring Jury Trial to Scheduled Offences In Northern Ireland*, (London: Cobden Trust, 1986).
62. SACHR, cited above n.60, pp.58–9.
63. *Independent*, 17 June 1989, p.12.
64. PTA, s.7.
65. PTA, s.5.
66. *Ireland v. United Kingdom* (1978) 2 E.H.R.R. 25, at pp.89–90.
67. R.J. Spjut, 'Internment and Detention Without Trial in Northern Ireland 1971–75: Ministerial Policy and Practice' (1986) 49 M.L.R. 712.
68. See M. Rees, Northern Ireland Secretary, cited in SACHR, Annual Report for 1975–76, H.C. 130 (1976–77), pp.9–10.
69. See generally C. Warbrick, 'The New Law on Extradition' (1989) Crim. L.R. 4.
70. *Cheng v. Governor of Pentonville Prison* (1973) 2 All E.R. 204.
71. G. Gilbert, 'Terrorism and the Political Offence Exemption Reappraised', (1985) 34 I.C.L.Q. 695, at p.698.
72. Gilbert, 'Terrorism and the Political Offence Exemption', pp.718–19.
73. 1978, c.26.
74. See S.I. 2146/1986.
75. 1982, c.16.
76. 1982, c.36, ss.1–3.
77. 1978, c.17.
78. 1982, c.28.
79. 1983, c.18.
80. K. Chamberlain, 'Collective Suspension of Air Services with States which Harbour Hijackers', (1983) 32 I.C.L.Q. 616.
81. Wilkinson, *Terrorism and the Liberal State* (note 3), p.268.
82. *Independent*, 6 May 1989, pp.1, 2.
83. Adams, *Financing of Terror*, (note 8), pp.45, 228, 310.
84. See Bonner, 'Combating Terrorism' (note 20); Greer, 'Supergrasses', cited above n.59.
85. Baker, cited above n.55, para.256.
86. PTA, s.18.
87. Kelley, *Longest War*, cited above n.2, p.242.
88. K. Boyle and T. Hadden, *Ireland: A Positive Proposal* (Harmondsworth: Penguin, 1985), pp.75–6.
89. Adams, *Financing of Terror* (note 8), pp.46–7.
90. Bishop and Mallie, *Provisional IRA* (note 7), pp.225–30, 269–86.
91. Spjut, 'Internment and Detention Without Trial', cited above n.67; Kelley, *The Longest War*, pp.236–7.
92. R. Dowden, 'An explosive test for Britain's hard line on terrorism', *Independent*, 28 April 1989, p.26.
93. Boyle and Hadden, *Ireland: A Positive Proposal* (note 88), Chs.4, 5.
94. O'Malley, *Uncivil Wars*, cited above n.13, p.356.
95. S.I. 2146/1986.
96. Cmnd. 9758 (1986).
97. Chamberlain, 'Collective Suspension of Air Services', cited above n.80.
98. *Independent*, 3 Feb. 1989, p.3.
99. Wilkinson, *Terrorism and the Liberal State* (note 2), p.282.
100. 1982, c.36, Part II.
101. Ibid., s.26.

102. Boyle, Hadden and Hillyard, *Ten Years On* (note 19), p.27.
103. *Independent*, 2 June 1989, p.3.
104. J. Stalker, *Stalker* (London: Harrap, 1988).
105. For more details, see Adams, Morgan and Bambridge, *Ambush* (note 9); J. Adams, *Secret Armies: the Full Story of the S.A.S., Delta Force and Spetsnaz* (London: Hutchinson, 1987).
106. Boyle, Hadden and Hillyard, *Ten Years On* (note 19), p.19.
107. Criminal Justice Act 1967, ss.60, 61.
108. Cited in *Findlay v. Secretary of State for the Home Department* (1984) 3 All E.R. 801, at p.808.
109. PTA, s.22.
110. PTA, s.23.
111. Report of a Committee to consider, in the context of civil liberties and human rights, measures to deal with with terrorism in Northern Ireland, Cmnd. 5847 (1975), p.34.
112. Bishop and Mallie, *Provisional IRA* (note 7), Ch.19.
113. SACHR, Annual Report for 1985–86, H.C. 151 (1986–87), pp.15–16, App.F.
114. Ibid., pp.17–18, App.G.
115. *Independent*, 13 April 1989, p.3.
116. As note 103.
117. SACHR, cited above nn.113, 114.
118. L. Curtis, *Ireland: The Propaganda War* (London: Faber, 1984). Adams, *Financing of Terror* (note 8), Ch.6.
119. See, e.g., Home Office Circular 26/1984, on the PTA 1984.
120. Fourth Report from the Home Affairs Committee, Special branch, H.C. 71 (1984–85), p.xii, para.15.
121. See S. Greer, 'Military Intervention in Civil Disturbances: The Legal Basis Reconsidered' (1983) P.L. 573.
122. See D. Hamill, *Pig in the Middle: The Army in Northern Ireland 1969–1985* (London: Methuen, 1985).
123. Stalker, *Stalker* (note 104).
124. Adams, *et al.*, *Ambush* (note 9), pp.92–3.
125. Taylor, *Beating the Terrorists*, cited above n.54; D. Walsh, 'Arrest and Interrogation: Northern Ireland 1981', (1982) 9 B.J.L.S. 37.
126. Adams, *et al.*, *Ambush* (note 9).
127. See for statistics, Flackes, *Northern Ireland* (note 12), pp.320–3.

Switzerland: Terrorism and Its Control

ALBERT A. STAHEL

This essay briefly describes the kinds of domestic and international terrorism experienced by Switzerland over the past several decades. While the domestic terrorism was primarily low-level violence, Switzerland has experienced some significant international incidents. The primary Swiss link with international terrorism is as a logistical base for arms traffic and money laundering, as well as being a transit station to neighbouring countries. The article also describes the special anti-terrorist groups in Switzerland, noting that, unlike other Western nations, no national unit exists.

The Terrorist Scene in Switzerland

As in neighbouring countries, a distinction can be made in Switzerland between right-wing and left-wing terrorism. While right-wing violence in the Jura constitutes a peculiarly Swiss phenomenon, left-wing terrorism in Switzerland has been strongly influenced by the terror scene just across the country's borders. This was particularly so with the Petra Krause gang.

From 1970 to 1974 the Swiss anarchist group of Daniel von Arb, Peter Egloff and Urs Städeli stole weapons and ammunition from some Swiss Army depots.[1] Besides guns and ammunition, they showed a special preference for Mk.60 antitank mines, Mk.59 antipersonnel mines, Mk. 43 hand grenades and Mk.49 scatter mines. Distribution of these weapons did not function properly at first, succeeding only when, in April 1974, Italian terrorists sent the German/Italian, Petra Krause (alias Anna Maria Grenzi alias Marina alias Annababi), who soon took over as leader of the anarchist group. Through her contacts, the Zürich underground bureau became Europe's most sought-after address among terrorist circles. Hand grenades and various types of mines were dispatched abroad in large quantities. For example, mines, grenades and guns were supplied to the Italian Red Brigades and the German Red Army Faction. A marksman's rifle and a Suomi machine pistol that Annababi had sold were found in the ruins of the German Embassy in Stockholm, which German terrorists stormed and blew up on 24 April 1975. But Greek terrorists also got hold of the Swiss Mk.49 scatter mines and Mk.60 antitank mines.

On 20 March 1975 the Zürich police arrested Petra Krause on the

Bellevue Platz. She was detained for 28 months. With three hunger strikes, an escape attempt, refusal to take exercise and by legal means, she repeatedly postponed her trial. As a result of accusations by Italian feminist groups, Italian women in parliament and the Italian press that Switzerland was violating human rights, Petra Krause was literally praised out of detention, and on 15 August 1977 was extradited to Italy without trial. There she remained in prison for five days. The following year, in Naples, she was discharged for lack of evidence. Later, she lived for some years in Paris. Her three accomplices were arrested, confessed and were convicted in 1977.

Swiss Links with International Terrorism

If only because of its international connections, especially the presence of international organizations, Switzerland has close relations with terrorism abroad and performs an important logistical function in supplying terrorists internationally with arms and ammunition. Although the number of international terrorist attacks against Switzerland, Swiss citizens and Swiss property has ostensibly diminished in recent years, they continue to take place. One example is the series of attacks in Switzerland or against Swiss facilities abroad by the Beirut-based Armenian underground organization ASALA (Armenian Secret Army for the Liberation of Armenia).[2]
- on 22 July 1981 a bomb exploded at Geneva's Cornavin railway station: one dead and three injured;
- on 9 June 1981 a staff member of the Turkish Consulate-General in Geneva was murdered;
- on 21 July 1981 an explosive detonated in a Lausanne department store: 15 injured.

Among the reasons given for these attacks was that claims of a Turkish genocide of Armenians had twice been met with silence and treated as a closed issue during conferences held in Switzerland.

An instance of more recent international terrorist acts against Switzerland is the prompt reaction to the arrest of Al Atat, a Lebanese, at Kloten airport on 18 November 1984.[3] He had in his possession an explosive device, intended for use in Italy. In response, Erich Wehrli, Switzerland's temporary chargé d'affaires in Beirut, was abducted on 3 January 1985. The kidnappers demanded the release of Al Atat. Following assurances of a fair and speedy trial for Al Atat, the abductors freed Wehrli on 7 January 1985. On 30 January 1985 Al Atat received a suspended prison sentence of 18 months and the next day was shipped off to Beirut.

National terrorism

Only a few attacks of any import have occurred in Switzerland since the youth riots of 1980/81. The situation is one of minor incidents attributed either to particular groups or to hooligans, lone individuals or political crackpots and the like. The aims pursued are revenge, vandalism, blackmail and anarchy. The adoption of terrorist methods by trouble-seekers illustrates the increasing use of violence for non-ideological protests as well.

Among these minor incidents figures the bomb attack in June 1982, at Muri (Canton Berne), on the home of the initiator of the Stauffacher development in Zurich. In an anonymous letter, signed by a *Kommando Grober Ernst* ('Deadly Earnest Squad'), he was even threatened with death if he did not abandon his plans. And abandon them he did. The property department of a big company in Zurich took over the project. In July 1983 there was a bomb attack on the home of the company's director. In a letter full of threats, responsibility was claimed by presumably the same group, but under the name '*Ernst Grob, Grober Ernstli & McRöschti*'[4] – presumably involving the same people as the *Kommando Grober Ernst*.

According to Helfer,[5] 94 politically motivated attacks (bombings, arson, serious damage to property, coercion and theft) were carried out in Switzerland during 1986. Of the chosen target groups (business, judiciary, military, etc.), business bore the brunt with 25 incidents. Of the 94 attacks, damage to property accounted for 27, followed by 22 cases of arson, 20 of coercion and 3 bombings. The ratio of explosions to arson is typical for Switzerland. Since bomb attacks call for better training and organization than arson, this says something about the general level of sophistication. The risk of being caught is greater with bombings than with arson. Because of this, arsonists tend to be less aggressive than bombers.[6] An evaluation of the letters claiming responsibility shows the following motives for the 1986 attacks, with the main emphasis on the first four:[7] destruction of the environment; shortage of housing and leisure space; the nuclear threat; the acquisitive society; imperialism; the capitalist system; repression and invasions of privacy.

Combating terrorism

At the international level, Switzerland is, like the other Western countries, a signatory to various agreements, such as those covering air travel. On the national level, control of terrorism is organized as follows: at the federal level, the federal police are in charge of co-ordinating counter-measures; however, the cantons and their own police forces are responsible for putting these into effect. In line with other Western democracies, Switzerland has taken the step of setting up special Anti-Terrorist (AT) groups. Such groups have been formed by the police forces Zurich, Berne, and Aargau cantons, as well as others. Unlike the professionals abroad, the 200 men in the AT groups of the Swiss cantons are policemen who perform normal duties when not on anti-terrorism missions. Their training is equivalent to that of AT groups in other countries. While the AT teams are trained regionally by the respective police forces, the training of cantonal AT instructors and field commanders is assisted by the Swiss Police Institute in Neuchâtel, together with the Federal Department of Justice and Police. What Switzerland lacks is an anti-terrorist unit at the central government level.

Conclusions

If Switzerland does not exactly occupy centre stage as far as terrorism is concerned, neither is it a blank space on the map of the terrorism war. Whereas, on a national scale, attacks in Switzerland are mainly the work of hotheads, the country's significance to international terrorism lies in the logistical sphere (weapons procurement and the laundering of money) and as a transit station. Neighbouring countries can be reached via Switzerland without the risk of close border control. It is regrettable that the step to create a national anti-terrorist unit has not been taken, and most likely never will, because of Switzerland's federal structure.

NOTES

1. E. Büchler, 'Terrorismus in der Schweiz: Waffen- und Sprengstoffbeschaffung für den Internationalen Terrorismus?', *Seminararbeit* MS II/86, Zurich, 1986 (Confidential), p.32f.
2. J.-P. Guélat, *Le terrorisme en Suisse*, Seminararbeit MS II/86, Zurich, 1983 (Classified), p.13.
3. Büchler, pp.24–5.
4. Ibid., p.29.
5. H.U. Helfer, *Politisch motivierte Anschläge in der Schweiz 1986* (Zürich: Presdok, 1987), pp.7–40.
6. Helfer, *Politisch motivierte Anschläge*, pp.30–1.
7. Ibid., p.35; A.A. Stahel, *Terrorismus und Marxismus, Marxistisch-Leninistische Konzeptionen des Terrorismus und der Revolution* (Huber Frauenfeld, 1987).

Terrorism in Austria: Experiences and Responses

HEINZ VETSCHERA

Before World War II Austria experienced significant political violence in two civil wars and from terrorism sponsored by Nazi Germany. Anti-terrorist legislation of that time anticipated various modern counter-terrorist initiatives. Since World War II Austria has suffered from both domestic and foreign terrorism, but to a lesser degree than other western European states. Domestic terrorism was mostly confined to individual violence and has never reached the level of coherent terrorist organizations. Foreign, 'imported' terrorism reached a higher intensity, but was not directed against Austria as the main objective. Austria served rather as a logistic base for German terrorists as well as a stage for Arab, Armenian and other violence related to the Middle East. In response Austria amended its already existing anti-terrorist legislation and took necessary measures, for example in intelligence and in the adaptation and creation of special police formations. On the international level Austria has on the one hand attempted to defuse regional conflicts prone to breed terrorism, and has on the other hand participated in (and in part also initiated) an intensified anti-terrorist cooperation among European states, but also within the United Nations.

With regard to terrorism, Austria differs significantly from other western European countries. Normally, Austria would not be associated by most people with modern terrorism at all. Despite some international terrorism incidents in Austria during the past two decades, the overall image of Austria would be that of a peaceful, non-violent country more or less unaffected by the major waves of terrorism or other forms of political violence during the past years. Consequently, neither has there been much to be heard about anti-terrorist measures taken by Austria. On the other hand, one must not ignore earlier experience with political violence in Austria. It predates in many cases modern transnational or international terrorism, as Austria had to cope *inter alia* with a major threat of state-sponsored terrorism by Nazi Germany in the 1930s. This has shaped many of the approaches taken in Austria to respond to political violence in general, and to terrorism in particular. Thus, the issue of experiences with and responses to terrorism in Austria requires an approach differing from other European countries. It will of necessity emphasize the historical dimension without, however, ignoring recent developments.

The Historical Background: The First and the Second Republic

After the defeat in World War I and the end of the Austro-Hungarian Empire, the remaining Austria (the 'First Republic') went through often violent confrontations of conservatives, socialists and communists, and National Socialists (Nazis). Political violence in Austria gained a new dimension when Adolf Hitler came to power in neighbouring Germany. National Socialists were subsequently actively supported by a foreign government, making Austria the target of state-sponsored terrorism. In 1933 a conservative Austrian government disbanded the parliament, abolished the existing constitution and replaced it by authoritarian rule similar to Mussolini's government in Italy. When in June 1933 a policeman was killed in a Nazi grenade attack, the Austrian government banned all National Socialist organizations. It also banned the socialists, which finally led to civil war in Vienna between the government and the Social Democrats' armed formation in February 1934. According to official data, 314 people were killed during four days of fighting, but the real figures may be significantly higher.

In July 1934 a Nazi commando group attempted to capture the entire government during a cabinet meeting and seize power. They failed, but during the action shot the Federal Chancellor. Simultaneous provincial uprisings by Nazis failed, too, and were successfully overcome by the armed forces. Official figures claim 244 people killed and more than 600 wounded during several days of fighting. The government reacted with anti-terrorist legislation which has since then influenced Austria's actions against political violence and terrorism. Also, a special guards battalion of the armed forces was established in Vienna for military protection of the capital. Despite all legislative, military, police and other measures, including the establishment of concentration camps for National Socialists and Social Democrats, the government was unable to prevent the further escalation of political violence. In addition, both the Nazis and other groups frequently used 'non-violent actions', namely propaganda, violence against property and other actions not intended to hurt persons, but to subvert and destabilize the government. Finally, in March 1938, Austria collapsed. A Nazi became Federal Chancellor and led Austria into unification with Germany (*Anschluss*). Nazi Germany's campaign of state-sponsored terrorism against Austria now became part of the government terror exercised by Hitler's dictatorship.

After World War II Austria was occupied by the four allied powers – France, the United Kingdom, the USA and the Soviet Union – and regained full independence only in 1955 with the signing of the State Treaty. After the last foreign soldier had left Austria, she declared permanent neutrality. In contrast to the development between the wars, the 'Second Republic' was based upon consensus rather than conflict between the major political forces. Nevertheless, even the 'non-violent' Second Republic was confronted with political violence.

National and International Challenges in the Field of Political Violence

Even without a genuine domestic terrorist movement comparable to other European countries, Austria has not been immune against several acts of domestic political violence. Austria has also been the stage for several terrorist acts by transnational groups, especially of Middle Eastern origin. To a certain extent, Austria has even been involved in active support for terrorism.

Domestic Terrorism

Most acts of domestic terrorism were related to minority issues. First, Austria was to a certain degree involved in violence in the Italian (South) Tyrol, inhabited by a large German-speaking regional majority. After harsh suppression by Mussolini's Fascist government, this group was granted minority rights by postwar Italy in an agreement with Austria in 1947. As the Italian side ignored its obligations, the regional population organized protest actions which in 1961 escalated into violence and terrorism. Parallel to the escalation in Italy, right-wing extremists in Austria committed arson and bomb attacks against Italian targets. In addition, between 1963 and 1967, Austrian extremists increasingly became involved in terrorist actions in Italy, both by providing explosives, and by actively participating in bomb attacks which cost several lives.

On the other hand, Italian terrorists conducted several counter-attacks in Austria between 1961 and 1963, which also cost several lives. Although Austria supported the minority's struggle morally and politically, Austrian and Italian authorities cooperated closely in preventing any escalation into terrorism. Austrian police arrested both Austrian and German-speaking Italian members of the resistance movement. Most of them were tried and convicted in Austria. In 1967 Austria even sent the Federal Army (*Bundesheer*) into action to prevent terrorist infiltration into Italy. Conversely, Italian authorities arrested and imprisoned the Italians involved in the bombing 'counter-attacks' in Austria.

A separate wave of domestic political violence was also related to minority issues. In the Austrian State Treaty, Yugoslav minorities (both Slovenes and Croats) in the provinces of Carinthia, Burgenland and Styria, had been granted minority rights, including bilingual topographical terminology and signposts. When Austria delayed the establishment of bilingual topographical signposts, the Slovene minority in Carinthia initiated a protest campaign in 1970, including the painting of Slovene names over German inscriptions. Two years later, a federal law was passed for bilingual signposts in the areas concerned. However, German nationalists prevented its execution by acts of civilian resistance, for example, removing bilingual road signs. A series of reciprocal bomb attacks was then initiated against memorials of the Yugoslav partisans (normally associated with the Slovene minority) and against memorials for the anti-Yugoslav Carinthian defense (*Abwehrkampf*) in 1920 (normally associated with the German-speaking majority), but also against power lines and railway lines. It was more by good luck than by accurate planning that most of the attacks caused only material damage but took no lives. Bombings took place even after the political end of the conflict, which was agreed between Austria and Yugoslavia in 1977.

Both the minority struggles in South Tyrol and in Carinthia also triggered waves of German nationalist and neo-Nazi violence. Some violent activists supporting the 'German case' in South Tyrol were also involved in several right-wing extremist organizations which were outlawed under the postwar anti-Nazi laws. In the 1960s they attacked not only Italian, but also American targets, in consonance with the 'enemy' images of their ideology. During the 1970s they were apparently linked to anti-Israeli Arab terrorists. During the early 1980s their attacks increased slightly. In some cases, attacks were either instigated or even executed by radicals from Germany. There has been a further increase in the number of attacks since 1986. The means have been relatively primitive, however, comprising either Molotov cocktails or bombs built from pressure-cookers filled with gunpowder. These attacks have been seen more as being of a symbolic nature than as a real terrorist threat. Those involved were, however, sentenced to up to five years in prison.

German Leftist Terrorism in Austria

The emergence of left-wing extremism and terrorism in the Federal Republic of Germany also afflicted neighbouring Austria, mainly because of the common language. Connections between the German and the Austrian extreme left were discernible in several violent demonstrations in the early 1970s. From the mid-1970s onwards, Austria increasingly became a potential hiding place, but also a logistic base for German terrorists. In 1976 a district office (*Bezirkshauptmannschaft*) was raided in Landeck in Tyrol, and several documents were stolen in order to provide Austrian identities for Red Army Faction terrorists. In December 1976 two members of the Red Army Faction attempted to rob a bank in Vienna. After a shoot-out with the police, one of them, Waltraud Boock, was caught and later sentenced to several years in prison. Five days after her arrest, sympathizers exploded a bomb in the Central Police Office in Vienna. Some arson attacks against the Austrian branch of the British firm Marks & Spencer in 1977 were also ascribed to sympathizers of the Red Army Faction or the IRA, although there has been no definitive proof.

In November 1977 German terrorists of the 'June 2' movement, assisted by Austrian extremists, abducted the millionaire M. Palmers, owner of a major textile firm, and demanded a ransom of several million Austrian schillings. After the money had been handed over, the terrorists released their hostage. Within a few days, the Austrians involved in the abduction were arrested at the Swiss border. They had arms with them and some of the ransom. They were later brought to trial and convicted. When the 'June 2' merged with the Red Army Faction in June 1980, they brought in something like a million marks of the Austrian ransom, which gave the Red Army Faction financial autonomy for the following two years. Since that time, no major actions of German terrorism have taken place in Austria. This does not exclude, however, the use of Austria as a hiding place or as a logistical base for German terrorists.

Palestinian Terrorism in Austria

For several reasons, Austria has also become involved in Middle East terrorism. In 1970 Austria's foreign policy took a distinct turn in favour of a clearly pro-Arab policy in the Middle East. In part, this was meant to avoid involvement in the emerging Palestinian terrorism of the early 1970s, but its main objective was apparently a higher profile in the Third World, and in the United Nations (UN).

By tradition, Austria had been a transit station for Soviet Jews emigrating to Israel. In September 1973 a Palestinian commando attacked a train with Jewish emigrants from the Soviet Union at the Czechoslovak-Austrian border. They took several hostages. After the Austrian government promised to close down a transit camp (which up to then had been run in effect by Israeli authorities), and allowed the terrorists and their hostages to go, the action was brought to an end without bloodshed. The 'Eagles of the Palestinian Revolution', associated with the Syrian-backed 'Saika' movement, claimed responsibility for this action. In 1979 the same group conducted a bomb attack against a synagogue in Vienna which fortunately caused only material damage.

In December 1975 a Popular Front for the Liberation of Palestine (PFLP) commando of Germans and Palestinians led by 'Carlos' Ramirez attacked the headquarters of the Organization of Petrol Exporting Countries (OPEC) during a conference of petroleum ministers. They shot three people and took 70 hostages, among them most of the ministers. After lengthy negotiations, they were finally allowed to depart with some hostages to Algeria, where the ministers were released.

In November 1980 a bomb detonated at a hotel in Salzburg just before a lecture on Israel was scheduled to take place. It was later attributed to the leader of a Palestinian commando which in the following year conducted the most severe attacks in Austria. On 1 May 1981 City Councillor Heinz Nittel, President of the Austro-Israeli Friendship Society, was assassinated in Vienna. In July 1981 some Arabs were arrested at Vienna airport when they attempted to smuggle weapons and explosives into Austria for a planned attack on Egyptian President Anwar Al Sadat, who was to visit Austria three weeks later. In this incident, the representative of the Palestine Liberation Organisation (PLO) to the UN in Vienna was involved. On 29 August 1981 three members of the Abu Nidal group attacked the Vienna synagogue with sub-machine-guns and grenades, killing two and injuring more than 20 people. They were arrested. The apparent purpose of the attack was to disturb the peace process in the Middle East. During interrogation, one of them also confessed to the assassination of City Councillor Nittel four months earlier. Further information led to the arrest of the group's leader, who had been involved in the 1980 incident in Salzburg.

The latest act of Palestinian terrorism was an attack by the Abu Nidal group on Vienna airport on 27 December 1985. The attack cost the lives of two passengers and one terrorist, and left 47 wounded. A simultaneous attack on Rome airport killed 13 and wounded 50 people. Again, the purpose of the attack appears to have been the torpedoing of a negotiated solution in the Middle East.

Anti-Turkish Terrorism in Austria

Since the early 1970s, Turkish diplomats abroad have increasingly become the victims of Armenian terrorists ostensibly seeking revenge for the genocide that took place in Ottoman Turkey in 1915–16. In October 1975 a commando group of three stormed the Turkish embassy in Vienna. After virtually executing the Ambassador, they managed to escape. The next day, the Turkish Ambassador in Paris was assassinated as well. Then, in June 1984, another Turkish diplomat, who in fact was a high-ranking intelligence officer, was killed by a bomb attached to his car. Finally, in November 1984, a Turkish director of the UN Industrial Development Organization (UNIDO) in Vienna was shot in his car while driving to his office. For all these attacks, Armenian organizations claimed responsibility. In September 1987 an arson ·attack against a Turkish Airlines office was committed by the (illegal) Turkish Communist

Party–Marxists/Leninists to mark the anniversary of the military coup in Turkey.

Other Foreign Political Violence

The war between Iran and Iraq, as well their civil war with Kurdish minorities, also spilled over into Austria. In 1980 a Kurd was killed in Vienna while preparing a car bomb. In 1982 the Iraqi embassy and the Iraqi airline were bombed by an Iraqi dissident organization. In the same year, Islamic extremists bombed the French embassy and the Air France office in Vienna. In August 1983 an Islamic commando hijacked an Air France plane en route from Vienna to Teheran. Then, in 1986, a letter bomb was sent to the Iranian embassy in Vienna. In 1987 shots were fired against a Kurdish club in Vienna. In 1988 shots were fired from the Iraqi embassy against Kurdish demonstrators in front of the building. The most severe incident, however, took place in 1989, when three exiled Kurdish dissidents were shot at a secret meeting in Vienna, most probably by Iranian agents. Letter bombs were sent to Austrian firms who had traded with Iraq in 1987.

Other incidents include the attempt by nine Pakistanis in 1984 to take hostages at a hotel in Vienna to free 200 political prisoners in Pakistan. They were apprehended before executing their plans. A former Libyan diplomat was attacked, both in 1985 and in 1987. While it has been suggested that political motives might have been involved, as he had opposed Colonel Gaddafi's regime, it is more probable that the attack had personal reasons. Attacks by unidentified persons include a bomb attack on a branch of a Hungarian bank at Vienna in 1985 and an attack at the Saudi Arabian airlines in 1986, just after a conference of the Austrian and the Saudi interior ministers.

Conclusions

Both the figures and the structure of political violence in Austria differ sharply between the First and the Second Republic. According to a recent source,[1] 338 major actions of political violence (including the two civil wars of 1934) took place in Austria between 1918 and 1938, which cost at least 836 lives and more than 2,000 wounded. For the Second Republic, the figures until the end of 1988 are 184 incidents (including violent clashes of opposing groups) with 16 dead and 112 wounded. To these victims, the three exiled Kurds assassinated in 1989 have to be added.

There are also qualitative differences. Major waves of domestic political violence were triggered by the minority issues in the 1960s and the 1970s which could be overcome, however, by the political defusing of the underlying conflicts. The remaining cases were of low intensity, despite a slight increase in numbers. Most of these, however, appear to be spontaneous acts of individuals, rather than the outcome of organized terrorism. In many cases, it may be unclear whether violence really served as an instrument for a political cause, or whether ideology served as a vehicle to legitimize the individual drive for destruction. This fact should not make us ignore the few cases of organized movements (as for example by some neo-Nazi groups, who have consciously planned violence), but should put it in proper perspective.

The acts of political violence of foreign origin, although not directed against Austria as such since the end of the South Tyrol crisis, were more serious. With regard to western European terrorism, Austria has served as a logistical base especially for German terrorists, due to the links between Austrian and German radicals on both sides of the political spectrum. With regard to Middle Eastern terrorism (Palestinian, anti-Turkish and 'surrogate warfare' in the Iran-Iraq conflict), Austria as well as many other western European countries became the stage rather than the target for attacks between conflicting parties. These acts had nothing to do with Austria's existence, her political system, or her political objectives. Violence was not directed against Austria, although in some cases against individual Austrians, as in the murder of Austrian policemen in the OPEC hostage case, and in the assassination of City Councillor Nittel, and in the synagogue attack.

The Response of Government and Society

Austria's experience with terrorist threats has been mainly in the interwar period. Correspondingly, the response of the official side, especially with regard to legislation, has also been shaped in history rather than in the recent past. Modern terrorism has induced adaptations rather than innovation in the legal, political and organizational approaches to counter-terrorism.

Legal Measures

Austria's legal system has always included several provisions against political violence. The Criminal Code of 1852 made an implicit distinction between political crimes, meaning to threaten the state, and ordinary criminal acts. Political crimes included acts like high treason and espionage, but also any violent or non-violent interference with the work of authorities. For example, organized, violent resistance against the authorities was qualified as the crime of insurgency (Articles 68 and 69). Threatening violence against authorities or offering individual violent resistance against the acts of authorities was labeled a crime of coercion

(Art.81). Non-violent resistance, or exhorting people to it, against acts of the authorities, constituted the lesser crime of rioting (Art.279). In addition, the Criminal Code included provisions against disturbances of public order, as for example the instigation of hate against the state, the system of government, or the constitution (Art.65), but also the instigation of hostility against nationalities, religious or other communities, or classes of the population. The latter provision appears especially important from the historical perspective, as Austria at that time was a multinational state which had to cope with increasing nationalism.

The purely criminal contents of political violence, however, were treated strictly as ordinary crimes, as for example murder, bodily injury, arson, etc. A Law on Explosives (*Sprengstoffgesetz*, RGBl. 1885/134)[2] not only regulated normal conduct with regard to explosives but also included criminal provisions against the use of explosives to endanger the life or health of human beings, or to damage property. It provided the legal basis to prosecute all forms of bombing.

Specific anti-terror legislation was initiated to counter Nazi Germany's state-sponsored terrorism in the 1930s. The Law on Explosives was amended in 1934 and 1935 (BGBl. 1934/II/7 and 1935/197). In 1935 quasi-censorship was introduced by means of the Law against Publications Hostile to the State (*Bundesgesetz zur Bekämpfung staatsfeindlicher Druckwerke*, BGBl. 1935/33). In 1936 a special Law on the Protection of the State (*Staatsschutzgesetz*, BGBl. 1936/223) was enacted. It was directed against secret armed or militarily organized associations, and against associations hostile to the state (Arts.1 and 4). It made it a crime to establish, join or support such organizations or to provide them with any type of combat, transportation, or communication equipment. On the other hand, reporting to the authorities exempted informers from punishment (Arts.3 and 6). The law also punished the secret or illegal production, storage, accumulation or distribution of means of combat understood in a broad sense, including tear-gas or similar means to disturb public events (Art.10 and 11).

When Austria regained independence from Germany in 1945, the Criminal Code of 1852 was reinstated (StGBl. 1945/25). In a similar way, the Law on the Protection of the State remained in force. A constitutional law prohibited any re-establishment of the National Socialist party or any of its organizations, and declared such acts criminal offences (StGBl. 1945/13). On the other hand, laws incompatible with the democratic, liberal character of the Second Republic have been abolished subsequently, for example, the Law Against Publications Hostile to the State. The legal situation remained basically unchanged until the early 1970s, when a completely new Criminal Code was introduced.

Work on the new Criminal Code had already been conducted in the 1950s and 1960s. It took its final shape in the late 1960s but could not be enacted until January 1974. It came into force on 1 January 1975. Its origins thus predate the emergence of modern terrorism, but during the latest stage of parliamentary considerations, specific anti-terrorist clauses have been included. The new Criminal Code covers, in principle, the same political crimes as the former criminal Code and the Law on the Protection of the State. It lists as crimes the founding, leading, joining or supporting of associations hostile to the state (Art.246), that is, aimed at attacking by illegal (but not necessarily violent) means the independence, the constitutional system or a constitutional body of the State; threats or coercion against the Federal President, any legislative body, any (federal or regional) government or any of the supreme courts or their members (Arts.249, 250, 251); violent resistance or violent attack against the acts of authorities (Arts.269 and 270); any forms of associations to commit future crimes (Arts.277 and 278); the founding, leading, training or supplying of organizations armed or to be armed (Art.279); the accumulation, keeping or distributing of means of combat (Art.280). Simultaneously, the Law on the Protection of the State was declared obsolete.

With regard to acts typical of modern terrorism, Articles 185 and 186 protect civilian aviation against acts of piracy or other acts intended to endanger its safety. Both articles have been included to conform to the Montreal Convention for the Suppression of Unlawful Acts Against the Safety of Civil Aviation of 23 September 1971, which was ratified by Austria in 1974 (BGBl. 1974/248). The taking of hostages is dealt with in a separate Article (Art.102). According to the parliamentary reports of the Committee on Justice, the draft text of this Article has been explicitly reshaped to make it applicable against terrorist hostage-taking. Most of the acts typical of modern terrorism would, however, be covered by the ordinary crimes enumerated in the criminal code, for example murder, bodily injury, arson or deprivation of personal freedom, but also the forging of documents, or other criminal acts necessary for the clandestine preparation of terrorist acts. Austria has explicitly rejected the idea of separate anti-terror legislation and prefers to treat terrorism within legislation on criminal law in general.

The only specific case has, however, been the Law Prohibiting the Bringing of Dangerous Objects into Civil Aircrafts of 13 July 1971 (*Bundesgesetz über das Verbot des Einbringens von gefährlichen Gegen-ständen in Zivilluftfahrzeuge*, BGBl. 294/1971). It has been the legal basis for several preventive measures at civilian airports, for example the screening of luggage, or the body-check of persons. Another area of legal prevention of terrorism has been the arms legislation. The Law on Arms (*Waffengesetz*) has been amended in 1980 (BGBl. 1980/75) explicitly to prohibit the possession of war materiel. Although legislation in this specific case was overdue as the Law on Arms enacted in 1967 (BGBl. 1967/121) had left the issue open, and no specific reference was made of its anti-terrorist character, the law now allows far better prevention in this area.

Similar to the area of criminal law, no specific legislation has been introduced with regard to criminal court procedures, or with regard to specific or extraordinary powers for security forces. The few serious cases of terrorism have not induced any such steps. The only reference to criminal acts originating from abroad is Art.64 (1) of the criminal code which establishes prosecution by Austrian courts for certain criminal acts committed abroad. The only reference to political crimes is Art.14 (1) of the Criminal Procedural Order (*Strafprozessordnung*) which establishes that certain political crimes should be judged by a jury. However, this rule was established long before the emergence of modern terrorism and has not been specifically induced by it.

With regard to extradition policies, Art.14 of the Law of 4 December 1979, on Extradition and Assistance in Legal Matters (BGBl. 529/1979), prohibits extradition in the case of merely political crimes (e.g., treason) but also of 'relative' political crimes, namely, crimes with a political motivation. In the latter case, however, an exception is made if the criminal character of the crime outweighs the political motivation. This rule is based on Art.3 of the European Convention on Extradition which has been ratified by Austria (BGBl. 320/1969). In a similar way, the European Convention on the Suppression of Terrorism of 27 January 1977 (ratified by Austria, BGBl. 446/1978) provides that an extradition must not be rejected on grounds of a political motivation if terrorist acts against civil aviation or against diplomats are involved. These rules also guide Austria's policy with regard to extradition in terrorist cases. For example, the Red Army Faction terrorist Waltraud Boock was extradited to the Federal Republic after ten years in prison in Austria.

Economic Measures

Austria has not taken any specific economic measures to counter terrorism, or any sanctions against states suspected of supporting terrorism. Rather, a reverse tendency is noticeable. While most western European states distanced themselves from Arab states (especially those apparently associated with terrorism), Austria expanded economic relations. This was partly due to the guiding principles of Austria's foreign policy in the Middle East at that time, but also due to economic interests which hoped for expansion towards markets with reduced

Western competition. A special case was the increase in commercial and political relations with Libya at a time when Colonel Gaddafi was strongly suspected of supporting international terrorism.

As far as financial rewards for information about criminal acts are concerned, these form an integral part of Austria's police procedures and have not been specifically introduced to counter terrorism.

Political Measures

Austria's basic approach to countering political violence has been on the political level, the overarching idea being to defuse the underlying causes. This was the case in the minority conflicts both in Italy and in Carinthia, but to a certain extent even with regard to the Middle East conflict. On the level of actual incidents, one has to make a distinction between cases in which time allowed the government to find a solution and those where the government could react only after the event had already taken place.

On the domestic level, Austria has developed a mixed pattern of resisting and yielding to demands supported by political violence. The criteria appear to be determined by the level of public support for the demands, and the level of violence. In some cases of non-violent resistance against government measures, the government was apparently willing to implement action against non-violent resistance, until the danger of escalation into violence emerged. Then, the government gave in to avoid escalation. This was the case, for example, during the minority dispute in Carinthia. The parliament had passed a law on bilingual topographic signposts. When road signs were installed in 1972, German-speaking extremists removed them. As the extremists had the backing of the local population, and escalation into violence could not be excluded, the government tacitly tolerated the actions, until the road signs could be installed five years later, after the situation had cooled down.

A similar pattern was apparent in 1984, when demonstrators illegally occupied an area where a power plant was to be built along the Danube. After initial attempts by the police to remove the occupants, the government finally decided to yield rather than to escalate the conflict. A major factor in this case was apparently the support for the demonstrators' demands by a major newspaper which until then had mainly supported the government. Another factor was the danger of escalation into violence as could be witnessed in parallel events in Germany. On the other hand, squatters in illegally occupied houses have usually been tolerated until they became a burden to the surrounding population. Then, however, they were removed by force, as it was clear that they would not get any support from the public.

Domestic incidents where the time factor precluded the possibility of political decision-making were treated by the police as normal criminal matters, both in terms of repression and investigation. With regard to foreign political violence, the same distinction can be made. When time allowed it, the usual policy has been to yield to the terrorists' demands and allow them to depart, in order to save the lives of those involved. This was the line taken both in the hostage case of the Jewish emigrants at Marchegg in 1973, and that of the OPEC ministers in 1975. In the Palmers case of 1977, the government virtually treated it as a private matter of the hostage's family, until the subsequent arrest of the Austrians involved in the case. In single phase incidents, including the attacks on the Vienna synagogue and the airport, the policemen on guard evidently acted under instruction not to abstain from action. They intervened by armed force and overcame the terrorists.

Normally, after terrorist acts have been committed, criminal investigations have taken their usual course. However, after the assassination of three exiled Kurds in Vienna in 1989, arrest warrants against suspected Iranians who had found refuge in the Iranian embassy were delayed until they had left Austria. There were indications that the government had acted out of fear of further terrorist attacks against Austrians both at home and abroad. This was, however, officially denied.

International Diplomatic Initiatives

During the 1970s and the early 1980s foreign policy was emphasized as the main instrument of Austria's security policy. This fact was also reflected in Austria's international activities against terrorism. Austria joined and ratified the Tokyo Convention on Offenses and Certain Other Acts Committed on Board of Aircraft of 14 September 1963 (BGBl. 1974/247), the Montreal Convention for the Suppression of Unlawful Acts against the Safety of Civil Aviation of 23 September 1971 (BGBl. 1974/248), the Convention for Suppression of Unlawful Seizure of Aircraft of The Hague of 16 December 1970 (BGBl. 1974/249), the Convention on the Prevention and Punishment of Crimes against Internationally Protected Persons, including Diplomatic Agents, of 12 December 1973 (BGBl. 1977/488), and the European Convention on the Suppression of Terrorism of 27 January 1977 (BGBl. 1978/446).

The emphasis was, however, on Austria's diplomatic engagement in the Middle East. Whereas most other western European countries sided for a long time with Israel and avoided contacts with the PLO as well as with the Libyan leader Colonel Gaddafi, Austria definitely sought contacts with them at an early stage, even when their involvement in terrorist operations and in training European terrorists could not be excluded. The then Federal Chancellor frequently met Chairman Yasser Arafat and

Colonel Gaddafi and invited them to Vienna. Austria was the first Western state formally to recognize the PLO, which was allowed to open offices both with the UN special organizations in Vienna, and with Austria.

These steps should not be seen as a distinct policy to counter international terrorism, but rather as being determined by a highly personalized anti-Israeli bias on the part of the then Federal Chancellor Bruno Kreisky, which was evidently not shared by the majority of Austria's foreign policy elite.[3] However, they necessarily influenced Austria's position *vis-à-vis* terrorism. For example, when in the early 1980s some Arabs raided a bus in Israel and killed several schoolchildren, the then Foreign Minister of Austria who happened to be on a visit in an Arab country formally condemned the attack but stated that there was a 'certain connection with Israel's policy in the occupied territories'.

Military and Police Measures

The military and the police are strictly separated in Austria. According to the Federal Constitution, the task of the military is military defence, that is, to counter violent threats from abroad (Art. 79 (1)). The task of the police is to maintain public order and security, which falls under the task of 'civilian defence' within the framework of the Comprehensive National Defense. However, the Federal Constitution also provides that the military can be called in by the civilian authorities to assist in maintaining public order and security (Art.79 (2) 1. a). During the First Republic, this provision was seen mainly in the perspective of the 1934 civil wars. In the present situation, it is more likely to be applicable to counter a terrorist threat. For example, the only case – apart from assistance in natural disasters – where the civilian authorities have called in the armed forces was the sealing of the Italian border in 1967, in order to prevent Austrian terrorist infiltration into Italy.

In general, however, the issue of terrorism has been mostly ignored by the Austrian military, despite the fact that the National Defense Plan (*Landesverteidigungsplan*) explicitly enumerates threats below the level of conventional warfare, for example terrorism, as threats to Austria's security. As the main task of Austria's armed forces has been seen as preserving permanent neutrality *vis-à-vis* potential future belligerents in Europe, conflict scenarios have been mostly based upon conventional warfare. Phenomena of low-intensity conflict have been mostly ignored. In contrast to other armed forces, those of Austria have not yet become the target of terrorist threats or attacks, apart from some hoaxes mostly in the late 1970s. The topic of terrorism is, therefore, quite remote for the average soldiers and officers. It may be assumed that within the armed forces' intelligence and counter-intelligence offices and staff branches some precautions will be taken against the emergence of terrorist threats, but there is no information available. As far as it is visible, however, the Army has, until now, done little to protect itself against terrorism or to develop any specific capability for counter-terrorist actions. This is primarily seen as a task for the police.

Police measures include the establishing of several special units. These will be dealt with below. Special measures have also been taken to protect threatened persons and objects, for example diplomatic representatives or international organizations. Such measures have been taken to fulfil obligations of the Convention on the Prevention of Crimes against Internationally Protected Persons, as well as agreements between Austria and the respective international organizations. Protection includes patrolling by uniformed police and detectives, guarding of objects (for example embassies) by uniformed police, and the installation of alarm communication facilities to dispatch police units in case of an attack. Measures to protect persons include escorts by armed detectives. Foreign representatives are sometimes allowed their own armed bodyguards. This does not, however, reduce Austria's responsibility for their safety. In the case of warning against and intelligence on impending terrorist threats against persons or objects, protective measures are intensified in proportion to the threat.

Other measures include special protection of airports as they have frequently become targets of terrorist attacks. Surveillance and protective measures have been intensified, and Austrian airports have been equipped with modern anti-terror devices, for example for the screening of luggage. Emphasis is given to Vienna airport, as it is an open gate to the Middle East, and has already been the object of terrorist attacks. These measures are to be expanded along with the further expansion of the airport. In addition, police measures include tighter control of lodging, border-crossing and the issuing of visas. Terrorist alerts are the basis for concentrated search actions, and information on dangerous persons is regularly issued to police offices. Granting of Austrian visas has been restricted, and the privilege of visa-free entry to Austria for owners of diplomatic passports has been abolished by Ministry of the Interior decree in February 1986, shortly after the attack on Vienna airport. As another consequence of this attack, visas were re-introduced for Tunisia, as the terrorists had used Tunisian passports. Only after Tunisia began to issue forge-proof passports was this measure revoked.

Prison Measures

No specific measures have been taken with regard to the terrorists in Austrian jails. In 1988, 15 terrorists were serving their terms in Austrian prisons. Austrian law courts and prison authorities have taken the normal procedures and have not yielded to any pressure to release imprisoned terrorists or to give them any special status. Terrorists are treated as ordinary criminals.

Psychological Measures

No specific psychological measures have apparently been taken, as the psychological climate in Austria has not been favourable for terrorism. Sympathy for the struggle in South Tyrol decreased when it escalated into terrorism and cost lives. The 1970s unrest in Carinthia polarized public opinion to some extent, with pro-minority sentiments generally on the left, and pro-majority sentiments generally on the right. However, the use of violence and the bombing attacks were generally rejected.

Terrorism was even more strongly rejected when it came from abroad. With regard to the Middle East, public opinion in Austria was generally pro-Israeli, with anti-Israeli sentiments only on the extreme right (because of traditional anti-Semitism) and on the extreme left (because of the siding with the PLO as a 'progressive force'). In addition, the first Arab attack took place against a humanitarian transport of emigrants, which gave terrorism a cowardly image. These feelings may have been enhanced by an emotional rejection of any acts of irregular warfare, due to personal experience of the elder generation in World War II, and by widespread anti-communism.

This, in turn, was the result of ten years of occupation of eastern Austria by the Soviet Union, its violent suppression of the Hungarian uprising in 1956, and the invasion of Czechoslovakia in 1968. Since the PLO was seen as a Soviet proxy in the Middle East, this also contributed to a rejection of both its policy objectives and its means. It also contributed to a widespread rejection of left-wing West European terrorist movements, such as the German Red Army Faction, or the Italian Red Brigades, but also of the violent demonstrations by the extreme left in Austria. Finally, foreign terrorists' actions were generally seen as disturbing Austria's domestic peace, and therefore rejected.

The media usually reflect these sentiments. In Austria, the audiovisual media are public institutions, while the printed media are private. There are only a few nationwide daily papers, and they conform to the mainstream of public opinion. Normally, they report on terrorist incidents as on any other form of crime, without, however, fuelling any sort of hysteria. This may be due to the normally good relationship between the media and the police which has been disturbed only in a few cases. In most clashes between the police and violent demonstrators, however, the media sided with the forces maintaining public law and order. This fact has influenced public opinion of anti-terrorist measures, as well as the impact of terrorist propaganda. Normally, public opinion accepts anti-terrorist measures, such as the security screenings at airports, as they are seen as necessary for one's own safety. Propaganda favourable to terrorist movements has not had much chance in Austria, except with small fringe groups on the respective sides of the political spectrum. For these reasons, there was little need for countering propaganda.

By tradition, students have been prominent among the radicals on both sides of the political spectrum. Whereas in the early 1960s, and especially during the crisis in South Tyrol, student extremism was stronger on the right – there was even one person killed during violent clashes between right-wing students and left-wing demonstrators in Vienna – it has since then declined. Right-wing extremism now recruits its followers mainly from uneducated strata of society. During the 1970s Marxist and anarchist groups flourished but have declined during the 1980s. Elections to the students' parliaments show a general decline in interest with extremely low voting rates, and a general turn towards the centre, with some residual inclination towards extremist positions. There has never been a pattern of explicitly siding with terrorism, as for example in the Federal Republic (e.g., the 'Mescalero' pamphlet). Nevertheless, the Austrians involved in the Palmers case had a background in extreme leftist student circles.

Organization of Anti-Terrorist Units and Bureaucracy

Austria is a federal state. According to the Federal Constitution (Art.10), the maintenance of public order and security is exclusively a matter of the federation (*Bund*). Thus, in contrast to other federal states, for example Switzerland or Germany, the provinces (*Länder*) have no police authority. According to the Federal Law on the Federal Ministries (*Bundesministeriengesetz*, BGBl. 1973/389), the maintenance of public order and security is the task of the Ministry of the Interior (*Bundesministerium für Inneres*).

By tradition, the Austrian police has always included a component of political police (*Staatspolizei*). Its task has been to protect the constitutional order, but also to execute some administrative functions, for example the registration of foreigners, the issuing of passports, the regulation of associations and gatherings. By definition, the political police in Austria are oriented towards both the prevention and the suppression of acts against the state and its security. The protection of endangered persons and objects, as well as political intelligence, are seen as its major task. This task includes the prevention of terrorism, but also investigations in those cases where terrorist acts have occurred.

The political police in Austria has never been organizationally separated from the ordinary police. Its tasks have been fulfilled by the regular police authorities with the Ministry of the Interior on top, security directorates (*Sicherheitsdirektionen*) for the provinces, and district offices (in the countryside) or separate police directorates (in major towns) on the lowest organizational level. Police directorates normally run several 'commissariats' (*Komissariate*) and police posts within their area. Within the Ministry of the Interior, a 'general directorate for public security' (*Generaldirektion für die öffentliche Sicherheit*) is the lead agency for both ordinary and political police matters. It also includes a department for the political police. The lower organizational units of the police (security directorates, police directorates) follow a uniform pattern. One department deals with political matters, another with criminal matters, and a third with administrative matters, for example drivers' licenses. District offices, on the other hand, do not follow these patterns as they are established not by the federation but by the different provinces and therefore follow their own patterns.

The police forces in Austria have two separate branches, the Federal Police (both uniformed and detectives) attached to the police offices (directorates, commissariats and police posts) and the Federal Gendarmerie in the countryside. The latter falls under the central guidance of the Ministry of the Interior, with regional commands in each province except Vienna (which is exclusively covered by the Federal Police), district commands and detached stations. It operates under instruction of the district offices to supplement the police forces they are lacking.

Modern terrorism has not changed this structure, but has led to several special units being formed within the standing forces. A special Gendarmerie unit was established in 1974, mainly as a reaction to the hostage incident in 1973, in order to provide protection for endangered persons. Following the international trend exemplified by the 1972–73 establishment of the *Grenzschutzgruppe 9* (GSG-9) in the Federal Republic of Germany, it was transformed in 1977 into a quick reaction team (*Gendarmerie-Einsatzkommando* or GEK). The GEK is directly subordinated to the Ministry of the Interior and consists of Gendarmerie personnel who, after special training, serve for a certain period with the team, before being returned to their normal duties. The duties of the standing force encompass emergency actions for hostage rescue and other forms of extraordinary violent crime (not necessarily of a political motivation). Their duties also involve providing armed guards on certain flights of Austrian Airlines to prevent any hijacking.

In 1984 special action units (*Sondereinsatzgruppen* or SEG) of the Gendarmerie were established in each of Austria's provinces, except Vienna, as there is no Federal Gendarmerie in the capital. The SEG consist of former members of the GEK, an arrangement which provides them with adequate training and experience. Their task is to intervene in the first instance against terrorist or similar incidents and to contain the situation until the GEK arrives from its base near Vienna, and to support local police or Gendarmerie formations in dangerous incidents. Since 1985 action units (*Einsatzeinheiten* or EE) have been established within each Gendarmerie province command to assist in normal police duties connected with terrorism or similar incidents or activities. They receive special training for their duties, yet not necessarily on a level comparable to the GEK or the SEG.

Like the Gendarmerie, the Federal Police have also developed action units. Its first force was the 'alarm group' (*Alarmabteilung*) of the police directorate in Vienna, consisting of three companies. This group was already established before the emergence of modern terrorism and has functioned *inter alia* as riot police. It saw action during the OPEC incident in 1975. It was then restructured in 1978 to conform to the tasks of a modern mobile anti-terror unit. Between 1983 and 1985 mobile action groups (*Mobile Einsatzkommanden* or MEK) were established within 12 police directorates. They perform normal police patrol duties but are trained and equipped to counter emerging terrorist threats or similar violence.

Due to Vienna airport's special needs, a special police station was established there in the mid-1970s which was to include a special police action force. After the terrorist incident in 1985, the force was restructured in 1987 and adapted and equipped to counter terrorist threats against civil aviation. The police station is responsible for normal security duties, for example security checks at the gates, but also for immigration control and other functions of the political police. The special force should deter terrorist attacks by its presence at the airport, and guards the airport against attacks from the outside. Its equipment encompasses the only armoured personnel carrier in Austria's public security forces, and other anti-terrorist devices. It also includes co-operation with the Ministry of the Interior helicopter wing.

On the preventive side, a special detective group was established within the police directorate of Vienna in 1978. In 1987 it was replaced by a plain-clothes special department for suppressing terrorism (*Einsatzgruppe zur Bekämpfung des Terrorismus* or EBT) within the Ministry of the Interior. It covers the whole of Austria and is intended to prevent violent and subversive acts. Its main task is to anticipate terrorism by adequate intelligence. Its members are recruited from the normal detective force of Austria's police and specifically trained for their anti-terrorist role.

International Co-operation

Austria closely co-operates with other western European states in suppressing terrorism, while not yet being a member of the European Community. Bilateral informal contacts between Austrian and foreign security agencies include regular exchanges of information and experiences with regard to terrorism, but also contacts and co-operation in emergencies. In addition, regular meetings between the Austrian Minister of the Interior and high-ranking officials take place with their counterparts in European countries, the USA and Arab states. Topics include information on the situation of terrorism in the respective countries as well as the establishment and intensification of co-operation in combating terrorism. In several cases, bilateral contacts have been formalized, for example with the interior ministries of Italy in 1986, of Spain in 1987, and of the Federal Republic of Germany in 1988. Agreements usually establish formal police co-operation in the areas of terrorism, narcotics and other forms of organized crime. The GEK has also established working contacts with several anti-terror units abroad, exchanging personnel for training and sharing information which allows it to adapt tactics and technical equipment to international standards.

On the multilateral level, Austria co-operates within several bodies to counter terrorism. Austria has regularly supported UN resolutions in this field. Austria has also joined and ratified the Convention on the Prevention, Prosecution and Punishing of Criminal Acts against Persons Protected by International Law, including Diplomats, of 14 December 1973 (BGBl. 1977/488) and the International Agreement against Hostage Taking, of 18 December 1979 (BGBl. 1986/600). With regard to civil aviation, Austria cooperates within the International Civil Aviation Organisation (ICAO) and has joined and ratified the Tokyo, Hague and Montreal Conventions. The agreement on security at airports of 1988 is still under ratification (status as of 1990).

When the *Achille Lauro* incident proved that the legal instruments against terrorist acts on the high seas were inadequate, Austria, together with Italy and Egypt, took the initiative in 1986 for a maritime anti-terror convention. The convention was concluded in 1988 in Rome. Austria has even joined several agreements with regard to maritime security against terrorist attacks, notwithstanding the fact that she is a land-locked country.

Austria also closely co-operates in countering terrorism through the

Council of Europe. Austria was the first state to ratify the Council's European Convention on the Suppression of Terrorism, of 27 January 1977. At the Council's conference in Strasbourg (France) in November 1986, of the ministers responsible for combating terrorism, Austria was active in the preparations as well as during the conference. The Austrian Minister of the Interior was even appointed vice chairman of the conference. The conference's results have been practical guidelines for the Austrian Ministry of the Interior in suppressing terrorism, and for its closer co-operation with foreign authorities. The conference has also established a committee of high-ranking officials of the pertinent ministries, and Austria too participates in this committee.

As early as 1978 Austria took the initiative to establish a closer co-operation of the Ministers of the Interior of Austria, France, Italy, the Federal Republic and Switzerland. A conference led to the 'Vienna Club' of these ministers, with its main topic being transnational cooperation against terrorism. Since then, frequent meetings of the ministers or high-ranking officials from these countries have taken place. Since other countries have also been interested in this form of co-operation, a widening of the 'Vienna Club' is probable. Austria also co-operates in the TREVI (Terrorism, Radicalism, Extremism and political Violence) group of EC countries, despite the fact that Austria has not yet become a member of the EC. First contacts were established during the European Council's Strasbourg conference in 1986. Since then, regular meetings have been held between the Austrian Minister of the Interior and the 'Troika' of the TREVI group (the chairman, his predecessor and his designated successor). Within the TREVI group, Austria's position is similar to the USA and Canada. She is entitled to present her views before the meetings of the group, even without formally belonging to the group, and to send personnel to seminars established by the group. Co-operation goes beyond the narrow area of terrorism and includes *inter alia* training and equipment of police forces, but also matters of immigration and granting asylum, as well as border control and visa policies.

Criteria and Methods for Evaluating Acceptability and Effectiveness of Anti-Terrorist Measures

Austria's anti-terrorist measures have been shaped by Austria's specific situation. They originated in many cases from the severe threat of state-sponsored terrorism in the 1930s and proved both sufficient and effective when modern terrorism emerged in the 1970s and 1980s. The only major modification was the reaction towards terrorist threats against civil aviation, which has induced legislation both in criminal law in the narrow sense, and in shaping a legal basis for protective measures.

There are, however, some criteria discernible within Austria's approach to counter-terrorism. On the level of overall anti-terrorist policies, Austria's official policy clearly distinguishes between political and purely criminal factors within terrorism. Austria has on some occasions, on the political level, supported the causes advanced by groups with terrorist means. Yet she has not refrained from taking effective counter-measures against the terrorism surrounding them. The underlying idea is that finding a political solution may remove the reason for terrorism. This must not be misinterpreted, however, as acceptance by Austria of terrorism as a means for advancing political objectives. As an example of how the policy works, Austria has politically supported the minority's claims in South Tyrol, yet has not hesitated even to send the armed forces to seal the border against terrorist infiltration into Italy.

Austria has also attempted to contribute to a political solution in the Middle East, even at the expense of a clear bias in favour of groups associated with terrorism, but has not refrained from taking anti-terrorist measures against Arab terrorism, either. Here, however, Austria's official policy has made several oscillations. During the 1970s it was evidently determined by the wish to avoid a confrontation with terrorist groups. Both in the case of the Marchegg hostage taking and the OPEC raid, Austria allowed the terrorists to leave with their hostages, the official line being that saving their lives was the overriding principle. However, it may also have conveyed the impression that the official policy used humanitarian reasons as a pretext to avoid any confrontation as soon as radical Arab interests were involved. This position has evidently changed with regard to Arab radicalism, as Austria has put those Arabs involved in the 1981 assassinations on trial and sent them to prison. On the other hand, the case against the Iranians suspected of the assassination of the Kurds in 1989 has again aroused suspicion that they were tacitly allowed to leave Austria, in order to avoid further terrorist attacks. Thus, the basic line of separating the political cause from the criminal phenomenon in terrorism, and treating the criminal part of terrorism as ordinary criminal acts, has been sometimes blurred by political considerations.

With regard to the democratic acceptability of counter-measures taken by Austria, the legal basis was shaped at a time of authoritarian rule but subsequently adapted to the requirements of a liberal democracy. The mere existence of laws concerning state security has prevented the painful necessity of introducing anti-terror legislation at a time when it might have been a controversial issue, as it was the case in the Federal Republic of Germany. Anti-terrorist legislation came as a disappointment for

liberal optimism there, whereas Austria could avoid similar emotiona-
lized controversies. The reaction by the public to anti-terrorist measures
has generally been positive. First, the terrorist challenge has been less
intensive in Austria than in other European countries, such as the
German Federal Republic, requiring less visible anti-terrorist measures.
Moreover, the issue has never had the emotional dimension in Austria as
elsewhere. Also, the potential for political violence is relatively limited,
with about one per cent of the public approving it, according to opinion
polls.[4]

Finally, the overall political climate in Austria has not favoured
extremism on the right or on the left. Radical groups have gained only
marginal votes in elections.[5] Extremism on the right is identified with
Nazism, which brought the loss of Austria's independence in 1938 and the
suffering of World War II. Although there is some tolerance in Austria
for the historical dilemma of those who erred in favour of National
Socialism at that time, the majority does not tolerate today's Nazis, who
have not learned the lessons of history. Extremism on the left has been
identified with communism, rejected in Austria mainly due to the
experiences with Soviet occupation until 1955, and the violent
suppression of freedom in Hungary and Czechoslovakia. Thus, both
domestic terrorism and foreign terrorism, which has also been seen
mainly in the context of the East-West confrontation, has had no positive
response with Austria's public. On the contrary, anti-terrorist measures
were readily accepted.

With regard to effectiveness, criteria are not easily established, as it
would mean evaluating a non-event. It is evident that Austria has been
afflicted by modern terrorism less than other countries, yet has not been
completely immune from it. It is not clear whether the situation is due to
terrorists' lack of interest in Austria, or by their use of Austria as an area
not for action but to hide in, or by the effective counter-measures taken
both in prevention and suppression of terrorism by the Austrian
authorities. Reasons could be advanced for each of these factors. There
are, however, some indications of a certain effectiveness in Austria's anti-
terror measures. International co-operation and exchange of intelligence
– and especially contacts with the Middle East – have allowed the
anticipation of impending terrorist actions and have led to the arrest of
commandos before they could become operational. Furthermore, even if
protective measures could not prevent terrorist attacks completely, they
could at least keep the casualty figures lower than in similar attacks
abroad. For example, the terrorists attacking the synagogue in 1981 were
driven off after the first shots and were overcome within minutes. Also, in
1985, at Vienna airport, the police prevented a massacre similar to that in

Rome, instantly driving the terrorists off the passenger area and fighting them in the open. Furthermore, investigations in most cases were successful and terrorists could be tried and imprisoned.

National Lessons for Europe 1992

For several reasons, Austria's experiences with terrorism as well as anti-terrorist measures cannot be easily applied to other European states, and could even less be made a model for the European Community. First, terrorism has been less of a concern in Austria than in most other European countries, making a high profile on this issue less of an imperative. Because the legal basis for anti-terrorist measures already exists, there is again no need for a high profile in adapting the security apparatus to the task of combating terrorism. Finally, the political climate has allowed anti-terrorist measures to be taken without much opposition, avoiding any controversies and thus giving the issue of terrorism a low profile.

Nevertheless, Austria's anti-terrorism measures appear appropriate and not at all ineffective. They have been taken quietly and apparently also operate quietly. Since modern terrorism often requires a spectacular act in public in order to communicate its message, keeping terrorism as well as anti-terrorism measures out of the limelight may prove an efficient way to reduce the terrorist danger.

NOTES

This study was completed in 1991 and does not therefore include the further surge of right-wing terrorism. However, the assessment of this phenomenon appears still valid for 1992.

1. R. Benda and I Gabriel. *Terror rot/weiss/rot. Politische Kriminalität in Österreich* (Zurich: Pres Dok/Vienna: Morawa, 1989).
2. Official Law Series: *Reichsgesetzblatt* (RGB1., until 1918); *Staatsgesetzblatt* (StGB1., immediately after World Wars I and II); *Bundesgesetzblatt* (BGB1.; during the existence of the Federal Constitutions before 1938 and after 1945).
3. Hanspeter Neuhold, 'Internationale Entwicklungen bis zur Jahrtausendwende aus der Sicht eines Teils der "aussenpolitischen Elite" in Österreich', *Österreichische Zeitschrift für Aussenpolitik* 20/3 (1980), pp.208–11.
4. Khol, Ofner, Stirnemann (eds.), *Österreichisches Jahrbuch für Politik, 1986* (Vienna/Munich, 1987) pp.902–3.
5. Khol, Ofner, Stirnemann, *Österreichisches Jahrbuch für Politik, 1991* (Vienna/Munich, 1992), pp.1025–39.

PART III
WESTERN AND EUROPEAN
RESPONSES

Towards a European Response to Terrorism: National Experiences and Lessons for 1993

F. KORTHALS ALTES

This essay discusses the importance of the Schengen Agreement as a first step towards making the free movement of persons in Europe a reality after 1992. The removal of borders will have to be balanced by the introduction of computer checks on persons, the harmonization of visa policy and the abolition or transfer of goods inspection, as well as the harmonization of long-term residence rights, social welfare policies regarding migrants, and controls on the sale of firearms. There is also a need for increased inter-state police co-operation, such as in the area of the right of pursuit. While the free movement of persons should only apply to European citizens, not extra-European persons, in practice this is only feasible at external borders and at national ports and airports. An intensification of certain types of controls (e.g., on aliens) and the upgrading of international contacts and information exchange will be necessary to compensate for the greater freedom of land traffic in the post-1992 Europe.

In the past two decades the international community has been confronted by a rising tide of terrorism. Measures to combat, or should I say control, terrorism have therefore demanded increasing attention on the part of governments. One problem that arises is the sheer number of forms that terrorism can take, each quite different from the others. Some terrorist groups confine their activities to arson or other forms of sabotage designed to damage property only, whether key targets or otherwise. Other organisations go further and resort to violence against people. Their victims may be political leaders or officials who might be regarded as being responsible in some part for the political system or course of conduct to which the terrorist is opposed. Sometimes however, the people who fall victim to the violence are entirely unconnected with the companies or governments which the terrorists are trying to pressure to meet their demands.

The different degrees of violence used, the form that this violence takes, the range of targets, physical and human, at which it is directed and the varying political objectives of terrorist groups have made it extremely difficult to find a definition that would encompass the many facets and forms of terrorism. Such a definition is necessary to facilitate discussion in international political fora about the way in which terrorism should be tackled. It is inevitably a very wide definition and the combating of different forms of terrorism accordingly calls for a differentiated approach. The problem could be compared to that of defining and tackling 'crime'. The question of how to prevent crime cannot be answered without first specifying precisely what crime entails. Common crimes require a different approach than that for organized crime.

This does not mean to say, however, that terrorist acts, no matter how much they differ, do not have a number of features in common. One shared feature of virtually all terrorist acts is that the perpetrators are not motivated by their own benefit but by a more general political goal. This means that the psychology of the terrorist, his motivation and determination, and the extent to which he is prepared to take risks, are on the whole of quite a different order than those of the person who commits serious criminal offences. This fact will accordingly have to be taken into account when deciding upon the measures to be taken to combat terrorism.

Combating terrorism, both in political and operational terms, is therefore a highly complex matter. This complexity must be constantly borne in mind whether we are concerned with taking preventive or repressive measures. Moreover, terrorism is not a static phenomenon. The activities of both individual terrorist groups and terrorists as a whole are in a state of constant flux. Recognizing these problems, the governments of Western countries and of the EC Member States in particular have come to realise that substantial results can only be achieved through joint efforts. Talks about the policy and operational aspects of combating terrorism have been held at ministerial and civil servant levels with increasing frequency since the mid-1970s. At a general political level, consultation takes place in various international fora. In 1984 the multi-disciplinary working group of senior officials responsible for the combating of terrorism was set up within a Council of Europe framework. Arriving at a clear and effective strategy has not been without its problems, however. Progress is hindered by the differing intentions of the various countries involved and by the fact that for some of them, such as Norway and Switzerland, this is the only forum in which terrorism is discussed, while for others it is only one of several.

In the context of European Political Cooperation, the decision was taken on 27 January 1986 to establish a permanent working group responsible for intensifying co-operation between the Twelve in relation to the combating of international terrorism. The working group's terms of reference are to study the causes of and background to terrorism, to make practical recommendations on preventive measures and to prepare the response of the Twelve to terrorist acts, in each case taking into account the activities of other consultative structures such as TREVI (Terrorism,

Radicalism, Extremism and political Violence). Besides consultation at a political level, collaboration also takes place in the operational sphere. Informal links between police forces were established back in 1978, partly to improve exchange of information and therefore the chance of tracking down terrorists. It is generally felt that this forum, in which all the member states participate, succeeds in meeting practical needs at the police level.

Finally, there are the TREVI talks. Following a decision by the Council of Europe in 1975, a resolution was passed at the first meeting of the competent EC ministers on 29 June 1976 to intensify efforts to combat international terrorism. On the basis of this resolution, four consultative groups were set up, one bringing together the directors general of the various ministries and the other three being permanent working groups. These working groups are charged with improving the exchange of information and analyses and making recommendations on the organisation and equipping of bodies concerned with combating terrorism. One working group, instituted in June 1985 by a decision of the TREVI ministers, is also concerned with international organized crime. Measures to combat this form of crime have some points in common with those to combat terrorism. Moreover, it would appear that some terrorist groups rely heavily on funding from profits earned, for example, through international drug trafficking.

International political consultation has led in the first instance to the formulation of general principles with regard to antiterrorism measures. The European Council, for instance, concluded in 1986 that their joint efforts against terrorism and those who support terrorist activities should be based on the following principles: no concession should be made to terrorists or their sponsors, even under pressure; the member states must be united in their efforts to prevent terrorist offences and bring the perpetrators to trial; and third, joint action must be taken in response to terrorist attacks in the territory of a member state when there is evidence of external involvement. In January 1986 the Ministers of Foreign Affairs of the Twelve once again stressed that terrorist acts could never be condoned or regarded as a legitimate means of achieving political goals.

What is the link between anti-terrorism measures and European unification? The completion of the internal market by the end of 1992 will see the removal of internal border controls. For the Netherlands, however, the Schengen Agreement matters far more for the immediate future. Its implementation will mean the removal of border controls between the Benelux countries, France and Germany even before the completion of the European internal market. I would therefore first like to consider the progress made in implementing the Schengen Agreement.

The Netherlands' primary concern is to secure agreement on the main issues, in other words, the conditions without which the abolition of internal border controls would be a perilous undertaking. An important prerequisite in my view is the free movement across borders not only of persons but also of goods. The two should coincide, since the liberalisation of the international movement of goods is of great economic significance for the Netherlands. I am prepared to accept the disadvantages associated with the free movement of people only if economic benefits are enjoyed in return.

The first condition is that the border control officials on the *external borders* should have at their disposal all the instruments necessary to carry out thorough checks on individuals. The parties to the Schengen talks have sought the solution to this problem in computerization. The Schengen countries will not be able to put full trust in one another's external border controls until such time as a computerized system linked to a data base is in operation. Intensive talks are in progress on a computerized system of this type. It will need to be accessible via terminals on the external borders, and also available for use by the national police.

The second condition, laid down explicitly in the Schengen Agreement, is that visa policy should be harmonized completely. France's decision in September 1986 to require visas from all non-EC nationals made it far more difficult to put this aim into practice. However, the Netherlands is still convinced that harmonization of policy on visas is an essential condition for eliminating checks at internal borders. France has now eased its visa requirements by exempting all Council of Europe member states except Turkey.

A third condition which is becoming increasingly vital is the need to strike a balance between the abolition of checks on individuals and those on goods. Negotiations on the elimination of goods inspections are proceeding slowly. Consequently, there is a danger that, while the Netherlands will be compelled to make a major investment to compensate for the abolition of checks on individuals at internal borders, this will not benefit the average traveller or company, given that customs checks at the internal borders will remain intact. In my view, checks on individuals and checks on hand luggage should be abolished at the same time.

Fourth, the Netherlands has emphasized within the Schengen negotiations that the supplementary agreement cannot be viewed separately from the need for gradual harmonization of longterm residence rights and those social welfare facilities to which aliens are entitled. It is also becoming increasingly clear from the talks that the vast majority of migrants will move to those countries where residence and social conditions are most attractive, unless a certain degree of harmonization takes place in these fields. Although there is no pressing need for negotiations on this subject to yield immediate results, discussions have now been initiated under the Schengen Agreement.

There will have to be clear progress in these four areas before the Netherlands can sign the supplementary agreement. On the other hand, the Netherlands has fewer problems in other areas causing serious headaches for its partners. Current negotiations on the harmonization of arms legislation are a prime example. That weapons, the acquisition and ownership of which require a licence in the Netherlands, can be bought freely – or, at any rate, without too much difficulty – in France or Belgium, as is the case at present, is unacceptable. Although progress is being made in the talks on this issue, it should not be forgotten that Belgium and France will need to amend legislation and give undertakings to implement it, if the desired aims are to be achieved. Belgium has declared that it is willing to do so and is now preparing a new scheme. However, there is still considerable resistance on the part of France. After all, the French national anthem contains the stirring exhortation: '*Aux armes, citoyens!*'.

Nor has any general agreement yet been reached on the precise nature of measures relating to international co-operation between the police and the criminal justice authorities. The Dutch negotiators are emphasizing that agreements at a regional level, the creation of regional consultative structures and the co-ordination of channels of communication will be required if such co-operation is to be improved and intensified. There are plans to step up international police contacts. Under the Schengen Agreement, there will be a need for regular, structured consultation on numerous topics, such as measures to combat terrorism and serious crime, including drug-trafficking and the illegal firearms trade. To promote and expedite police co-operation between the countries party to the Schengen Agreement, plans have been made for bilateral agreements on the secondment of liaison officers. Their tasks would include facilitating the exchange of information on the combating of crime and terrorism, both preventive and repressive, complying with requests for assistance from the police and the criminal authorities in criminal cases and assisting the work of border control authorities on the external borders. However, as things stand the police force in the Netherlands is inadequately equipped for international consultation of the type which future developments will demand. Clearly, the level and degree of intensity of future international consultation and co-operation will also require financial investment. Existing budgets will not suffice.

In a Europe without frontiers, it is unthinkable that border obstacles should be abolished for passenger and goods traffic only, while they continue to impede the work of the police and criminal justice authorities. Accordingly, plans are being made to regulate certain forms of police co-operation in the implementation treaty. One example is the right of pursuit (*droit de poursuite*). It is most important that international surveillance should be well-regulated if terrorism and organised crime are to be tackled effectively. Naturally, it will be necessary to stipulate in some detail the conditions on which this can be arranged. Another major item on the agenda is the issue of whether and, if so, how the international pursuit of suspects should be regulated.

Major issues which count as far as the Netherlands is concerned there-fore include three conditions which have yet to be satisfied: introduction of an operational computerized information system, harmonization of visa policy, and abolition or transfer of goods inspections. A fourth condition, which seems to have every chance of being fulfilled in the near future, is discussion on the gradual harmonization of long-term residence rights and the social welfare facilities available to migrants. As regards the other areas referred to, the Netherlands is satisfied with the solutions reached in Schengen and it is to be hoped that other countries will be able to set aside any reservations which they may still have.

This brings me to the implementation of the second stage, the European internal market. The European Community will be confronted with essentially the same problems as the countries party to the Schengen Agreement, though on a larger scale. Achieving uniformity among the five Schengen partners and achieving it among the 12 EC member states are, of course, two quite different matters, and this will be reflected in the checks carried out at the external borders. Moreover, the EC member states have differing allegiances and preoccupations, according to their geographical position. In this connection I would single out the obligations of the Danes to the other countries of the Nordic Council and the pressure of migration from North Africa to which the countries of Southern Europe are subject.

What is the exact significance of the European market? According to the definition given in the Single European Act, it means the free movement of goods, persons, services and capital. It should be borne in mind that this concept has an economic dimension. The aim is that the European internal market should give a fresh economic impulse to the EC, including European economic traffic. How far is passenger transport for noneconomic purposes included, and to what extent can non-EC nationals share in these benefits? In my view and that of most of my ministerial EC counterparts, the free movement of persons in the context of the Single European Act means the free movement of European

Community nationals. However, non-EC nationals will, for practical reasons, also be allowed to cross internal borders freely and without being subjected to checks.

Free movement, of course, relates only to the territory of the 12 member states. It follows that free movement must be confined to crossing internal borders by land. Most EC member states regard inner national ports and airports as forming part of the external border. However, opinions differ on this issue. We know that the European Commission prefers to regard international ports and airports as *not* being part of the external border where vessels or aircraft from other EC member states are concerned. But here I foresee problems with passengers in transit from countries outside Community territory.

Even this brief description shows that the scope of the European internal market is, in fact, rather limited. Moreover, a significant number of the rights to which I have referred have already been introduced under current EC legislation. After all, the free movement of workers and services which increasingly includes tourism is a *fait accompli*. And this accounts for the major part of cross-border traffic. If the European internal market is to be given a broader dimension comparable to that created by the Schengen Agreement, it is essential that there should be informal co-operation between governments. The negotiation process then, will only work effectively if there is proper co-ordination between on the one hand the decision-making process in Community institutions, the purpose of which is to give substance to the concept of a European internal market, and, on the other, inter-governmental co-operation, the aim of which is to draw up measures to reinforce the effects of the European internal market.

Finally, the other compensatory measures drawn up under the Schengen Agreement will eventually need to be introduced in the EC as well. This refers to the harmonization of firearms legislation and increased co-operation between the police and criminal justice authorities of different states. As in other instances, negotiations on the larger forum constituted by the 12 community member states will be more difficult than those between the five Schengen states. On the other hand, results achieved in the EC as a whole are naturally more significant, as, once approved, they will affect a much larger area. I both hope and expect that the results attained under the Schengen Agreement will have an impact at the Community level, thus conferring upon Schengen the initiatory role originally planned for it.

A few final observations: implementation of the Schengen Agreement and 'Europe 1992' is bound to bring about radical changes. Europe will become more open. In the future, the movement of persons and goods within the community will no longer be obstructed by barriers. This will, first and foremost, serve the economic interests of all of us. In my view, however, it would be unacceptable if this development were to lead to compromises on security. In fact, the compensatory measures of which I spoke earlier – such as the computerized information system to be set up when controls are shifted to the external borders, intensifying the surveillance of aliens in the individual states, upgrading international contacts between police and criminal justice authorities, and, finally, the exchange and analysis of information within this context – should help to improve the efficiency and effectiveness of the measures to combat terrorism and organized crime. New impetus and ideas are essential to make society safer.

The European Response to Terrorism

MELITON CARDONA

This essay argues that military-strategic anti-terrorist measures must be balanced by judicial and political controls. It therefore focuses on legal measures, agreeing with Alex Schmid that terrorism can be considered 'the peacetime equivalent of war crimes'. It criticizes the notion of 'international terrorism', claiming that all terrorism has a national origin as well as international connections, especially within a unified Europe. The effectiveness of various conventions against terrorism is reviewed and it is concluded that all too often non-implementation renders the statement of principle devoid of practical effect. While global conventions are hard to implement, there is more hope for a sectorial, European approach, but such a response must be both collective and democratic. In the long run, adherence to the rule of law makes the fight against terrorism successful. The study discusses the working of the European Convention for the Suppression of Terrorism, the TREVI group and the measures taken by the European Political Co-operation (EPC) in the area of state-sponsored terrorism and concludes that a set of common principles has been arrived at, but that putting these into practice is the challenge that lies ahead.

No matter how barbaric or apparently absurd their ways seem to be, no matter how similar their profiles might be to those of common criminals, there is always a peculiar logic of terrorist actions that can only be grasped from the particular point of view of their perpetrators. Understanding terrorism is the first step in successfully combating it. Yet it is a fact that police action has taken the lead over politicians' conceptual frameworks. Efforts to understand and analyze terrorism in the framework of historical context lag behind military-security anti-terrorist measures.

As a phenomenon whose name routinely evokes emotional reactions, the issues raised by terrorism are somehow of a moral nature. No one describes himself as a terrorist and some former terrorists enjoy or have enjoyed the respectability of statesmen. There has been an understandable but dangerous historical trend to label as terrorist all acts of political violence that have challenged situations of domination, as there is today a certain tendency to use the concept of terrorism indiscriminately as one that must command automatic reactions of loathing and rejection. Being one of those words that elicit immediate responses of condemnation, everyone rejects terrorism just as everyone has a natural impulse to reject arson or rape.

One can also hear from time to time reminders of the disparity between the violence of terrorist groups and that of police forces or conventional armies. It has even been suggested that terrorists' atrocities may stem from this very frightening imbalance of forces and might be a deviant form of calling public attention to their claims on specific issues. The widespread agreement in expert literature that no real definition of terrorism is actually possible seems rather disturbing too. Nevertheless, the preceding statements should not lead us to conclude that terrorism cannot be defined or should not be rejected, useful as it may be to bear in mind the complex political and moral issues raised by the systematic recourse to terrorist methods.

It has been repeated *ad nauseam* that one man's terrorist is another man's freedom fighter. So he is, but it should not be so. It is essential to a terrorist to be the actual agent of destruction. Allow me to illustrate this point with an example taken from one Spanish writer[1] who has made an effort to understand and reveal the intrinsic moral perversion of terrorist logic. A soldier might even feel relieved if the man he has to kill dies as a result of an accident, say by lightning, before he can pull the trigger. Should this happen to a terrorist's target, he will feel deprived of his goal and consider that the accident has frustrated his action.

Terrorist killings invert the relationship existing between fact and news. Fact becomes a function of news and not the opposite. For terrorist killing is news-oriented. It is news-generating too, in that terrorists kill in cold blood, with neither hatred nor passion, rejecting personal motives as if this lack of personal involvement could confer an aura of rationality or even justice upon their deeds. This moral perversion of means and ends constitutes the definitive trait of terrorist violence. And the more remote and unattainable their 'Cause', cause with a capital 'C', the greater the amount of gratuitous violence that will be put to its service, as if mere violence and destruction were palpable proof of its actual feasibility.

Responses to Terrorism

Military-strategic thought has had well-known consequences in the field of international relations and it is regrettable that this kind of approach has initially had the upper hand in combating terrorism. It is often said that terrorist violence must be fought with equal, if not greater, state violence. No matter how attractive this oversimplification can be, this exclusively authoritarian approach has led to unfortunate delays and misunderstandings. Suffice it to say with Juliet Lodge,[2] that the more stringent anti-terrorist measures a state introduces, the more terrorist groups will be able to claim that such measures are proof of the state's devious and fascist intentions.

Recourse to special legislation has also been frequently advocated. In fact, experience has shown that special legislation is always welcomed by terrorists. They literally love repressive legislation, the more draconian the better, since they use its very existence as proof of their own relevance and as a means of justifying their violent actions. Democracies tend to equate terrorism with criminal violence, against which legal remedies must be used. The rule of law is specially relevant in this context. I share the opinion that European democracies are bound to balance military-security anti-terrorist measures by judicial and political controls.[3] Hence the emphasis I want to place on legal measures, to which I shall turn next.

As Professor Carrillo Salcedo[4] has stated in his 1988 course devoted to international legal aspects of terrorism, the only international text in force prohibiting terrorism in general is Article 33 of the Fourth Geneva Convention of 1949 on the protection of civilians in wartime. This text can only be applied to international armed conflicts and is thus unadapted to terrorism in peacetime. Yet I adhere to the proposal set forth by Alex Schmid that acts of terrorism can be understood as a special kind of violence: the peacetime equivalent of war crimes.[5]

Many authors and agencies have attempted to draft typologies of terrorism. A much publicized category nowadays is so-called 'international terrorism'. Under this attractive label, the origins of which would be interesting to trace, many authors confusingly subsume anti-imperialism, anti-colonialism, nationalist conflicts, wars of independence and state-sponsored external terrorism.[6] While this typological category has gained some favour in international fora, including the European Political Cooperation, for those concerned with the political aspects of the problem, typologies of terrorism are far less important than the need to derive a workable legal standard that will distinguish between permissible revolutionary activity and prohibited criminality in public international law.[7]

So-called domestic or indigenous terrorism has aggravated the threat in Western Europe in general and in specific states in particular. Many European states enjoy the dubious privilege of having to deal with both domestic and international or transnational terrorism. It would certainly be ironic to try and limit European co-operation in combating terrorism to the latter. This is not only because terrorists are only relatively bound, like any other mortals, by space limits, but because as internal border relaxation in Europe advances, any terrorist act perpetrated in Europe, no matter its origins or motivations, shall eventually be considered as against all EC members.

All terrorism has a national origin and international connections and so-called 'international terrorism' confusingly subsumes many categories of terrorist activities. As Alex Schmid has pointed out, each definition of a problem prejudices to some extent, the area where we look for solutions.[8] It is no wonder that respected experts have even suggested that NATO be put in charge of co-ordinating anti-terrorism in western Europe. If one interprets terrorism as surrogate war, there is a certain logic to such a proposal. On the other hand, if one interprets it as a serious offence, the framework and scope of anti-terrorist measures will change in a radical way.

Over the past 55 years considerable efforts have been made at the international level to find ways and means of combating terrorism. The first attempt to bring about a comprehensive legal international regulation relating to terrorism was made in 1937, when a conference convened by the League of Nations drew up a 'Convention for the Prevention and Punishment of Terrorism' that never came into force. As has happened ever since, a central problem encountered by the 1937 conference was the need to find an internationally accepted definition of terrorism. This problem has recently gained renewed immediacy in connection with a Syrian proposal to convene a UN Conference to define terrorism and thus differentiate it from struggles for national liberation. It is almost certain that the Syrian proposal will not gather the necessary support, the Community and other major Western countries being opposed to it on the grounds that no cause justifies the systematic use of certain methods.

In view of the impossibility of bringing about a general convention, international efforts since the 1970s have been directed towards singling out certain categories of crime that can be internationally agreed upon to be acts of terrorism. This sectorial approach has led to the conclusion of several conventions under the auspices of the International Civil Aviation Organization (ICAO), the International Maritime Organization (IMO) and the UN. Within the framework of ICAO, they include the 1971 Convention for the Suppression of Unlawful Acts against the Safety of Civil Aviation, the 1970 Hague Convention for the Suppression of Unlawful Seizure of Aircraft, the 1963 Tokyo Convention on Offences and Certain Other Acts committed on board Aircraft and the 1986 Supplementary Protocol to the Montreal Convention of 1971. Within the UN framework, there are the 1973 Convention on the Prevention and Punishment of Crimes Against Internationally Protected Persons, including Diplomatic Agents, and the 1979 Convention against the Taking of Hostages. Against the background of the seizure of the passenger liner *Achille Lauro* in October 1985, a draft Convention for the Suppression of Unlawful Acts against the Safety of Maritime Navigation was put forward in the framework of the IMO, which convened an international conference in Rome in March 1988 that produced the Convention for the Suppression of Unlawful Acts against the Maritime Security and the Protocol for the Suppression of Unlawful Acts against the Safety of Fixed Platforms located on the Continental Shelf.

International anti-terrorist conventions are both difficult to formulate and often hampered by lack of ratification and, what is even worse, by non-implementation. They seem no more than statements of principle devoid of practical effect. In this sense, they provide a practical example of the existing tension in the international community between state sovereignty and international law.

The European Response to Terrorism

Although an internationally accepted definition of terrorism seems practically impossible to arrive at, Spain believes that EC members should work out a definition of terrorism that undoubtedly could play an important role in combating terrorism at the European level. The idea was first suggested by Belgium in 1979 but has been delayed ever since. If global anti-terrorist conventions are difficult to reach, one could assume that a regional group of democracies such as the European Community would be better placed to carry out a concerted supranational action. One should expect that a common view on terrorism would easily derive from the unanimity of their democratic commitments, a relatively similar degree of economic development, a set of homogeneous legal traditions and, above all, multiple common interests. The EC existence, with its ability to deliver certain binding decisions upon its member states, apparently reinforces the idea that at least the EC would be able to speak with one voice and react unanimously against terrorism.

While this is essentially true, it is also a fact that Europe is not a state and this type of unanimous response is difficult to reach. The nature and type of terrorist threats differ greatly from country to country and the political culture and tradition of each European state confronted with terrorism has influenced the type of response delivered. Sharing those experiences and learning from them is one of the advantages that derive from European anti-terrorist co-operation. The existence of different European fora in which debate and concerted action can take place may be perceived as a supplementary advantage, not only because complementarity can be put ahead of competition, but because there is a record of successful co-operation in many other fields already.

And yet, disadvantages are also patent. First of all, there are the problems derived from a multiplicity of sovereignties and jurisdictions. Different legal practices add to the difficulties too: common law systems like that of the United Kingdom are different from civil law ones like the French or Spanish. Institutions like the right of political asylum create many sensitivities, especially in France and Ireland. In this latter country, even constitutional issues are raised by extradition agreements. Last but not least, the Treaty of Rome did not commit member states to the pursuit of common foreign policies. This is to be regarded as a major setback in the efforts to implement common views on major international issues.

In spite of it all, it can be contended that European countries in general and EC members in particular have developed what could be termed a European policy on terrorism. Two principles have gained widespread support:

- Terrorism is a collective threat that requires a collective response;
- Terrorism is a threat to democratic values that requires a democratic response.

These principles are guided by democratic solidarity and the need to move towards European integration. The need for co-operation is implicit in the first principle and real, threefold European co-operation has developed at three key levels: the legal, the operational and the diplomatic.

The European response to terrorism is above all respectful of the rule of law. Paul Wilkinson has pointed out that in liberal democracies the aim is to balance military-security anti-terrorist measures by judicial and political control.[9] This balance is difficult to reach as nothing is more welcome to terrorist groups than repression. Curtailing individual rights and liberties can be perceived by terrorists as a certain kind of victory. The Spanish ETA terrorist group has long had as an avowed goal to induce a spiral of violence and repression leading to a popular uprising. The rule of law must be preserved if the fight against terrorism is to be successful in the long run. One should be extremely careful not to destroy the very democratic values whose preservation is the basis of our common endeavour. It is not surprising that the Council of Europe has pioneered the fight against terrorism in Europe.

The European Convention for the Suppression of Terrorism (ECST) originated within the Council of Europe. Its members put the emphasis on ensuring that terrorists would not be able to evade punishment by unduly exploiting national extradition laws and international extradition treaties. As is well known, those legal instruments usually exclude from their provisions both political and politically inspired offences. The main purpose of the Convention was to establish the principle *aut dedere aut judicare* – some say *aut dedere aut punire*, or *aut dedere aut persequi* – for certain categories of crime. Thus, Article 1 forbids considering as political or politically motivated the following offences: those within the scope of the 1970 Hague Convention (Unlawful Seizure of Aircraft) and the 1971 Montreal Convention (Safety of Civil Aviation), serious offences against internationally protected persons, including diplomatic agents, serious offences involving kidnapping, the taking of a hostage or serious unlawful detention, offences involving the use of a bomb, grenade, rocket, automatic firearm or letter or parcel bomb if this use endangers persons.

Its main weakness stems from Article 5:

> Nothing in this convention shall be interpreted as imposing an obligation to extradite if the requested state has substantial grounds for believing that the request . . . has been made for the purpose of prosecuting or punishing a person on account of his race, religion, nationality or political opinion or that person's position may be prejudiced for any of these reasons.

Furthermore, Article 13 allows signatory states to enter a reservation permitting them to reject a request for extradition on the grounds that the offence is of a political character, notwithstanding the fact that a listed offence is involved. This seems to be a contradiction negating the basic assumption that terrorist offences be regarded as crimes and punished as such. And yet, this possibility is not absolute, because the state having entered a reservation is compelled duly to take into account the character and effects of the offence. According to Carrillo Salcedo this is an example of the limits put by international law on state sovereignty.

Although the Convention has been widely criticised, its apparent weakness is no more than an attempt to accommodate political and even constitutional problems that would have otherwise prevented some states from ratifying it. As often happens in international law, state sovereignty imposes limits to international co-operation that would otherwise be simply impossible to bring about.

The second legal instrument for combating terrorism at the more restricted EC members level is the so-called Dublin Agreement of 1979, which is a more regionally confined and more concerted effort of European co-operation. In drafting the Agreement, the Community members' priority was to ensure that the ECST would be applied uniformly among them, basically seeking to ensure its application without qualification and reservations in the extradition proceedings between EC member states. Nevertheless, EC states wishing to maintain the 'political offence' reservation under ECST Article 13 have to make a further declaration under Article 3 of the Dublin Agreement. Denmark, France and Italy have retained theirs and Ireland entered a reservation on Article 1 stating that it would try offenders domestically.

Although both legal instruments are open to justified criticism, they reflect the maximum degree of attainable consensus at the moment they were drafted. As has been pointed out before, legal systems, traditions, practices and institutions are quite different from country to country within the EC. Matters of extradition require a satisfactory uniform regulation among EC states. Harmonising national criminal laws in the Community would remove the emphasis on extradition proceedings but for the time being this seems a quite remote goal. Nevertheless, political willingness as a means of overcoming technicalities should not be underestimated. Short of breaking constitutional principles, EC states can gradually harmonise their legal views on terrorism. In fact there have been calls for the establishment of common anti-terrorist laws administered by a European Court.

At the operational level, special mention must be made of the so-called TREVI (Terrorism, Radicalism, Extremism and political Violence) Group, which was established following a decision of the European Council while meeting in Rome in December 1975. It is mainly a forum for discussion and co-operation on police and intelligence matters. The Ministers of Justice or of the Interior initiated regular systematic work concerning terrorist threats against EC member states in order to facilitate the apprehension and subsequent prosecution of terrorists. Exchange of intelligence information among EC members, compiling a blacklist of terrorists, analysis of the so-called external threat and sectorial studies on specific terrorist groups are some of its main activities. The fact that an exchange of information has been set up as a result of TREVI endeavours on intelligence and other related matters is especially remarkable in view of the well-known reluctance of several European intelligence-gathering bodies to share their findings.

Special mention should be made at this point of the efforts to combat terrorism in the framework of the European Political Co-operation. It is well known that the Treaty of Rome does not commit member states to the pursuit of common foreign policies. By the mid-1970s, timid steps towards a greater exchange of EC members' views on foreign policy matters began by the establishment of consultative arrangements. This was the germ of the institutionalized European Political Co-operation (EPC), further reinforced by the ratification of the Single European Act. EPC is an intergovernmental arrangement designed not so much to formulate a common foreign policy for the Community as to try to facilitate co-operation of a non-binding sort among its member states in the sphere of foreign policy. Its aims are to enhance credibility of

Community responses and limit the chances of third parties exploiting the often divergent interests of EC members.

EPC discussion of terrorism can be said to have taken off in spring 1984, on a British initiative following Libyan embassy involvement in the murder of a British police officer in London. By September the EPC Foreign Ministers' meeting reached an agreement on several guidelines for combating this special form of state-sponsored terrorism. In January 1986, against the background of the terrorist actions in Rome and Vienna airports, the Foreign Ministers of the Twelve adopted a declaration stating their willingness to co-ordinate and intensify their efforts to fight terrorism. A permanent EPC working group was set up to that end. The group is competent to prepare the reactions by the Twelve to terrorist incidents, study their causes and recommend concrete measures to prevent their occurrence. It has established a close liaison with the ongoing co-operation between the justice and interior ministers of the Twelve and with the working group on Judicial Co-operation. It co-ordinates common action by the Twelve in the framework of international fora and may submit to the Political Committee recommendations regarding the possibility of co-operation with third countries.

EC reactions to acts of state-sponsored terrorism exclude any military initiatives. Measures taken are based on political and commercial sanctions as well as on diplomatic pressure. Those criteria are in full harmony with basic rules of international law for the peaceful settlement of disputes as contained in the UN Charter. General principles with respect to anti-terrorist responses have been enunciated. EC states openly doubt the wisdom and utility of military retaliation and some of them feel that attention should be paid to the roots of Middle East terrorism. EC countries are well aware of linkages in international affairs and believe in the need to preserve the rule of law, whether domestically or internationally.

Nevertheless, much must be done if credibility of the Twelve is to be preserved. Democratic solidarity must be put before commercial gain and a certain renunciation will be unavoidable. Those EC countries that openly and repeatedly break consensus in international matters or prevent reaching it must reflect on the wisdom of this line of action. Consistency and correspondence between public declarations and private action is a must in a successful fight against terrorism. The Single European Act challenges centrifugal forces at the Community level. Whereas a Community corpus of principles in combating terrorism has gradually emerged, what is needed now is concerted action to put it into practice.

NOTES

1. Rafael Sánchez Ferlosio, 'Notas sombre el terrorismo', *El Pais*, 11 March 1980.
2. Juliet Lodge, 'Terrorism and Europe: Some General Considerations', in Juliet Lodge (ed.), *The Threat of Terrorism* (Brighton: Wheatsheaf, 1988).
3. Paul Wilkinson, *Terrorism and the Liberal State* (London: Macmillan, 1986).
4. J.A. Carillo Salcedo, *International Legal Aspects of Terrorism* (The Hague, 1988).
5. Alex P. Schmid, 'Force or Conciliation? An Overview of Some Problems Associated with Current Anti-terrorist Response Strategies', *Violence, Aggression and Terrorism* 2/2 (May 1988), pp.149–78. See also idem, this volume pp.12–13.
6. Lodge, *Terrorism and Europe*.
7. R.A. Friedlander, 'The Origins of International Terrorism', in Y. Alexander and S.M. Finger (eds.), *Terrorism: Interdisciplinary Perspectives* (NY: John Jay Press), 1979.
8. Schmid, 'Force or Conciliation?'.
9. Wilkinson, *Terrorism and the Liberal State*.

The West's Counter-Terrorist Strategy

L. PAUL BREMER III

This essay provides an American perspective on the Western approach to counter-terrorism. Beginning with a retrospective look at why the international response to terrorism in the 1970s was so weak and confused, the study then focuses on the development of strategic policy objectives and the specific measures to achieve them. By putting pressure on states that supported terrorism and by applying the rule of law to terrorists to delegitimize them and portray them as criminals, some successes were achieved during the 1980s. The analysis then focuses on tactical measures, such as information exchange and target-hardening, and outlines some of the more recent successes in prosecuting international terrorists.

International terrorism is a global problem, and no country, no region, no people are completely immune from terrorist violence. An effective strategy for fighting it becomes more pressing with each new act of barbarism. In 1988, a few days before Christmas, Pan Am Flight 103 flying from Frankfurt via London to New York was destroyed in mid-air by a bomb. This tragedy resulted in the deaths of 259 passengers and 11 people from the small Scottish town of Lockerbie. These 270 innocent people were the victims of a gross act of terrorism. Pan Am 103's destruction and other bloody terrorist incidents remind us that terrorism is still a major issue on the international agenda, one which demands our attention and requires our action. I would like to describe how the US Government – with the help of other Western democracies – is responding to the challenge of international terrorism.

Dealing with Terrorism is a Long-term Problem

Within the past 25 years we have experienced many different forms of terrorism. We have seen terrorism live and in colour in our living rooms. But in spite of the impression that many of us have, terrorism is not something new. It has been around for centuries. The group whose name gives us our word for assassin arose in Persia about 900 years ago and later flourished in Syria. The assassins recognized that a tiny group of men prepared to die during their attack could paralyse a larger foe, and that fear of such attacks could give them power beyond their numerical strength. During the Napoleonic Wars, partisan forces pushed carts laden with explosives into the ranks of soldiers, causing significant damage. These were the predecessors of today's car bombs. By the late nineteenth century, the telegraph, newspapers, and rising literacy led Russian anarchists to recognize the shock value of violence. They referred to their terrorist attacks as 'Propaganda by Deed'. They knew that the audience for their acts was wider than the immediate victims.

Given the persistence of terrorism over centuries, it is unreasonable to expect we can eliminate it completely. But our governments can, and must, take vigorous action to limit terrorism. And the signs are that, after an initial period of uncertainty, the West is finally developing a coherent counter-terrorist strategy.

In the 1970s the West was on the Defensive

When modern terrorism burst on the scene some 25 years ago, the international community, especially in the United Nations, reacted in a befuddled fashion. We in the West lacked a strategy and we were on the defensive against both domestic and international terrorism. There were various reasons for this confusion:

- Many nations had recently emerged from colonialism; in some cases they considered terrorists as fellow revolutionaries who would soon join them in the community of nations;

- In the late 1960s and early 1970s the prevailing political and intellectual climate in many Western countries promoted an extraordinary tolerance of violent political action. This allowed terrorists to demand and receive public attention for their 'causes'. Terrorist acts – even kidnapping, kneecapping and murder – acquired an aura of romance and adventure;

- The Vietnam War increased anti-American sentiment around the world and led to an intellectual environment in which anti-American activism was easier to justify;

- In the Middle East, Israel's stunning military successes shattered the hopes, nourished by some Palestinians, that the front-line Arab states would destroy Israel and by military force create a Palestinian state. Many of them began to think of terrorism as a way to continue the war by different means;

- Finally, the tremendous growth in air travel and worldwide television in the 1960s gave terrorists increased mobility, more vulnerable targets, and a ready-made worldwide audience for their vicious acts.

The West Develops a Counter-terrorist Strategy

By the end of the 1970s outrage at terrorist acts slowly began to turn the tide of public opinion in the West. Increasingly, people realized that nothing justified what they were seeing. Perhaps more than anything, the ever-expanding circle of targets for terrorist attack brought about change. People and governments began to realize that terrorists could and would attack anyone, including erstwhile sympathizers. In America, the 1979 seizure of the US Tehran Embassy galvanized public opinion and led to demands for effective government action. As a result of these changes, the West began to develop a clear, overall strategy to deal with terrorism. We have also put in place the supporting tactics necessary to implement that strategy. Action on two levels was needed: the development of political will to counter terrorism and the allocation of more resources to the fight.

Development of a Strategy: Political Vision and Political Will

Our strategic objective is to reduce terrorism to a point where it no longer diverts attention from other important foreign policy questions. We can only achieve this objective with a firm, concerted effort sustained over time. Our goal is to make the general political, economic and psychological climate in which terrorists operate more hostile. The targets of our counter-terrorist measures, therefore, are not particular terrorists or groups but the community of nations and the overall strategic environment in which terrorists must act.

The key element in developing a counter-terrorist strategy is the nurturing of political vision and political will to carry out the fight. To nurture political will, the West had to change the whole dynamic of the international discussion of terrorism. We had to move away from the early 1970s defensive, muddled reaction to terrorist violence and re-assert, clearly and decisively, democracy's willingness to fight terrorism. We had to shift the public debate on terrorism from understanding 'root causes' to condemning the crimes terrorists commit. We cannot, of course, ignore the causes. But we must also deal with the effects.

Specific Measures to Accomplish the Strategic Objective

To pursue this strategic objective, the West has adopted specific measures. For example, until recently, the international political environment made it relatively easy for terror-supporting states like Libya, Syria and Iran to operate against the West. A major element of our counter-terrorism policy, therefore, is to put pressure on states that support terrorism. If the West can make it clear that supporting terrorists is unacceptable international behaviour, then terrorists will be denied important financial, military and other backing from state supporters.

Another important measure of our overall strategy is applying the rule of law to terrorists. Terrorists are criminals. They commit criminal actions like murder, kidnapping and arson, and countries have laws to punish criminals. So we have sought to delegitimize terrorists, to get society to see them for what they are – criminals – and to use one of democracy's most potent tools, the rule of law, against them.

Counter-terrorist Measures Succeeding

These counter-terrorist measures are beginning to succeed. In a major show of collective political will, in 1986 the nations of Western Europe took a series of concerted actions to close down Libya's terrorist infrastructure of embassies, 'businessmen' and 'students'. These actions, combined with the American military strike against terrorist facilities in Libya, led to an immediate decline in Libyan-supported terrorism. Indeed, we detected Libyan involvement in only six terrorist incidents in 1988 compared to 19 in 1986. Colonel Gaddafi no longer openly brags about his use of terrorism. Most important, the political environment was shifted. The West at long last had taken decisive action against a terrorist state. That was a major breakthrough in the development of a Western counter-terrorist strategy.

In a similar way, in late 1986 the US and the EC imposed sanctions on Syria after Syrian officials were proven to have supported specific terrorist operations. These steps were possible because the countries of Europe had set the pattern of responding to state terrorism with their earlier measures against Libya. Again, the political environment had shifted. Again we had success. In June 1987 Syria expelled Abu Nidal, a notorious and particularly vicious Palestinian terrorist. In February 1989 the EC responded forcefully to Ayatollah Khomeini's call for the execution of the British author Salman Rushdie. The EC foreign ministers simultaneously recalled all their ambassadors in Tehran and suspended all high level official exchanges with Iran. They also condemned the Iranian death threat against Mr Rushdie. President Bush expressed strong support for the European actions.

As a result of concerted Western pressures, terrorists are finding it harder to get refuge and overt support. The Abu Nidal organization was expelled from Iraq in 1983 and from Syria in 1987. In Eastern Europe a successful diplomatic campaign seriously disrupted a network of enterprises of the Abu Nidal organization. Newspaper stories about the terrorist links of a Syrian family named Qassar, notorious for arms trafficking with terrorists, led to action against them by several European countries in 1987.

Our limited success in keeping terrorists on the move and pressuring their state supporters should not lead to complacency. Indeed, Libya, Syria and Iran continue to support some of the most violent and vicious international terrorist groups. There are indications that Libya in particular may have turned to using surrogates to hide Libya's hand in acts of international terrorism.

During the past decade, the West has elaborated an international legal structure grounded in bilateral and multilateral agreements to extradite or prosecute terrorists for their crimes. The first steps in an international legal framework were taken in the early 1970s with the Hague Convention on aircraft hijacking. Since then, further agreements have been reached in Montreal and at Summit meetings of the seven leading industrialized nations in Tokyo, Bonn, and Venice.

In spite of Lenin's insistence that the revolutionary must never abandon terrorism, by 1989 the former Soviet Union was saying that it opposed 'all terrorism'. While the Soviet definition of terrorism could be convoluted from our point of view, during the late 1980s the Soviets specifically condemned some acts of terrorism, including the attempted hijacking of a Pan American flight in Karachi. The Soviets also helped in drafting new counter-terrorist conventions on maritime and airport safety. Finally, where earlier attempts to cope with terrorism in the United Nations deteriorated into endless apologies for terrorists, in 1987 and 1988 the UN passed important resolutions condemning terrorism and hostage-taking. Diplomatic efforts were also made to gain UN approval for a general resolution condemning hostage-taking.

So we have made a real start during the 1980s in developing a strategy to change the overall environment in which the terrorists must act. Responsible countries have joined a new consensus against terror and have taken concrete steps. No one of these measures itself will solve the problem or reduce terrorism to a tolerable level. However, these and other measures, relentlessly pursued over time, will achieve our strategic objective.

Anti-terrorist Tactics to Obstruct and Deter Terrorists

Just as the West had to fortify its collective political will before it could develop a coherent counter-terrorist strategy, so it had to dedicate greatly increased resources to anti-terrorism before our tactics could succeed. The strategy demands will; the tactics demand money. Our tactical objective is to confound and thwart terrorists – to reduce their options and make their operations more complicated and perilous.

For the most part, anti-terrorist tactics are measures that better protect the most likely targets from terrorist attacks. How do they work? In much the same way as you protect your home from burglars. Putting heavy dead-bolt locks on your doors, a bar on sliding glass doors and keeping a dog or installing a burglar alarm will not stop a truly professional thief willing to run substantial risks. But each of them reduces the likelihood of a break-in at your home. Taken together, they can achieve your purpose – protecting your property, lowering your insurance rates and increasing your peace of mind. Anti-terrorism measures work much the same way to complicate and deter terrorist operations. In contrast to counter-terrorist measures, anti-terrorist steps are largely defensive in nature and can be unilateral or taken in concert with others. But they cost money.

More Resources to Anti-terrorist Fight Contribute to Success

One of the most important developments in the 1980s has been the public outrage throughout the world directed at terrorist violence. This strong public reaction has pressured politicians to make more money available to the anti-terrorist fight in the United States and abroad. These new resources form the hard core of our revitalized anti-terrorist tactics. Not surprisingly, the police and intelligence agencies first dedicated these new resources to the fight against their own domestic terrorists, particularly in Europe. So not surprisingly, the first successes of anti-terrorist measures were seen here. In Italy, anger at the 1978 kidnapping and murder of former Prime Minister Aldo Moro led to actions which shattered the old Red Brigades. In Germany, the Baader-Meinhof gang was broken through aggressive intelligence collection and vigorous law enforcement. The same has happened with French efforts to counter *Action Directe* and in Belgium with the Fighting Communist Cells.

As nations developed better tactics for dealing with their home-grown terrorists, they turned their attention to international co-operation. The West European countries have established the so-called TREVI (Terrorism, Radicalism, Extremism and political Violence) Group made up of Ministers of Justice and Interior. In succeeding years the TREVI Group has expanded considerably the amount of police and intelligence co-operation among the 12 EC members. For example, the ministers now regularly produce an agreed assessment of the terrorist threat facing the EC countries and they have developed a mechanism to exchange specific information on the movements and operating methods of terrorists. The International Police Organization (INTERPOL), which had resisted dealing with terrorism because of its political overtones, finally began co-ordinating information on terrorism in 1985 at US request. The American Federal Bureau of Investigation, for instance, can now notify the INTERPOL secretariat of arrest warrants it has out on terrorists. INTERPOL then sends the names by alert to all of its member countries.

Specific anti-terrorist measures developed by the West include:

- Near universal screening of all airline passengers for metallic objects, so that terrorists can no longer simply stroll aboard a flight with a pistol or bomb in their pockets;
- Tighter security at diplomatic installations so that an attack on an embassy is likely to require the attackers to suffer casualties, thereby making an attack less likely;
- 'Watch lists' of terrorists for border police to stop terrorists entering countries; and
- Measures to sow dissension within terrorist groups through black and grey covert operations.

Tactical Measures Succeeding

As we have had success in developing and implementing a counter-terrorist strategy, now our tactical measures are showing signs of working. Although the tragedy of Pan Am 103 reminds us of an airline's vulnerability to assault, over the past 15 years there has been steady progress in developing comprehensive anti-terrorist measures to protect air travellers. In the 1970s there were 18 to 20 terrorist hijackings each year, with substantial casualties and damage. In 1988 there were only two hijackings. Similarly there has been a significant decline in terrorist attacks on our diplomatic establishments. The 'watch lists' we have developed are in the hands of border police in many countries. Border police are becoming much more attentive to suspicious travellers. As a result, terrorists run considerable risks crossing international borders. Finally, because of increased attention to anti-terrorism by Western governments, terrorist groups can no longer be sure they have not been penetrated by Western intelligence agencies.

As countries dedicate more resources to the fight against terrorism, they are catching and prosecuting increasing numbers of international terrorists:

- In February 1989 a US federal court in New Jersey sentenced a Japanese Red Army terrorist, Yu Kikumura, to 30 years for transporting explosives. An alert New Jersey state trooper stopped Kikumura on a highway for acting suspiciously. A search of his car revealed that Kikumura was carrying three home-made anti-personnel bombs;
- In November 1988 a Maltese court sentenced the sole surviving terrorist in the November skyjacking of an Egyptian airliner to 25 years imprisonment – the maximum sentence allowed under Maltese law;

- In October 1988 a Sudanese court passed the death sentence on
  five Palestinian terrorists for their attack on Khartoum's
  Acropole Hotel and Sudan club;
- In 1989 a West German court convicted Muhammed Hammedi,
  a Lebanese terrorist implicated in the 1985 TWA hijacking which
  resulted in the death of an innocent American seaman, Robert
  Stethem;
- In Washington, DC, another Lebanese terrorist named Fawaz
  Younis stood trial in 1989 on hostage-taking charges arising from
  the hijacking of Jordanian Airlines flight 401 in June 1985.

As with the strategic steps mentioned earlier, no single tactical measure
or even group of measures will solve the problem, but, the cumulative
effect of the measures helps achieve our strategic purpose.

Conclusion

Terrorism has by no means disappeared from the world scene. We are
making progress in countering terrorism in some areas, but new
dimensions to this problem continue to emerge with distressing
frequency. There is no magic solution to this international scourge. Yet
over the years we have developed the strong political will and the clear
political vision to confront the terrorists. Our available resources are
carefully used and our technical expertise is improving. With the
persistence and patience that must surely mark our counter-terrorism
effort, I am optimistic that terrorism will diminish as an issue which
demands our attention.

Negotiating with Terrorists

RICHARD CLUTTERBUCK

This essay examines the record of government responses to some of the more highly publicized cases of terrorist blackmail from 1968 to 1989 and assesses, in light of this experience, the problems of government policy in the area of negotiations and concessions. The following policy issues are addressed: whether governments should ever make concessions; the effectiveness of international agreements; whether governments should prohibit the payment of ransoms; and government and corporate contingency planning and crisis management. The study concludes that concessions by specific governments have contributed to further targeting of those governments, although this was not a generalized pattern. Concessions also appeared to play a role in providing momentum to various 'fashion waves'. While responses such as refusing to negotiate at all or prohibiting negotiation by corporations or families, as well as international agreements and media coverage, have all proved problematic, yet on the other hand taking a firm stand, good contingency planning and crisis management, and target-hardening have all provided good results in dealing with terrorist blackmail.

Terrorist Blackmail: Questions of Responses

In a perfect world, no-one would ever make concessions to terrorist blackmail; as with any other blackmail, this encourages the crime. The same applies to street robbery, but few people would refuse to part with ten dollars at gunpoint, and legislation to forbid this would be unrealistic. How far can government policy or legislation prevent or discourage making concessions or giving money to terrorists? How should governments assess the balance between life, assets, principles and the encouragement of further terrorism and crime?

Clearly, governments should not release captured or convicted terrorists who are likely to kidnap or kill again, but does 'should not' mean 'should never'? And what about other concessions? Should they ever change their policies or pay ransoms to save the lives of one or a hundred or a thousand of their citizens? And should they legislate to ban corporations and families from negotiating with illegal organizations or from paying ransoms to save their own staff and children's lives? How strong is the evidence to support the general assumption that governments, corporations and families which make concessions to terrorist and criminal blackmail once are more likely to be picked as targets for extortion again? To what extent will democratically elected governments be influenced by public opinion? What are the effects of the media on their handling of this blackmail? And what kind of crisis management organization do governments need? How do corporations and individuals differ from governments in handling such crises? In what respects can government legislation help or hinder them? How should corporations approach the problems of contingency planning, crisis management and negotiation?

Political terrorist blackmail of governments began to become a serious problem in 1968. There were two main reasons for this. First, The Popular Front for the Liberation of Palestine (PFLP), frustrated by the loss of almost every territory giving direct access to Israel from Syria, Jordan and Egypt in the 1967 war, decided to pursue their objectives by international terrorist attacks, especially against aircraft. Second, left-wing guerrilla movements in Latin America, frustrated by the failure of rural guerrilla tactics, especially those of Che Guevara in Bolivia in 1967, switched to urban terrorism, initially concentrating on the kidnapping of foreign diplomats.

Governments' Response to Terrorism: 1968–1971[1]

In January 1968 two US Army officers were shot dead in Guatemala and, in August 1968, the US Ambassador, John Mein, was also killed, both cases appearing to be kidnap attempts. On 31 March 1970 the same guerrilla group kidnapped the German Ambassador, Count von Spreti, and demanded the release of 17 prisoners with 700,000 dollars. Despite pressure from the German government, the demand was refused and von Spreti was murdered on 4 April. A change of government followed and that terrorist group was ruthlessly suppressed, but terrorism continued at a high level in Guatemala.

In September 1969 the Brazilian government released 15 prisoners to secure the kidnapped US Ambassador. In March 1970 they released five more in exchange for the Japanese Consul-General in São Paulo, and in June a further 40 for the US Consul-General in Porto Allegre. The escalation reached its peak in January 1971 when 70 were released to free the Swiss Ambassador. The government, however, had been playing for time and by 1971 they were ready to crack-down ruthlessly on the terrorists, at considerable cost to civil liberties, and Brazil has been largely free of insurgent terrorism (though not of violent crime) ever since.

In Uruguay during 1970–71 the Tupamaros kidnapped a series of diplomatic hostages, one of whom (an American police adviser) they killed. Again, public disgust contributed to a hardline government being swept to power, soon followed by a military regime, which abruptly finished off the Tupamaros but with a prolonged denial of democracy and civil liberties for the people.

In October 1970 the Quebec Liberation Front (FLQ) in Canada, inspired by the Tupamaros, kidnapped a British diplomat and a French Canadian politician, eventually murdering the latter. The Canadian government introduced the War Measures Act with overwhelming political and public support and, though many later accused the Prime Minister, Pierre Trudeau, of over-reaction, terrorism was rapidly crushed.

Meanwhile in Europe, the international terrorist campaign by the Palestinians had begun. On 22 July 1968 an El Al Boeing 707 aircraft was hijacked 20 minutes after take-off from Rome by three PFLP terrorists and ordered to land in Algiers. The Algerians released all the non-Israeli passengers, and held the three hijackers, the crew and 12 Israeli passengers in military custody. The PLO sent a delegation to Algiers, demanding the release of 1,200 Arab prisoners from Israeli jails. Other Arab governments joined in, Egypt, Syria and Jordan demanding the withdrawal of Israeli troops from territories occupied in the 1967 war – Sinai, the Golan Heights and the Old City of Jerusalem.

In mid-August the International Federation of Airline Pilots Associations, and various western European airlines, announced that they would boycott Algeria from 19 August unless the hostages were released. On 1 September an Italian aircraft flew all the hostages to Rome and a French crew flew out the hijacked aircraft. On 2 September the Israeli government announced that, as a humanitarian gesture suggested by the Italian government, 16 Arabs captured before the 1967 war would be released. The Algerians later released the three terrorists, two of whom reappeared in further hijackings in 1972.

Following this incident, El Al installed locked bullet-proof partitions between cabin and flight deck, placed armed guards among the passengers, and instituted a much fuller check-in procedure for El Al flights. Since then, though the Arab terrorists would rather attack El Al aircraft than any other, such attacks have in fact been very rare and virtually never successful. The Algerian government played an ambivalent role in this incident, generally humanitarian and constructive, but allowing Arab terrorists to go free. They have continued this role in, for example, the release of US Embassy hostages from Iran in 1981 and the resolution of the Kuwait Airlines hijack in 1988.

In September 1970 Palestinian terrorists hijacked three aircraft (US, British and Swiss) with about 400 passengers, including unaccompanied British schoolchildren returning from holidays with parents stationed overseas. They were held on a remote desert airstrip, Dawson's Field, in Jordan. Eventually the hostages were all released in exchange for seven Palestinian prisoners, including Leila Khaled who was held in Britain following an unsuccessful hijack attempt on an Israeli aircraft which made a forced landing in London. Contrary to many predictions, the release of Leila Khaled did not result in any further Palestinian attacks on British targets, though she herself continued work with the PFLP as an organizer, trainer and international propagandist, her face having become too well known for her to take any further part in international terrorist operations.

The government of Jordan was so incensed by the affront to their sovereignty that their army was ordered to drive the entire armed Palestinian guerrilla organization out of Jordan, and this they did, inflicting heavy casualties. The survivors took refuge in Iraq, Syria and Lebanon, which have remained the principal bases of their various factions ever since. In mourning for this, younger members of Al Fatah, to whom Yasser Arafat turned a blind eye, formed a fanatical group called Black September, which carried out several attacks, including those at the 1972 Munich Olympics and the murder of diplomats at the Saudi Arabian Embassy in Khartoum in 1973.

One of their first attacks was on 28 November 1972, when Black September assassinated the Jordanian Prime Minister in Cairo, Wafsi Tal. The four assassins were captured by the Egyptians, but later released. Previously, on 15 December 1971, an Algerian terrorist working for Black September wounded the Jordanian Ambassador in London, Zaid al-Rifai, in an assassination attempt. The terrorist escaped to France, where he was arrested in Lyons. The Lyons court's recommendation to grant the British request for extradition was overruled by the French Ministry of Foreign Affairs, who decided to send him to Algiers, whose government had allegedly invented a charge against him for that purpose. This was one of several cases in which the French government has been accused of devious tactics, including the release of Abu Daoud in 1977, and an alleged deal for the release of French hostages from Lebanon.

Governments' Response to Terrorism: 1972–1977

Some of the passengers in the three aircraft hijacked to Dawson's Field in 1970 were West Germans, and the seven Palestinian prisoners released in exchange for them included three from West Germany. The West German government was known to have pressured the British and Swiss governments to join in releasing their prisoners earlier than they actually did. The German readiness to give way did not pass unnoticed, and this may have played a part in German targets being selected for other terrorist attacks during the next few years, to which they repeatedly gave way, until Chancellor Helmut Schmidt stopped the pattern in 1975. These were halcyon years for terrorists all over the world because, though some governments did stand firm, including the US, Irish, British and Dutch, the Japanese government also showed a depressing readiness to give way quickly to terrorist blackmail.

In February 1972 a German Boeing 747 was hijacked to Aden and the German government paid a five million dollar ransom. Then, at the Munich Olympics on 5 September 1972 eight Palestinian guerrillas kidnapped 11 Israeli athletes. Under the pretext of allowing them to fly out with their hostages, the Bavarian police attempted a rescue at the airport, which was bungled. The terrorists killed all 11 hostages and five terrorists were killed. The remaining three were captured alive. On 29 October the Palestinians hijacked another German aircraft to Zagreb. The three captured terrorists were at once flown from Munich to Zagreb. The German aircraft then flew them all – hijackers and captured terrorists – to Tripoli, where they were released. Some commentators even suggested that the Germans, realizing that the Palestinians would mount an operation to secure the release of three captives, secretly agreed to go through the ritual of the Zagreb hijack to complete the process with less risk of bloodshed.

The US government led the way in trying to stem the tide in March 1973, when Black September terrorists seized the Saudi Arabian Embassy in Khartoum and held three diplomats hostage – two Americans and one Belgian – demanding the release of 60 Palestinian prisoners held in Jordan and the Palestinian assassin of Senator Robert Kennedy imprisoned in the USA. When the US government refused to give way, all three diplomats were murdered. Even the Arab world was shocked by this, and the Sudanese government went through the motions of arresting and convicting the murderers, but released them a year later.

The international trend towards a firmer stance, however, was set back by the Japanese government in February 1974, when a mixed group of Palestinian and Japanese Red Army (JRA) terrorists hijacked a ferry after an abortive attempt to blow up an oil refinery on a small island off Singapore. The Singapore government took a hard line, and blockaded the ferry, with the terrorists holding the passengers and crew as hostages. The Palestinian/Japanese terrorist organizations thereupon spread their operation to Kuwait, where they seized the Japanese Embassy. Despite Singaporean and Kuwaiti protests, the Japanese government provided an aircraft to fly the terrorists from Singapore and Kuwait to freedom.

In July 1974 one of the released JRA terrorists, Yoshiaki Yamada, was arrested in Paris trying to smuggle counterfeit dollars to Europe to finance a proposed JRA kidnap operation in Germany. In September, assisted by the Palestinian commando based in Paris, three JRA terrorists seized the French Embassy in the Netherlands, threatening to kill the French Ambassador and ten other hostages unless Yamada was released. The French government conceded, insisting that the Dutch government allow the three terrorists to leave, and flew Yamada and the terrorists to Damascus, where they were allowed to rejoin their comrades in Lebanon.

In September 1977 six JRA terrorists boarded a Japanese Airlines DC8 aircraft at Bombay and hijacked it to Dacca, Bangladesh. Threatening to kill the passengers, they demanded the release of six JRA activists imprisoned in Japan. Again the demands were met by the Japanese government, the six JRA prisoners being flown to Dacca and, with the six hijackers, released with six million dollars. This incident was the climax of a highly successful series of JRA operations and Japanese government submission to them, in which some 20 known terrorists or imprisoned activists were allowed to go free to the Middle East. Yet, surprisingly, the JRA confined itself generally to nonviolent propaganda activities for the next nine years until it briefly (and unsuccessfully) tried to resume international operations in 1987–88 in the run-up to the Seoul Olympic Games, in which some of those released were rearrested. The reasons for this suspension of activity, however, were probably due more to events in the Middle East than to any change in Japanese government policy.

Meanwhile the German government, too, was making more concessions to terrorists: On 27 February 1975 the Second of June Movement kidnapped Peter Lorenz in Berlin, demanding the release of six imprisoned terrorists. Lorenz was one of the candidates for the mayoral election, due in three days time. His opponent – the incumbent mayor – felt that he could not abandon him to his fate, and five prisoners were released (one of the six preferring to complete his sentence and return to normal life). Those released included 22-year-old Gabriele Kröcher-Tiedemann. On 21 December 1975 she was one of a combined team of Palestinian and German terrorists which abducted 11 oil ministers of the Organization of Petroleum Exporting Countries (OPEC) at a meeting in Vienna. Three policemen and guards were killed, two of them allegedly by Kröcher-Tiedemann. The Austrian government then allowed the terrorists to be flown to Algiers, where they released their hostages. It was rumoured that some of the Arab oil countries paid a total ransom of 25 million dollars to get their ministers released.

The new German Chancellor, Helmut Schmidt, had been mortified by the release of the five terrorists in Berlin, but was in no position to overrule the incumbent mayor in the special circumstances. He wasted no time, however, in showing that he intended to take a firmer line than his predecessor. On 24 April 1975 six terrorists of the Red Army Faction seized the German Embassy in Stockholm and held 23 hostages, including the German Ambassador, demanding the release of 26 Red Army Faction prisoners held in German jails. Schmidt encouraged the Swedes to stand firm. The terrorists threatened to shoot the Military Attaché unless the Swedish police withdrew, and when this was refused, they shot him. When Schmidt maintained his refusal to release prisoners, they killed another hostage. At this point, the Swedish police decided to attack but, before they could do so, the terrorists made a bungled attempt to blow up the building, wounding all the hostages and killing two of themselves. The other four terrorists were captured and imprisoned in Germany. Though the Red Army Faction hijacked an aircraft in 1976 and committed three more murders in 1977, the Stockholm incident marked the beginning of their decline.

During the same period, the Irish, British and Dutch governments stood firm when two IRA terrorists kidnapped a Dutch industrialist, Dr Herrema, in the Republic of Ireland on 3 October 1975: and, two months later, when four more IRA terrorists being pursued by the police, barricaded themselves with two hostages in a house in Balcombe Street, London. Both incidents ended in a siege by the police: all the terrorists were arrested and convicted and the hostages released unharmed. The IRA gang arrested in London proved to be one which had killed 13 people in the previous 18 months.

The Dutch government continued to stand firm against a series of attacks by South Moluccan terrorists from 1975 to 1978. There is an element of tragedy about the South Moluccans, whose islands became part of the newly independent Indonesia in 1949. Many South Moluccans who had been loyal soldiers in the Dutch Army chose emigration rather than absorption into Indonesia and to this day bitterly maintain a refusal either to accept repatriation or integration into Dutch society. On 2 December 1975 a group of young South Moluccans hijacked a passenger train at Beilen, killing two of the 75 hostages during the seizure and later a third, in cold blood, when the Dutch government refused to concede to their demands; these included the release of 25 South Moluccans held in Dutch prisons for other terrorist offences, and the 'recognition' of a South Moluccan Republic to be independent of Indonesia. On 4 December, to reinforce their demand, they seized the Indonesian Consulate in Amsterdam where they killed another hostage. The Dutch government negotiated skilfully to save the other hostages but made no concessions and by 19 December all the terrorists had surrendered, later receiving prison sentences of up to 14 years.

In May 1977 their comrades hijacked another train near Glimmen, and took over a school, to get the 1975 hijackers released, but the Dutch government sent in a marine commando, which killed six terrorists and captured the remainder, saving all the hostages except two who were killed during the rescue. In March 1978 South Moluccan terrorists seized a local government office in Assen, killing one of the 69 hostages before the Dutch Marines, in another highly professional operation, rescued the remainder and captured the terrorists.

Meanwhile, the tendency to stand firm was dramatically reinforced when, on 27 June 1976, a mixed gang of Palestinians and Germans hijacked an Air France aircraft with 257 passengers to Entebbe, where President Idi Amin connived with the hijackers and provided them with additional weapons. Non-Jewish passengers were segregated and released, about 100 Jewish passengers being retained as hostages in the airport terminal. The Israelis played for time by negotiating while preparing a rescue operation. Despite a strong Ugandan Army presence on the airfield, on 4 July an Israeli commando team rescued all the hostages except three who were killed, and killed the seven terrorists who were guarding them. This was an exceptionally daring and hazardous raid, and the courage and military skill of the commandos was fully matched by the political courage of the Israeli government, for whom it would have had disastrous consequences if it had failed.

Six months later, however, the French government gave a boost to Arab terrorist moral when they released Abu Daoud, who was widely believed to have organized the Munich Olympics operation in 1972. On 7 January 1977 Daoud entered France from Beirut on a false Iraqi passport with a false name, to attend the funeral of a murdered PLO representative. He later claimed that his visit had been approved, with a guarantee of immunity, by the French government. Acting on an Israeli tip off, the French police arrested him, apparently without the knowledge of the Foreign Office. The Israeli and German governments applied for his extradition, the Israelis requesting that he be held for 60 days to give time for extradition proceedings. The French government, under pressure from Arab governments with whom they wished to maintain friendly relations, refused the Israeli request on the grounds that Munich was not in Israel, and claimed that the Germans had not sent the necessary follow-up documentation. (There were suggestions that the German government was dragging its feet lest the imprisonment of Daoud in Germany lead to further terrorist attacks to force his release). The French courts accepted Daoud's false name and passport and released him; on 11 January he was flown to Algiers – with remarkable haste.

Throughout 1977 the German government maintained their firm

stand. In April, the Red Army Faction murdered the Public Prosecutor, Siegfried Buback; then in July the Chairman of the Dresdener Bank, Jurgen Ponto, was murdered by a Red Army Faction gang led by Suzanne Albrecht, who was his goddaughter and had treacherously used this family friendship to gain access to his guarded home. Then, on 5 September, they kidnapped in Cologne Dr Hans-Martin Schleyer, a director of Mercedes Benz and President of the German employers' federation, and demanded the release of 11 of their leaders from prisons. Helmut Schmidt skilfully played for time; while announcing publicly that there would be no concessions (as governments always do), he authorized Schleyer's family to try to negotiate a ransom, though with no hope of success as they had no power to release the prisoners. He also arranged for government ministers and officials to be seen in such places as Algiers and Damascus, to which prisoners might well be released, and the media rose to the bait and conjectured on the reasons. As a result, despite repeated ultimatums, the Red Army Faction kept Schleyer alive and moved him from place to place. Due to a mixture of bad luck and a ponderous intelligence system, the German police twice missed rescuing him by about a day, but this was not the fault of Helmut Schmidt.

The case took a dramatic turn when, on 13 October, a Lufthansa aircraft was hijacked by four Arab terrorists demanding the release both of the Red Army Faction's 11 leaders and some additional Arab prisoners. The hijackers had boarded the plane in Majorca, it had refuelled in Rome, Cyprus, Bahrain and Dubai (where they murdered the Captain whom they accused of giving messages to the authorities) before landing at Mogadishu in Somalia. In the final stages, the aircraft had been shadowed by another German aircraft carrying the German rescue commando Grenzschutzgruppe 9 (GSG-9), accompanied by a British SAS officer and sergeant who had local knowledge of the Gulf and 'stun grenades' which might be useful in a rescue. While the Dubai government had refused to allow them to act on its soil, the Somali government did authorize them to do so. They carried out a masterly raid at 2am on 18 October, rescuing all the hostages alive, killing three of the hijackers and wounding and capturing the fourth. When this news reached Stammheim prison where the Red Army Faction leaders were imprisoned, four of them committed suicide; and on 19 October the body of Dr Schleyer was found in the boot of an abandoned car in Mulhouse, close to the German border with France.

The US government has a declared policy of making no concessions to terrorists in order to secure the release of government employees and it usually sticks to this, especially in the case of diplomats. In some cases, however, there are differences in perception over who is or is not a government employee. Richard Starr was a Peace Corps volunteer in Colombia and was kidnapped by chance during a raid by the self-styled *Fuerzas Armadas Revolutionarias Colombianas* (FARC) guerrillas on a rural police station on 14 February 1977. The guerrillas did not at first realize that he was an American but, when they did, they put it out that he was a 'CIA agent' (a standard accusation against Peace Corps volunteers) and demanded an exchange with a FARC member in prison for murder. After complicated three-way negotiations with the Colombian government, the prisoner was released on a legal technicality but Starr was not handed over. FARC then demanded a 250,000 dollar ransom in a letter to the US Embassy, instructing them to insert a newspaper advertisement to indicate acceptance. For fear that Starr would otherwise be killed, they inserted the advertisement, even though they had no intention of paying. This torpedoed a parallel negotiation being conducted by Starr's mother together with a congressman, but they eventually raised 250,000 dollars in conjunction with a well-known journalist, Jack Anderson, and Starr was released on 12 February 1980.

Governments' Response to Terrorism: 1978–1989

In Rome, on 16 March 1978, terrorists of the Italian Red Brigades (BR) kidnapped the former Prime Minister, Aldo Moro, in an operation clearly modelled on the Schleyer kidnap. They demanded the release of BR activists convicted or undergoing trial. The Italian government's response was hampered by argument between its coalition partners and by a recent politically inspired weakening of the intelligence organization, but, though it tried to play for time by negotiation, it resolutely refused to release any BR prisoners. Aldo Moro's body was found on 9 May in the boot of a car in Rome.

In 1979–81 there was a brief but intense surge in the incidence of embassy seizures, sometimes to extort money and other concessions, but more often to obtain publicity for a political cause. There were 35 such seizures in 1979, 42 in 1980 and 25 in 1981, after which the fashion declined as rapidly as it had grown. Of these 102 seizures, 46 were in Latin America, 35 in Europe and 21 elsewhere. The hostages included 32 ambassadors, and in all 59 people were killed, most of them terrorists during rescue operations.

By far the most significant instance was the seizure of the US Embassy in Tehran on 4 November 1979, initially with 60 hostages, though this was reduced to 50 by the release of female and black hostages two weeks later. These 50 were held for 444 days. The original seizure was by 3,000 young Islamic militants and, because these were the kind of people to whom the Ayatollah Khomeini was most sympathetic, he threw the whole weight of the army and police force behind the holding of the embassy and its diplomatic hostages – probably the most flagrant breach of the Vienna Diplomatic Convention in history. President Carter, after a disastrous attempt at a military rescue operation in April 1980, eventually negotiated their release with the Algerians as mediators during the period between his failure to secure re-election and the inauguration of President Reagan in January 1981. Carter's concessions were the release of some of the Iranian assets frozen in US banks when Khomeini had seized power in February 1979.

The most spectacular and successful instance was the seizure of the Dominican Embassy in Bogota, Colombia, by April 19 Movement (M-19) terrorists on 17 February 1980. Masquerading as two football teams on the University playing fields across the road, they pulled on track suits with weapons concealed in them and ran into the embassy in well-rehearsed formation, killing a guard, and seizing 75 hosts and guests – including 14 ambassadors – attending a reception on the first floor. They released non-diplomatic staff but held the remainder under threat of death for two months, demanding the release of 300 M-19 prisoners and a ransom of 50 million. The Colombian government refused to negotiate on either demand but eventually a consortium of businessmen from some of the countries whose ambassadors were held paid a ransom of 2.5 million dollars upon which the Colombian government agreed the terrorists and hostages would be flown to Cuba and released. The greatest success of the operation, however, was the publicity it gained for the M-19 movement, which was probably its primary aim. With ambassadors from 14 countries held hostages, the whole event was front-page news throughout the two months.

Publicity was also the primary aim of the seizure of Khomeini's Iranian Embassy at Princes Gate in London on 30 April 1980 by six Iranian Arabs from the south-west Province of Khuzestan, demanding the release of prisoners by the Iranian government – a demand which they knew would not be accepted. The embassy was quickly surrounded and, of the 26 hostages, five who were sick or pregnant were soon released as a result of patient negotiation by the police. As the Embassy was situated across the road from Hyde Park, the whole event was given massive world publicity through the huge array of television and press cameras which assembled in the Park. Tension was further eased when the terrorists were notified of the time that reports were going out on the BBC World Service, to which they listened with delight. Having achieved their primary aim, they reduced their demand to one of safe custody out of the country.

It soon became clear, however, that the British government had no intention of conceding this or any other demand. The terrorists therefore killed one hostage (a member of the Embassy staff) and threatened to kill another every 40 minutes until this demand was met. The British government, with Khomeini's authority to enter the Embassy, ordered in the rescue force of the army Special Air Service (SAS) Regiment, who killed five of the terrorists and arrested the sixth, rescuing all the remaining hostages unharmed except for one whom the terrorists shot dead (also wounding two others) before the rescue force reached the room where they were held. This rescue, due to its spectacular success in front of the world's cameras, encouraged other governments to stand firm and marked the start of the rapid decline of embassy seizures.

Another terrorist fashion – the seizure of foreign technicians assisting the economic development of Third World countries – was also checked by firm concerted action by both the host and the foreign governments concerned. These seizures became prevalent in Kurdish Iraq, in Angola (by UNITA guerrillas) and in the Sudan in the early 1980s, where they forced the suspension of two major development projects in 1984 – the Jonglei Canal by a French consortium and the Bentiu oil project by the US Chevron Corporation. These kidnaps tended to alienate the local population, however, and they had largely gone out of fashion by 1985.

The kidnap and murder of Aldo Moro had shown up serious weaknesses in the Italian police and intelligence services and in the laws as they affected terrorism. In 1979–81 the Italians made great strides in all these fields, and placed an outstanding officer, General Dalla Chiesa, in charge of anti-terrorist operations. The improved intelligence services, the offer of leniency to repentant terrorists ('*pentiti*') and the training of a successful hostage rescue force played their part in the discovery and rescue of US Brigadier General James Dozier 43 days after he was kidnapped by BR in Verona on 17 December 1981. This gave a major boost to police confidence and to the defection of terrorists and their supporters, dramatically reducing the number of terrorist murders from hundreds in 1976–80 to a trickle from 1983 onwards.

The incidence of hijacking was greatly reduced by improved security in the 1970s, falling from a peak of 90 in 1969 to an average of less then 20 per year since 1981. Nevertheless, hijacks, when they occur, have a dramatic effect on public confidence and achieve massive publicity, thanks largely to irresponsible exploitation by the media. The most notorious example was the hijacking of a TWA Boeing to Beirut in June 1985, when US TV channels competed by arousing a degree of public hysteria and conjecture about President Reagan's options which eventually left him one option only – to make deals with the Shia leaders, Nabih Berri and President Assad of Syria, to persuade the Israelis to release 700 prisoners and allow the hijackers to go free in exchange for the lives of the hostages. A similar situation was created for the Kuwait government in April 1988 when one of their aircraft was hijacked to Algiers. The media again co-operated with the terrorists in broadcasting hysterical interviews with terrified hostages at gunpoint. Though the Algerians negotiated the release of all the passengers except those already murdered earlier in the hijack, all the terrorists went free to a hero's welcome.

In October 1985 the US government did manage to intercept the Egyptian aircraft carrying the hijackers of the cruise ship *Achille Lauro* on their way to Tunis, and forced it to land in Italy, where four of them were later sentenced to long terms of imprisonment. The Italian government, however, for reasons never fully explained, allowed the organizer behind the hijack, Abu'l Abbas, to go free on the day he was captured.

Of all international 1980s terrorist operations, the most successful at forcing concessions by Western governments was the series of suicide bomb explosions by Shia fundamentalist terrorists of the Party of God (Hizbollah) in Lebanon in 1983. At the request of President Gemayal, a Multinational Peacekeeping Force (MNF) with US, French, British and Italian contingents was established in Lebanon. Hizbollah were determined to drive it out. On 18 April 1983 they bombed the French and US embassies in Beirut, killing 50 people. On 23 October 1983 they bombed the main US and French MNF bases, killing 240 US Marines and 60 French paratroops. The end result was that all the MNF contingents were withdrawn early in 1984.

At the original time of writing, there were about 20 Western hostages still held by Islamic fundamentalist Hizbollah terrorists in Lebanon, some of whom had been held for over three years. There were suspicions that the French, Germans and Americans made secret concessions to secure the release of some of their hostages. Alfred Schmidt, a Siemens executive kidnapped in Beirut on 21 January 1987, was released in September of that year and Hizbollah claimed that there had been 'guarantees and promises' by the German government; there were also suggestions that a ransom of two million dollars had been paid for him, with a promise of a further three million dollars for the release of a second German hostage, Rudolf Cordes. On 29 November 1987 the French government released an Iranian diplomat, Wahid Gordji, arrested and charged with masterminding a spate of bombings in Paris in September 1986, in exchange for the release of French hostages in Lebanon. In February 1989 a government spokesman in Iran accused France of failing to honour a promise made by the Chirac government in 1985 to release Anis Naccache, imprisoned in 1982 for the attempted murder (approved by the Ayatollah Khomeini) of former Iranian Prime Minister Shapour Bakhtiar in Paris.

Britain stood firm over her three hostages, and they were eventually released late in 1991, without any government concessions. One of the three, the Archbishop of Canterbury's special envoy Terry Waite, was known to have left word before the visit to Lebanon during which he was kidnapped in 1986 that he wished no concessions to be made on his behalf. Hans-Martin Schleyer did the same before he was kidnapped in 1977. In both cases this inspired their governments to match their courage.

Should Governments Ever Make Concessions?[2]

'Never say never'. Governments obviously should not give way to blackmail, yet it is easy enough to think of scenarios in which they would have no option. Israel has the hardest of hardline policies, backed by an embattled people who know that weakness could mean rapid extinction, yet they have on several occasions had to make concessions, including the release of prisoners. In 1970 during the Dawson's Field hijack of three planes, the British Prime Minister, Edward Heath, advocated a harder line than the Germans or the Swiss – all three governments held prisoners whose release was demanded by the hijackers – but with a lot of unaccompanied British schoolchildren marooned in the desert at that point he could not have carried the British public with him if he had refused to release Leila Khaled when the other governments were ready to hand over their own six prisoners to get their hostages out.

Nevertheless, only in extreme circumstances should governments release terrorists who have killed and are likely to kill again. There are other concessions for which terrorists may be ready to settle, such as publicity. Britain, like Germany, has been flexible over this, but has not, so far as is known, released any terrorists who have killed, hijacked or kidnapped, other than Khaled.

It is on the face of it surprising that, during 1970–77, the governments of two of the world's most robust nations, Germany and Japan, seemed to be the most ready to give way to terrorist blackmail. The likeliest explanation is that both these countries were trying to live down the impression made on the world by their years of fascist government, that they had little concern for human life. Their succession of capitulations, the Germans in Jordan (1970), Zagreb (1972) and Berlin (1975) and the Japanese in Singapore and Kuwait (1974), Malaysia (1975) and Dacca (1977) must almost certainly have given encouragement and momentum to the JRA, the Palestinians and the Red Army Faction during this period.

The Germans clearly decided to check this momentum firmly in 1975 and ceased to be regarded as an easy target, but with Japan it would appear that the JRA offensive's suspension was due to internal developments in the JRA and the Middle East rather than to action by the Japanese government of the day. The JRA's chief sponsor, Wadi Haddad, died in 1978; he had been the leader of the faction of the PFLP which had broken away from the more moderate leadership of George Habash, who had come to the conclusion that international terrorism, as distinct from attacks on Israel, was proving counter-productive. The motivation and practical backing for worldwide operations carried out on Haddad's behalf by the JRA in 1972–77 died with him. Then, when Israel invaded Lebanon in 1982, the JRA Middle East cell had to move out in a hurry, and they spent the next four years on an 'ideological reappraisal' before resuming operations in 1986 – with their sights on Japan and the 1988 Seoul Olympics rather than the Middle East.

When governments have the initiative, such as in a siege of a building or of a hijacked aircraft in one of their own airports, it is easier to stand firm than in the case where the precise location of the hostages is unknown (e.g., in Lebanon) or when they are beyond its control (e.g., in an aircraft held at a foreign airport). The examples given above indicate a growing firmness in cases where the government does have the initiative.

Governments should not, however, refuse to negotiate at all, even when they have no intention of making concessions. The art of negotiation is to ensure that the other party always believes that there is more to be gained by continuing to talk than by cutting its losses and carrying out the threat (e.g., killing the victim). Moreover, it is only by negotiation that the police and others concerned (e.g., psychologists) can obtain information, make judgments and gain time in which to secure a release or mount a rescue. The example set by Helmut Schmidt in the 1977 Schleyer case was an excellent one.

International Agreements to Co-operate Against Terrorism

There is a traditional principle of jurisprudence that a state which has an extradition agreement with another has the alternative of prosecuting the offender in its own courts. This, however, will only work fairly if the judiciary is genuinely free from the influence of its government, and reaches its verdict on strictly legal grounds. Despite French government claims to the contrary, it was widely believed, both in France and elsewhere, that the decision of the court to release Abu Daoud in 1977 was influenced by the perceived national interests of France in its relations with Arab states.

The Tokyo (1963), Hague (1970) and Montreal (1971) international conventions against hijacking and other 'unlawful acts against the safety of civil aviation' were ratified by a majority of countries in the world (107, 113 and 111 respectively); all were based on the 'extradite or prosecute' principle, but they also permitted any state to relieve itself of its obligations if it considered the offence to be 'political'. This loophole is even wider in such conventions as have been attempted by the United Nations, which are so worded as to condone virtually any international terrorist offence by claiming that it was carried out against a 'military imperialist', or 'economic imperialist', or 'neocolonialist', or 'oppressive' government. These definitions can be applied, on its own appraisal, to any government in the world by any state which finds it convenient to condone a terrorist attack.

A determined attempt was made by the Council of Europe, in its European Convention for the Suppression of Terrorism (1977), to overcome this problem by the signatories agreeing that certain offences would *not* be regarded as 'political' for the purpose of extradition, including kidnap, hijack, hostage-taking or endangering life by use of bombs or automatic guns (Article 1). To get it signed at all by some countries, however, the Council had to insert two additional articles which totally defeated this object: that there was no obligation to extradite if there were substantial grounds for believing that the accused person might be prosecuted on account of race, religion, nationality or political opinion (Article 5); and that, notwithstanding Article 1, any state may reserve the right to refuse extradition for any offence which it considers to be political (Article 13). This means in practice that no state need take any notice of Article 1 if it considers it more in its national interest to evade it. And – to make sure of this – Article 14 permits any state to withdraw from the Convention, instantly, simply by notifying the Council of Europe that it has done so.

The conclusion is that the only effective way in which governments can be pressured into refusing sanctuary for terrorists is a boycott threatened by enough of the others to make it hurt. At the Bonn Summit in 1978, the USA, Canada, Japan, France, Germany, Italy and the UK agreed to a total air boycott of any country which failed to extradite or prosecute captured hijackers. Since these seven countries operated 80 per cent of the non-communist world's commercial air traffic, this boycott really would hurt, and a reminder of the possibility of it has on occasions been effective. But it is easy enough to get out of it by prosecution and acquittal. And would all these seven countries apply the boycott if they judged it contrary to their national interests? The Abu Daoud case suggests that the answer is doubtful.

Should Governments Ban the Payment of Ransoms?

It is unrealistic for governments to try to legislate to compel corporations or families to stand as firm as they would themselves hope to do. If governments make it a crime to pay a ransom or to insure against it, or if they try to prevent this by freezing corporate or family assets, or by blocking the release of currency, they will in practice be more likely to drive the firm or family to settle secretly behind the backs of the police. When an executive is kidnapped in a high risk area, his corporation knows that if they abandon him to his fate they will lose more, in terms of staff morale, public image and future recruitment of people willing to serve them in such places, than the cost of paying a ransom. And obviously the parents of a kidnapped child will not allow a law to stand in their way if they think obeying it is likely to result in the death of their child.

Where such restrictions have been imposed, this has simply resulted in numerous ransoms being paid without the authorities being notified at all, with the terrorists or criminals receiving their full demand and with no chance whatever of the police getting information leading to arrest or conviction. These restrictions were attempted in Italy and Argentina in the 1970s, and the arrest rate of kidnappers was between five and ten per cent. By contrast, in the USA, where the FBI publicly declare a policy of giving every possible assistance to the firm or family, negotiation and ransom delivery are carried out in full cooperation with the police, resulting in an average arrest rate of 90 per cent. There have been numerous cases in Europe where co-operation between the police and corporations and families of hostages in negotiation and payment of ransoms have resulted in the arrest and conviction of kidnappers.

Government Contingency Planning and Crisis Management

Every government has some kind of structure for dealing with emergencies, whether they are natural disasters, international incidents, threats to public order or terrorist threats. In any large country, this will probably exist in shadow on three levels; national, regional and local (i.e., at the site of the incident). The crisis management structures in Britain and the Netherlands have been developed and used successfully through such emergencies over the past 15 years, so they have been selected as illustrations.

At the national level, the crisis management committee in Britain is known as COBRA (a loose acronym for the Cabinet Office Briefing Room). It is chaired by the Secretary of State for Home Affairs (the equivalent of a Minister of the Interior) and its permanent secretariat is run by a senior civil servant in that department. It meets regularly for contingency planning and its composition varies with the contingency which is being considered. The police will almost invariably be represented. If the contingency is an air disaster or hijack, the transport and aviation ministers will be co-opted. If terrorism is involved, COBRA will also co-opt the intelligence services, the Ministry of Defence and probably also the Brigadier commanding the SAS Brigade, who is based in London and has a role of advising the government on countering terrorism when required. If there is a foreign country affected, the Foreign and Commonwealth Office will be represented. The Central Office of Information will handle public relations, and other experts will be co-opted as required, such as international lawyers or technical experts.

When an actual crisis occurs, COBRA is at once convened with the appropriate composition. Its task is to decide policy and take strategic decisions. A small executive committee, typically the permanent secretary of COBRA with a police representative and (in terrorist incidents) the SAS Brigadier and a member of one of the intelligence departments, will handle events and information on an hour by hour basis as they arise, will consult other members as needed, keep the Secretary of State informed and advise him to convene a plenary session if necessary.

At the regional level, the crisis is handled at the police headquarters responsible. If the incident is in Greater London, this will be the Metropolitan Police Headquarters at New Scotland Yard. If it were at, say, Stansted Airport, the Chief Constable of Essex would handle it from his headquarters in Chelmsford. His responsibility would be the tactical handling of the crisis and he, like COBRA, would co-opt whatever members were appropriate, almost always including a psychiatric adviser.

Handling the incident on the ground would be an improvised police headquarters established in a nearby building. In the case of a hostage or hijack situation, this headquarters would be termed a negotiating team and would, as soon as possible, establish a direct telephone link to the terrorists in their building or aircraft cockpit. This direct line is particularly important in a hijack negotiation; otherwise, radio negotiations will be intercepted by both domestic and foreign media, and both sides will assume postures which will prejudice any chance of meaningful negotiations.

In nearly 20 years of handling such incidents (i.e., since 1974), the British police have developed a highly skilled team of police negotiators. These officers are expert in keeping terrorists or criminals talking – and hoping. They are of middle rank, so that they can avoid being rushed into decisions ('I will have to refer that to my boss'), and frequently succeed in establishing a cordial working relationship with the terrorist negotiator. This, however distasteful to them, can be an important factor in saving the lives of the hostages.

The decision to call on the SAS to effect a rescue is normally initiated by the officer in command of the negotiating team on the site, when he judges that the lives of the hostages are in such imminent danger that the defensive use of firearms by the police is insufficient to save them and that military force must be used to kill or capture the terrorists before any (or any more) hostages are killed. He will normally refer this decision upwards through the Chief Constable to COBRA and the Secretary of State, though, if he judges that immediate action is essential to save life, he may ask the SAS to start deployment pending approval and be prepared to justify his action in retrospect if communication failures or other causes result in the Secretary of State's approval being delayed. He will give the SAS officer a specific task, probably 'to rescue the hostages', and this request is normally confirmed on the spot in writing. (This was certainly done in the Iranian embassy siege in London in 1980.) How the SAS carry out this task is the responsibility of the SAS officer and when it is complete he at once hands responsibility back to the police, with the aircraft or building, captured terrorists and hostages. The SAS officer does, however, remain answerable to the law and, if he or his men were to act in clear breach of that law, it would be the duty of the police to charge them.

The success of the SAS is due largely to their methods of selection and training. A man is only eligible to apply for secondment to the SAS if he has already been a fully trained soldier in another regiment. Since they get plenty of such applications they only invite the very best for test and assessment at their headquarters, and even of these they only select about one in ten. The tests are extremely rigorous, both physically and psychoogically, because the war role of the SAS man is to act in clandestine and highly dangerous surveillance tasks, often in enemy territory, as one of a very small group, typically of two or four men on their own. Thus mental stability and resilience are no less important than physical courage, endurance and skill at arms. The intensity of competition for selection, and the enormous pride and prestige of being selected, is such that it engenders a determination for the man to keep his place in the team, just as a member of a national football squad will play every match in the knowledge that holding his place depends on it. Any SAS soldier whose fitness, reflex actions, skills or mental stability fall away is liable to be returned at once to the regiment from which he was seconded.

The Dutch government crisis management system has many features in common with the British, the two developing side by side in 1974–80, especially through the five hostage seizures by South Moluccan terrorists. This development in the Netherlands was set in motion in September 1974, with the seizure of the French Embassy in the Hague by JRA terrorists, where the Dutch desire to stand firm was frustrated by French insistence on giving way, and in October 1974 when two Dutch and two Arab convicts seized 15 hostages in Scheveningen Prison, who were successfully rescued by the Dutch Marines rescue force (BBE) after the convicts had been worn down by five days of skilful negotiation with the help of a psychiatric adviser.

At the Dutch Cabinet level is the Crisis Centre, similar in structure and role to the British COBRA. It is headed by the Minister of Justice, who is responsible for law enforcement, is also Head of the Public Prosecution Service and controls the National Police (*Rijkspolitie*). The Minister of the Interior will always be a member, as he is responsible for public order through the mayors who in turn control their municipal police forces; he also controls the Department of Internal Security (BVD). Other members will usually include the Prime Minister; also, where air or surface transport, universities, schools or foreign interests are involved, the Minister of Transport and Public Works, Education and Foreign Affairs. Professional co-ordination of the Crisis Centre is by the Secretary-General of the Minister of Justice (a senior civil servant), whose office becomes the communication centre to the Policy Centres and Command Posts.

The Policy Centre is usually in a local government building as close as possible to the site of the incident. It is chaired by the Attorney General or sometimes the District Attorney (who is in any case a member). Other members include the mayors of municipalities involved and the chiefs of the municipal (and sometimes the national) police. There are also professional public relations and behaviourial advisers – the latter in all the cases described being the psychiatrist Dr Dirk Mulder, who had a remarkable record of success and has promulgated much of his expertise to the rest of the world.

At the site of the incident there is a police command post which is almost identical to its British counterpart, the negotiating team. In the case of a siege or hijack, it controls the surrounding marksmen, surveillance operations, medical services, delivery of food, and negotiation. It also keeps unauthorized people off the site.

The Dutch intelligence services again compare closely with their British equivalents, the BVD equating roughly to the British Security Service (MI5), the Central Investigation Information Service (CRI) to Special Branch at Scotland Yard, and the LBT, which collects information about terrorist crimes and reinforces local police as necessary, to the British Anti-Terrorist Branch (SO13) at Scotland Yard.

Specialist military forces are more diffuse, including police and military marksmen, and the Military Police (*Marechaussee*) which in civil matters is always subordinate to the regular police. The nearest equivalent to the SAS are the Special Assistance Units (BBE) of the Dutch Marines. They differ in that they are not long-service regulars but short-service marine conscripts who are rigorously selected from those who volunteer for this duty. BBE comprises two active platoons in readiness and one training platoon which becomes active when one of the others becomes due for demobilization. Though the individual marines may lack the long professional experience of the SAS troopers, their performance in the cases described has proved beyond doubt that the system does work.

One of the biggest problems experienced by the Dutch has been to prevent the media from prejudicing the success of siege and rescue operations. Though many journalists do have some conscience about putting Dutch hostages' lives at risk, others – especially some foreign journalists – have no such scruples, and will stop at nothing to get the sensational stories they want. The police normally operate two concentric cordons, the outer one admitting residents only and the inner one admitting no unauthorized persons at all. There is, however, no Dutch law to prevent a resident from accepting huge fees for the use of his house and its windows, and the media are willing to spend unlimited money to get round the police controls. They do so under the banner of freedom of speech, but the price of their freedom may be paid in hostages' or policemen's lives.

Dutch experience has been that the first two days of a siege are highly dangerous, when the terrorists are volatile and excitable, and liable to use violence if they feel thwarted. The aim of crisis management during the next three to five days is to allow a fragile equilibrium to develop between terrorists and hostages and also between terrorists and negotiators. In this they have been highly successful and, although there were between one and three hostage casualties in four of the seven sieges in the Netherlands between 1974 and 1978, they made no concessions whatever and captured or killed every terrorist (excepting only, on French insistence, the three Japanese who seized the French Embassy in 1974). No government, or its crisis management organization, can match that record.

Corporate Contingency Planning and Crisis Management

About 90 per cent of kidnaps for extortion are by criminals rather than political terrorists, and the great majority of these have been against business rather than government targets. Since the mid-1970s even political terrorists have more often picked corporations than govern- ments as their targets, because they believe them to be more ready to pay. During 1971–74 the Monteneros (a Marxist-Peronist movement in Argentina) extorted 240 million dollars in ransoms from business firms, including the world's record ransom of 60 million for the release of the two sons of the Chairman of the Argentinian Bunge Born Corporation. In 1978–79 the guerrilla organization Farabundo Marti National Liberation Front in El Salvador kidnapped executives of multinational subsidiaries from five countries (Japan, Netherlands, Sweden, UK and USA), playing one off against the other to raise 40 million dollars in ransoms, which they used as capital to create the organizational structure for their prolonged campaign to overthrow the government.

Corporations can lose enormous sums from terrorist extortion. In addition to the 60 million dollars quoted, others paid ransoms of five or ten million dollars in the same period. If this is accompanied by several months of negotiation, they can lose almost as much in management disruption and loss of trade. It is therefore wise for any corporation with operations or subsidiaries in high-risk areas to make contingency plans and to set up and rehearse shadow crisis management teams, just as governments do. As with governments, this structure will probably need two or sometimes three tiers. For example, a Dutch corporation might have its Corporate Crisis Management Committee (CMC) in Amsterdam, a Regional Committee in Bermuda or Bogota, and Incident Management Teams (IMTs) ready in five or ten high-risk subsidiaries in various Latin American countries.

These Committees should prepare contingency plans, taking as many policy decisions in advance as possible. Regular rehearsals and simulation exercises will reveal where such policy decisions are needed – e.g., how to respond to bomb, kidnap or extortion messages, whether to negotiate, in what circumstance if any to agree to pay a ransom to save life and, if so, the maximum sum to be contemplated; also, whether to enlist a specialist consultant, first to advise on contingency planning and then to be summoned to join the CMC if a crisis occurs. A pro forma should be placed beside every telephone to which calls are likely to come, indicating how to keep the caller talking, what questions to ask, what to note (e.g., voice characteristics), and whom to inform. All such calls should be taped.

If a crisis occurs, the CMC will be convened, and a crisis coordinator should be appointed. He is a key man and should be an able executive, fit for the task, who should be freed at once from other duties under the contingency plans. After the first meeting, it should be possible for the crisis to be handled day-to-day by the crisis coordinator (with a specialist consultant if he has one), calling in the chairman and other CMC members (e.g., security, personnel, finance, legal and public relations) only when decisions need to be discussed with them. Much the same applies at the IMT level, where the negotiator (again perhaps with a consultant) will handle all day-to-day business. One of the main benefits of a good crisis management organization is that most of the executives will be freed to carry on the normal commercial activities of the company.

A corporate CMC will have four main factors to consider if it is negotiating for someone's life. First will be moral considerations, for example, the relative values of material assets and lives. Second will be commercial considerations, concerning direct losses and the cost to a corporation's public image; in these respects, an insensitive approach to moral factors may indirectly cost more in the end. Then there are the legal factors, that is, acting within the law of the land bearing in mind legal liabilities to employees, stockholders and trading partners. Finally, there is the public policy factor, namely, not to encourage or reward terrorism and crime. The art of negotiations, as with government, is to ensure that the adversary always sees more to gain in continuing to talk than in carrying out his threats.

Conclusions

The humiliating concessions to terrorism by the German and Japanese governments between 1972 and 1977 probably did contribute to their being repeatedly selected as targets. The same may to some extent apply to French and US concessions in the 1980s. There is, however, little evidence that this is of general application; the Austrian government gave way twice but was not picked again. There is even less evidence of corporations being picked a second time, because terrorists have probably observed that a corporation, once bitten, markedly improves security, making it a less attractive target than others. There is, however, reason to believe that concessions do encourage a general and sometimes worldwide fashion or momentum in the selection of a particular type of target which seems to yield results. Examples were the series of kidnaps of diplomats in Latin America in 1968–71, of kidnaps of expatriate business executives in Argentina in 1971–74, of kidnaps and hijacks by JRA, Red Army Faction and Palestinian terrorists in 1974–77, of embassy seizures in 1979–81 and of bombings and kidnaps in Lebanon in 1983–88.

A firm stand by a government or group of governments has, as a corollary, had a generally suppressive effect on terrorism, such as that by the Dutch, British and Germans (after 1975) and by the US government generally in relation to kidnapped government employees, especially diplomats.

Governments should not release terrorists who have killed, hijacked or kidnapped, since they often repeat the crime, but it is a mistake to refuse to negotiate with terrorists at all, since without negotiations there is little hope of gaining time and information. Both sides should perceive advantages in continuing to talk.

Laws to inhibit negotiation by corporations or families are usually counterproductive, since they encourage settlements behind the backs of the police, who are therefore denied any chance of getting the time and information necessary for making arrests and convictions.

International agreements have a poor record of success since governments, both in drafting and executing them, will usually find loopholes whereby to put their national interests first.

Good contingency planning and crisis management pay handsome dividends both for governments and for corporations. The Dutch and British government organisations provide good models, as do those of several Dutch corporations.

Irresponsible use of freedom of the media by both electronic and print journalists may result in a big price being paid by governments and corporations and sometimes in individual lives.

A final conclusion is that both professional criminals and political terrorists usually carry out detailed reconnaissance and surveillance for several months in selecting their targets. If these reveal alert and positive security precautions, experience suggests that they will usually turn away and seek a softer target.

NOTES

1. The main sources for the facts and case studies presented in this article are as follows: *Control Risks Information Services Briefing Book Monthly*, 1981–1989 (London: Control Risks, 1981–89); Edward F. Mickolus, *Transnational Terrorism: A Chronology of Events, 1968–79* (London: Aldwych, 1980); Lester A. Sobel (ed.), *Political Terrorism Volume 1, 1974–1978* (Oxford: Clio Press, 1978); *TVI Journal*, Vols.5 to 8 (1984–89); *The Economist* (London), 1972–89; *The Times* (London), 1974–89. Some of the case histories briefly described in this article were covered more fully in Richard Clutterbuck's *Kidnap and Ransom* (London: Faber, 1978) and *Kidnap, Hijack and Extortion* (London: Macmillan, 1987).

2. The philosophies summarised in this chapter are based on what the author learned in his ten years as a non-executive director of Control Risk Ltd., from discussions following his lectures to police and business conferences, and from undertaking consultancy projects for governments and corporations in the United Kingdom and overseas. These philosophies are more fully explored in his own book, *Kidnap, Hijack and Extortion* and in two chapters he contributed to Brian Jenkins' *Terrorism and Personal Protection* (see below). These and other recommended books are as follows: Y. Alexander and R. Kilmarx, *Political Terrorism and Business* (NY: Praeger, 1971); Clutterbuck, *Kidnap, Hijack and Extortion* (London: Macmillan, 1987); R.D. Crelinsten and D. Szabo, *Hostage-Taking* (Lexington, MA: D.C. Heath, 1979); Martin F. Herz (ed.), *Diplomats and Terrorists: What Works, What Doesn't* (Washington, DC: Georgetown Univ. 1982); Brian M. Jenkins (ed.), *Terrorism and Personal Protection* (Boston and London: Butterworths, 1985); Brian M. Jenkins, Pamphlets published by the RAND Corporation, Santa Monica: 'Should Corporations be Prevented from Paying Ransoms' (1974);

'Embassies under Siege' (1981); 'Diplomats in the Front Line' (1982); 'Talking to Terrorists' (1982); 'The Lessons of Beirut' (1984); P. Koch and K. Hermann, *Assault on Mogadishu* (London: Corgi, 1977); Abraham Miller, *Terrorism and Hostage Negotiations* (Boulder, CO: Westview, 1980); The *Observer, Siege: Six Days at the Iranian Embassy* (London, Macmillan 1980); Yehuda Ofer, *Operation Thunder: The Entebbe Raid* (London: Penguin, 1976); Susanna Purnell and Eleanor Wainstein, *The Problems of US Business Operating Abroad in Terrorist Environments* (Santa Monica: RAND Corporation, 1981); Andrew Selth, *Against Every Human Law* (Canberra: Australian National Univ. 1988); Grant Wardlaw, *Political Terrorism* (Cambridge, UK: CUP, 1982); Paul Wilkinson, *Terrorism and the Liberal State* rev. ed. (London: Macmillan, 1986); idem and A.M. Stewart (eds.), *Contemporary Research on Terrorism* (Aberdeen: Aberdeen UP, 1987); John B. Wolf, *Fear of Fear* (NY: Plenum Press, 1981).

Combating Terrorism: Report to the Committee of Legal Affairs and Citizens' Rights of the European Parliament

M.P.M. ZAGARI[1]

This study traces the history of the European Parliament's efforts to deal with international terrorism from 1975 through 1988. It also examines the European Convention on the Suppression of Terrorism, efforts at intergovernmental co-operation (the Dublin Agreement, TREVI, the European Political Cooperation), anti-terrorist legislation, and extradition. It is argued that the establishment of a European judicial area is essential in a unified Europe, so as to overcome the legal and procedural barriers that exist between nations. The political and legal spheres must develop in parallel, necessitating a harmonization of legislation and increased coordination of the judiciary and of security forces. The essay concludes that creating a European Court would resolve the dilemma of countries refusing either to extradite or try a suspect. In such cases, the suspect would be tried before the European court.

A grave threat hangs over Europe: the threat of terrorism. The scale of the problem and its injurious consequences to public life, the political stability of states and the safety of their citizens have made it the subject of recurring topicality in the debates of the European Parliament and its bodies. In all the resolutions which have been adopted, one finding comes through as a constant thread: terrorist attacks seek to destroy Western democracies' defences, terrorism aims to destabilize and constitutes an assault on the democratic organization of states and is a threat to international relations. Recognition of this scenario requires of Europe's democrats a fundamental rethinking of how security can be achieved without sacrificing democracy, the fundamental principles of the rule of law, the basic rights and freedoms of the individual and the rules of justice traditionally observed in democratic states.

Activities of the European Parliament

The European Parliament's interest in the problem of terrorism was first evidenced on 10 July 1975 when the resolution on the terrorist attack in Jerusalem was adopted (OJ No. C 179, 6.8.75, Doc. 190/75). A year later, on 10 July 1976, the European Parliament adopted a resolution on combating international terrorism (Doc. 22/76, OJ No. C 178, 2.8.76).

Two days later, at the meeting of 12–13 July 1976, the European Council meeting in Brussels adopted the declaration on international terrorism in which the taking of hostages was condemned.

A great many other resolutions were adopted in due course. Some called on the Member States to ratify the 1977 European Convention on the Suppression of Terrorism, others stressed that anti-terrorist legislation, whether at the Community or the state level, should respect traditional democratic rights, still others reaffirmed the need to intensify joint efforts in the face of the international spread of terrorism. Condemnations were issued not only of terrorists but also of states which participated in their activities directly or facilitated such activities by holding hostages; calls were made for efforts on the part of the law-makers and of the appropriate authorities to avert the danger of a reawakening of fascism, anti-semitism, racism or xenophobia; governments were urged to take immediate steps for the creation of a European judicial area.

On 9 July 1982 came the adoption of the Tyrrell resolution on the European judicial area. This concluded, from an examination of the Treaties, that alternative legal bases existed for Community action with regard to the judicial area. It also concluded that the Commission should adopt a working document first and, subsequently, a proposal for a directive on the suppression of terrorism, on extradition, the transfer of prisoners, mutual assistance in criminal matters, the taking of witness statements, etc. On 16 September 1982 the European Parliament adopted a resolution (OJ No. C 267, 11.10.1982) in which the creation of a European Court to judge terrorist crimes was proposed. There followed a stream of resounding resolutions condemning terrorism, but no practical measures were taken.

The European Parliament adopted numerous resolutions[2] on this particular problem, attempting to respond to terrorist activities with the only means at its disposal – condemnation and an appeal to Member States to adopt a common policy against terrorism and against all actions which are directly or indirectly inspired by a policy contrary to the principles of democracy. In one resolution,[3] the European Parliament called on the presidency of European Political Cooperation to adopt a more effective policy and requested to be allowed to take an active part in its work.

In the series of resolutions referred to above, attention was first of all drawn to the international links between the various terrorist movements which aim to destabilize democratic governments. In order to combat such activities it was therefore deemed necessary to co-operate at the international level and it was recognized that such co-operation requires the co-ordination of measures to be adopted and a rapid exchange of information. The struggle against terrorism, it was argued, must be carried out fully observing the principles of democracy and of individual freedoms. Abuse of the right to political asylum, it was stressed,[4] results in impunity for terrorists which cannot be tolerated. Other resolutions stressed the need quickly to create the European judicial area and to establish common measures concerning extradition.

The Presidents-in-Office of the Conference of the Ministers of Justice have approached the Committee on Legal Affairs and Citizens' Rights on the problem of combating terrorism – Mr Scalfaro on 20 March 1985 and Mr Krieps on 13 September 1985. On both occasions, members of the committee put forward the idea of the creation of a European judicial area and raised the issue of the right to asylum within the European Community (EC), the problem of extradition and the idea of the possible creation of a European Court; they also asked for further information on the meetings of the TREVI (Terrorism, Radicalism, Extremism and political Violence) Group. On 11 September 1986, following terrorist attacks in Karachi and Istanbul and concluding a topical and urgent debate, the European Parliament adopted a compromise text backed by the Socialist Group, the European Democratic Group, the Liberal and Democratic Group, the RDE, the Communists and the EPP. By 193 votes to 11, with two abstentions, the European Parliament voted for more effective co-operation among the security services and forces, strict application of the rules on extradition and a proposal to establish a Community office for combating terrorism.

Recently, the problem's equivocal nature has emerged even more clearly and the European Parliament is required to play an extremely difficult role in maintaining the necessary balance. On the one hand, there are political differences and the demands of the various countries, whilst on the other, there is an awareness that the only way for us to guard against being 'mere victims' is at least to have operational co-ordination and be united politically, irrespective of the difficulties and priorities of each Member State. As early as 1972 the Consultative Assembly of the Council of Europe recognized the need for co-ordinated action in Western Europe against terrorism and adopted Recommendation 684 (on 23 October 1972) concerning international terrorism. Following the adoption of Recommendation 703 (1973), the Committee of Ministers adopted (on 24 January 1974) Resolution 74 on international terrorism, the contents of which may be seen as the basis of the principles laid down in the European Convention on the Suppression of Terrorism of 1977.

At the conclusion of the Conference of 4–5 November 1988, attended by Ministers of the Interior and of Justice and by those responsible for public order and security in the governments of the 21 member states, provisions to consolidate co-operation in the struggle against terrorism were adopted. It was decided, *inter alia*, to set up a group of the Ministers' closest advisers to examine how co-operation among states could be increased; to establish co-operation between the TREVI Group, to which the Twelve belong, and the remaining countries of the Council of Europe; and to consider introducing stricter criteria for the accreditation of foreign diplomats.

European Convention on the Suppression of Terrorism: Critical Analysis

The European Convention on the Suppression of Terrorism focuses on extradition as a particularly effective means of ensuring that the perpetrators of terrorist acts will not go unpunished. To this end, in Articles 1 and 2, several crimes are defined which should not or cannot be regarded as political crimes. It should be noted (and this is also true of an earlier Council of Europe Convention on Extradition, that of 1957) that no precise definition is given of 'political crime', of 'terrorist acts' or of 'terrorism'.

The fact that the European Convention concerns itself with political terrorism – and the concept of political crime which it recognizes seems to be very broad: political offences, offences related to a political offence or an offence inspired by political motives (Articles 1.1 and 2.1) – has aroused severe criticism. In addition, and independently of the Convention's provisions, states are able to use a procedure which has now become customary, though it remains debatable: that of expulsion or *l'extradition déguisée*. The removal of *personae non gratae* from a state's territory in fact achieves the same purpose as extradition. It has been, and continues to be, used by France, particularly as regards Basques.

The application of the principle *aut dedere aut judicare*, which we have seen is at the heart of the Convention in question, gives rise to another problem, or more precisely another risk, for a country of refuge to which an application for extradition has been made. If that country refuses to extradite a suspect for any reason (and that reason might be a reservation it has declared at the time of ratification, for which Article 13 of the Convention provides), it must, pursuant to Article 7 of the Convention, 'submit the case, without exception whatsoever and without undue delay, to its competent authorities for the purpose of prosecution', that is, it must *judicare* (judge) and hence possibly convict.

Intergovernmental Co-operation

Numerous resolutions adopted by the European Parliament have been accompanied or followed by many declarations on the issue of terrorism by the European Council. Let us recall here the one at the close of its meeting on 7–8 April 1978 in which the Council, declaring its deep distress at the kidnapping of Aldo Moro and the murder of his escort, stressed its firm resolve to do everything to protect the rights of individuals and the foundations of democratic institutions and agreed that 'the relevant Ministers will increase their mutual co-operation and will as soon as possible submit their conclusions on the proposals before them for a European judicial area.'

It was thus that the concept of a 'European judicial area' was first consecrated, to be subsequently taken up by the Ministers of Justice at their meeting on 10 October 1978. On that occasion, the working party which was preparing what was to become known as the Dublin Agreement[5] was instructed to consider the problems relating to extradition and, in addition, those concerning mutual assistance in criminal matters, the notification of criminal sentences and the transfer of prisoners. Based on their studies, the group of experts drew up a draft Convention on co-operation in criminal matters among the EC Member States. The Convention was about to be signed in Rome on 19 June 1980 when the Netherlands' Minister of Justice declared his opposition and it was never opened for signature. The principal reasons for the Dutch opposition seem to have been that the Convention's aims were not considered as being sufficiently broad, that it did not contain clauses allowing one of the contracting parties to withdraw, that no procedure was provided for the settling of disputes, that there was no provision for referral for interpretation to European courts and that it would have had an adverse effect on the Council of Europe's Convention.

Following the Netherlands' refusal, France in turn refused to ratify the Dublin Agreement and the 1977 Convention. Thus things were at an impasse: the Dublin Agreement was inoperative because, though signed, it had not been ratified; the Convention on co-operation in criminal matters among the EC Member States had not even been opened for signature; the Badinter proposal had been rejected; the Council of Europe's 1977 European Convention on the Suppression of Terrorism, even though much restricted by the reservations option of its Article 13, had been ratified by very few EC Member States.

Following a spate of terrorist attacks in 1987 and 1988, numerous declarations were issued by the Ministers meeting in political co-operation in which they proposed to set up, within the framework of political co-operation, a permanent working party with the specific task of monitoring the implementation of measures concerning security at airports, visa policy, etc.

Little publicity surrounds the activities of the TREVI Group (consisting of the justice and interior ministers of the EC member countries), presumably mainly because of the sensitive problems with which it deals. Replying on 5 September 1986 to a Written Question (199/86) by Mrs Lizin, the Foreign Ministers of the Twelve explained the role of the TREVI Group as follows: the TREVI I working group is concerned with the exchange of information on terrorist activities and mutual assistance in specific cases; the TREVI II working group is concerned with the exchange of technical information on combating terrorism and disturbances of public order; and the TREVI III working group deals with international organized crime.

Following a series of terrorist attacks in France, the TREVI Group held an extraordinary meeting in London on 25–26 September 1986 at which it was decided that a new telecommunications system (telecopier/coded facsimile reproduction) would be installed for very rapid exchange of information between police forces. In addition, the TREVI 'Troika' would henceforth analyze and compile the information gathered and would also maintain contacts with third countries. At the meeting of 20 October 1986 the TREVI Group decided to further increase co-operation in combating terrorism and the narcotics trade. A working party was given the task of studying the problems of improving checks at the Community's external frontiers, the co-ordination of national visa policies and co-operation in combating passport fraud. Following the thwarted attempt to place a bomb on a plane in London, and the resulting Hindawi trial, the Twelve met in political co-operation at Luxembourg on 28 October 1986. On the agenda was the question of the attitude to be adopted with regard to Syria. Common guidelines were established, but Greece refused to accept them.

Given the proliferation of European-level bodies concerned with combating terrorism – the TREVI Group, the EC Political Cooperation Working Party, the Council of Europe Working Party or the 'alter egos' of the Ministers concerned, the WEU and the group of co-ordinators – there seems to be a need for setting up a permanent secretariat, or at least a co-ordinating centre that would monitor the measures which are adopted, their practical implementation and the application of the legislation in force, including legal and judicial as well as formal aspects. Another reason why this is important is to prevent the emergence within European territory of parallel legal areas as a result of these bodies' parallel activities, or of bodies not subject to any control. It should always be borne in mind that the ultimate aim is to achieve a common legal and judicial area that could serve as an example and a pole of attraction for other countries willing to enter without reservations the area that we create.

Anti-terrorist Legislation: Legal Aspects

The growth of terrorism, particularly from 1970 onwards, has forced the countries most affected to create various legal instruments for the defence of their institutions. All the countries which in one way or another have suffered from terrorism, from the Federal Republic of Germany to Italy, from France to Spain, from Ireland to the United Kingdom and Canada, have introduced special provisions in criminal law, criminal proceedings and the judicial system, as well as police measures, in order to adapt the legislation in force to the specific features of terrorism's objectives and methods of combat.

The considerable degree to which it has been possible to respect the principles and legal guarantees of the constitutional system is all the more impressive when it is remembered that in other countries, even those with well-established democratic traditions, ample recourse has been had, if only for limited periods, to exceptional measures such as the setting up of special courts, sometimes comprising military judges (as in the State Security Court in France or the special court located in Madrid with jurisdiction over the whole territory of Spain), the use of the military against terrorists and their detention without trial (Northern Ireland), or the severely repressive limitations of the right of defence and the possibility of holding terrorist prisoners in total isolation (Federal Republic of Germany).

The mandate conferred by the Assembly on the Committee on Legal Affairs and Citizens' Rights[6] implies, *inter alia*, the duty of maintaining close and permanent contact with the appropriate parliamentary committees of the Member States in order to enable our committee to keep up to date with developments in these countries.

Extradition Between Member States

The mere concept of extradition between the Community's Member States implies an approach contrary to the integration of the Twelve and the establishment of a 'European judicial area'. Extradition, in fact, means the consigning of a person to a completely separate sphere of sovereignty, to a judicial area foreign to that of the state from which the extradition takes place; on the other hand, in a federation of states, or at any rate within a judicial area unified in terms of criminal law, it is no longer a question of 'extradition' but simply of transfer and consignment of suspects or prisoners. Thus, for instance, in the Constitution of the USA it is laid down that: 'A Person charged in any State with Treason, Felony, or other Crime, who shall flee from Justice, and be found in another State, shall on Demand of the executive Authority of the State from which he fled, be delivered up, to be removed to the State having Jurisdiction of the Crime.'

It is true that the EC is still a long way from achieving the stage of 'federation of states', but if that indeed is the goal we mean to achieve, if the sovereignty of the Member States has already been diminished in favour of Community bodies and if, lastly, we really mean to try and start creating a single judicial area for penal law among the Twelve, then it seems inadvisable to put at the heart of any 'new' conventions to be concluded by the Twelve a concept such as that of 'extradition' which is more appropriate to relations between states that do not form part of the same community – a concept that in its very definition contains the assertion of that clear separation between different judicial areas that we want to abolish.

In the legislation of countries, extradition, which is the handing over of a person from one to another sphere of sovereignty, is subject to many strict safeguards, some of them constitutional in nature, which generate impediments and motives for refusal that, on reflection, are seen to have no *raison d'être* in relations between the Twelve, and only persist because of nationalist reluctance towards change and the slowness with which traditional legal forms evolve. As to the constitutional obstacles which in some Member States prevent extradition for political crimes, given the requisite goodwill, these could be overcome by means of a progressive interpretation which takes account of the fact that the territory of a Community Member State is by no means 'foreign' to that of another Member State. It is not foreign for the workers who can no longer be regarded as 'emigrants' within the Community, and it should not be 'foreign' (and thus constitute a safe refuge) for political criminals, whose transfer should not therefore be regarded as 'extradition' in the true sense of the word.

There should be no room for the right of asylum in relations between the Twelve, for not only are all the Community States bound by the provisions of the Council of Europe Convention for the Protection of Human Rights and Fundamental Freedoms (which lays down minimum rules for trial and detention procedures and prohibits persecution for political, religious, etc. reasons), but respect and upholding of human rights are regarded as quintessential to the very membership of the EC and the European Court of Justice has on several occasions declared that these are part of the fundamental principles of Community law of which it is the guardian.

The process of integration of the Twelve presupposes that the Member States recognize the affinity of their political structures and moral values and that they recognize one another as partners equal in every sense. It follows that a Member State cannot, by invoking the right of asylum, refuse a request for extradition from another Member State as this would effectively mean that it was claiming greater independence and impartiality for its own courts and was setting itself up as more respectful of human rights. If ever this were not to be a mere pretext for refusing extradition, and if there really were serious reasons to believe that in an EC Member State there was a danger of systematic violation of human rights (in the form of persecution on grounds of race, religious or political belief, etc.), this would be a matter of such seriousness that it would not only justify the refusal to hand over the person demanded by that State, but would put in question that state's continuing membership in the EC.

Co-operation Among the Member States in the Judicial Area: Establishment of a Judicial Community or 'European Judicial Area'

The close links of economic co-operation among the EC Member States entail the need for equally advanced co-operation as regards courts in these States and their operation. The new situation created by the establishment of a European area of free movement of persons, goods, services and capital must inevitably find its counterpart in the removal, or at least considerable reduction, of the judicial and procedural barriers currently existing between community countries. The absence until now of even an inchoate 'European judicial community' (or 'European judicial area') is one of the major obstacles not only to the further progress of European integration but even to the effective implementation of achievements already theoretically attained.

What is basically needed in order to create a single judicial area comprising different national legal systems is therefore not homogeneity of legislation among these systems but, first, identity of fundamental values and essential principles and, second and above all, mutual confidence among the national systems in the proper functioning, fairness and impartiality of the various judicial mechanisms. Where there is mutual confidence and identity of fundamental principles and values (respect for human rights, observance of the right to defence, etc.), a unified judicial area can be achieved even in the face of considerable differences in the legislation. As for mutual confidence, it is enough to recall that among states 'determined to lay the foundations of an ever closer union among the peoples of Europe' (first recital of the Preamble to the Treaty of Rome), confidence must be regarded as present by definition, for in the contrary case it would not be possible to continue on the common road towards 'ever closer union'.

As to the identity of fundamental principles and values, we know that in the 35 years since the foundation of the EC several essential values have come to be defined, the respect of which is an essential condition of membership in the Community and which can therefore be regarded as constituent elements of the 'European identity'. This European identity has basically been defined in the Copenhagen Declarations (1978) where respect of fundamental democratic freedoms, the maintenance of representative democracy and above all respect for human rights are set down as essential factors of Community membership. The Court of Justice of the European Communities has also on many occasions declared[7] that fundamental human rights are an integral part of Community law, of which the Court is the guardian, and has stated that in guarding these rights it is inspired by the common constitutional tradition of the Member States.[8]

The emergence of the 'European identity' implies two important limitations on the sovereignty of the Member States, for which there is no provision in the Treaties, in areas related not to economic and commercial activity but to those States' very constitutional life: a state which has joined the Community can no longer, if it wishes to continue its membership, introduce a dictatorial form of government and, second, should such a state ever systematically violate human rights, it would not merely be infringing the Treaties, *but, by failing to conform to one of the fundamental elements of 'European identity', such a State could no longer continue in the Community.*

The Member States so far have not drawn the evident conclusions in the judicial field in respect of judicial co-operation from the emergence of the 'European identity'. For instance, they continue to deny to their fellow Members extradition of perpetrators of political crimes, as if representative democracy were not the political system of Europe and as if the suppression of crimes against that system were not of equal concern to all the Community States. They deny extradition by invoking the 'right of asylum' despite the fact that, by definition, a Community Member State cannot systematically violate human rights and any Member State which, by claiming the contrary, refused extradition requested by another Member State on these grounds, could not confine itself to refusing the extradition but, drawing the inevitable legal consequences of such a claim, should also demand the expulsion of the other State from the Community.[9]

In conclusion, given that both the identity of fundamental legal values and mutual confidence in the probity of the respective judicial mechanisms must be assumed to exist, the establishment of a 'European judicial community' among the Twelve would be a step for which preconditions have existed for a long time now; and if so far, with one exception, no progress has been made towards this goal, the reason seems to be the conviction that everything to do with the conduct of trials and the execution of sentences is, because it is the direct expression of the state's coercive power and dominion, indissolubly linked to state sovereignty. It is this link that is the obstacle and the objection to the achievement of a 'judicial Community', an objection imbued with legal formalism that still draws its inspiration from the traditional concept of national sovereignty. There is no substantial conflict of interest in this area between the Member States – on the contrary, given the severe overloading of the judicial systems in practically all Member States, it would be very advantageous for each of these States to save much time and expense by the automatic, or nearly so, recognition of the judicial decisions of other Member States.

Practical Measures to Combat Terrorism

It is clearly stated in the preamble to the 1986 Single European Act that the Member States undertake to act in close co-ordination to safeguard the ground rules of democracy, the constitutional state and respect for fundamental rights. At the same time they undertake to co-operate in safeguarding peace and security.

On various occasions the representatives of the Member States have pointed to the need to step up co-operation. At a meeting of the group of co-ordinators, set up according to decisions taken at the 1988 Rhodes summit, it was clearly stated that the completion of the internal market poses problems in connection with the public safety implications of the abolition of border controls. Discussion of the legal aspects was postponed because of the slant the presidency wished to put on the talks. It preferred to tackle the question of the instruments which would be needed and could be adopted in the short term. Nevertheless, it seems that this question will be raised again by virtue of the list of priority subjects under discussion, such as right of asylum, extradition and co-ordination between security forces. The prime instrument of democratic control in this area is still legislative harmonization and in fact the problem has merely been postponed pending, above all, the drawing up of concrete intervention measures.

For this reason, it would seem expedient to back the creation of an effective policy of inter-institutional co-operation and the setting-up of a study group consisting of jurists, judges and representatives of the security forces to examine and report back on the possibility of setting up stable forms of co-ordination between the judiciary and the security forces and the harmonization of penal legislation. The two spheres, the political and the legal, can only advance in parallel. At the end of the five-year period referred to in Article 30, paragraph 12 of the Single European Act, we should be in a position to take effective decisions, no matter what the present circumstances are.

The considerably complex present situation (European Council, TREVI Group, the Council of Ministers of the Interior, European Political Cooperation and the group of co-ordinators) must be considered as temporary even if all the avenues it opens up must be explored. On the other hand, political co-operation calls for unequivocal legal instruments. The European Parliament must be ready with proposals aimed at supporting more effective co-operation between states and bringing the competent authorities nearer to the Community legal system, so that it may play its proper role as a guardian of democratic principles. For all these reasons, the adoption of common procedures to combat terrorism, better co-ordination between the competent authorities, closer collaboration between them and the European Parliament, the creation of permanent bodies for co-operation between the security forces and between the judicial authorities, are priority objectives in the creation of a 'Common legal area', which is the only instrument capable of guaranteeing that the ground rules of democracy are observed.

If, therefore, our common desire is to make a harmonious and co-ordinated, that is, European, response to international terrorism, then, in the light of what has been said above and in order to obviate otherwise inevitable problems and risks, the only way out seems to be to set up a European court competent to deal with all crimes which by their very nature elude detection because of the borders between States – in particular terrorist crimes. During the debate, some European MPs, while recognizing the considerable difficulties standing in the way of the setting-up of a European Court, nevertheless saw fit to show their support for the project, not least because the implementation of such a measure would constitute progress from the institutional point of view. In the past, a similar project was carried out by the League of Nations, which on 16 November 1937 opened for the signature of its member states a Convention on the Establishment of a European Criminal Court. At the time, very few countries felt it necessary to sign the Convention and none ratified it.

To summarize, the principles to be applied ought to be the following: (1) *aut dedere aut judicare*; (2) depoliticization of terrorist crimes; and (3) the option for a country (of refuge) which cannot (or will not) – for the reasons listed above – agree to extradition and must therefore proceed to judge the suspect, of transferring him or her for trial to the European Court. In essence, recourse to the 'European Court' offers the state of refuge the possibility of avoiding both the obligation of extradition and of putting the suspect on trial before its own courts.

NOTES

1. Excerpt from the Report drawn up on behalf of the Committee on Legal Affairs and Citizens' Rights on problems relating to combating terrorism. European Communities, Strasbourg, European Parliament. Session Documents. (Document A2-0155/88 Series A, 2 May 1989, Section B). Some editing was done for this volume.
2. Motions for resolutions by Mr Boesmans Doc. B 2-670/88, Mr Staes and others Doc. B 2-733/88, Mr Von Wogau and others Doc. B 2-961/88, Mr Prout and others Doc. B 2-1137/88, Mr Beyer de Ryke Doc. B 2-1095/88, Mr Arendt and others Doc. B 2-1120/88, Mrs Lenz Doc. A 2-310/88, Mrs Ewing and others Doc. B 2-1301/88, Mr Hutton Doc. B 2-1239/88, Mr Cervetti and others Doc. B 2-1292/88, Mr Arbeloa Muru and others Doc. B 2-958/88, Mr Arbeloa Muru and others Doc. B 2-1208/88, Mr Pearce Doc. B 2-1335/88, Mr Ephremedis and others Doc. B 2-488/88, Mr Fitzgerald Doc. B 2-794/88, Mr Cinciari Rodano and others Doc. B 2-1208/88, Mrs Veil and others, Doc. B 2-1251/88, Mr Robles Piquer and others, Doc. B 2-1108/88, Mr Cervetti and others, Doc. B 2-1157/88.
3. Motion for a resolution by Mr Poettering and others, Doc. B 2-953/88.
4. In Doc. 2-1643 and Doc. 1618/84.
5. The agreement on the application of the European Convention on the Suppression of Terrorism was opened for signatures during the European Council of December 1979 in Dublin. This agreement lays down rules for the application of the 1977 Strasbourg Convention pending its ratification without reservations by all the EC Member States; once this happens it is to lose effect. However, the agreement, signed on 4 December 1979 in Dublin by all the Member States, is still inoperative: it has been ratified by only three Member States.
6. At the conclusion of the debate on the written question (Doc. 2-1451/85/rev. II).
7. Judgment of 14 May 1974 in Case 4/73.
8. In fact, many Third World countries recognize that the doctrine of human rights is a particular contribution of Western Europe.
9. It is interesting to note in this connection that the Italian Constitutional Court has since 1965 followed a similar line of reasoning: when it declared (in Judgment No. 98/65) that it could not overrule Community Regulations on the grounds of constitutionality, it stated that these Regulations must, on principle, be assumed to conform to the Italian Constitution, but that should ever a Regulation violate the principles of the Italian constitutional system or the inalienable rights of the individual, then the Constitutional Court would not just have to overrule that Regulation but would be faced with the much more important question of verifying whether the Treaty of Rome was still compatible with the fundamental principles of the Italian system.

Keeping Track of Terrorists After 1992

RICHARD CLUTTERBUCK

This study examines the dilemma of striking a balance between ensuring internal security within a unified Europe with no internal borders and safeguarding civil liberties from security-related abuses. Terrorism, particularly of the indigenous nationalist variety, will likely persist, as well as less structured movements and single-issue groups willing to cooperate with them. International crime rings involved in computer fraud and drug trafficking pose an even greater danger. Technological methods for checking identities and detecting impersonation that are cost-effective and reliable do exist, as well as computerized means of information exchange. The problem is to prevent abuse, such as discriminatory use of identity checks to intimidate specific groups, for example, young immigrants, and corruption, such as use of stored information for commercial purposes.

The European Dilemma

From 1 January 1993 every citizen and every foreign visitor will be free to cross internal frontiers within the EC, as freely as between States in the USA. The Council of Ministers has decided to compensate for this by tightening the external frontiers, but it is very easy to get from outside into some of the EC countries, either through lax immigration checks, or in small boats along the thousands of miles of coastline, with their mass of tiny inlets and sandy beaches. There is therefore some concern that it may be very difficult for police and intelligence services to keep track of indigenous or foreign terrorists and criminals. The problem will be how to ensure the internal security of Europe without unacceptable erosion of civil liberties.

Unlike the EC, the USA faces little domestic threat from indigenous or visiting foreign terrorists, though it does have a high rate of violent crime. There are both Federal and State courts and laws, but these all operate on the same legal principles, and there is a fully integrated police intelligence and investigative system. The EC nations have vastly different judicial systems and legal traditions and are extremely unlikely to develop an integrated intelligence system to which all members would entrust their secrets.

The Terrorist and Criminal Threat

Terrorist movements in the EC are analyzed elsewhere in this volume, so a brief reminder should suffice here. The left- and right-wing ideological movements which plagued Europe in the 1970s and 1980s, such as *Brigate Rossi* in Italy, the *Rote Armee Fraktion* in Germany and *Action Directe* in France, have been decimated by arrests, but their surviving activists, either individually or in small cells, will continue to offer safe houses and other facilities to foreign terrorists who fight their battles on European streets, especially Palestinians, Libyans, Syrians and other Arabs, and nationalist movements such as the Armenians. Other foreign terrorist groups will emerge. One problem is that there will always be sympathizers with these groups among the immigrants temporarily or permanently in Europe. Foreign terrorist groups are likely to continue to be responsible for most of the terrorist murders in Europe outside Northern Ireland and Spain.

Some of the less structured terrorist movements in Europe, such as the German Revolutionary Cells and the Autonomous Groups, are likely to persist, though their targets are more often property than persons and especially the 'Military Industrial Complex' (MIK), including NATO. These are notoriously difficult for intelligence services to pin down as they usually consist of independent cells of part-time activists, mainly living in middle-class family homes, with no need for safe houses, central committees, directives and couriers who may be followed or intercepted. Members of single-issue groups (e.g., anti-NATO, anti-nuclear, conservationist or animal rights groups) will sometimes find shared aims and join or co-operate with these cells. This pattern is likely to continue and perhaps to spread, with great potential for damage and disruption at low risk.

The indigenous nationalist terrorist groups, such as ETA in Spain and the IRA in the United Kingdom, though much weaker than they were, are unlikely to disappear. ETA have a loyal base of sympathizers in South West France, and the IRA operate clandestine 'active service units' in Belgium, France, the Netherlands and Germany, where they enjoy cover and logistic support from indigenous left-wing and anti-NATO movements.

Perhaps most dangerous of all are the international crime rings, notably those involved in computer fraud and drug trafficking. The Mafia are strongly established in Italy, the Netherlands and Britain, and the Triad secret societies among Chinese immigrants from Hong Kong are highly active in drug trafficking both in Britain and the Netherlands. Drug addiction, which in many cases proves incurable, will continue to spread unless firmly checked, because drug addicts can only finance their addiction by crime or, as their success at this inevitably declines, by recruiting new addicts to whom they can sell drugs to pay for their own.[1] The drug traffickers who supply them are thus ruining more and more people's lives, often with fatal results, and it is urgent to detect them and lock them up in prison.

Identification and Detecting Impersonation

The only effective deterrent against crime or terrorism is a high probability of arrest and conviction. To achieve this, the police need to be able to identify people who are in an area where they believe that an offence may be or has been committed. This is not new. After a spate of terrorist bombs in Paris in 1986, the French police were empowered to prevent people leaving the scene of a crime and to demand proof of identification, failing which a magistrate could order photographs and fingerprints to be taken. Identity cards are required in Germany, and there is a scheme in readiness to replace these with machine-readable cards, should conditions justify this. There is also a plan to issue machine-readable Europassports. The data on the card or passport would be referrable instantaneously to the German national police computer.

By 1993, if the Council of Ministers so decided, it would be practicable for all EC countries to issue similar machine-readable identity cards and passports. Their national police or intelligence computers could be linked to each other (as many are now), so that relevant data about the person on any one of their computers could be made available to whichever police force or immigration service was investigating the case. It would be possible for machine-readable visas to be issued by consular offices as a condition of entry to the EC from countries which do not themselves co-operate in the European data link system. Machine-readable passports from such countries as the USA, Switzerland, Norway, Japan, etc., could well be linked to the EC system and the need for the special visas might thus be confined to those tourists, visitors (e.g., officials, businessmen and journalists), students and temporary workers who come from countries such as Libya and Syria.

One essential feature of all such machine-readable data would be the inclusion of personal biometric data to prevent impersonation. This would be necessary to prevent such incidents as the kidnap and murder by German terrorists of a young US airman in 1986 purely to use his military identity card to gain entry to a US Air Force Base, where they planted a bomb which killed two civilian workers.

There are several recently developed technologies for detecting impersonation which are either already on the market or shortly to go into manufacture. The most promising is the fingerprint scan. The unique data from the holder's fingerprint is recorded digitally in a microprocessor on his card or passport, or on a host computer memory, or ideally on both. This system is already in production and the card with microprocessor costs only two or three pounds. The finger placed on the scanner and the card placed in the slot can be matched or rejected instantaneously; if the data is called up from the main computer memory by dialling a Personal Identification Number, the matching still takes only four seconds.

The vein pattern of the back of the hand is as unique as a bar code on a bottle of sauce in a supermarket, and can be read just as quickly by passing a diode across it; this too can be matched instantaneously to a card in the slot, or in a few seconds to data on the main computer. The retina scan is equally reliable but involves pointing a laser gun into the eye, which arouses some consumer resistance! Other methods on the market include the digital recording and matching of voiceprints and signature dynamics. The analysis of DNA molecules in body fluids requires some hours of laboratory tests and is therefore not applicable to instant identity checks, but it has proved best of all for forensic evidence in court (e.g., in rape or murder cases) and this could be applied to a wide range of criminal and terrorist offences.

Possible Erosion of Civil Liberties

The technology is available for immediate and reliable checks of identity, at relatively small cost once the initial computer network has been installed – and much of it already exists in national police computer systems. The inconvenience to the public would be minimal, since the checks themselves take only a few seconds – as everyone with a bank cash-point card knows. There are, however, grounds for serious concern that the system could be abused.

Wider powers to demand identification could be used by unscrupulous police officers to intimidate people they dislike; young immigrants, especially, already have reason to complain that they are 'picked on' by police in most EC countries. On the other hand, since the proof of identity and the clearance of suspicion would be immediate and reliable, this might result in people being harassed less and released more quickly. Much would depend on the selection, training and supervision of policemen.

The requirement to prove identity at any time could also sometimes be a social embarrassment in the form of invasion of privacy. An obvious example is the married man who keeps a mistress but has managed to conceal this from her parents or his wife. This is perhaps a form of privacy which it is not very important to protect, but other forms of deception may be more innocent. The demand for electronic proof of identity could not, however, be made by anyone other than an authorized person with access to the necessary equipment (policemen, immigration officials, etc.), who have an obligation of confidentiality, but there would undoubtedly be scope for abuse.

There is also a serious risk of corruption. Policemen or officials (especially those working in the computer centre) would have access to personal data which would be of commercial value to such organizations as finance and insurance companies or employment agencies. Some of these would be willing to pay generous retainers to officials willing to look for certain types of information and pass it on. This abuse might be hard to trace, since nothing need be in writing; the corrupt official could memorize the data, or jot it down in note form, and pass it on discreetly and verbally at periodic assignations in a pub or public park.

Prevention or Detection of Abuse

If full use is to be made of the emerging technological capabilities to preserve lives and property against crime and terrorism, it will be essential at the same time to develop reliable means of preventing abuse of these capabilities or, where prevention fails, to detect that the abuse has taken place *and to detect who did it.* By far the most important is the selection and vetting of staff who have access to the computer systems and software containing confidential and personal data. Access to these must be strictly controlled so that no one can enter without a card or pass backed by a biometric scan (probably of a fingerprint) to guarantee against impersonation. The electronic monitor which reads the card can also record the time at which the person entered and left.

Within the system, access to specific information must be kept strictly to those who need it for a particular and authorized purpose. Both the authority and the time and date when that person did receive the information must also be electronically recorded. The parallel computer systems now coming on stream will have ample capacity for recording and processing this mass of information, and especially for instant detection of links between bits of data. The vast majority of data would remain dormant in the computer memory until and unless some such unsuspected link called attention to it.

Striking a Balance

The human suffering and disruption caused by terrorism, violent crime, fraud and drug trafficking is far greater than just the number of deaths and injuries they cause. Though EC police forces have had some success in wearing down the structured European terrorist movements of the 1970s and 1980s, they have had less success against the autonomous groups and independent cells which have become more fashionable, and which will continue to co-operate with foreign terrorist groups which wish to fight their battles on European streets. Violent crime, computer crime and drug trafficking are all increasing. The opening of European frontiers in 1993 may make the task of the police and intelligence services more difficult.

Effective technological means to combat these evils, especially by identification, detection of impersonation and obtaining conclusive evidence for conviction, are already available or under development. Their financial cost would be small in the context of national expenditure. The challenge will lie in the parallel development of means to prevent or detect their abuse, in order to safeguard civil liberties. This presents a political dilemma for the European Commission and for the elected ministers who direct it.

The essential moral principles are unassailable. Crime, the ruin of other people's lives for personal gain, and the use of terrorism to influence the political process are not civil liberties; nor is the concealment of identity; nor is impersonation; nor, above all, are kidnap or murder. We must never preserve the 'right to kill' claimed by a tiny minority, at the expense of the most fundamental civil right of the community, the right to live.

NOTES

1. Alternative drug control policies do exist, of course, such as in the Netherlands, where addicts are provided free drugs on a regular basis. This provides the opportunity for needle exchanges, distribution of educational material and sometimes counselling. The fact that other countries in Europe maintain different, more 'hard-line', law-and-order drug policies underscores the complexities that underlie calls for harmonization of national policies, not only in the judicial and policing areas (see Zagari, this volume), but also in broader social areas as well (see Korthals Altes, this volume) [eds.].

Western Responses to Terrorism:
A Twenty-Five Year Balance Sheet

RONALD D. CRELINSTEN and ALEX P. SCHMID

This concluding essay surveys the kinds of responses that have been developed by Western nations over the past 25 years, both domestically and internationally, and also considers the kinds of responses that have not been adequately developed. Special attention is devoted to the military dimension, which has received considerable notice in recent years, and the propaganda dimension, never adequately addressed in the literature. The study also examines the effectiveness and democratic acceptability of the various response options: sometimes it is the effectiveness of certain options that can be questioned, while at other times it is the acceptability of a particular option for a democratic state that is more in doubt. Finally, the question to what extent the balance between acceptability and effectiveness has been achieved in various democratic states faced with varying forms and degrees of terrorism is addressed. What factors affect this balance and under what circumstances is one side of the equation favoured over the other?

He who fights with monsters might take care
lest he thereby become a monster.
Friedrich Nietzsche
Beyond Good and Evil (1886)

The terrorist and the policeman both
come from the same basket.
Joseph Conrad
The Secret Agent (1907)

For 25 years Western democracies have been struggling with the problem of how to control and maybe even prevent the use of terrorism in political life without sacrificing or jeopardizing those very principles that make a democratic way of life possible in the first place. The emergence of the European Community (EC) single market at the start of 1993 – this volume's nominal point of departure – and the difficulties for Member States to agree upon and to co-ordinate counter-terrorism policies in the areas of, for example, extradition, asylum rights, and co-ordination of security forces,[1] demonstrate how Western responses to terrorism have both domestic and international components and how the two can sometimes work at cross purposes; national interests and regional co-operation can come into conflict despite a commonly perceived threat.

Such jurisdictional conflicts can occur even within the confines of a single nation state, as evidenced for example by the Canadian case,[2] where co-operation between different police forces or between federal and provincial or municipal authorities can be strained during a major terrorist incident, whether purely domestic or international. With the reunification of Germany, and the incorporation into a Western nation of a former member of the Soviet bloc, the possibilities of such intranational strain are multiplied.

A. J. Jongman has shown how the distinction between domestic and international terrorism can lead to misleading data bases that distort the real extent of the terrorist problem in certain countries, for example the United Kingdom and Northern Ireland.[3] The interpenetration of domestic and international politics poses the same difficulties for classifying options for counter-terrorist responses and assessing their effectiveness as it does for classifying terrorism itself and assessing its prevalence. If classification and assessment are based solely on the international dimension, then certain response options, such as economic sanctions, would have little relevance for the purely domestic context, except perhaps to the extent that foreign sponsors were involved in funding, training or harbouring domestic terrorists or subverting domestic political life. If, on the other hand, classification and assessment were based solely on domestic experience, then certain options, such as the diplomatic approach, would not really be applicable, except where international conventions were translated into national legislation.

All the cases presented in this volume show how Western responses to terrorism share domestic and international features. As such, any survey of response options must address both features, plus their interplay. In view of the profound restructuring of the world order that has taken place, it is no longer acceptable to confine one's analysis strictly to the international dimension or to assume that domestic problems have no significance beyond national borders, especially when new states are emerging and old ones restructuring.

What are the consequences, for *domestic* political life and social control, of regional policies that are developed in the context of a larger geopolitical entity, such as the EC? What is the impact on such larger, multi-nation policies of differential *national* experiences across Member States within the same supranational community? Germany's approach to counter-terrorism, for example, reflects its particular history and the concept of 'militant democracy' that emerged after the collapse of the Weimar Republic.[4] The resulting impact on legal procedure, the rule of law and civil liberties such as freedom of expression, as described by Kurt Groenewold in this volume, might not be acceptable for other nations that have not experienced the same history, nor the same level or form of terrorism.

The United Kingdom's approach to counter-terrorism is greatly influenced by its colonial past and its history of counter-insurgency, hence the heightened use of the military in Northern Ireland. Yet its strong legal tradition has also led it to confine its counter-terrorism within the rule of law despite a persistently high level of terrorism. The result has been the introduction of special laws and legal procedures that tend to undermine the legal tradition for which the British are so respected. France's approach has always been influenced by its determination to play an international role independent of the United States and the United Kingdom and this is perhaps why France has often been more willing to negotiate openly and to accommodate terrorist demands than her Western partners. Canada's approach has been greatly influenced by its powerful neighbour, the United States, and by its previous colonial master, the United Kingdom, yet it was the first Western nation to experience a political kidnapping at home and chose ultimately to deal with it by suspending due process and invoking special emergency powers.[5]

Do all these different approaches constitute the 'Western' response to terrorism or do some have greater influence than others? And are they all equally 'democratic' or are some more democratic than others? To answer these questions, we must first examine the panoply of responses that have been applied to the problem.

Classifying Response Options

The most common way to differentiate among response options is to separate them into the *soft line* (e.g., addressing root causes) and the *hard line* (e.g., President Reagan's 'swift and effective retribution' coupled with a firm no-negotiations policy). Peter Sederberg, for example, distinguishes between conciliatory and repressive responses,[6] while Alex Schmid distinguishes between conciliation and force.[7] The two most common forms of *conciliatory* response are *accommodation* (including direct negotiation with terrorists and the possibility of giving in to specific demands) and *reform* (usually addressing the grievances raised by terrorists without directly dealing with the terrorists themselves). The two most common forms of *repressive* response are the legal-repressive and the military or what Ronald Crelinsten calls the *criminal justice model* and the *war model*, respectively.[8] In the former case, counter-terrorism policy adheres to the rule of law while treating terrorism as crime. In the latter case, counter-terrorism adheres to the rules of war while treating terrorism as a special form of war or low-intensity conflict (LIC).

A second approach to classifying response options is to consider the time required for such responses. One distinction that can be made is between *short-term* and *long-term* responses:[9] those that address the immediate threat or attempt to resolve a particular incident here and now, and those that look to the future, either in terms of prevention (such as deterrence) or long-term reform. Another time-oriented distinction, more typical of policing in general, is reactive versus proactive. *Reactive* policies tend to be incident-oriented and, as a result, short-sighted, focusing on the past rather than the future. As a result, they tend to overlook potential side effects and unintended consequences. This can be particularly problematic when attempting to strike a balance between effectiveness and acceptability.

Proactive responses look beyond the immediate to the long term, to the possible emergence of novel forms of terrorism from newly emerging political conflict as well as to new ways to prevent old forms of terrorism, such as by improved target-hardening. In addition, proactive responses must consider the consequences, both domestic and international, of specific options. The use of identity cards or special technological means of identification, as described by Richard Clutterbuck,[10] hold great potential for the successful tracking and monitoring of terrorists, but they may also lay the groundwork for irrevocable damage to the democratic principles of free movement and free expression that we have grown accustomed to take for granted. Technological advances coupled with bureaucratic efficiency have greatly facilitated anti-democratic forms of repression in the past, including mass murder and genocide. The storage and retrieval of information on large numbers of people may be effective, but it is not necessarily acceptable when we attempt to focus on unintended consequences as well as anticipated ones.

A third way to classify response options is to distinguish between those that address the *coercive capabilities* of the terrorist and those that address the *political capabilities* of the terrorist.[11] One set of responses deals with the violent dimension of terrorism, the terrorist's combined use and threat of violence, while the other set of responses deals primarily with the propaganda dimension of terrorism, that is, its communicative nature.[12] The former would include much of the legal-repressive and military options referred to above, while the latter would include reform and possibly accommodation, although direct concessions are usually intended more to end immediate terrorist violence or coercion than to meet political demands. Ronald Crelinsten refers to a 'communication model' of counter-terrorism, whereby the state attempts to address the root causes of the terrorist problem by means of reform, to distinguish a more political approach from the coercive approaches of the criminal justice and war models.[13] It is true, however, that coercive approaches do possess communicative elements, in the form of deterrence or demoralization. For this reason, the distinction between political and coercive or repressive approaches (including communication) seems more appropriate.

Because political recognition is what terrorists are usually seeking, few governments negotiate with terrorists about meeting their grievances, although some have attempted to institute reforms that would render the terrorist enterprise superfluous. In some cases, such as in Canada, this has led political activists to abandon the terrorist cause and to work within the system again. In other cases, such as in Spain, terrorism has persisted despite considerable reform. As Ariel Merari has pointed out,[14] whether or not the terrorists' specific political agenda is addressed, there are three principal dangers in dealing directly with 'root causes'. First, political concessions may compromise the essentials of the democratic policy-determining process. Second, they may trigger counter-grievances in potentially terroristic groups on the other end of the political spectrum. Third, they may reinforce terrorism as a method of obtaining political and personal goals.

Less often considered among those response options that address political capabilities are what Martha Crenshaw terms 'de-legitimation',[15] that is, policies and practices designed to decrease the legitimacy of the terrorists or to undermine their political support. Here, the media can play a central role and have been specifically targeted by counter-terrorist policies in some countries.[16] Counter-terrorism policies that recognize the multiple audiences that are addressed – intentionally or unintentionally – by terrorist violence and that develop strategies and tactics to counteract and influence the perceptions of these audiences could ultimately reduce the political credibility or legitimacy of the terrorist. In doing so, such policies might obviate the necessity to resort to repressive violence in dealing with terrorists and their supporters or sponsors.

While coercive responses may be effective either in the short term or in reducing the coercive capabilities of the terrorist, they may be less effective in the long run, either by triggering cycles of violence and counter-violence, revenge and counter-revenge, or by enhancing the *political* capabilities of the terrorist by increasing public sympathy for the terrorist cause, stimulating recruitment to the terrorist movement or provoking public antipathy to the state's coercive response.

A fourth way to distinguish between response options is to differentiate between domestic and international responses. *Domestic* responses include legal and administrative policies that are applicable within a single nation, such as the creation of special laws, as in the British Prevention of Terrorism Act or Germany's *Berufsverbot*; special courts, such as Northern Ireland's Diplock courts or other juryless courts (e.g., France, Italy, Spain); special rules of procedure, such as allowing informers to testify anonymously (e.g., Northern Ireland's 'supergrasses') or restricting client-lawyer interactions (as was done in Germany); special regimes of imprisonment, such as the Maze Prison in Northern Ireland or Stammheim Prison in Germany; or special police powers. They could also include creating special assault forces or special negotiation teams for hostage situations, increased security and hardening of potential domestic targets, and a wide variety of policy declarations and more politically oriented initiatives.

International response options typically include the *political-diplomatic* approach, such as strengthening the international legal instruments dealing with terrorism; the *economic sanctions* approach, such as sanctions against states that sponsor terrorism by financing, training or harbouring individuals or groups involved in or accused of terrorism, or actions designed to disrupt support mechanisms like the drug trade or the arms trade; and, finally, the *military* approach, such as the use of pre-emptive strikes (e.g., Israel), retaliation (e.g., the American bombing of Libya) or even military intervention (such as Israel's 1982 invasion of Lebanon or its more recent incursions against the Hizbollah). The political-diplomatic approach has clearly predominated throughout the 25-year history of Western responses to terrorism, while the economic sanctions approach and the military approach have received commensurately much less attention, until the early 1980s, when the phenomenon of 'state-sponsored terrorism' began to attract the attention of Western policy-makers.[17]

On the whole, the main focus in policy discourse over the entire 25 years has been on international terrorism, with its special impact on international air·travel, the tourist population and the diplomatic community. Yet many Western nations have at various times and for differing periods of time experienced domestic forms of terrorism far more serious than the threat emanating from international terrorism. In some cases, the distinction between international, transnational or domestic terrorism is difficult, even misleading: domestic groups operate at home, abroad, or move back and forth across borders; foreign terrorists carry on their battles within the confines of nations far removed from the battlefield and are subject to the domestic legislation in force in the country in which they are apprehended. Sometimes successful control 'at home' depends largely on co-operation from a neighbouring state not to provide asylum or to permit safe haven 'abroad', as in the case of Spain or Austria.[18]

Counter-terrorism policy in certain countries has evolved in response to both international and domestic incidents or campaigns as, for example, in the Netherlands or Canada.[19] Even the United States, which seems preoccupied with international terrorism, has experienced varieties of domestic terrorism.[20] With the dramatic geopolitical changes of the past few years, the interplay between domestic and international political life has only been accentuated. For this reason, a clear-cut distinction between domestic and international responses can lead to an artificial separation between response options that can have an equally significant impact on democratic life at the national, regional or international levels.

Western Trends in Counter-terrorism

Some of the basic principles of strategy are to attack the opponent where he is weak rather than strong, and to attack him when and where he does not expect it, by means he cannot easily match. In the fight against insurgent terrorism, democratic governments have, though to a lesser degree than non-democratic ones, shown an inclination to answer violence with violence, and sometimes even with counter-terror. From a purely strategic point of view, this recourse to violence to fight violence is sound insofar as it involves means which the non-state opponent cannot easily match. Given the enormous discrepancy in means of destruction which governments possess when compared to social-revolutionary as well as ethnic terrorists, there is usually little doubt about the outcome of an armed confrontation. Except for some colonial situations (Palestine, Algeria, Aden, Cyprus), Western democracies have always won. What is more, when the public is alarmed by wanton acts of destruction and murder, calls for revenge, retaliation or pre-emptive strikes can be politically useful as well. As such, coercive response options have tended to predominate over conciliatory ones, especially in the areas of declared policy and international co-operation.

In light of the chequered history of negotiations provided by Richard Clutterbuck in this volume,[21] it is clear that the predominance of coercive responses over conciliatory ones during the past two and a half decades has applied principally in the short term and in the public domain. While much public debate and political-diplomatic action concentrated on apprehending terrorists, many terrorists that were apprehended and even convicted and imprisoned were quietly released once the spotlight of media and public attention had faded. In other cases, they were simply exchanged for hostages during subsequent incidents. Even the most hardline countries have negotiated in secret while toeing the hard line in public, witness the Iran-Contra affair.

This apparent contradiction between short-term, public repression and long-term, secret conciliation or negotiation underscores the importance of the political aspect of any response option. This is particularly true in democratic states, where public opinion can have a much greater impact on government than in non-democratic ones, simply because the concepts of open government and public accountability are taken seriously. It often pays to be inflexible in public, for the benefit of domestic constituencies, and flexible in private, when dealing with state sponsors of terrorism. The existence of multiple audiences for any response option or policy initiative and the danger that the wrong message can go to the wrong audience – probably one of the main sources of unintended consequences – leads almost inevitably to the coupling of public stances for some audiences with private communication to different ones. This propaganda element in counter-terrorism is largely neglected in the literature and we shall return to it later.

Among the repressive options, it was legal-repressive responses that predominated throughout the 1970s, with the criminal justice model prevailing in the domestic context and the strengthening of international legal instruments by a variety of international bodies in the international context. Within a criminal justice model of counter-terrorism, the use of force is usually a police responsibility. One consequence of this has been a trend during the 1970s toward a certain militarization of the police, particularly when the *domestic* threat of terrorism is perceived to be severe. One manifestation of this has been the creation of special forces or 'third forces' that are mandated to use force, such as to terminate hostage sieges. During the 1980s, while legal-repressive responses still continued to play a central role in Western approaches to counter-terrorism, the military or war model began to gain considerable prominence, particularly within the international context, with greater emphasis on maintaining a military option as one element in a counter-terrorist strategy.

Counter-terrorist policy in the West has consistently emphasized the rule of law,[22] yet calls for a military approach to counter-terrorism became louder and ever more insistent during the last decade. Academic and professional discourse during the 1970s and early 1980s did not focus at length on the military option, although this was always considered one of a range of possibilities, perhaps most appropriate for rescue operations in hostage sieges. As early as 1970 the Canadian government abandoned the criminal justice model for the war model in its handling of a combined domestic and international kidnapping (a provincial politician and a foreign diplomat – the first and only such case in North America), but this was quite rare and was seen as a last resort.[23]

By the late 1980s and, in particular, in the wake of the 1986 American bombing of Libya, the war model had assumed a more central role in counter-terrorism discourse. Peter Sederberg, for example, includes a range of military options in his survey of response options, although he does underscore their weaknesses.[24] Neil Livingstone argues forcefully for the war model's importance in an overall response strategy.[25] Preliminary research by Ronald Crelinsten on the images of terrorism and counter-terrorism in media, policy and scientific discourse between 1965 and 1985 suggests that war images became more prevalent during the 1980s and that the source of this imagery was the policy discourse of the Reagan administration.[26] During the 1980s the military approach to counter-terrorism clearly prevailed in the United States. After all, it was President Reagan who declared that he wanted to deal with terrorism 'in the spirit of Rambo'. For this reason, we shall focus on the US when discussing the ascendancy of the military option and the war model of counter-terrorism during the 1980s.

Combating Terrorism by Military Means: the American Example

The choice of basic approach to counter-terrorism is important. Before you start combating a monster you have to understand its nature and *modus operandi*. For this, you need a good description of its characteristics – a workable definition. A wrong definition – like the Ptolemaic definition of the earth as a flat disk – makes certain solutions impossible because they are not thinkable in that particular framework. The intimate link between conceptions of terrorism and types of response models is clear when one examines the American perception of terrorism and the framework for dealing with it over the past several decades.

The *Nixon administration* (1969–74) attempted a *collective security system* approach. It was held that if a sufficient number of states would agree to a system of denying sanctuary to terrorists and would apprehend, prosecute or extradite them to states desiring to punish them, then the problem would be solved. The *Carter administration* (1977–80) regarded international terrorism more as a symptom of larger human rights issues, arising from poverty, injustice and repression. Solutions were sought in dealing with the underlying problems, such as the Arab-Israeli conflict. The *Reagan administration* (1981–88), on the other hand, distanced itself from the unheroic approach of its predecessor and sought to develop military instruments for solving the problem of international terrorism. These three different approaches correspond to a criminal justice model, a communication model and a war model, respectively.[27] In the American case, however, these three approaches were generally applied to the international context rather than the domestic context. In fact, American counter-terrorism policy, like American data bases,[28] tends to focus almost exclusively on the international dimension and it is very difficult to find any cogent analysis of *domestic* anti-terrorism policy.[29] Yet the Nixon administration in particular was faced with considerable domestic violence, including terrorism.

The rhetoric of the Reagan administration's anti-terrorist policy was clearly based on a war model of counter-terrorism. William Casey, for example, claimed that 'international terrorism has become a perpetual war without borders'. The logical response to terrorism was therefore, almost by definition, a military one. When welcoming home the American hostages from Tehran in 1981, Reagan promised 'swift and effective retribution' rather than deterrence, let alone negotiation or reform. The culmination of this policy came on 15 April 1986 when Colonel Gaddafi's home and headquarters in Tripoli and Benghazi (and three other sites) were bombed in an assassination attempt disguised as a larger military operation. Despite the failure of obtaining its covert objective, the attack was widely hailed as a landmark in counter-terrorism. It had a cathartic effect on the American public while the European public was worried about the risks of escalation into war.

Statistical analysis of international terrorist incidents before and after the raid on Libya revealed no significant change apart from a slight shift from acts of hostage-taking to bombings. In the first 45 days after the raid, five terrorist incidents with possible Libyan connections took place. Only two days after the raid, a Libyan grenade attack on an American officers' club in Ankara, Turkey was foiled. This would indicate revenge rather than deterrence at work, although the attack may have already been planned and initiated without additional instructions from the Libyan 'people's bureau'. The raid on Libya might have had a deterrent effect on other state-sponsors of terrorism, although Iran, one of the most 'deserving' targets, probably felt little pressure, given its secret dialogue with the White House.

One unintended effect of the raid was that, for European policy-makers, it provided an incentive to become more serious in imposing various sanctions on Libya. The expulsion of more than 100 Libyans, mostly 'diplomats', and other counter-measures taken by 14 European nations might have weakened the Libyan terrorist infrastructure and thereby prevented further attacks more effectively than the deterrent effect of the raid itself. However, the downing of Pan Am 103 less than three years later, if indeed two Libyan agents were responsible, highlights the short-term impact of either possibility. The main irreversible unintended consequence of the raid was the death of more than one hundred civilians in a residential area near the French embassy, caused by a stray laser-guided bomb emanating from a plane that was hit by Libyan fire.

Looking beyond the raid on Libya, there are several fundamental problems with the military option in counter-terrorism. First, the transformation of the confrontation from the political to the military level is part of the anticipated reaction of terrorists and serves, in their perception, their long-term strategy – the provocation of repression that, in turn, will provide the terrorists with sufficient recruits, supporters and sympathizers to mount the truly military operation that was not possible before. Terrorists usually attack civilian targets because they are less well protected.

When they attack military targets, which they do only occasionally,[30] it is generally done for the psychological rather than the material effect. When they do target the military, such as German and Belgian terrorists targeting NATO with sabotage and assassination, it is usually in a non-combatant context: soldiers are killed while on leave, eating out in restaurants, or while sleeping in their barracks. While military terminology is widely used by terrorists, this cannot hide the fact that they cannot engage in a sustained counter-force strategy. They basically follow a counter-value strategy or a 'politics of atrocity'.[31] By using a military response to terrorist outrages, a state plays into this strategy.

The second problem pertaining to a war model of counter-terrorism is intimately related to the first problem: the existence of two armed parties confronting each other creates a symmetry in the perception of the onlooker, permitting the terrorists to portray themselves as soldiers rather than as criminals or terrorists. The essentially different manner of fighting of soldiers, on the one hand, and terrorists on the other is lost sight of. The potential political cost is a gain in legitimacy for the terrorist and a commensurate loss of legitimacy for the legal government and that is exactly what the terrorist wants.[32]

A third problem arising from the use of the military in counter-terrorism relates directly to the issue of democratic acceptability. In using a war model of counter-terrorism to defend itself against terrorist attack, a democratic state might in the process be transformed into a different type of regime. In doing so, a victory may be won against terrorism, but democracy would be defeated in the process. In the domestic context, history has shown how the use of the military against insurgent terrorism has usually led to the creation of anti-democratic military regimes, such as in Uruguay, Argentina or Turkey. Usually, the definition of who is terrorist widens to include anyone or any group that disagrees with the policies of the regime in power. In the international context, retaliatory strikes are often of questionable legality even if they seem morally justifiable, while pre-emptive strikes can make the attacking state look no better than the terrorist. Given the problems of accuracy when reliable intelligence is not assured and the resulting high probability of collateral damage, the use of military strikes can also cause considerable strain for international or regional co-operation to deal with international terrorism.

A fourth problem with the military option pertains to its effectiveness. We have already seen that a deterrent effect is difficult to establish even when there is a drop in terrorist activity. The record of military rescue missions indicates that the risk of failure, either due to lack of intelligence or unexpected resistance, is quite high. The *Mayaguez* rescue in Cambodia (1975) cost about as many lives of the US rescue force as there were hostages. Later, it turned out that the release of hostages had little to do with the rescue effort. The Israeli Entebbe rescue mission of July 1976 cost the lives of only three out of 103 hostages, while one Israeli, seven terrorists and 20 Ugandans were killed. The rescue operation by Egyptian commandos in Cyprus on 19 February 1978 cost the lives of 15 commandos, while 22 others were wounded, apparently mainly because the Cypriot National Guard was not informed. The storming of the Iranian Embassy in London on 5 May 1980 by Special Air Service troops cost only the lives of five terrorists. On the other hand, the Colombian raid against the Palace of Justice in Bogota on 7 November 1985 led to a massacre in which more than one hundred people were killed. According to one study, the chances of hostages dying during a rescue mission are higher than their dying at the hands of their captors during negotiations.[33]

As for pre-emptive or retaliatory strikes, it is extremely difficult to trace the whereabouts of terrorist groups and to clearly to pinpoint individual actors responsible for specific attacks. Even if intelligence can provide direct demonstrable involvement of specific groups or individuals, few nonstate terrorists have fixed headquarters where they can be hit. The headquarters they have are often hard to find and well protected in that they are housed in areas with a high population density so that a military attack would create much collateral damage among civilians. There is also the logistical problem of time: often the time needed to prepare and mount a successful military attack makes a rescue mission or a retaliatory strike impossible.

During the 1985 *Achille Lauro* incident, for example, the American intervention came only after three days of preparation. While Italian and

American warships began to follow the terrorist-seized passenger ship, a military response came only after the hostages were already released. Yet still there were problems. When the Egyptian plane carrying Abu'l Abbas was intercepted and forced to land in Sigonella, Italy, the Italian government had not been consulted, apparently for reasons of secrecy, and initially refused permission to land until the Egyptian pilot cited a low-fuel emergency. The incident led to an armed confrontation between Italian Carabinieri and US Navy Seals in Sicily. If a unilateral military response in a friendly country like Italy is so difficult, a response in a neutral or hostile environment is likely to be even more difficult.

When evaluating the potential effectiveness of the military option, however, it is the unintended consequences of such an approach that are the most serious. The use of the military in counter-terrorism could lead to an escalation of violence to a level where an international crisis with a 1914 Sarajevo-type chain reaction can occur, such as the escalation of retaliation into a war with allies of the punished country or, at the very least, the staging by nonstate actors of solidarity acts of terrorism against Western targets of opportunity. For example, the 1986 raid on Libya led to revenge murders of American and British citizens in Lebanon, Sudan, Israel and North Yemen, as well as attacks on American targets in Mexico, Great Britain, Pakistan and Tunisia. During the 1991 Gulf War, while many predicted an Iraqi-directed campaign of terrorism against Western targets, most actual incidents were terrorist bombings against American targets of opportunity by already existing groups expressing solidarity. In the domestic context, when the Indian Army was used in 1984 to attack the headquarters of Sikh militants in the Golden Temple, Amritsar, the result was a revenge assassination of Prime Minister Indira Gandhi by two Sikh bodyguards which, in turn, triggered widespread anti-Sikh violence by Hindu mobs out for revenge.

Those who expect a deterrent effect from a military punitive expedition or strike probably also underestimate the willingness to suffer and die for the 'just' cause which motivates many terrorists. Although martyrs are rare even among terrorists, the prospect of retaliation and punishment is probably less of a deterrent for terrorists than for ordinary political actors. In the Israeli case, military retaliatory strikes have led to an endless action-reaction pattern between terrorist and counter-terrorist. As Ariel Merari points out, the Israeli retaliatory policy has more to do with boosting morale at home (revenge) than true deterrence.[34]

Even a full-scale military intervention designed to crush the infrastructure of a terrorist group or regime can have unintended consequences. The Israeli invasion of Lebanon in 1982, the Vietnamese intervention in Cambodia in 1978 and the Indian intervention in Sri

Lanka in 1987 all led to unexpected consequences that included increased violence. The Israeli and Vietnamese armies both became embroiled in protracted conflict from which it was difficult to extricate.[35] When the Israelis finally withdrew, the Palestinians simply returned; in recent years, it has been the Hizbollah that has persisted despite military incursions into their territory. In Cambodia, the continuing Vietnamese presence contributed to the persistence of the Khmer Rouge as a viable partner in the country's reconstruction, despite its genocidal past. In Sri Lanka, the Indian Army also became caught in the crossfire between Tamils and Sinhalese, and former Prime Minister Rajiv Gandhi himself became the victim of a terrorist act of revenge in May 1991.

One terrorist leader, himself a former military professional, General George Grivas, head of the Greek Cypriot EOKA terrorists in 1955–59, once commented on the military anti-terrorist tactics of the British with these words: 'one does not use a tank to catch field mice – a cat will do the job better'.[36] This impressionistic assessment by a participant is shared by the author of one of the few studies on the comparative effectiveness of various anti-terrorist policies. Looking at terrorist campaigns in five countries, Christopher Hewitt found on the basis of time and correlation analysis:

> It does not appear that troop strength or military activity, in itself, reduces terrorism immediately, and in fact military activity and terrorism are usually positively and significantly correlated. These results could be interpreted in two ways; either that military activity provokes terrorism or, more plausibly, that military activity is frequently a response to terrorism. The statistics do not suggest that military activity reduces terrorism in subsequent months. In only two cases do we find a negative lagged correlation, and in neither case is the correlation significant.[37]

While the use of the military might be unavoidable in certain situations, particularly in a hostage situation where a rescue mission has a high probability of success, it should be used as an instrument of last resort, rather than as a first line of defence. A military response creates irreversible facts and calls for revenge. As one anti-terrorist expert once put it: 'When you cannot kill them all, don't kill them; they will come back stronger'.[38] Given these considerations, a 1986 proposal by Paul Wilkinson to put NATO in charge of co-ordinating anti-terrorism in Western Europe has to be judged as of doubtful wisdom.[39] In earlier writings, Wilkinson has been more critical of using the armed forces and more concerned about its dangers.[40]

Within the Reagan administration, Secretary of Defense, Caspar W.

Weinberger, was generally more hesitant than his colleague George P. Shultz, the Secretary of State, when it came to military intervention. In November 1984 he laid down five conditions which have to be met for military force to be used: the force must be *timely*, *appropriate*, have *public support*, have a *high probability of success* and should be used only as a *last resort*.[41] These pragmatic conditions partly reflect those of just war theory, which attempts to find a working solution to the conflict 'between the prohibition to inflict harm and the obligation to prevent harm'. Just war theory considers war as an evil but realizes that there are cases of 'tragic necessity' when innocents have to be protected from aggressors, in which case a just war can be seen as a 'lesser evil' than inaction. A war is just when force is employed in the cause of justice and in strictly regulated form. In particular:

> It is legitimate to use force only when it is declared by proper authority, as a last resort, for a justifiable cause, with just intentions, in which the total good is expected to outweigh the evil, and with the reasonable hope of success. In the conduct of war, violence must be both discriminate (immunity for non-combatants) and proportional (means appropriate to ends).[42]

In conclusion, then, there are serious limits and drawbacks to a military response to terrorism. In the international context, these are chiefly the political consequences of using such an approach, particularly as a first line of defence, and its limited utility when it is used. In the domestic context, the use of force is usually the responsibility of the police rather than the army, at least in democratic nations. In some countries, specialized 'third' forces have been created within the police, such as in Canada,[43] although other countries place them with the military, such as Great Britain. In extreme cases, the military has been used in aid of civil power, primarily to protect potential targets during a crisis and to help police with arrests and searches. This is what happened in Canada in 1970, but the military always remained under the authority of civil authority, namely the police.

Some commentators have mistakenly assumed that martial law was invoked in Canada,[44] but this did not happen. In martial law, civilian courts are replaced by military ones; in Canada the regular courts continued to try terrorist cases. In some countries, such as Turkey, specialized courts with military judges deal with terrorist cases even when martial law is not in force. Thus, in the domestic context, there is a gradation in the use of the military ranging from military aid to civil power, where civilian authority remains supreme, all the way to a military regime where the civilian authority is completely replaced by a military one. In Western democracies, the dangers of alienating the population, legitimizing the terrorist, and provoking a popular backlash against the government generally mitigate against the military option in time of peace, even when dealing with serious and persistent terrorist threats.

The Propaganda Dimension of Counter-terrorism

While there is much literature on legal, diplomatic and military responses to terrorism, particularly the more coercive/repressive kinds of responses, there is little on economic counter-measures and practically none on what can be called 'psychological' counter-measures. Economic sanctions and boycotts against terrorist organizations and their sponsors can only be a forceful weapon when they are used with consistency and moral legitimacy. So far, little progress has been made in this area.[45] As we saw in the Swiss case,[46] the laundering of money and the procurement of arms are two areas where terrorist groups can sometimes even benefit from government economic policies.

As for the psychological domain, we have already noted the multiplicity of audiences involved in the dialogue between terrorists and counter-terrorists. Terrorists are not so much interested in their direct victims as in the effect of their victimization on various audiences. As such, terrorists fight not for physical territory but for mental space – the hearts and minds of those watching and listening. If terrorism is a form of psychological warfare, then the propaganda dimension becomes an important element in counter-terrorism as well. What is at stake is to obtain attitudinal and behavioural results with relevant target groups. These results can consist of either a strengthening or a modification of existing beliefs; in this sense, they can be labelled *defensive* and *offensive* respectively. If we distinguish between two target groups, one's own reference group and that of one's opponent, then four fields emerge. Psychological operations (psyops) can then be divided into four main categories:[47]

1. *Offensive internal psyops*: aiming to *promote* desired perceptions, images, opinions or attitudes among members of the actor's *own* organization;
2. *Defensive internal psyops*: aiming to *prevent* undesired perceptions, images, opinions or attitudes among the members of the actor's *own* organization;
3. *Offensive external psyops*: aiming to *promote* desired perceptions, images, opinions, or attitudes among the members of *another* actor's organization;
4. *Defensive external psyops*: aiming to *prevent* undesired percep-

tions, images, opinions or attitudes among the members of *another* actor's organization.

If we apply these four categories of psychological operations to the problem of counter-terrorism, several areas can be identified where democracies can usefully improve their nonviolent armoury. In doing so, however, we should keep in mind that 'psychology' is not a tool, *per se*, as Ariel Merari has pointed out:

> Strictly speaking, there is no such thing as 'psychological tools'. The means at the disposal of a government are legal, economical, informational, diplomatic, and military. These, however, should be used in accordance with sound psychological principles in a co-ordinated fashion.[48]

Merari's point is important: while we have examined the coercive and repressive aspects of legal, diplomatic and military means in some detail, including a glimpse at less coercive economic means, it is clear that all of these means have communicative aspects as well. All response options convey information of some sort to different audiences; they are expressive and symbolic as well as instrumental. Yet the particular messages that are *received* by a particular audience may not be what the sender intended to convey; this is part of the unintended consequence problem mentioned before. What Merari calls 'informational' comes closest to a direct concern with conveying explicit, *intended* messages to specific audiences; this is the propaganda dimension of counter-terrorism. It should not be forgotten, however, that all response options do have their communicative dimension as well.

Offensive Internal Psyops

Here, we are talking primarily about 'delegitimation' of the terrorist and of the use of terrorism and violence in democratic political life. In order to create or maintain a political climate in which terrorists are not supported by the population or sections thereof, the public must be educated about the threat posed by terrorist organizations. One method is to treat all terrorism as crime and to deal with terrorists within the rule of law, as in the criminal justice model. One variant of this could be a 'no-policy policy',[49] where the declared policy is that there is no official anti-terrorist policy distinct from ordinary criminal justice policy. In the words of one American psyops instructor:

> The PSYOP should always stress the inhumanity and immorality of the terrorist's activities while emphasizing that the actual impact (death, injuries, and property losses) is relatively small.[50]

It is ironic that the media tend to sensationalize the violence and victimization of people by terrorism, along with the terrorist's inhumanity and immorality. The result is to increase the impact of the terrorist's actions rather than to minimize it. An explicit policy to downplay the actual physical impact while at the same time condemning the terrorism could help to promote the idea that terrorism is unacceptable in democratic society while at the same time minimizing the risk of public calls, fuelled by insecurity and terror, for repressive measures that undermine the rule of law and individual rights.

People tend to be willing to sacrifice freedom when their security seems to be seriously threatened, even when a democratic tradition is strong. Scapegoating and indiscriminate labeling are two of the most pernicious anti-democratic symptoms of generalized public fear and insecurity. It is therefore important that the public learns to distinguish between those political actors who try their utmost to prevent the use of violence, on the one hand, and those who use violence as a first rather than a last resort, or as unrestrained provocation, rather than as a means to prevent the occurrence of further violence. There is much moral confusion as to which violence is action and which is reaction, which side is legitimate and which is not. There is much confusion between legitimate armed resistance against non-democratic regimes which have neither been elected by a majority nor respect the rights of minorities and clandestine armed attacks by tiny groups on unarmed civilians in peaceful societies. Confusion among the populace also arises when a democratic government uses non-democratic methods abroad or at home, thereby losing legitimacy *vis-à-vis* the terrorists.

On the other hand, one cannot expect a democratic regime to be perfect either. In the words of Merleau-Ponty, 'we do not have a choice between purity and violence but between different kinds of violence'.[51] As Jean-François Revel points out: 'We fall into a trap laid by the terrorists and the totalitarians when we endorse the idea that we have no right to be free from attack unless we attain perfection, a duty they do not have.'[52] By containing the official use of violence and repression within the rule of law, the criminal justice model attempts such an approach. By retaining the war model as a means of last resort and by using it only in extreme cases and for a short period of time, according to the principles of just war theory outlined previously, a government can maintain legitimacy even when using military force. There is clearly a task of educating the public about democratic values and terrorist values. In order to be credible, a sound human rights policy and a respect for the rule of law are essential points of departure.

Defensive Internal Psyops

While public education can be seen as an offensive strategy aimed at one's own constituency, there are also defensive measures which a government can take to prevent undesired public perceptions. Terrorist attacks against democratic regimes are in part meant to show the strength of the terrorists and the weakness of the government. If the terrorist is viewed as stronger, public demands to yield to terrorist demands can intensify. If the government stands firm and terrorist violence increases, such demands can intensify further if the public attributes the increased threat to the government's hard line. Conversely, the public might call for impossible or ill-advised responses from the government, such as a quick end to a hostage siege or a massive crackdown on dissidents, and a cautious government might then be perceived as being cowardly or vacillating. If, on the other hand, a government makes concessions, to prevent violence either immediately or in the future, it can be seen as weak. Such conflicting public perceptions can have a serious impact on public trust and confidence in government: 'Like a child clamoring for forbidden toys, the public expects the government simultaneously to give in and to hold fast.'[53]

In order to establish a relationship of trust with the public, democratic governments must be willing to share more and more accurate information about terrorist organizations, their aims and their capabilities. Only then can the public realistically assess what is possible and impossible for a government to do. The media play a central role in this relationship, as public perceptions are shaped not so much by the terrorist's atrocities themselves as by the way in which the media report on them and on the government's reactions to them. As terrorism provokes a competition for allegiance – either to the terrorists or to the government – the media are in a key position to determine whether the population supports the government or acquiesces to the terrorists.

The relationship between government, media and terrorists in situations of a clear terrorist threat is still not well enough understood.[54] It is clear though that media coverage of terrorist events is fuelled by two conflicting ideologies: on the one hand, the concept of newsworthiness leads the media to promulgate official perceptions of the terrorist event and to ignore alternative perspectives; on the other, the media play a watchdog role, criticizing government action and defending the public's right to know.[55] A defensive strategy would therefore do well to address this contradiction by using the privileged access to the media enjoyed by the official perspective to inform the public of the nature and seriousness of the terrorist threat. This might prevent the kinds of panicky and contradictory perceptions that undermine public trust in government and fuel public demands for the quick fix or the impossible solution.

On the other hand, officials must be prepared to allow the media to provide objective coverage of terrorist groups and their goals without knee-jerk accusations that the media are thereby legitimizing terrorism. The Thatcher Government's 1988 move to ban broadcast interviews with both the IRA and Sinn Fein highlights a prevalent belief in government circles that truly balanced reporting – a feature of most media guidelines and codes of ethics by the way – functions to legitimize the terrorist and his cause. Part of a defensive strategy aimed at one's own constituency would be to prevent this from happening without resorting to censorship.

Offensive External Psyops

Democratic governments can try to promote desired perceptions among individual members of terrorist organizations, their sympathizers, and their foreign backers. One perception governments like to create is that of terrorism as a strategy without any reasonable prospect of success. This tactic is likely to have some effect if the government is also able to apprehend and punish terrorists; faced with tangible evidence of their lack of success, terrorists and their supporters can become demoralized. However, governments are rarely so effective that deterrence is achieved in this way. Reform-minded governments can try to meet at least some of the grievances professed by the terrorists, thereby conveying the message that terrorism is unnecessary to achieve certain goals. This can create internal dissension within or between terrorist groups over the proper course to take. In Spain, for example, certain government reforms led some groups to abandon terrorism and to pursue a dialogue with the government.

By granting amnesties to imprisoned terrorists in exchange for assurances of future legal activities, governments can attempt to bring extremists back into conventional politics. While this worked in Italy, it can also backfire, as in the case of the members of *Action Directe* in France, who were granted such an amnesty by the government of François Mitterrand in 1981. In that case, the terrorist violence came back much stronger than before 1979, with a move from bombing to assassination. Yet the apparent failure of this conciliatory response is not as clear-cut as might be assumed at first glance:

> Although 80 per cent of the amnestied prisoners did not return to violence, the resurgence of a more murderous *Action Directe* made the government appear naive and weak. Nevertheless, the much

smaller organization, even more committed and cohesive, was also more vulnerable to police penetration. When key leaders were arrested in 1987, the organization was effectively destroyed.[56]

For the majority of prisoners, the strategy did work. The smaller core that persisted and escalated the violence made the government look bad, but their smaller numbers made them more vulnerable to eventual defeat.

Offensive external psyops are often directed at the vulnerabilities of terrorist organizations, attempting to create uncertainty, suspicion, internal dissension and rivalries between groups. According to McEwen, these can include 'rumours of spies and informers, allegations of special treatment of officers and/or leaders, and amnesty/incentive programs for terrorists who surrender'.[57] As McEwen points out, however, many of these tactics, particularly those aimed at triggering rivalries between specific groups, require access to good intelligence and it is often very difficult to obtain reliable or credible information on clandestine groups operating underground. The greatest danger of such an approach is that the main targets of such operations become those groups that are easiest to penetrate, namely radical organizations that may share the goals or ideology of terrorist groups but who do not engage in violence or terrorism. Obviously, offensive psyops explicitly directed at such organizations go against democratic principles of freedom of expression and freedom from government interference.

Psychological operations can also be directed at external publics that may possibly identify with or sympathize with terrorist groups. In the case of Armenian terrorists in Turkey, the government portrayed young Armenian activists as drug dealers and communist puppets,[58] hoping to achieve general condemnation by Western democracies of Armenian terrorism. Given the dubious human rights record of the Turkish regime, the effort was less than successful. However, much more attention could be given by democratic governments to countering terrorist propaganda by answering their ideological writings in a serious way. Terrorist writings are too often dismissed as mere propaganda not worth being taken seriously. Insofar as the terrorists themselves and their sympathizers do take it seriously, it should not be so readily dismissed. Terrorist writings, like much extremist political literature, generally depict the world in black and white terms: one is either on the right side or on the wrong side, part of the solution or part of the problem, and there is no room for doubt, for compromise, or for a middle ground. Those who do opt for that middle ground are often targeted for special vilification; mediators, moderates and reform-minded officials are typical targets of terrorist groups. In terrorist propaganda, the opponent is dehumanized and described as being evil beyond redemption. The creation of such an enemy image is important, for it gives the terrorist's conscience a clean moral bill for killing those who stand in the way of progress, the revolution, the just cause.

In view of the importance of terrorist propaganda for justifying the use of violence and facilitating the commission of violence against specific kinds of targets, terrorist writings should not go unanswered. While it might not be possible to establish a dialogue with the terrorists in the underground, some imprisoned terrorists as well as their sympathizers might be more receptive to such an approach. If a dialogue can be established and imprisoned terrorists can be persuaded to change sides, to return to humanity, the impact on a terrorist movement can be tremendous. In the case of West Germany, the televised dialogue between the liberal Minister of the Interior, G. Baum, and Horst Mahler, one of the founders of the Red Army Faction, had such an impact. In Italy, the testimony and the memoirs of Patrizio Peci[59] had a similar but weaker effect, though the outcome was tragic for his brother, who was kidnapped by the Red Brigades and killed in revenge. In Peci's case, the fundamental message was that terrorism is not a viable strategy of social change as it criminalizes the entire left and fails to obtain its objectives.[60]

Defensive External Psyops

The fourth variation of psychological operations involves the prevention of undesired perceptions among terrorists and their constituency. Offensive and defensive psyops that are directed at the terrorist camp are intimately connected: promoting the notion that terrorism cannot work, either by deterrence or by reform, can also prevent potential terrorists or supporters from believing that terrorism *can* work. Yet there are two major areas where defensive external psyops might help to prevent certain beliefs that serve to bind individual members to the terrorist group: the idea that once violence has been committed, you cannot go back, and the idea that the group is the only place where a sense of identity, belonging, importance or existential meaning can be achieved.

One of the ways in which individual members are inducted into the world of terrorism is to give new recruits small tasks to perform that are auxiliary to the main mission and typically do not involve the use of violence. In this way, individuals who are sympathetic to the cause and want to help out in some way are not immediately forced to confront their own consciences and their own feelings about violence and victimization. Many people who are attracted to extremist groups, including terrorist groups, are seeking ineffable affective ties as much as they may be seeking instrumental political goals. They may be seeking a sense of purpose in life, a feeling of doing something important, of being involved in something socially, politically or even existentially significant. By feeling useful to the group and feeling that they are gradually accepted by the group, these more emotional goals begin to be fulfilled. The new recruit begins to enjoy the *esprit de corps* within the group and begins to feel part of the group. At the same time, of course, they are being tested by the group – for their commitment, their particular skills and their general usefulness to the group.

Finally, they are asked to participate in the commission of violence and, once this violence threshold is crossed, the new member is told that there is no way back, that they will go to jail and that their friends and family will never forgive them for what they have done. At this point, those who still may have doubts about the course they have taken commit themselves fully to the cause because they feel that exit is now impossible. Others, who have perhaps found for the first time that sense of belonging or meaning that they were seeking in the first place, accept whatever task they are given so as to maintain their emotional fulfillment.

Laws that provide reduced sentences for co-operation with authorities or that offer amnesty for renouncing violence, coupled with official statements, perhaps publicized through the media, that convey similar messages stating that exit from the group is always possible and that those who co-operate and who renounce the use of violence in political life can be accepted back into society, could help to prevent certain individuals from remaining trapped in the self-contained world of the terrorist via a deepening commitment to the group and the continued use of violence.

A balance must be struck between the 'delegitimation' of terrorism in political life, typical of offensive operations, and leaving open the door to those who wish to come back, typical of defensive operations. To this end, violence and coercion might not always be the best method of coping with terrorism. The more coercive and repressive methods might strengthen the terrorist organization and its hold over its members. Anti-terrorist strategies might be directed, on the one hand, to preventing new recruits from joining terrorist organizations and, on the other, to facilitating the exit of older members from existing organizations. To achieve this, positive incentives have to be created so that, beyond victory and defeat, the conflict can be carried on at a different level. Nobody is born a terrorist. Nobody should die a terrorist. A dead terrorist is likely to become a martyr and an inspiration for further violence.

For democracies, the terms 'propaganda', 'psychological warfare', 'political warfare', 'war of ideas', 'war of nerves', 'agitprop', 'campaign of truth', 'perception management', 'political advocacy' or 'persuasive communications' tend, for very good reasons, to have a pejorative connotation, conjuring up images of Big Brother and the Thought Police of Orwell's *1984*. However, if terrorism, like war, begins in the minds of men, as a UNESCO declaration says, it is on this front that it has to be countered as well. If terrorism is 'propaganda by the deed', a form of communication by means of violence and threat of violence, then countering terrorism must involve countering not only the violence but also the communication.

Counter-terrorism and Democracy: In Search of a Democratic Solution

Western democracies have been faced with domestic and international terrorism for more than two decades, yet they are still far from a solution to the problem. Contemporary nonstate terrorism creates its terror predominantly through countervalue targeting. In democratic societies where each life is valued, there is an abundance of targets, civilian or otherwise. The protection of all possible targets in open societies is impossible without turning them into draconian police states. Short of this unacceptable solution, there is no complete effectiveness against terrorism.

The dilemma posed by terrorism to democracies can be depicted by a simple 2 × 2 matrix:

	Acceptable	*Unacceptable*
Effective	I	II
Ineffective	III	IV

The elusive ideal is an effective solution that is acceptable to any democratic society (I). In attempting to achieve a balance between these two criteria, two kinds of problem areas can result: those solutions to the terrorist problem that may be effective but are unacceptable democratically (II) and those solutions that might be democratically acceptable but prove to be ineffective (III).

The most common scenario in democratic states has been when politicians or law enforcement officials feel that traditional methods of policing or criminal justice are not sufficient to deal with a persistent or serious threat or that the procedural safeguards built into the rule of law actually undermine effectiveness. In this case, there can be calls for any number and variety of special measures – laws, police powers, courts, trial procedures, rules of evidence, sentences, or prisons – that undermine to a greater or lesser extent the rule of law, the prerogatives of due process or the rights of individuals, accused or otherwise. In this volume, we have seen how several states have resorted to such measures either on a temporary basis or a more permanent one. In the United Kingdom, what was originally conceived as a temporary measure – the Prevention of Terrorism Act – eventually became permanent, although it has undergone periodic revision along the way in an attempt to adjust the balance between effectiveness and acceptability.

Hardline solutions that resemble the state terror of totalitarian regimes clearly fall into the category of unacceptable. Their effectiveness determines whether they fall into category II (effective but unacceptable) or IV (ineffective and unacceptable). It is probably no coincidence that during the breakup of the Soviet Union political violence, including skyjackings and terrorism, increased dramatically.[61] Recent disclosures of the pervasiveness of a totalitarian political system, with its elaborate system of informers, highlight how difficult any kind of dissident political activity can be, let alone insurgent violence such as terrorism. It is the coercive/repressive models of social control that seem to be favoured by anti-democratic regimes and they seem to be very effective, particularly when unfettered by any concerns for civil liberties or minority rights.

It is precisely this tension between effectiveness and acceptability of repressive models of counter-terrorism that lies at the crux of the demo-cratic response problem. While the coercive/repressive models have clearly predominated in Western responses to insurgent and international terrorism, they have taken a different form more congruent with demo-cratic principles such as the rule of law. This is precisely what makes them acceptable. It is when they begin to move away from these principles that their acceptability becomes questionable.

As for effectiveness, coercive/repressive models are widely seen to be more effective than conciliatory models of control, which are often seen as encouraging further terrorism or, at best, circumventing the legitimate political process. Conventional wisdom seems to be that when the threat is sufficiently great, effectiveness must take precedence over democratic acceptability. This usually means that repressive models predominate because of their presumed effectiveness and that, the worse the threat, the more willing we are to compromise on democratic acceptability. We have seen, however, that the effectiveness of hardline repressive policies, such as military reprisals or indiscriminate legal repression, can be questioned on purely operational grounds, regardless of the acceptability dimension. Sometimes repression leads not to deterrence but to revenge and increased solidarity.

In such cases where unacceptable solutions prove ineffective, we would enter category IV: unacceptable and ineffective. While it is true that for many critics of conciliatory solutions addressing the grievances of the terrorist in any way whatsoever is both unacceptable and ineffective, the standard of acceptability in this case differs somewhat from what we might call 'democratic acceptability', in that it focuses more on the dangers of encouraging further terrorism rather than on the dangers of undermining democratic principles. However, where conciliatory models of control begin to undermine public security and confidence in government or to circumvent the rights of other groups in society, be they the majority or some other minority, then one can argue that they, too, are unacceptable democratically. The question of their effectiveness remains.

Clearly, what is acceptable democratically depends on the nature of the threat and the nature of a society on the defensive. The case studies in this volume clearly show that when the threat is persistent and severe, the willingness to accept limits to democratic principles is greater (e.g., the United Kingdom and the Federal Republic of Germany). At the extreme, such as in Peru in April 1992, where the president suspended the parliament and imposed a state of emergency in part because of a persistent and vicious terrorist campaign, public opinion can even support the suspension of due process and the rule of law. Similarly, most people – whether English-speaking or French-speaking – supported the Canadian government's decision to impose emergency regulations and to suspend due process during the October crisis of 1970.

The standards for effectiveness are also flexible. While conciliatory policies were successful in some countries (e.g., amnesty laws in Italy), they were less successful in others (e.g., structural reform in Spain or amnesty in France). Clearly, the nature of the terrorist threat, including the kind of group involved (e.g., revolutionary or nationalistic) and the cultural tradition of the specific country involved are important elements in determining potential effectiveness. We have also seen that effectiveness can vary between the short term and the long term, as in the case of France, where Mitterrand's amnesty had a negative short-term impact, but a more positive long-term one, so that assessments of effectiveness become very difficult. Any dichotomy remains heuristic only in so far as it helps us understand how the two sides of the coin interact. The danger is that we treat the two sides as separate entities that behave independently of each other. The very effectiveness of any *democratic* solution to the terrorist problem must include a determination of the political dimension and the impact of that solution on democratic political life. If terrorism is eliminated at the expense of democracy or the rule of law, via either too much repression (dictatorship) or too much accomodation (anarchy), is such a solution really effective?

We have seen that Western responses to terrorism typically fall into two basic repressive models. In the criminal justice model, terrorism is treated as crime and the onus of response is placed upon criminal prosecution and punishment within the rule of law. The problem here is that the political nature of most terrorism has strained the procedural controls imposed by the rule of law and has led in certain cases where the terrorism has been particularly severe – or *perceived* to be particularly severe – to serious departures from conventional judicial processing and sentencing.[62]

The limitations of the criminal justice model have led some states to adopt a *war model*, particularly in dealing with serious domestic campaigns and with international and state-sponsored terrorism. Here, the onus is placed on the military and the use of special forces, retaliatory strikes and, at the very least, troop deployment in peacetime. Some have even argued for a permanent covert force capable of conducting retribution campaigns.[63] The problem with the war model is that, by treating terrorism as war, the political role of the terrorist is acknowledged and possibly legitimized, perhaps thereby encouraging more insurgent violence. What is worse, the war is often directed at those who may share the terrorists' political goals, but not their means, but because they do not operate secretly are easier targets for the state.

Ronald Crelinsten describes how the state can slide into a grey zone of state terrorism that separates these two models of counter-terrorism:

> From one end, the police bend the rules of due process, arrest and search warrants are obtained illegally or not obtained at all, charges are laid without sufficient evidence and . . . 'political justice' becomes more prevalent as use of the criminal justice system becomes politicised. From the other end, the military starts to target civilians, to use torture to obtain information, death squads are formed. As the sharp distinction between the police and the military breaks down and the imperatives of due process and the rules of combat are replaced by the demands of national security, the controller slides into the grey zone of terrorism 'from above'.[64]

Thus there are two primary routes by which a democratic state, using the coercive apparatus of the nation state to counter terrorism from below, can begin to threaten the democratic nature of the state itself: the criminal justice route or the military route. Neither route leads inevitably to a fullblown policy of state terror and it is not necessary to call a state 'terrorist' if it adopts extraordinary measures that move in one or the other direction. Yet such a conceptualization does help to identify the kinds of measures that might typically presage a movement towards a more generalized anti-democratic counter-terrorist policy.

The case studies in this volume suggest that *it is primarily by the criminal justice route that Western responses to terrorism have moved away from democratic acceptability*, although examples of the military route exist as well. This reflects the fact that most Western nations, except Israel, favour the criminal justice model over the war model. In fact, Israel is the exception that proves the rule. The unique context in which terrorism occurs in Israel has tended to favour a war model approach to counter-terrorism.[65] The most common measures adopted along the criminal justice route have been the creation of special legislation, the increasing of police powers, changes in rules of evidence and procedure during trials (e.g., anonymous testimony by witnesses or informers, without the right to cross-examine), and in some cases the creation of special courts or jurisdictions and the creation of special regimes of imprisonment for convicted terrorists.

The cases in this volume highlight one particular measure that appears regularly in any special powers accorded to the police: *the prolongation of the period of detention for which a suspect can be detained without access to a lawyer or without laying specific charges*. While usually justified as 'preventive detention' or as a necessary means to obtain information before others can be warned of the suspect's arrest (e.g., via the lawyer), such a measure increases the likelihood of abuse of power, mistreatment and intimidation of suspects and, in the case of suspects who are detained not because of any suspected criminal activity but because of their beliefs or political affiliation, serious damage to democratic principles and individual civil rights. Furthermore, as Fernando Jiménez points out, it is the area of detention and interrogation that is most sensitive to exploitation by terrorist propaganda.[66]

When the military route is taken, the two most common variants are the use of troops in aid of civil power, such as troop deployment for the protection of vulnerable targets, or the use of special forces for what might otherwise be normal police work. While the former solution can lead to an unacceptable situation akin to martial law or even a military *coup d'état*, it has been very rare in Western democracies that states of emergency or widespread use of the military in aid of civil power has persisted to the point of undermining the legitimacy of the democratic regime. The more prevalent solution has been the use of special forces for apprehension of suspects, searches and seizures and, in the case of barricaded hostage situations, termination of the incident by means of assault.

The most common problem associated with the use of special forces, whether within the military, the police or some paramilitary 'third force', is the question of the level of force that is appropriate to a democracy and the locus and degree of accountability when excessive force is used.

Police typically use the minimal level of force needed to apprehend a suspect, while the military are trained to use maximal force to ensure that the enemy is put out of commission.[67] In the latter case, the individual soldier is not held accountable for his action while in the former case, the police officer is.

During the late 1960s and the 1970s in the United States, both left-wing revolutionaries, such as the Weather Underground, and Black nationalists, particularly the Black Panthers, were dealt with primarily by means of legal repression, namely, the criminal justice model. With the Black Panthers, however, it can be argued that the police adopted a more military approach that circumvented the rule of law, relying more on violent police raids that ended in the death of suspects rather than their arrest. This *militarization of the police* in response to Black violence in the 1970s is reminiscent of the British response to Irish terrorism in the 1980s and 1990s, particularly the accusations of a shoot-to-kill policy carried out by the Royal Ulster Constabulary and the Special Air Service (SAS). When agents of the state begin *consistently* to shoot suspects without bothering to arrest them, or to mistreat them during interrogation in order to force confessions, then the state has moved far along the road to a regime of terror. That such a route can be taken by either the police or the military simply highlights the problems surrounding the use of force in any counter-terrorism strategy, be it a criminal justice model or a war model.

The second lesson that can be drawn from the case studies in this volume is that *movement away from democratic principles has been most evident on the domestic scene*, where the state is dealing with domestic groups operating domestically, although again, exceptions do exist when international terrorism has been involved, such as the American bombing of Libya in 1986. While it is much more difficult for separate nations to achieve consensus on the need for extraordinary measures to combat international terrorism, individual nations are more able to bring public opinion along when dealing with domestic terrorist threats. Even within a nation, however, there is differential application of emergency powers or draconian measures. In Canada, in 1970, while emergency powers were adopted nationwide to deal with the terrorist threat in Quebec, local politicians elsewhere in Canada who attempted to use these powers to deal with social or political problems in their jurisdictions were sharply warned by the Federal Minister of Justice that this was not acceptable.

In the United Kingdom, the powers applied to Northern Ireland are generally more draconian than those applied in Great Britain itself. And in Israel, the repressive response is greater in the occupied territories than in Israel proper. Once again, the standard of acceptability is subject to differing interpretations depending upon where the counter-terrorist policies are applied, even within a single nation. This flexibility in acceptability can help to preserve democratic traditions, as in limiting severe measures to areas where they are most needed. On the other hand, especially in pluralistic democracies with large or diverse minority populations, such flexibility can be transformed into selective democracy for favoured groups within the society, at the expense of those minorities or communities deemed to be the 'sea' in which the terrorist fish swim.

As for the international context, treating most acts of terrorism as the peacetime equivalent of war crimes, as suggested by Alex Schmid,[68] achieves a balance between the two traditional control models by adopting their strengths while avoiding their weaknesses. By treating acts of terrorism as war crimes, the criminal nature of such acts is highlighted even while recognizing their political context. Creating special courts or procedures in this case would not be the same as creating special courts or procedures in the traditional criminal justice model, since the special nature of the crime is explicitly recognized. Yet by treating them as the *peacetime equivalent* of war crimes, this approach highlights the absence of a formal state of war and thereby obviates the recourse to a military approach and its inherent dangers to a democratic way of life. If the military is used, it is explicitly in aid of the civil power, with full accountability resting on the civilian authorities.

This approach is consistent with Amnesty International's recent decision to recognize the possibility that national liberation movements and non-state actors fighting against oppression can also engage in human rights violations (HRVs). HRV perpetrators in such contexts would receive the same condemnation as state perpetrators of HRVs now do, regardless of ideology, cause or political goal. Freedom fighters who use terrorism as their principal method of waging conflict would be treated like war criminals rather than liberation forces.

From a response point of view, then, this redefinition of terrorism as the peacetime equivalent of war crimes could open the way to a wider level of international co-operation within a legal framework that transcends the more narrow confines of national legal systems. As such, it minimizes the risk inherent in the criminal justice model of undermining the rule of law within any one nation state, while minimizing the risk inherent in the war model of collateral damage to the very principles inherent to the notion of democracy. The greatest challenge for this definitional solution, however, lies in its supranational impact. When nation states band together to create larger regional entities, such as the EC, individual member states find it difficult to cede control to supranational bodies, such as a special European court with special jurisdiction on terrorist offences.[69]

The cases in this volume also make it clear that *conciliatory responses have not been totally ignored in the fight against terrorism*, despite the prevailing wisdom that they constitute signs of governmental weakness and only serve to encourage further terrorism. Conciliatory solutions, both in the short term and the long term, can play a very important part in countering terrorism by addressing audiences other than the terrorists themselves – their sympathizers, the general population, the international community, and potential victims or targets of terror. While they may be ineffective in reducing the coercive capabilities of the terrorists in the short term, amnesties, reforms or even concessions may reduce their political capabilities, particularly in the long term. This could also lead in the long term to a reduction in their coercive capabilities. Our survey of the psychological aspects of counter-terrorism makes it clear that the political dimension of counter-terrorism is particularly important in democratic society. If the general public and especially the mass media were to understand the differences between coercive and political capabilities, between short-term loss and long-term gain, and between domestic and international policy concerns, then a more flexible counter-terrorist strategy that can balance the needs of effectiveness and acceptability might be more feasible.

By considering the communicative aspects of different control models, repressive or conciliatory, short term or long term, political or coercive, domestic or international, governments can perhaps discover more innovative ways to deal with the problem of terrorism that are both effective and acceptable to our democratic way of life. In doing so, they might succeed in avoiding the trap identified by Friederich Nietzsche when he warned: 'He who fights with monsters might take care lest he thereby become a monster'. Nietzsche continues: 'And if you gaze for long into an abyss, the abyss gazes also into you'. This reciprocal relationship between controller and controlled, with its inherent danger of mirroring the monster that one is fighting, lies at the root of the problem of democratic control. If governments fail to heed Nietzsche's warning, then Joseph Conrad's observation that 'the terrorist and the policeman both come from the same basket' can too easily become fact.

NOTES

1. See, e.g., M.P.M. Zagari, this volume.
2. See G. Davidson Smith, 'Canada's Experience With Modern Terrorism', *Terrorism and Political Violence* 5/1 (Spring 1993), forthcoming.
3. A.J. Jongman, this volume.

4. John E. Finn, *Constitutions in Crisis: Political Violence and the Rule of Law* (NY: OUP, 1991).
5. See Ronald D. Crelinsten, 'Power and Meaning: Terrorism as a Struggle Over Access to the Communication Structure', in Paul Wilkinson and A.M. Stewart (eds.), *Contemporary Research on Terrorism* (Aberdeen: Univ. of Aberdeen Press, 1987), pp.419–50.
6. Peter C. Sederberg, *Terrorist Myths: Illusion, Rhetoric, and Reality* (Englewood Cliffs, NJ: Prentice Hall, 1989).
7. Alex P. Schmid, 'Force or Conciliation? An Overview of Some Problems Associated with Current Anti-Terrorist Response Strategies', *Violence, Aggression and Terrorism* 2/2 (May 1988), pp.149–78.
8. Ronald D. Crelinsten, 'Terrorism as Political Communication: the Relationship between the Controller and the Controlled', in Wilkinson and Stewart (eds.), *Contemporary Research on Terrorism* (note 5), pp.3–23; Ronald D. Crelinsten, 'Terrorism, Counter-Terrorism and Democracy: The Assessment of National Security Threats', *Terrorism and Political Violence* 1/2 (April 1989), pp.242–69.
9. Sederberg, *Terrorist Myths* (note 6).
10. Richard Clutterbuck, 'Keeping Track of Terrorists After 1992', this volume.
11. See Jeffrey Ian Ross and Ted Robert Gurr, 'Why Terrorism Subsides: A Comparative Study of Trends and Groups in Terrorism in Canada and the United States', *Comparative Politics* 21/4 (1989), pp.405–26 for a similar distinction applied to the question of how terrorism ends.
12. See Alex P. Schmid and Janny de Graaf, *Violence as Communication: Insurgent Terrorism and the Western News Media* (Beverly Hills: Sage, 1982); Crelinsten, 'Terrorism as Political Communication' (note 8).
13. Ronald D. Crelinsten, 'International Political Terrorism: A Challenge for Comparative Research', *International Journal of Comparative and Applied Criminal Justice*, 2/2 (1978), pp.107–26.
14. Ariel Merari, 'Problems Related to the Symptomatic Treatment of Terrorism', *Terrorism* 3/3&4 (1980), p.280.
15. Martha Crenshaw, 'How Terrorism Ends', Paper presented to the American Political Science Association, 1987.
16. See David Bonner and G. Davidson Smith (see note 2) for the examples of the UK and Canada, respectively. For more general discussion, see Ronald D. Crelinsten, 'Terrorism and the Media: Problems, Solutions, and Counterproblems', *Political Communication and Persuasion* 6/3 (1989), pp.311–39.
17. Of course, state-sponsored terrorism is nothing new. Heinz Vetschera (this volume) reminds us of Nazi Germany's 1930s sponsoring of terrorism in Austria. Several centuries before that, when sea piracy was at its peak, Western powers systematically provided 'letters of marque' to pirate ships (called privateers) that refrained from attacking their own merchant ships and promised to confine their attacks to merchant vessels from rival nations. The letters of marque protected the pirates from the issuing nation's navy. The system eventually broke down when pirates began 'abusing' the system by collecting letters from competing nations and attacking everyone while protecting themselves from every navy (William Chambliss, personal communication to RDC at 1985 Annual Meeting of the American Society of Criminology, San Diego, California).
18. See Fernando Jiménez, this volume, for Spain and Heinz Vetschera, this volume, for Austria.
19. See Alex P. Schmid, 'Countering Terrorism in The Netherlands', this volume and Smith, 'Canada's Experience With Modern Terrorism' (note 2).
20. See Stephen Sloan, 'United States Anti-Terrorism Policies: Lessons for the European Response in the 1990s and Beyond', *Terrorism and Political Violence* 5/1 (Spring 1993), forthcoming.
21. Richard Clutterbuck, 'Negotiating With Terrorists', this volume.
22. See, e.g., Paul Wilkinson, *Terrorism and the Liberal State* (London: Macmillan, 1982).
23. Crelinsten, 'Power and Meaning' (note 5).

24. Sederberg, *Terrorist Myths* (note 6).
25. Neil C. Livingstone, *The War Against Terrorism* (Lexington, MA: Lexington Books, 1982); idem, 'Proactive Responses to Terrorism: Reprisals, Preemption, and Retribution', in idem and Terrell E. Arnold (eds.), *Fighting Back: Winning the War Against Terrorism* (Lexington, MA: Lexington Books, 1986).
26. Ronald D. Crelinsten, 'Images of Terrorism in Media, Policy and Scientific Discourse', Paper presented at conference, Centre for Conflict Studies, University of New Brunswick, Oct. 1990.
27. See Crelinsten, 'International Political Terrorism' (note 13).
28. See Jongman, this volume.
29. See, however, Brent L. Smith, 'Antiterrorism Legislation in the United States: Problems and Implications', *Terrorism* 7/2 (March–April 1984), pp.213–31. For an excellent social historical study of domestic violence, see Daniel J. Monti, 'The Relation Between Terrorism and Domestic Civil Disorders', *Terrorism*, Vol.4 (1980), pp.123–41.
30. See Jongman, this volume.
31. David C. Rapoport, 'The Politics of Atrocity', in Yonah Alexander and Seymour Finger (eds.), *Terrorism: Interdisciplinary Perspectives* (NY: John Jay, 1977), pp.45–61.
32. Crelinsten, 'Power and Meaning' (note 5).
33. Brian M. Jenkins, J. Johnson and D. Ronfeldt, 'Numbered Lives: Some Statistical Observations from Seventy-Seven International Hostage Episodes', *Conflict* 1/1 (1978), pp.71–111.
34. Ariel Merari, 'Coping with Insurgent Political Violence: The Israeli Experience', *Terrorism and Political Violence*, forthcoming.
35. Sederberg, *Terrorist Myths*, p.148 (note 6).
36. Cited in Christopher Hewitt, *The Effectiveness of Anti-Terrorist Policies* (NY: Univ. Press of America, 1984), p.85n.
37. Hewitt, *Effectiveness of Anti-Terrorist Policies*, p.86.
38. Personal communication to A.P. Schmid.
39. Recommendation made at seminar in Bonn, 'Terrorism as Surrogate War', *Frankfurter Allgemeine Zeitung*, 16 Oct. 1986; cit. *Knipselkrant*, 1986, p.1281.
40. Paul Wilkinson, 'Proposals for Government and International Responses to Terrorism', in idem (ed.), *British Perspectives on Terrorism* (London: Allen & Unwin, 1981), pp.170–1.
41. Cited in Brian M. Jenkins, 'The US Response to Terrorism: a Policy Dilemma', *TVI Journal* (1985), p.34. These considerations are not specifically designed for intervention in terrorist situations.
42. Kermit D. Johnson, 'Just War and Nuclear Deterrence', unpubl. MS, n.d., p.1.
43. This specialized police unit was recently disbanded due to budget cuts and the Armed Forces will take over this responsibility.
44. See, e.g., Martha Crenshaw, 'How Terrorism Declines', *Terrorism and Political Violence* 3/1 (Spring 1991), pp.83–4.
45. See James Adams, *The Financing of Terror* (Sevenoaks, Kent: NEL, 1986) for a rare look at how some major nonstate groups have financed their terrorist operations.
46. Albert Stahel, this volume.
47. Rudolf Th. Jurrjens, *The Free Flow: People, Ideas, and Information in Soviet Ideology and Politics* (Amsterdam: Free University, 1978), pp.74–5.
48. Merari, p.283 (note 14).
49. Clark McCauley, 'Terrorism, Research and Public Policy: An Overview', *Terrorism and Political Violence* 3/1 (Spring 1991), p.139, citing D.C. Rapoport.
50. M. McEwen, 'Intelligence and PSYOP in Terrorism Counteraction', *Military Intelligence* (Jan.–March 1984), p.10.
51. Maurice Merleau-Ponty, *Humanism and Terror: An Essay on the Communist Problem* (Boston: Beacon, 1969), original French publication (Paris: Gallimard, 1947).
52. Jean-François Revel, 'Democracy versus Terrorism', in Benjamin Netanyahu (ed.), *Terrorism: How the West Can Win* (NY: Farrar, Strauss, Giroux, 1986), p.197.
53. Benjamin Netanyahu, 'On Terrorism', in Netanyahu, *How the West Can Win*, p.201.

54. But see Schmid and de Graaf, *Violence as Communication*; Crelinsten, 'Terrorism and the Media' (note 16); David L. Paletz and Alex P. Schmid (eds.), *Perspectives on Terrorism and the Media* (Beverly Hills, CA: Sage, 1992).
55. Crelinsten, 'Terrorism and the Media', p.312 (note 16).
56. Crenshaw, 'How Terrorism Declines', p.83 (note 44).
57. McEwen, 'Intelligence and PSYOP in Terrorism Counteraction', p.10 (note 50).
58. See, e.g., *International Terrorism and the Drug Connection* (Ankara: Univ. of Ankara Press, 1984). This is the final report of a symposium on international terrorism organized by Ankara University in April 1984 on 'Armenian Terrorism, its supporters, the narcotic connection [and] the distortion of history'.
59. Patrizio Peci, *Io, l'infame [I, the Scoundrel]* (Milan: Mondadori, 1983).
60. S.E. Moran, 'The Case of Patrizio Peci: a Character Sketch', *TVI Journal* (1985), p.34.
61. In remarks made at the 7th Annual International Symposium on Criminal Justice Issues, held at Chicago, Illinois in Aug. 1991, Col. Gennady Chebatarov of the Soviet MVD (Interior Ministry) revealed that 'numerous passenger train bombings, kidnappings, crop poisonings and other acts of violence occurred, resulting in 900 deaths [in 1991], plus the taking of 300 hostages, over one hundred assaults on the police and the theft of 3,000 automatic weapons'. Source: *Intelligence Newsletter*, No.176 (Sept. 1991), p.1.
62. Ronald D. Crelinsten, Danielle Laberge-Altmejd and Denis Szabo, *Terrorism and Criminal Justice* (Lexington, MA: Lexington Books, 1978); Finn, *Constitutions in Crisis*; David Bonner, this volume; Kurt Groenewold, this volume.
63. Livingstone, 'Proactive Responses to Terrorism', p.127 (note 25).
64. Crelinsten, 'Terrorism as Political Communication', p.9 (note 8).
65. See Merari, 'Coping With Insurgent Political Violence' (note 34).
66. Fernando Jiménez, this volume.
67. Grant Wardlaw, *Political Terrorism: Theory, Tactics, and Counter-Measures*, 2nd ed. (Cambridge, UK: CUP, 1989), p.90.
68. Alex P. Schmid, 'The Response Problem as a Definition Problem', this volume.
69. See Korthals Altes, Cardona, Zagari, this volume.

Bibliography

BELGIUM

DESCHUTTER, B. 'Prevention, legislation and research pertaining to terrorism in Belgium', in R.D. Crelinsten, D. Laberge-Altmejd and D. Szabo (eds.), *Terrorism and Criminal Justice: An International Perspective*. Lexington, MA: Lexington Books, 1978, pp.53–60.

LEGEBEKE, G. and H. SIMONSE. Vijf jaar bende van Nijvel. *Intermediair* 23/20 (1987), pp.11–15, 57.

INVERNIZZI, G. 'Belgium's two faces'. *World Press Review* 33 (1986), pp.55–6.

VANDER VELPEN, J. *De CCC: de staat en het terrorisme*. Berchem: Uitgeverij EPO, 1986.

JENKINS, P. 'Strategy of Tension: the Belgian terrorist crisis 1982–1986'. *Terrorism* 13 (1990), pp.299–309.

THE NETHERLANDS

Bedrijfsleven, politie en (politiek) geweld. 's-Gravenhage: Stichting Maatschappij en Politie – Stichting Maatschappij en Onderneming, 1988.

CHORUS, B., S. VAN HOUCKE and H. VERRIJN STUART. *De colonne eenmaal in beweging; oproerpolitie in Nederland*. Leeuwarden: Pamflet, 1981. 132pp.

CUPERUS, J. and R. KLIJNSMA. *Onderhandelen of bestormen; het beleid van de overheid inzake terroristische akties*. Groningen: Rijksuniversiteit Groningen, Polemologisch Instituut, 1980.

FIJNAUT, C. *Opdat de macht een toevlucht zij? Een historische studie van het politieapparaat als een politieke instelling*. Antwerpen: Kluwer/Arnhem: Gouda Quint, 1979. 2 dln. 1203pp.

FRACKERS, W. 'Control of Terrorism in the Netherlands'. *Abstracts on Police Science* 5/4 (1977), pp.211–14.

——— 'Organizational aspects of hostage-taking prevention and control in the Netherlands' in R.D. Crelinsten and D. Szabo (eds.), *Hostage Taking*. Lexington, MA: Lexington Books, 1979, pp.105–18.

GAAY FORTMAN, W.F. DE. *Rechtstaat en terrorisme*. Alphen aan den Rijn: Samson, 1979. 26pp.

Geweldgebruik door de politie; rapport van de commissie bezinning op het geweldgebruik door de politie. 's-Gravenhage: Ministerie van Justitie, 1987. 256pp.

HORN, J. 'Terrorismebestrijding in Nederland'. *Intermediair* 22/37 (1986), pp.35–9, 45.

HULSMAN, L.H.C. 'Gewelddadigheid, terrorisme en strafechtelijke normen'. *Delikt en delinkwent* 6/6 (1976), pp.299–303.

KLERKS, P. *Terreurbestrijding in Nederland, 1970–1988*. Amsterdam: Het Ravijn, 1989. 302pp.

REENEN, P. VAN. *Overheidsgeweld; een sociologische studie van de dynamiek van het geweldsmonopolie*. Alphen aan den Rijn: Samsom, 1979.

ROSENTHAL, U. *Rampen, rellen, gijzelingen; crisisbesluitvorming in Nederland*. Amsterdam: De Bataafsche Leeuw, 1984.

UYL, J.M. DEN. 'The Dutch Response' in B. Netanyahu (ed.), *International Terrorism: Challenge and Response*. New Brunswick, NJ: Transaction Books, 1981, pp.165–71.

SPAIN

ARANGO, E.R. 'Violence and terrorism' in E.R. Arango, *Spain: From Repression to Renewal*. Boulder, CO: Westview Press, 1985, pp.179–84.

BENEGAS, J.M. *Euskadi*. Barcelona: Argos Vergara, 1984. 218pp.

BRUNN, G. 'Nationalist violence and terror in the Spanish border provinces: ETA' in W.J. Mommsen and G. Hirschfeld (eds.), *Social Protest, Violence and Terror in Nineteenth and Twentieth Century Europe*. London: Macmillan, 1982, pp.112–36.

CLARK, R.P. 'Patterns in the lives of ETA members'. *Terrorism* 6/3 (1983), pp.423–54.

—— *The Basque Insurgents: ETA, 1952–1980*. Madison: University of Wisconsin Press, 1984. 328pp.

GARCIA DAMBORENEA, R. *La encrucijada vasca*. Barcelona: Argos Vergara, 1984. 250pp.

GURRIARAN, J.A. *La bomba*. Barcelona: Planeta, 1982. 310pp.

HAYES, R.E. and M.Y. SHIBUYA. *The impact of government behaviour on the frequency, type, and targets of terrorist group activity: the Spanish experience, 1968–1982*. McLean, VA: Defense Systems Inc., 1983. 123pp.

Le GAL ou le terrorisme d'état dans l'Europe des démocraties. Bern: CEDRI, 1989. 168pp.

MOXON-BROWNE, E. 'Spain and the ETA: the bid for Basque autonomy'. London: Institute for the Study of Conflicts, 1987. 17pp. *Conflict Studies* 201.

MUNOZ ALONSO, A. *El terrorismo en Espana*. Barcelona: Planeta/Madrid: Instituto de Estudios Economicos, 1982. 279pp.

ORRANTIA, M. *Euskadi, pacificacion?* Madrid: Ediciones Libertarias, 1980. 239pp.

PISANO, V.S. 'Spain faces the extremists: cannons to the left and cannons to the right'. *TVI Journal* 2 (July 1981), pp.10–16.

RIDDER, M.M. DE. 'Basque terrorism: evaluating governmental responses to ETA'. Paper presented to the 24th annual convention of the International Studies Association, Mexico City, 5–9 April 1983.

TREVINO, J.A. 'Spain's internal security: the Basque autonomous police force' in Alexander and K.A. Myers (eds.), *Terrorism in Europe*. London: Croom Helm, 1982, pp.141–53.

VISSER, C.J. *Spanje en de Baskische ETA: Terrorisme van dictatuur tot democratie*. The Hague: Staatsuitgeverij, 1982. 94pp.

WALDMANN, P. 'Die Bedeutung der ETA für Gesellschaft und Politik im spanischen Baskenland'. *Aus Politik und Zeitgeschichte* 45 (1988), pp.3–19.

FRANCE

BERTRAND, F. 'Le nouveau statut de la Corse'. *Regards sur l'actualité* 88 (1983), pp.47–56.

BIGO, D. and D. HERMANT. 'Simulation et dissimulation. Les politiques de luttes contre le terrorisme en France'. *Sociologie du Travail* 28/4 (1986), pp.506–26.

CASAMAYOR. *Et pour finir, le terrorisme*. Paris: Gallimard, 1983. 239pp.

CERNY, PH.G. 'France: non-terrorism and the politics of repressive tolerance' in J. Lodge (ed.), *Terrorism: A Challenge to the State*. Oxford: Martin Robertson, 1981, pp.91–118.

CHAUVIN, L. 'French diplomacy and the hostage crises', in B. Rubin (ed.), *The Politics of Counter-Terrorism: The Ordeal of Democratic States*. Washington, DC: The Johns Hopkins Foreign Policy Institute, 1990, pp.91–104.

CORNUT-GENTILLE, F. 'L'insécurité, les enquêtes' in *Opinion publique*. Paris: Gallimard, 1986, pp.121-29.

DRESSLER-HOLOGAN, W. 'Le statut particulier de la Corse à l'épreuve de la réalité insulaire'. *Les temps modernes* 41 (1985), no.463, pp.1479–1517.

GUENAIRE, M. 'Le régime juridique de la responsabilité administrative du fait des actes de violence. L'actualité juridique'. *Droit administratif* (1987), pp.227–49.

HAMON, A. *Action directe. Du terrorisme français à l'Euroterrorisme*. Paris: Seuil, 1986. 251pp.

JACQUARD, R. *Les dossiers secrets du terrorisme: tueurs sans frontières*. Paris: Albin Michel, 1985. 322pp.

—— *La longue traque d'Action directe*. Paris: Albin Michel, 1987. 235pp.

'LA MACHINE POLICIÈRE UNE FOIS LANCÉE . . .' Interview with George Moreas. *l'Autre journal* (June 1985), pp.15–20.

LEAUTE, J. 'Terrorist incidents and legislation in France' in R.D. Crelinsten, D. Laberge-Altmejd and D. Szabo (eds.), *Terrorism and Criminal Justice*. Lexington, MA: Lexington Books, 1978, pp.67–70.

'LES FRANÇAIS ET LE TERRORISME'. *Geopolitique* 14 (1986), pp.6–7 plus tables.

MORANGE, J. 'Le nouveau régime des contrôles d'identité'. *Revue française de droit administratif* 3 (1987), pp.85–8.

PEYREFITTE COMMISSION. *Résponses à la violence*. Paris: Presses-pocket, 1977. 2 vols.

PLENEL, E. 'La France et le terrorisme: la tentation du sanctuaire'. *Politique étrangère* 51 (1986), pp.919–36.

QUADRUPPANI, S. 'L'antiterrorisme en France ou la terreur integrée' 1981–1989'. Paris: La Découverte, 1989. 323pp.

TERRORISMES. Special issue. *Esprit* 94–95 (1986). 254pp.

WIEVIORKA, M. 'French politics and strategy on terrorism', in B. Rubin (ed.), *The Politics of Counter-Terrorism: The Ordeal of Democratic States*. Washington, DC: The Johns Hopkins Foreign Policy Institute, 1990, pp.61–90.

WEST GERMANY

ALTHAMMER, W. and B. ROMBACH. *Gegen den Terror: Texte-Dokumente*. Munich: Hanns Seidel-Stiftung, 1978. 213pp.

Anti-Terror Debatten im Parlament 1974–1978. Hamburg: 1978.

Anti-terrorist legislation in the Federal Republic of Germany. Washington, DC: Library of Congress Law Library, 1979. 143pp.

Auseinandersetzung mit dem Terrorismus, Mögligkeiten der politischen Bildungsarbeit. Bonn: Bundesministerium des Innern, 1981. 229pp.

BAKKER-SCHUT, P.H. *Deutschland, Deutschland. Staatschutz und Berufsverbote*. Tilburg: 1976, Hamburg: 1977.

—— *Stammheim: der Prozess gegen die Rote Armee Fraktion*. Kiel: Neuer Malik Verlag, 1986. 685pp.

BINDER, S. *Terrorismus: Herausforderung und Antwort*. Bonn: 1978.

BLANKENBURG, E. (ed.), *Politik der inneren Sicherheit*. Frankfurt a.M.: Suhrkamp, 1980. 239pp.

BLUM, J. 'The protection of persons and installations at risk: the German way'. *Police Studies 1*, (1978), pp.53–61.

CHLADEK, T. 'Le terrorisme en Allemagne fédérale'. *Politique étrangère* 51/4 (1986), pp.937–49.

COBLER, S. *Die Gefahr geht vom Menschen aus*. Der vorgelegte Staatsschutz. Berlin: 1976.

'CONTACT BAN BETWEEN PRISONERS AND THE OUTSIDE WORLD; INFORMATION ABOUT A LAW TO FIGHT TERRORISM' in M. Kravitz (ed.), *International Summaries: A Collection of Selected Translations to Law Enforcement and Criminal Justice*. Vol.3. Rockville, MD: National Criminal Justice Reference Service, 1979, pp.147–53.

CORVES, E. 'Terrorism and criminal justice operations in the FRG' in R.D. Crelinsten, D. Laberge-Altmejd and D. Szabo (eds.), *Terrorism and Criminal Justice: An International Perspective*. Lexington, MA: Lexington Books, 1978, pp.93–102.

DEUTSCHEN BEIRAT UND SEKRETARIAT DES 3. INTERNATIONALEN RUSSELL TRIBUNALS. *Zur Situation der Menschenrechte in der Bundesrepublik Deutschland*. Vol.4: *Einschränkung von Verteidigungsrechten*. Berlin: Rotbuch Verlag, 1979.

Dokumentation über Aktivitäten anarchistischer Gewalttäter in der Bundesrepublik Deutschland. Bonn: Bundesministerium des Innern, 1974.

Dokumentation zur Entführung von Hanns Martin Schleyer. Bonn: Bundesregierung, 1977.

EINSELE, H. and N. LOW-BEER. 'Political socialization and conditions of custody' in M. Kravitz (ed.), *International Summaries: A Collection of Selected Translations to Law*

Enforcement and Criminal Justice. Vol.3. Rockville, MD: National Criminal Justice Reference Service, 1979, pp.63–9.

ELLIOTT, J.D. *West Germany's Political Response to Contemporary Terrorism.* Gaithersburg, MD: International Association of Chiefs of Police, 1978.

FABRICIUS-BRAND, M. 'Women (terrorists) in isolation' in M. Kravitz (ed.), *International Summaries: A Collection of Selected Translations to Law Enforcement and Criminal Justice.* Vol.3. Rockville, MD: National Criminal Justice Reference Service, 1979, pp.55–62.

FETSCHER, I. 'Terrorism and reaction' in: M. Kravitz (ed.), *International Summaries: A Collection of Selected Translations to Law Enforcement and Criminal Justice.* Vol.3. Rockville, MD: National Criminal Justice Reference Service, 1979, pp.45–54.

—— and G. ROHRMOSER. *Analysen zum Terrorismus,* Vol.1: *Ideologien und Strategien.* Bonn: Westdeutscher Verlag, 1981.

GEMMER, K. 'Problems, means and methods of police action in the Federal Republic of Germany' in R.D. Crelinsten and D. Szabo (eds.), *Hostage Taking.* Lexington, MA: Lexington Books, 1979, pp.119–26.

GROENEWOLD, K. *The Charge of the Federal Prosecution against Kurt Groenewold as Defence Counsel of the Red Army Faction (RAF) Prisoners.* Hamburg: 1976.

—— *Angeklagt als Verteidiger.* Hamburg: Attica-Verlag, 1978. 212pp.

HORBATIUK, K.G. 'Anti-terrorism: the West German approach'. *Fordham International Law Forum* 3, 1980, pp.167–91.

HORCHEM, H.J. 'The German government response to terrorism' in Y. Alexander and R.A. Kilmarx (eds.), *Political Terrorism and Business.* New York: Praeger, 1979, pp.245–56.

—— 'Terrorism and government response: the German experience'. *Jerusalem Journal of International Relations* 4/3 (1980), pp.43–55.

—— 'Political terrorism: the German perspective' in A. Merari (ed.), *On Terrorism and Combating Terrorism.* Frederick, MD: University Publications of America, 1985, pp.63–8.

—— 'Fünfzehn Jahre Terrorismus in der Bundesrepublik Deutschlands'. *Aus Politik und Zeitgeschichte* 5 (1987), pp.3–15.

KLAUS, A. *Aktivitäten und Verhalten inhaftierter Terroristen.* Bonn: 1983.

KRAUS, D.M. 'Reform of criminal procedure law in the Federal Republic of Germany'. *Juridical Review* (Dec. 1979), pp.202–23.

KRIEGER, W. 'Worrying about West German democracy'. *Political Quarterly* 50 (1979), pp.192–204.

KRÜGER, M. and K. WAGENBACH. *Tintenfisch: Zehn Jahrbücher zur Deutschen Literatur von 1967–1976.* Berlin: 1981.

LOCHTE, C. 'Fighting terrorism in the Federal Republic of Germany' in B. Netanyahu (ed.), *Terrorism: How the West Can Win.* New York: Farrar, Strauss, Giroux, 1986, pp.171–4.

MOONS, E.J.H. 'The political and judicial approach to terrorism and anarchistic criminality in the Federal Republic of Germany' in M. Kravitz (ed.), *International Summaries: A Collection of Selected Translations to Law Enforcement and Criminal Justice.* Vol.3. Rockville, MD: National Criminal Justice Reference Service, 1979, pp.123–30.

OSTENDORF, H. *Das Recht zum Hungerstreik.* Frankfurt: Metzner, 1983. 289pp.

PRIDHAM, G. 'Terrorism and the state in West Germany during the 1970s: a threat to stability or a case of political overreaction?' in J. Lodge (ed.), *Terrorism: A Challenge to the State.* Oxford: Martin Robertson, 1981, pp.11–56.

RILL, B. and R. SCHOLZ (eds.). *Der Rechtsstaat und seine Feinde.* Heidelberg: Decker und Müller, 1986. 131pp.

RÜHMANN, F. *Anwaltsverfolgung 1970–1976.* Hamburg: 1977.

STUBERGER, U. (ed.). *In der Strafsache gegen Andreas Baader u.a. wegen Mordes. Dokumente aus dem Prozess.* Frankfurt a.M.: Syndikat, 1977. 280pp.

TOPHOVEN, R. *Politik durch Gewalt.* Bonn: Wehr- und Wissen-Verlagsgesellschaft, 1976. 173pp.

—— *GSG9: German Response to Terrorism*. Koblenz: Bernard und Graefe Verlag, 1984. 124pp.

WASSERMANN, R. (ed.). *Terrorism contra Rechtsstaat*. Neuwied: Luchterhand, 1976. 266pp.

WEISS, P. 'Joe McCarthy is alive and well and living in West Germany: terror and counter-terror in the Federal Republic'. *New York University Journal of International Law and Politics* 9 (1976), pp.61–88.

WITTKE, T. *Terrorismusbekämpfung als rationale Entscheidung*. Frankfurt: 1983.

WÖRDEMANN, F. *Terrorismus. Motive, Täter, Strategien*. Munich: Piper Verlag, 1976. 394pp.

Zur Zwangsernährung verpflichtet. Ein Ratgeber bei medizinischen und juristischen Fragen. Berlin: Ärtzegruppe Berlin, 1981.

ITALY

BERNARDI, A. 'Dissociazione e collaborazione nei delitti con finalita di terrorismo'. *Questione giustizia* (1982).

BERTONI, R. 'La legge sui 'pentiti'. Una prima valutazione d'insieme'. *Giustizia Penale* 2 (1982).

BRICOLA, F. 'Politicia criminale e politica dell'ordine pubblico (a proposita della 1. 22 maggio 1975, no.152'. *La questione criminale* 1975.

CASELLI, G.C. 'La questione dei petiti'. *Quaderni della giustizia* 4 (1981).

—— and A. PERDUCA. 'Terrorismo e reati associativi. Problemi e soluzione giurisprudenziali'. *Giurisprudenza Italiana* 4 (1982).

—— and D. DELLA PORTA. 'La storia della Brigate rosse. Strutture organizzative e strategie d'azione' in D. della Porta (ed.), *Terrorismi in Italia*. Bologna: Il Mulino, 1984.

CHELAZZI, G. *La dissociazione dal terrorismo*. Milan: Giuffre, 1981. 154pp.

CHIAVARIO, M. 'Un anno di fermo di polizia nella relazione del Ministro dell'Interno'. *La legislazione penale* 1981.

CROCE, D. 'La legge sui pentiti'. *Quaderni della giustizia* 8 (1982).

DE LUTIIS, G. *Moventi e motivazioni della dissociazione*. Working paper. Bologna: Instituto Cattaneo, 1988. 313pp.

—— *Storia dei servizi segreti*. Rome: Editori Riuniti, 1984.

DE RUGGIERO, L. 'I problemi posti dai processi di terrorismo' in Magistratura democratica (ed.), *La magistratura di fronte al terrorismo e all'eversione di sinistra*. Milan: F.Angeli, 1982.

DELLA PORTA, D. 'Recruitment processes in clandestine political organizations. Italian leftwing terrorism' in S. Tarrow, B. Klandermans and H. Kriesi (eds.), *From Structure to Action*. New York: Jay Press, 1988.

—— and M. ROSSI. *Cifre crudeli. Bilancio dei terrorismi italiani*. Bologna: Instituto Cattaneo, 1984.

—— 'Il Terrorismi in Italia tra il 1969 e il 1982' in G. Pasquino (ed.), *Il sistema politico italiano*. Bari: La Terza, 1985, pp.418–56.

—— and G. Pasquino. 'Interpretations on Italian leftwing terrorism in P.H. Merkl (ed.), *Political Violence and Terrorism. Motifs and Motivations*. Berkeley, CA: University of California Press, 1986, p.169–90.

FERRAJOLI, L. '1977: Ordine pubblico e legislazione eccezionale'. *La questione criminale* (1977).

—— 'Il caso "7 aprile". Lineamenti di un processo inquisitorio'. *Dei delitti e delle pene* 1 (1983).

FLAMIGNI, S. *La tela di ragno. Il delitto Moro*. Rome: Edizione associate, 1988.

FURLONG, P. 'Political terrorism in Italy: responses, reactions and immobilism' in J. Lodge (ed.), *Terrorism: A Challenge to the State*. Oxford: Martin Robertson, 1981.

GALLI, G. *Storia del partito armato*. Milan: Rizzoli, 1986.

GIAMBRUNO, S. 'Considerazione sulle ultime misure urgenti per la tutela dell'ordine democratico e dellea sicurezza pubblica'. *Giustizia penale* 1 (1980).

GREVI, V. 'La procedura speciale per i reati commessi in servizio dagli appartenenti alla polizia. Un privilegio non conforme al principio d'eguaglianza'. *Giurisprudenza costituzionale* 1 (1976).
—— 'Sistema penale e leggi dell'emergenza: la risposta legislativa al terrorismo' in G. Pasquino (ed.), *La prova delle armi*. Bologna: Il Mulino, 1984.
HAYES, R.E. and R.S. SCHILLER. *The Impact of Government Behaviour on the Frequency, Type and Targets of Terrorist Group Activity: The Italian Experience, 1968–1982*. Maclean, VA: Defense Systems Inc., 1983. 142pp.
MAGISTRATURA DEMOCRATICA. Osservazioni sul decreto legge 15 dicembre 1979 n.625 concernente misure urgenti per la tutela dell'ordine democratico e della sicurezza pubblica. *Foro italiano* 5 (1980).
—— 'Osservazioni sul disegno di legge approvato al Senato concernente misure per la difesa dell'ordine costituzionale'. *Questione giustizia* (1982).
MARCHESE, S. *I collegamenti internazionali del terrorismo italiano – dagli atti giudiziari*. Rome: Japadre, 1989. 250pp.
MOSCONI, G. 'Lo sterotipo del terrorista pentito. Natura e funzione in relazione al decorso legislativo'. *Critica del diritto* 25–26 (1982).
ONORATO, P. 'Processi di terrorismo e inquinamento della giurisdizione' in Magistratura democratica (ed.), *La magistratura di fronte al terrorismo e all'eversione di sinistra*. Milan: F.Angeli, 1982.
PALOMBARINI, G. *7 aprile: Il processo e la storia*. Venice: Arsenale, 1982.
PASQUINO, G. *I soliti ignoti: Gli opposti estremismi nelle analisi dei presidenti del consiglio*. Working paper. Bologna: Instituto Cattaneo, 1988.
PISANO, V.S. 'Terrorism and security: the Italian experience' in US Senate, Committee on the Judiciary, Report of the Subcommittee on Terrorism and Security'. 98th congress, 2nd sess. Washington, DC: GPO, 1984. 94pp.
PULITANO, D. 'Misure antiterrorismo. Un primo bilancio'. *Democrazia e diritto* 1–2 (1981).
RODOTA, S. 'La risposta dello stato al terrorismo: gli apparati' in G. Pasquino (ed.), *La prova delle armi*. Bologna: Il Mulino, 1984.
SALVINI, G. *La legge sui terroristi pentiti. Un primo bilancio*. Milan: Unicopli, 1983. 64pp.
—— 'Riflessioni sella gestione dei processi per reati di terrorismo e sulle nuovi disposizioni in tema di dissociazione dalla lotta armata. *Giustizia penale* 3 (1982).
SCARPARI, G. 'La vicenda del "7 aprile"'. *Questione giustizia* 3 (1982).
—— 'Processo a mezzo stampa: il "7 aprile"'. *Quale giustizia* 51 (1979).
VIOLANTE, L. 'Politica della sicurezza, relazioni internationali e terrorismo' in G. Pasquino (ed.), *La prova delle armi*. Bologna: Il Mulino, 1984.

UNITED KINGDOM

ADAMS J. *The Financing of Terror*. Sevenoaks: New English Library, 1986. 293pp.
—— *Secret Armies: The Full Story of SAS, Delta Force and Spetsnaz*. London: Hutchinson, 1987. 440pp.
—— R. MORGAN and A. BAMBRIDGE. *Ambush: the War between the SAS and the IRA*. London: Pan Books, 1988.
ALEXANDER, Y. and A. O'DAY (eds.). *Terrorism in Ireland*. London: Croom Helm, 1984. 277pp.
——, —— *Ireland's Terrorist Dilemma*. Dordrecht: Martinus Nijhoff, 1986. 279pp.
BISHOP, P and E. MALLIE. *The Provisional IRA*. London: Corgi Books, 1988. 374pp.
BONNER, D. 'Combating terrorism in Great Britain: the role of exclusion orders'. *Public Law* (1984), pp.262–81.
—— *Emergency Powers in Peacetime*. London: Sweet & Maxwell, 1985. 295pp.
—— 'Combating terrorism: supergrass trials in Northern Ireland'. *Modern Law Review* 51 (1987), pp.23–53.
—— 'Combating terrorism in the 1990s: the role of the Prevention of Terrorism (Temporary Provisions) Act 1989'. *Public Law* (Autumn 1989).

BOYLE, K., T. HADDEN and P. HILLYARD. *Law and State: The Case of Northern Ireland*. London: Martin Robertson, 1975. 194pp.
——, ——, —— *Ten Years in Northern Ireland: The Legal Control of Political Violence*. London: Cobden Trust, 1980. 119pp.
BOYLE, K. and T. HADDEN. *Ireland: A Positive Proposal*. Harmondsworth: Penguin, 1985. 126pp.
CARLTON, CH. 'Judging without consensus: the Diplock courts in Northern Ireland'. *Law and Police Quarterly* 3 (1981), pp.225–42.
CARROLL, T.G. 'Regulating conflicts: the case of Ulster'. *Political Quarterly* 51 (1980), pp.451–63.
CLUTTERBUCK, R.L. *Britain in Agony: The Growth of Political Violence*. Rev. ed. Harmondsworth: Penguin, 1980. 368pp.
COOGAN, T.P. *The IRA*. 6th rev., impr. and exp. ed. London: Fontana, 1980. 620pp.
EVELEGH, R. *Peacekeeping in a Democratic Society*. London: C. Hurst, 1978.
FLACKES, W.D. and S. ELLIOTT. *Northern Ireland: A Political Directory 1968–1988*. Belfast: Blackstaff Press, 1989.
FOLEY, T.P. 'Public security and individual freedom: the dilemma of Northern Ireland'. *Yale Journal of World Public Order* 8 (1982), pp.284–324.
GARRETT, J.B. 'Ten years of British troops in Northern Ireland'. *International Security* 4 (1979–80), pp.80–104.
GIFFORD, T. *Supergrasses: The Use of Accomplice Evidence in Northern Ireland*. London: Cobden Trust, 1984.
GREER, D.S. 'The admissibility of confessions under the Northern Ireland (Emergency Provisions) Act'. *Northern Ireland Legal Quarterly* 31 (1980), pp.205–38.
GREER, S.C. Military intervention in civil disturbances: the legal basis reconsidered. *Public Law* (1983), pp.573ff.
—— 'Supergrasses and the legal system in Britain and Northern Ireland'. *Law Quarterly Review* 102 (1986), pp.198–249.
—— and A. WHITE. *Abolishing the Diplock Courts: The Case for Restoring Jury Trial to Scheduled Offences in Northern Ireland*. London: Cobden Trust, 1986. 136pp.
HAMILL, D. *Pig in the Middle: The Army in Northern Ireland 1969–1985*. London: Methuen, 1985. 308pp.
HILLYARD, P. and PERCY-SMITH. 'Converting terrorists: the use of supergrasses in Northern Ireland'. *Journal of Law and Society* 11, 1984, pp.335ff.
HOGAN, G. and C. WALKER. *Political Violence and the Law in Northern Ireland*. New York: St Martin's Press, 1989. 342pp.
JACKSON, J. 'The Northern Ireland (Emergency Provisions) Act 1987'. *Northern Ireland Legal Quarterly* 39 (1988).
KELLEY, K.J. *The Longest War: Northern Ireland and the IRA*. London: ZED Books Ltd., 1988. 395pp.
LEE, A.M. *Terrorism in Northern Ireland*. New York: General Hall, 1983. 253pp.
McGUFFIN, J. *Internment*. Tralee: Anvil Books, 1973. 228pp.
MURRAY, R. 'Killings of local security forces in Northern Ireland'. *Terrorism* 7/1 (Jan.–Feb. 1984), pp.11–52.
NELSON, S. *Ulster's Uncertain Defenders*. Belfast: Appletree Press, 1984. 219pp.
O'MALLEY, P. *The Uncivil Wars: Ireland Today*. Belfast: Blackstaff Press, 1983. 481pp.
PATRICK, D. *Fetch Felix: The Fight Against the Ulster Bombers, 1976–1977*. London: Hamish Hamilton, 1981. 184pp.
RYDER, C. *The RUC: A Force under Fire*. London: Methuen, 1989.
SAMUELS, A. 'The legal response to terrorism: the Prevention of Terrorism (Temporary Provisions) Act 1984'. *Public Law* (1984), pp.365ff.
SCORER, C. *The Prevention of Terrorism Acts 1974 and 1976: A Report on the Operation of the Law*. London: National Council for Civil Liberties, 1976. 39pp.
——, S. SPENCER and P. HEWITT. *The New Prevention of Terrorism Act: The Case for Repeal*. 3rd upd. and exp. ed. London: National Council for Civil Liberties, 1985. 82pp.
SMITH, W.B. 'Terrorism: The Lessons of Northern Ireland'. *Journal of Contemporary*

Studies 5, 1982, pp.29–50.

SPILLANE, J.M. Terrorists and special status: the British experience in Northern Ireland. *Hastings International and Comparative Law Report* 9 (1986), pp.481–515.

STALKER, J. *Stalker*. London: Harrap, 1988. 288pp.

TAYLOR, P. *Beating the Terrorists? Interrogation in Omagh, Gough and Castlereagh*. Harmondsworth: Penguin Books, 1980. 347pp.

TOWNSHEND, C. *Political Violence in Ireland: Government and Resistance since 1848*. Oxford: Clarendon Press, 1983. 445pp.

WALKER, C. 'The Prevention of Terrorism (Temporary Provisions) Act 1984'. *Modern Law Review* 47 (1984), pp.704–13.

—— *The Prevention of Terrorism in British Law*. Manchester: Manchester University Press, 1986. 272pp.

WALSH, D.P.J. 'Arrest and interrogation: Northern Ireland 1981'. *British Journal of Law and Society* 9 (1982).

—— *The Use and Abuse of Emergency Legislation in Northern Ireland*. London: Cobden Trust, 1983. 138pp.

WILKINSON, P. (ed.). *British Perspectives on Terrorism*. London: Macmillan, 1986.

WOLF, J.B. *Provos versus the Crown: A Review of Terrorist and Anti-Terrorist Operations in Northern Ireland*. Gaithersburg, MD: International Association of Chiefs of Police, 1982.

—— 'British antiterrorist policy in Northern Ireland: legal aspects'. *Police Chief* (April 1983), pp.36–40.

AUSTRIA

BENDA, R. and I. GABRIEL. *Terror rot/weiß/rot. Politische Kriminalität in Österreich*. Zürich: PressDok/Vienna: Morawa, 1989.

BERTL, B. 'Österreich – Kein hausgemachter Terrorismus'. *Öffentliche Sicherheit* 9 (1989), pp.3–4.

Die Vorfälle vom 21. und 22. Dezember 1975 (Überfall auf die Teilnehmer der OPEC-Konferenz). Vienna: Bundeskanzleramt, 1976.

KÖBERL, I. 'Terrorismus als psychologisches Problem' in H. Neisser and F. Windhager (eds.), *Wie sicher ist Österreich?* Vienna: Österreichische Verlagsanstalt, 1982, pp.105–13.

Landesverteidigungsplan. Vienna: Bundeskanzleramt, 1985.

NEUHOLD, H. 'Internationale Entwicklungen bis zur Jahrtausendwende aus der Sicht einesee Teils der "außenpolitischen Elite" in Österreich'. *Österreichische Zeitschrift für Außenpolitik* 20/3 (1980), pp.208–11.

—— and H. VETSCHERA. *Austria's Security Policy*. Geneva: UNIDIR, 1984.

PALMER, E. 'The Austrian law on extradition and mutual assistance in criminal matters'. 1983.

Sicherheitsbericht. Vienna: Bundesministerium für Inneres, annual report.

SZIRBA, R. 'Staatspolizei – Institution, Aufgaben, Kompetenzen, Befugnisse'. *Zeitschrift für Verwaltung* 5 (1989), pp.464–68.

EUROPEAN AND WESTERN RESPONSES

ALEXANDER, Y. and K. MYERS (eds.). *Terrorism in Europe*. New York: St Martin's Press, 1982. 216pp.

—— and A. NANES (eds.). *Legislative Responses to Terrorism*. The Hague: Martinus Nijhoff, 1986. 327pp.

AMARAL NUNEZ, J.L.DO and L.J. SMITH. *Interim-report of the sub-committee on terrorism*. Brussels: North Atlantic Assembly/Political Committee, 1987. 32pp.

ASTON, C.C. *International Law and Political Terrorism*. Westport, CT: Greenwood Press, 1982.

BELL, J.B. *A Time of Terror: How Democratic Societies Respond to Revolutionary*

Violence. New York: Basic Books, 1978. 292pp.

BIGGS-DAVISON, J. 'Terrorism and the superpowers' in *RUSI and Brassey's Defence Yearbook 1987*, pp.205–16.

BREMER III, L.P. 'International terrorisme vergt internationale bestrijding'. *Atlantisch Perspectief* 1 (1987), pp.24–7.

BUSH, G. 'Prelude to retaliation: building a governmental consensus on terrorism'. SAIS (School Advanced International Studies) Report 7 (1986), pp.1–9.

BUSUTTIL, J.J. 'The Bonn declaration on international terrorism: a non-binding international agreement on aircraft hijacking'. *International and Comparative Law Quarterly* 31/3 (1982), pp.474–87.

CHLADEK, T. 'Die westlichen Demokratien im Kampf gegen den internationalen Terrorismus'. *Europa Archiv* 42/20 (1987), pp.577–86.

CLUTTERBUCK, R.L. 'Terrorism and the security forces in Europe'. *Army Quarterly* 111 (Jan. 1981), pp.12–29.

———— *Living with Terrorism.* London: Faber & Faber, 1975. 160pp.

———— *Kidnap, Hijack and Extortion: The Response.* New York: St Martin's Press, 1987. 228pp.

COLE, R.B. *Executive Security: A Corporate Study to Effective Response to Abduction and Terrorism.* New York: John Wiley and Sons, 1980.

CRELINSTEN, R.D. 'Terrorism as political communication: the relationship between the controller and the controlled', in P. Wilkinson and A.M. Stewart (eds.), *Contemporary Research on Terrorism.* Aberdeen: University of Aberdeen Press, 1987, pp.3–23.

———— Terrorism, Counter-terrorism and Democracy: The Assessment of National Security Threats. *Terrorism and Political Violence* 1/2 (April 1989), pp.242–69.

———— and D. SZABO (eds.). *Hostage-Taking.* Lexington, MA: Lexington Books, 1979.

———— D. LABERGE-ALTMEJD and D. SZABO (eds.). Terrorism and Criminal Justice. Lexington, MA: Lexington Books, 1978.

CRENSHAW, M. 'Introduction: reflections on the effects of terrorism' in M. Crenshaw (ed.), *Terrorism, Legitimacy and Power.* Middletown, CT: Wesleyan University Press, 1982.

DOBSON, C. and R. PAYNE. *Counterattack: The West's Battle Against the Terrorists.* New York: Facts on File, 1982. 198pp.

FALVEY, A. 'Legislative responses to international terrorism: international and national efforts to deter and punish terrorists'. *Boston College International and Comparative Law Review* 9 (1986), pp.323–59.

FIJNAUT, C. 'De politiëlle bestrijding van politiek terrorisme in westelijk Europa'. *Nieuw Europa* 12/2 (1986), pp.48–53.

FREEDMAN, L. *et al. Terrorism and International Order.* London: Routledge and Keegan Paul, 1986. 107pp.

FRIEDLANDER, R.A. 'Seeking legal remedies; domestic and international'. *International Society of Barristers Quarterly* 17/2 (1982), pp.296–306.

GAL-OR, N. *International Cooperation to Suppress Terrorism.* New York: St Martin's Press/London: Croom Helm, 1985. 390pp.

GILBERT, G.S. 'Terrorism and the political offence exemption reappraised'. *International and Comparative Law Quarterly* 34/4 (1985), pp.695–723.

GOLDIE, L.F.E. 'Combating international terrorism: the United Nations developments'. *Naval War College Review* 31/3 (Summer 1979), pp.49–60.

GREEN, L.C. 'Terrorism and its responses'. *Terrorism* 8/1 (Jan.–Feb. 1985), pp.33–78.

GREGORY, F. 'Policing the democratic state: how much force?' London: Centre for Security and Conflict Studies, 1986. 25pp. *Conflict Studies* 194.

HEWITT, C. *The Effectiveness of Anti-terrorist Policies.* Lanham, MD: University Press of America, 1984. 122pp.

HORCHEM, H.J. 'Terror in Europa: Akteure und Hintergrunde-Gengenstrategien'. *Beiträge zur Konfliktforschung* 16/4 (1986), pp.31–54.

HUBBARD, D.G. *Winning Back the Sky: A Tactical Analysis of Terrorism.* San Francisco: Saybrook Publishing, 1986. 140pp.

HURWITZ, L. (ed.). *The Harmonization of European Public Policy: Regional Responses to Transnational Challenges*. Westport, CT: Greenwood Press, 1983. 264pp.

International terrorisme: oorzaken, bestrijding. Special issue. *Jason* 11/4 (1986). 24pp.

JANKE, P. (ed.). *Terrorism and Democracy: Some Contemporary Cases*. Houndsmills, Basingstoke: Macmillan, 1992.

JENKINS, B.M. 'International terrorism: a new challenge for the United Nations' in *The United Nations and the Maintenance of International Peace and Security*, 1987, pp.407–21.

KALDOR, M. and P. ANDERSON (eds.). *Mad Dogs: The US Raids on Libya*. London: Pluto Press, 1986. 172pp.

KEIJZER, N. *Het Europees verdrag tot bestrijding van terrorisme*. Deventer: Kluwer, 1979. 36pp.

KERR, D.M. 'Coping with terrorism'. *Terrorism* 8/2 (March–April 1985), pp.113–26.

KITSON, F. *Low Intensity Operations: Subversion, Insurgency, Peace-keeping*. Hamden, CT: Archon Books, 1974. 208pp.

LAQUEUR, W. 'Reflections on terrorism'. *Foreign Affairs* 65/1 (Winter 1986), pp.86–100.

—— *The Age of Terrorism*. London: Weidenfeld & Nicholson, 1987. 385pp.

—— 'Terrorism reconsidered'. *NATO's Sixteen Nations* 32/7 (Dec. 1987), pp.33–4.

LEVENTHAL, P. and Y. ALEXANDER (eds.). *Preventing Nuclear Terrorism: the Report and Papers of the International Task Force on Prevention of Nuclear Terrorism*. Lexington, MA: Lexington Books, 1987. 472pp.

LEVITT, G.M. *The Western Response to State-Sponsored Terrorism*. New York: Praeger, 1988.

LIVINGSTONE, N.C. *The War against Terrorism*. Lexington, MA: D.C. Heath, 1982. 291pp.

—— and T.E. ARNOLD (eds.). *Fighting Back: Winning the War Against Terrorism*. Lexington, MA: Lexington Books, 1986. 268pp.

LODGE, J. (ed.). *Terrorism: A Challenge to the State*. New York: St Martin's Press, 1981, 247pp.

—— *The Threat of Terrorism*. Boulder, CO: Westview Press, 1987. 280pp.

LYNCH, E.A. 'International terrorism: the search for a policy'. *Terrorism* 9/1 (Jan.–Feb. 1986), pp.1–85.

MERARI, A. (ed.). *On Terrorism and Combating Terrorism*. Westport, CT: Greenwood Press, 1985. 188pp.

MILLER, R. 'Acts of international terrorism: governments' responses and policies. *Comparative Political Studies* 19 (1986), pp.385-414.

MOORE, J.N. 'Global order, low intensity conflict and a strategy of deterrence. *Naval War College Review* 39/1 (Jan.–Feb. 1986), pp.30–46.

MORRIS, E. and A. HOE. *Terrorism: Threat and Response*. New York: St Martin's Press, 1987. 210pp.

MURPHY, J.F. *Punishing International Terrorists: The Legal Framework for Policy Initiatives*. Totowa, NJ: Rowman and Allanheld, 1985. 142pp.

NETANYAHU, B. (ed.). *Terrorism: How the West Can Win*. New York: Farrar, Strauss, Giroux, 1986. 254pp.

O'BRIEN, C. Valt terrorisme te bestrijden. *Intermediair* 22/39 (1986), pp.13–17.

RIVERS, G. *The War Against the Terrorists: How to Win It.*. New York: Stein & Day, 1986. 250pp.

ROSENTHAL, B.R. 'Countering International Terrorism: Building A Consensus'. *Whittier Law Review* 8 (1986), pp.747–62.

RUBIN, B. (ed.) *The Politics of Counter-Terrorism: The Ordeal of Democratic States*. Washington, DC: The Johns Hopkins Foreign Policy Institute, 1990.

RUMPF, H. 'Völkerrechtliche Probleme des Terrorismus'. *Aussenpolitik* 36/4, pp.383–88.

SCHMID, A.P. 'Force or Conciliation. An overview of some problems associated with current anti-terrorist response strategies'. *International Forum* 12/2 (1988), pp.149–78.

—— A.J. JONGMAN *et al*. *Political Terrorism: A New Guide to Actors, Authors, Concepts, Data Bases, Theories and Literature*. Amsterdam: North-Holland Publishing Company, 1988. 700pp.

SCHULTZ, R.H. and S. SLOAN (eds.), *Responding to the Terrorist Threat: Security and Crisis Management*. New York: Pergamon, 1980, 261pp.

SMITH, G.D. *Combating Terrorism*. London: Routledge, 1990.

SOFAER, A.D. 'Fighting terrorism through law'. *US Department of State Bulletin* 85, 1985, pp.38–42.

—— 'Terrorism and the law'. *Foreign Affairs* 64/5 (Winter 1986), pp.901–22.

STOHL, M. (ed.). *The Politics of Terrorism*. 3rd rev. and exp. ed. New York: Marcel Dekker, 1988. 622pp.

SUTER, K. *An International Law of Guerrilla Warfare: The Global Politics of Lawmaking*. London: Pinter, 1984. 192pp.

TUCKER, H. (ed.). *Combating the Terrorists: Democratic Responses to Political Violence*. New York: Facts on File, 1988. 210pp.

TURNER, S. *Terrorism and Democracy*. Boston: Houghton Mifflin, 1991.

VERINE, S. 'La coopération internationale en matière de lutte contre le terrorisme'. *Political étrangère* 51/4 (Winter 1986), pp.977–84.

WALLACK, M. 'Terrorism and "compellance"'. *International Perspectives* (Nov.–Dec. 1987), pp.201–9.

WARBRICK, C. 'The European convention on human rights and the prevention of terrorism'. *International and Comparative Law Quarterly* 32 (1983), pp.82–119.

WARDLAW, G. 'State response to international terrorism: some cautionary comments' in R.O. Slater and M. Stohl (eds.), *Current Perspectives on International Terrorism*. London: Macmillan, 1987.

—— *Political Terrorism: Theory, Tactics & Countermeasures*. Cambridge, NY: Cambridge University Press, 1989.

WAUGH, W.L., Jr. *International Terrorism: How Nations Respond to Terrorists; A comparative Policy Analysis*. Salisbury, NC: Documentary Publications, 1982. 326pp.

WILKINSON, P. 'Proposals for government and international responses to terrorism'. *Terrorism* 5/1–2 (Jan.–April 1981), pp.161–93.

—— *Terrorism and the Liberal State*. 2nd ed. London: Macmillan, 1986.

—— 'State-sponsored international terrorism: the problems of response'. *The World Today* 40/7 (July 1984), pp.292–8.

WINDSOR, PH. 'Terrorism and international order'. *Atlantic Community Quarterly* 25/2 (1987), pp.201–9.

YARDLEY, M. 'MACE: a multi-national approach to countering terrorism'. *International Defense Review* 19/11 (Nov. 1986), pp.1621–5.

Notes on Contributors

Alex P. Schmid received his academic training as an historian at the University of Zurich, Switzerland. He is an Associate Professor of International Relations, Department of Political Science, Leiden University, The Netherlands, and a Senior Research Fellow at the Center for the Study of Social Conflicts. His published work includes *Violence as Communication, Soviet Military Interventions since 1945, Political Terrorism: A New Guide to Actors, Authors, Concepts, Data Bases, Theories, and Literature*. He is research director of the PIOOM Foundation, an interdisciplinary research organization analyzing the root causes of gross violations of human rights.

Ronald D. Crelinsten is Associate Professor of Criminology at the University of Ottawa in Canada. His published work includes *Terrorism and Criminal Justice* (Lexington, MA: Lexington Books, 1978) and *Hostage-Taking* (Lexington, MA: Lexington Books, 1979), plus articles and chapters on terrorism and counter-terrorism, images of terrorism in the media, and policy issues pertaining to media coverage of terrorism. He is a founding editorial board member of the quarterly journal *Terrorism and Political Violence* (London: Frank Cass) and is currently a Research Fellow with the PIOOM Foundation at Leiden University, where he is principal researcher on a project studying the career paths of torturers.

Albert J. Jongman majored in sociology at the University of Groningen in 1981. Before that, he worked as a research assistant at the Stockholm International Peace Research Institute (SIPRI). After being attached to the Polemological Institute of the University of Groningen, where he began preparing his doctoral dissertation on a quantitative study of war, armed conflict and political violence since 1980, he continued his scientific work as Research Associate at the Center for the Study of Social Conflict of Leiden University. At this institute he is involved in a project on the monitoring of human rights violations for the PIOOM Foundation. His research interests are in political violence, armament and disarmament issues and human rights. His 'World Directory of Terrorist and Other Organizations Associated with Guerrilla Warfare, Political Violence and Protest' was included in *Political Terrorism* 2nd edition (Amsterdam: North Holland Publishing, 1988) edited by Alex P. Schmid.

Fernando Jiménez is an international lawyer who received his degrees from the Universities of Valencia, Birmingham and the City College of London. He is a recognized expert in the area of terrorism and system vulnerabilities mitigation. He was appointed to the Council of Ministers for different assignments with the rank of General Director and Secretary of State. From 1966–70 he served in the Special Commission under Technical Assistance Service of the United Nations in Europe. Between 1977 and 1982 he was consecutively Governor of Salamanca, Asturias, Bizcaya and Alava, provinces of the Basque country where he was responsible for commanding strategies against terrorist groups. In 1977–79 Dr Jiménez participated in many conferences on Terrorism and NATO Defense Systems. Presently he is stationed in Washington, DC.

Gilbert Guillaume was born in Bois-Colombes, France on 4 December 1930. Since 1958 he has been a member of the *Conseil d'Etat*. From 1968 to 1979 he was legal adviser for the *Direction générale de l'aviation civile française*. In 1979 he was director of legal affairs for the Organization for Economic Co-operation and Development and, from 1979–87 served as director of legal affairs for the French Ministry of Foreign Affairs. Since 1987 he has been a Judge on the International Court of Justice. He is also President of the French Branch of the International Law Association (ILA), a member of the permanent Court of Arbitration and designated arbiter for the International Centre for Settlement of Investment Disputes, the International Civil Aviation Organization (UN) and the International Chamber of Commerce.

Kurt Groenewold is a lawyer in Hamburg. He also lectures at the Department of Political Science of Hamburg University and publishes regularly. He is founder and co-editor of the journal *'Strafverteidiger'* and is a partner in the publishing house Europäische Verlagsanstalt. In the 1960s he defended students of the anti-Vietnam war movement. In the 1970s he was the legal defender of several members of the Red Army Faction, including Andreas Baader and Ulrike Meinhof. In the Stammheim trials he was excluded from the defence and a preliminary decree was issued prohibiting him from practising law. In 1979 this decree was revoked. He has also been a lawyer for the defence in other 'political' trials. He participated in a group of observers monitoring the trials in Athens during the Greek Colonels' regime. He also represents writers and is president of the Erich Fried Association in Vienna.

Donatella della Porta, sociologist, received her Ph.D. at the European University Institute. She was a 1992 Awardee of the H.F. Guggenheim Foundation at the Wissenschaftszentrum Berlin für Sozialforschung where she was involved in a comparative research project on terrorism in Italy and in West Germany. Her research fields include social movements, political violence, political corruption and the police. Among her publications on terrorism are *Terrorismo e violenza politica. Tre casi a confronto* (Bologna, 1983, co-editor); *Terrorismi in Italia* (Bologna, 1984, editor); *Cifre crudeli. Bilancio dei terrorismi italiani* (Bologna, 1984, co-author); *Il terrorismo di sinistra* (Bologna, 1990, author); and *Social Movements and Violence: Participation in Underground Organizations* (Greenwich, CO, 1992, editor).

David Bonner studied law at Leicester University (UK) and at Queen's University, Kingston, Ontario. He is a Senior Lecturer at Leicester University where he teaches on civil liberties and human rights, anti-terrorist powers, immigration law, social security law and welfare law. His principal publications are: *Emergency Powers in Peacetime* (London: Sweet & Maxwell, 1985); *No Means Tested Benefits: The Legislation* (London: Sweet & Maxwell, 1985, 7th ed. 1992); *Combating Terrorism: Supergrass Trials in Northern Ireland* (1988); *Combating Terrorism in the 1990s: The Role of the Prevention of Terrorism (Temporary Provisions) Act* (1989).

Albert A. Stahel studied economics and political science at the University of Zürich, Switzerland, strategic studies at the University of Lancaster and the University of London. He has been teaching at several Swiss universities on aspects related to national security. He has authored several books, including *Terrorism and Marxism* (1987, in German).

Dr **Heinz Vetschera** is a Lieutenant Colonel in the legal branch of the Austrian Federal Army/militia. He studied law and criminology (1967–71) and political science and international relations (1972–74) at Vienna University. He was a Research Fellow at the International Institute for Strategic Studies (IISS) in 1980–81 and at the Institute for East-West Security Studies (IEWSS) in New York in 1983–84. From 1972 to 1989 he was with the Institute for Strategic Research at the National Defence Academy in Vienna. Since 1989 he has been with the legal and presidial section of the Federal Ministry of Defence in Vienna and is a lecturer on security policy at the National Defence Academy, the Institute for Political Science at Vienna University and the NATO Defense College in Rome. He is a Member of the

Academic Advisory Board of the Austrian Institute for International Affairs.

Frits Korthals Altes was Minister of Justice in two Dutch cabinets (1982–89). In this capacity he wrote the article for this volume. Mr Korthals Altes received his law degree from Leiden University in 1957. Before he became a Minister he had been practising law in Rotterdam since 1958. From 1975 until 1981 he was chairman of the Liberal Party (VVD), having been secretary of this party since 1963. After having served in the government he joined the Rotterdam office of the law firm, Nauta Dutilh, in 1990. He is also a member of the First Chamber (Senate) of the Dutch Parliament.

Meliton Cardona is a lawyer by training. He is also a graduate of International Studies from the Diplomatic School in Madrid. He subsequently joined the Diplomatic Corps. He has served in various capacities representing his government in Maputo, Nouakchot, Agadir and Frankfurt. His present rank is Consul-General of Spain in Düsseldorf, Germany.

Ambassador **L. Paul Bremer, III** graduated from Yale University, *Institut d'Etudes Politiques* in Paris and Harvard Graduate School of Business. He entered the Foreign Service in 1966 and as a junior officer was first assigned to the US Embassy in Kabul, Afghanistan. In 1968–71 he served as economic/political officer in Blantyre, Malawi. In 1971 he returned to the Department where he served as special and executive assistant to the Secretary of State until 1976. He was Chargé d'Affaires at the American Embassy in Norway the next three years and served as Executive Secretary of the Department of State in the Reagan administration. From 1983–86 he was US Ambassador to the Netherlands and from 1986–89 was Ambassador at large for Counterterrorism. In June 1989 he joined Kissinger Associates.

Richard Clutterbuck was a non-executive director of Control Risks Ltd. from 1977–87. He was in the British Army for 35 years, retiring as a Major-General in 1972, and he was then Senior Lecturer and Reader in Political Conflict at the University of Exeter until 1983. He has a Cambridge MA in Mechanical Sciences and a London Ph.D. in Politics. He now travels widely as a consultant in security and political risks and lectures mainly to police and business audiences. He has given over 300 broadcasts and written about 100 articles and 15 books, including *The Media and Political Violence* (1983), *Kidnap, Hijack and Extortion*

(1987), *Terrorism and Guerrilla Warfare* (1980) and *Terrorism, Drugs and Crime in Europe after 1992* (1990). There have been 10 translations of his books, into French, German, Japanese, Portuguese and Spanish.

M.P.M. Zagari was born in Milan, Italy, and is a journalist, an economist and a politician. During the Second World War he helped reorganize the Socialist Party of Proletarian Unity, where he served as a member of the Executive Committee. After the party split, he became a member of the Executive Committee of the Social Democratic Party and worked for unification of the actual PSI. He was elected to the Constituent Assembly as a member of the Chamber of Deputies. He also attended the first European Parliament at Strasbourg. He was elected to the Chamber of Deputies in 1963, 1968, 1972 and 1976. He served as Under-Secretary for Foreign Affairs, Minister of Foreign Trade (1970–71), and Minister of Justice (1973–74). He was a member and Vice-President of the European Parliament (1979–84 and 1984–89) and is President of the Italian Council of *Movimento Europeo*. He is also editor of *Iniziativa Europea*, *Sinistra Europea* and *Unita Socialista*. His publications include *Le Sfide Europee* and *Superare le Sfide*.

Index